Fay Summers

CHAIN BREAKERS – FROM DARKNESS TO LIGHT

AUSTIN MACAULEY PUBLISHERS™

LONDON ∗ CAMBRIDGE ∗ NEW YORK ∗ SHARJAH

A CIP catalogue record for this title is available from the British Library.

ISBN 9781398460997 (Paperback)
ISBN 9781398461000 (ePub e-book)

www.austinmacauley.com

First Published 2022
Austin Macauley Publishers Ltd®
1 Canada Square
Canary Wharf
London
E14 5AA

My huge thanks go to my 'three wise men'. Without their help this book would never have been printed. They are awesome. Geoff Knight, Jeff Rudkin and Peter Jackson—what would I have done without you. And then Bid Pettitt, who typed out what I had written back in 2008. She wanted me to finish it. Well Bid, I did. I thank you all and I thank God for you all too.

Table of Contents

Mexborough

WHENEVER I SMELL VINEGAR, my mind takes me back to being three years old. My Dad was drunk and angry; he had hit my Mam and she was unconscious on the kitchen floor. I was crying and clinging to Dad's legs; he kicked me away and screamed "SHUT IT!" I watched and tried to hold in my sobs as he picked up a saucepan from the cooker. Mam had made poached eggs in vinegar water earlier and the pan was full of cold, smelly water. He slowly poured it onto Mam's face. She coughed and spluttered and he screamed "GET UP BITCH!" He screamed a lot, my Dad; he was a very scary man.

Mam was 19 and was so in love with Dad that she put up with everything, from his violence towards her and us, to his drinking, fighting, thieving and even his womanising. He wasn't very good at thieving. He usually got caught and finished up fighting the police who came to talk to him, so most of his prison sentences were for GBH to policemen.

He was a boxer and when he wasn't fighting in the ring, he was fighting outside clubs, pubs or anywhere he could. He loved it; violence was his answer to everything, even with Mam and us.

I ought to start at the beginning which, as far back as I can remember, is in Mexborough, South Yorkshire—39 Schofield Street to be exact. My great Grandad, 'Grandad Collins', lived there. He was a large, plain-speaking Yorkshireman in his late 80s. He was my Gran's Dad and so it was her 'duty' to look after him after her Mam died. So Gran and her second husband, 'Grandad Ned', also lived with him.

When Dad went to prison, Mam took Phil, my eldest brother, back to Schofield Street and Gran took her in. It was only a two-up two-down terraced house with a backyard and an outside loo. Mam and Phil lived in the front room and that was where I was born on 7 December 1951.

It was around this time that Gran and Grandad Ned were offered their own council house. They were thrilled and moved into 30 Hawthorn Crescent,

13

Highwoods Estate. It had its own inside and outside toilets and three bedrooms, so naturally, Grandad Collins went with them, which left Mam and us children with nowhere to live.

This was when Mam found temporary digs. Here she was, 20 with two kids, with no idea how to cope and nowhere to live. She wasn't very good at the 'mothering' thing. I have the scars to prove it!

She was going to bathe me in an enamel bowl. She had filled it with water and, just as she was about to put me in, Phil decided he wanted a drink so Mam put the bowl on the kettle stand. It was an old-fashioned fireplace with a coal fire and the kettle stand was attached to the front of the fire grate, heating whatever you stood on it. When Mam finally got back, she lifted the bowl off the fire and felt the water with her elbow but not the back of the bowl. It had been in the fire and was white hot so when she put me in, I screamed. She took me out immediately but the skin from my back stayed in the bowl!

I was very poorly for a long time, having to have treatment for my back for months. Mam, still with nowhere permanent to live, asked my Gran to look after Phil until she got a place. Mam took me, still very poorly, to walk the streets looking for somewhere to live. I became very ill with meningitis and then pneumonia. The landlord took pity on us and allowed us to stay for about three months.

Mam nursed me at home and the doctor would come regularly to give me lumbar punctures. Mam would go outside and sit in the loo with her hands over her ears so as not to hear my screams. For a long time, she didn't know if I would survive but I began to get slowly better. She hadn't slept much the whole time I had been ill and was at the end of her tether; no home, no money, no husband to help and this sick baby to take care of. She was physically and emotionally drained.

When Dad came home, the first thing he did was to give Mam a good hiding for what she had done to me. Nice bloke! It never occurred to him that had we been in proper housing with electricity like a normal family, the whole scenario would never have happened. That was down to him, but he never took the blame for anything. It was always someone else's fault.

Then he moved us into a squat; a dilapidated house by the canal. This was OK until it rained and the canal flooded and in turn flooded the downstairs of the house. When the water came in so did the rats which meant we only lived in the bedroom, if you can call it that. It was a filthy little room, about nine feet square, with a broken window and a fireplace. Luckily, we had a dog. Dad always had a bull terrier, which would stand at the top of the stairs and catch the rats as they came upstairs. He loved it and Mam said she felt safer knowing Butch was standing guard. Occasionally, while he was sleeping, one would find its way into the room. Mam would be hysterical as the rat ran around the room, up into the pram and across the mantelpiece. Butch, having been rudely awakened by all the commotion, would generally have it in his mouth in a flash and he would eat them too!

It was while we were living there that Mam had a nervous breakdown. She was just worn out. Dad had no idea what she had gone through while he had been in prison with a roof over his head and three meals a day and no worries over money. She, on the other hand, had had a dreadful time and was mentally and physically shattered, having coped with no husband, no home, no money and a sick baby. When Dad came home, I think Mam had the idea that he would provide a home and security for us but he took us to a leaky, stinky, rat-infested squat. It was no surprise that she had this breakdown and went into a sanatorium. Dad couldn't cope with us, so he took us to live with Gran and Grandad Ned. Gran didn't like Dad at all—she would have us kids but not him—so he went to stay with his foster parents. Mam was in hospital for about six weeks.

When she came home, she took us to live with Dad at his foster parents, Jim and Eva Phillips and, while we were there, my brother John was born. He was a huge baby—11 lbs! Phil went to stay with Gran yet again. Dad was fighting again, professionally now, and earning a few quid. Mam was saving and they were able to buy a little two-up two-down terraced house in Roman Terrace. Dad was so chuffed with his ability to provide for his family.

After a couple of years, we moved to a house in Dollcliffe Road. This was slightly bigger but we're not talking flash, it was just a two-up two-down again. Dad was doing OK with his boxing but, as I said, it always spilled over and he was always fighting somewhere else. One day he got angry about something and punched the wall, breaking his hand. He was due to fight for good money and I remember watching him with the plaster off, determined to fight. He fought and he won! He was so big-headed. "Even with a broken hand, I can beat these idiots," he said. Mam was chuffed because he gave her some money! Due to fight again, he had been drinking and was fighting outside the pub when he got nicked yet again. He punched a policeman and went to prison and, once again, we were left to fend for ourselves.

This time Mam decided the only way to cope was to take in lodgers. She hated having to ask Gran for help because it gave Gran the opportunity to say what a no-good useless article my Dad was, which was true but Mam didn't want to hear it. She took in a friend of Dad's and his lady friend. As we only had two bedrooms, it meant Mam had to move in with us kids.

It was here that my baby brother, Kenneth Craven Lancaster, was born on 20 March 1957. After the birth, Mam became seriously ill with septic fever and had to go into hospital. She used to tell us how they put her in a bath full of ice—I have no idea why or even if they actually did.

The baby went to Gran and Grandad's while John and I stayed at home with the lodgers who were meant to look after us, but they had other ideas. They loaded up their van with all Mam's things; furniture, bedding and anything valuable. We hadn't much of value but whatever we had they took, leaving John and me to fend for ourselves. I was seven and John was only three. I remember thinking, "I'm the boss and I've got to look after John". So I did. We had cornflakes for breakfast and we would walk up to Gran's to have dinner. I didn't tell Gran that we were on our own or that the lodgers had taken everything, because Mam would be cross. I knew to keep my mouth shut about what went on in our house. Mam would quite often say, "Don't tell your Gran" if Dad had been drunk and shouting and hitting us, so it was ingrained in me to keep stumm!

We would have dinner at Gran's. She would always give us bread and anything else that she had baked to take home with us. We would walk home, play for a bit and have a jam sandwich at tea-time and then go to bed. Because the lodgers had taken all the blankets, the only thing I could find to cover us up with was my Dad's very expensive Crombie coat which he loved. It was a kind of ritual when he was going out. He would get this heavy black coat and brush it with his clothes brush until there was not a bit of fluff or hair on it. He would put in on, turn up the collar and don his trilby, look in the mirror admiring himself and then he would be ready. Well, here we were cuddled up together underneath this lovely coat and John, bless him, weed on it! I remember lighting the fire in the grate every morning and putting Dad's coat in front of it to dry! The smell was delightful but it worked and we had a dry blanket. I can't remember what happened to that coat but I guess Dad didn't fancy wearing it after that.

Mam came home from the hospital after about four weeks. She couldn't believe what the lodgers had done. I remember feeling very proud that I had been 'boss' and looked after Johnny really well, in my eyes anyway. We hadn't had a bath or anything like that. I bet we smelt gorgeous but we survived.

It must have been soul-destroying for Mam. Every time she got a home together, Dad went inside and she had to sell stuff to survive, but this was worse. So-called friends, who knew her situation, knew Dad was away, knew she had just had a baby and was ill, yet, instead of helping her, they robbed her and left two kids in a house on their own. With friends like these, who needs enemies?

I can remember starting school. I went to Roman Terrace Primary. I have vague memories, one of which is sitting in class and the teacher taking the register and collecting the dinner money and putting the money in a tin. I was asked to take the tin and register to the office. I remember opening the tin and taking out a two-shilling piece. I wanted it! I didn't have anywhere to hide it, no pockets, so I put it in my mouth.

When I got back from the office the teacher asked me if I found the office OK. I panicked and swallowed the two shillings. I thought my throat would split and I couldn't breathe but I couldn't let on what I'd done. I could feel it slowly moving down my throat; it was *so* painful my eyes were watering. The teacher must have wondered what on earth the matter was with me. I remember worrying all day as to the whereabouts of my two bob but the next morning I stopped wondering! Parting with it was almost as painful as swallowing it but at least I had the cash to show for it. Sweeties all round! I was a little thief even at that age and devious with it. When I think about it now, it makes my eyes water.

When we moved to Dollcliffe Road, I started at a new school, Dollcliffe Primary. I remember so clearly the little canvas beds we had to take a nap on after lunch. I can't remember the teacher's name but her face is imprinted on my memory. She didn't like me for some reason. I remember her shouting at me. She questioned me about something and when I answered her, she obviously didn't like my answer. She picked up a ruler and smacked me on the side of my face. I was shocked; I wanted to cry but held it in. *You nasty old cow bag*, I thought, but I was used to being hit so I just took it in my stride. It stung like mad and I still had the welt on my face when I went home. I told Mam how I got it and she went mad.

The following day she marched into school with me, took me into my classroom and picked up a ruler. She walked up to the smiling teacher, smacked her face with the ruler and said, "How do you like it?" She was obviously shaken and didn't know what to do. I remember wishing Mam would hit her again, teach the old cow bag to hit me! Mam said, "Nobody hits my kids but me, understand?" I think she did because she never hit me again.

Life continued to be a struggle for Mam. She would often take us up to Gran's. We would all have something to eat and Gran would give Mam bread to take home. Also, because Grandad Ned worked at the pit, they got free coal, so Gran and Mam would load up the pram with it. We looked a right sight, with coal piled in the pram along with groceries, Kenny at one end and John at the other, while I dragged behind. Poor Mam would have to push this load for miles. To cap it all, we lived at the top of a very steep hill.

I remember vividly trying to help Mam push the pram up this blasted hill when this goat came from nowhere and started ramming the pram. We were terrified! The blinking thing kept ramming the pram and we were all screaming. Mam was whizzing this great big old pram round and round trying to avoid the goat while I was hanging onto the handle and the boys were hysterical. After what seemed like hours, the goat got fed up and went away. Poor old Mam! She was exhausted and, to make it worse, we still had the hill to face.

The pram had taken quite a battering from the goat but we pressed on. I was hanging onto the handle, pushing with all my might, constantly looking over my shoulder to make sure the goat wasn't coming back for another go at us when, suddenly, we were all in a heap on the floor. We had pushed the pram body off the wheels! There was coal everywhere, Kenny was screaming, the wheels were racing back down the hill and Mam was crying. "Don't cry, Mam. I'll get 'em back," I said, running back.

A very kind gentleman stopped the wheels, pushed them back up to Mam and helped her put the pram back together. The body was held onto the wheels by two leather straps and, during the encounter with the goat, these straps had snapped. So this lovely man took off his braces and did a Heath Robinson repair on the pram, bless him, and, after replacing the coal and boys, we struggled back up the hill and home. Later that evening Mam and I did laugh about the whole 'goat episode' as she called it as we sat in front of the lovely fire eating toast, all courtesy of Gran and Grandad.

When Dad came home from prison, the council told us they were going to knock down the houses in Dollcliffe Road and our house was under a compulsory purchase order. Great stuff! We were offered our money back and a brand new council house in Cedar Avenue. Dad said it was a win-win situation. We moved in shortly after. It was so exciting, another new home. It was bigger, with three bedrooms, though we kids still all slept in the same room. It never occurred to us that the empty room could be used for one of us. I guess the reason was that we all slept on one double mattress.

Dad was back boxing again and making quite a bit of money so it wasn't long before all the stuff that had been nicked by the lodgers had been replaced. Even so, Dad said if ever he came upon either of them he would kill them. I was quite pleased about that because even Johnny and I thought what they did to us was horrible and they deserved everything Dad was going to dish out!

Dad soon got himself another new dog, though this time it was a white English bull terrier. He had given Butch, our lovely little Staffy, to his drinking partner 'Nack' Hully to prove his friendship! So our new dog was called Laddie and it was completely mad. We had all been used to Staffordshire bull terriers which were so good with us kids. We would wrestle with them, ride them, even take them to bed on cold winter nights. They were better than any hot water bottle; so we automatically thought we could treat this new dog the same. How wrong can you be!

We were all playing with our new dog. I was wrestling with Laddie when all of a sudden his legs went stiff, his eyes went strange and he just growled, staring at me. I was lying on the floor underneath him and was petrified. Dad came rushing in from the kitchen and said, in a very quiet voice, "Keep very still." He began talking to the dog which just growled periodically and kept looking at me, willing me to move. Needless to say, I didn't and I hardly dare breathe, all the time Dad was talking to the dog in this sotto voice.

I must have lain there for about twenty minutes, though it seemed like an eternity. Then as suddenly as he went stiff and peculiar, he was back to being playful. I got up very slowly and carefully. Nonetheless, I never liked that dog after that. Dad told us that no matter what we were doing, if Laddie's legs went stiff in future, we were to stand very still.

I can remember one of Dad's friends; Digger was his name and he was a real tough guy. Dad and his drinking pals had come home one Sunday afternoon and he challenged them that they wouldn't have the bottle to feed his dog. Digger took up the challenge. He got some bread (he was very drunk at the time) and the dog jumped up onto Digger's lap, put his front legs onto his shoulders and went stiff-legged so Digger was eyeball to eyeball with this mad dog. Dad and all the other mates thought this was hilarious but Digger was terrified. Dad eventually told Digger to be quiet and keep very still. Dad talked to the dog in the quiet voice again until the dog finally 'came round'. He was a *very* frightening dog and *very* unpredictable.

Punchbag Time

WE HAD LIVED IN CEDAR AVENUE FOR A FEW MONTHS when, late one evening, Dad came home with his face in such a mess and his clothes covered in blood. He had already been to the hospital and been stitched up. Apparently, some bloke in the pub wanted to fight the tough guy but Dad turned him down and before he knew it, this bloke rammed a pint glass into Dad's face. If the glass had gone a fraction one way, he would have lost an eye, a fraction the other way and it would have hit his jugular vein and he would have bled to death. During the night Mam woke up (itself a miracle since when she was asleep a bomb wouldn't have woken her), only to find that Dad had burst his stitches and was bleeding. Mam always maintains that had she not woken up and sorted him out he would have bled to death. Many are the times I have wished she hadn't woken!

When Dad was home, life was different. We had money because Dad was fighting and supplementing his income with thieving. He was also drinking and he was hateful. He was horrible to be around when he had been drinking. Some people get really jolly and silly when they drink. Not my Dad; he got nasty and violent! Sometimes when he was drunk he would teach the boys to box and I was the punchbag. Dad and his mates found this entertaining.

I was as tall as I was wide, a little dumpling, so Dad would make me stand in the middle of the room while the boys took it in turns to punch me. "Give her a left jab, now a right cross, no, not like that, put some umph into it." When they knocked me over they would all laugh because I couldn't get myself back up again but once up, it would be "Again Phil, now you John, come on, punch her in the guts, now an uppercut." I hated being hit, and even though I was used to it, I figured I had to start hitting back or this would only get worse, so I started boxing and I was good too, thank goodness!

Dad would take us down to the gym and would get us to spar for everyone. He enjoyed showing us off to his mates. He would have us skipping, shadow boxing and doing the speedball. He would lift me up to the speedball and it seemed that I was a natural. He would tell everyone that I could make that ball talk. I didn't understand what he meant and every time he would lift me up I remember listening intently for this ball to talk to me.

I have strange memories of Mam at that time. It was while we were living at Cedar Avenue, I must have done something wrong to make her mad at me because she gave me a thrashing. She would hold onto my hair and punch me with the free hand and as I tried to evade her hand, she would kick me. All the while I was begging her to stop. When she was finished, she threw me outside in my vest and knickers and told me to piss off, she didn't want me! I remember sitting on the doorstep in the covered passageway.

It was weird because I remember thinking I didn't want to go anywhere, this was all I knew, she was my Mam and this was where I belonged. I must have sat there for about an hour. I was crying and wondering what to do, it was dark and I was cold and scared. Then Mam opened the door and said, "I told you to piss off, why haven't you gone?" I said I had nowhere to go. She grabbed my hair and pulled me into the kitchen and said, "Get to bed." I ran upstairs and dived into my bed, relieved to be allowed back in.

Dad had been out with his drinking buddies and didn't come home. It was late and Mam was in a state. The next morning we learned that he had been arrested yet again. He went to Lancaster Prison and Mam took us to visit him. I thought he must be a special person to have his own prison.

While Dad was away Mam managed to get a house swap with a lady who lived directly opposite my Gran and Grandad in Hawthorn Crescent which was great. Gran was a woman who appeared very hard on the outside but she was so soft on the inside and her door was always open to us. I was never frightened of Gran or Grandad Ned like I was of Mam and Dad. It also meant that we got to see Phil more because since Kenny was born, he had just stayed with Gran and Grandad. I thought he was so lucky. He had his own room and lots of things of his own. He had a pedal car and he let me ride down the hills in the boot, but only if I pushed it back! Gran and Grandad loved him, he was their favourite, but they loved us too.

Gran was always very hard on our John, poor thing; he suffered most when Dad went to prison. Dad was at home when John was born so he was Dad's boy and John loved him, so when Dad went to prison John really missed him and was forever asking for his daddy. He became so clingy to Mam; she even had to hang out the washing carrying John on one hip and the washing on the other. Often she would leave us with Gran while she went shopping and John would start to cry as soon as Mam left. Gran never picked him up and cuddle him. She would say to him, "You can't come into my house till you stop making that racket" and she would put him outside the back door until he shut up.

He got so used to it that as soon as Mam left, he would take himself outside and sob. When he had cried himself dry, he would knock on the door and she would let him back in. Poor little fella would come flying across to me with his snotty nose and swollen eyes and cling to me saying, "Where's Mam? When is she coming back?" I always thought they were so unkind to poor John. It didn't take a genius to work out he was frightened that, like Dad, Mam might go out one day and not come back!

I liked living there best of all because when Mam hit me, I had somewhere to run to. Also Gran would often make us dinner when Mam couldn't be bothered or there was nothing in the cupboards to cook.

One of the things I liked too was when Grandad Ned got his free coal delivered. That happened three times a year. The lorry would tip a ton of coal outside their house, then you had to move it into your coalhouse or the 'coal ole' as it was known. Well, Grandad Ned would give Phil and me half a crown each to shift it. We would work like mad all day with a barrow and shovel, traipsing back and forth to the coal ole until we had shifted the lot. We were bright black at the end of the day but we'd be rich; 2/6d each, and boy, did we enjoy doing it.

Dad's foster parents lived on the same estate just along the road from us but he didn't have any time for his foster mother. I think he quite liked his Dad Jim although I can understand why he didn't like Eva; she was so cruel to him. I have a very vivid memory of the time Eva died. They lived in a small bungalow so if you stood in the doorway of the kitchen you could look into the living room straight ahead and the bedroom to your right. I was only little, maybe four, and we had word that Eva was ill. Mam said Dad should go. They argued a bit but finally they got ready and we all went round there.

When we went inside it was very quiet. Eva was in the bedroom in bed and Jim was on a bed settee in the living room. So, as I said, by standing in the kitchen doorway I could see them both. Mam went into Eva and started talking to her but there was a weird response, she started groaning and making strange noises. I remember being quite frightened.

As this was going on, I watched my Dad going through all their drawers and cupboards. I knew what he was doing; he was looking for her money. Jim meanwhile was having an epileptic fit on the bed settee. It was really scary! We stayed there for quite a while. By the end of the day Dad had been through all their things. I desperately wanted Dad to take the two china dogs on the mantelpiece; lovely red spaniels facing each other and I really liked them. He didn't take them.

He went into the bedroom in which Eva was dying. She knew it too. She had a great pile of pillows but she kept sliding down the bed and she was very frightened, that was obvious even to me. Eva kept grabbing onto Mam and I just watched as Mam kept pulling her back up the bed-time after time, almost as if as long as she sat up she could stave off death. I watched as Dad went into the bedroom, calm as you like. He went over to the bed and took Eva's hand. I thought he was being nice to her then I realised he was taking off her wedding ring! Eva looked at him as he did it, both of them with hatred in their eyes. He didn't say a word to her. Not long after that she died.

We were living in Hawthorn Crescent when Phil, John, Ken and I did our first 'job' together. I think it must have been a weekend. I was looking after the two little ones; Kenny was about 18 months old and in a pushchair. We decided to go and play in the school playground so we all trooped up to Highwood Infants School. We played 'tiggy' for a bit until we got fed up. That was when Phil noticed that the toilet window was open so we thought it would be good fun to climb in. I remember feeling a bit scared but I did it anyway.

First we pushed John through and told him to stand in the sink and open the side window which he did. I climbed in, then Phil lifted Kenny and passed him to me, then Phil climbed in. Both Phil and I were scared. This was Phil's school, nevertheless this was exciting. We all wandered around the classrooms. Nothing much to do in there we thought so we found our way to the headmistress's office. This looked more promising. Phil didn't like her. It was all very orderly. She had a budgie in a cage so we thought it would be kind to let it out, so we did.

Then we noticed the chocolate biscuits on a tray by the window, so we ate them. We found a tin with some cash in it which we took. Not a great deal of money but it was to us, we felt dead rich. When we got fed up we decided to go and spend our cash. For some strange reason we decided it would be funny to turn all the taps on, so we did, then climbed back out of the window. We were so stupid!

We went to the shop and spent our ill-gotten gains on sweets and stuffed ourselves all afternoon. We laughed about what we had done and how big we were. We promised not to tell a soul about it and we did a spit handshake, unbreakable!

It was teatime when a policeman came to the door. He told Mam he wanted to speak to the Lancaster kids. Apparently, Phil had been bragging to his mates about breaking into the school. Big mouth! So much for the spit handshake, I thought. Anyway, Mam pointed to Kenny who was asleep in his pushchair. "Well, that's Kenny." A snotty-nosed John came to see what was going on. "And that's John," said Mam.

"You can't be serious." The policeman didn't know what to say. Then Mam told me to go to Gran's and get Phil. We were both scared silly. I remember him asking us if we had been in the school. We denied it of course. I'm sure he didn't believe us for one minute but we were too young to be charged. He gave us a lecture about telling the truth, not taking things that didn't belong to us. He scared us by taking his truncheon out and began slapping it into the palm of his other hand as he was talking to us. He was saying something about not going into other people's property without being invited.

We were listening but were more concerned with what he was going to do with his truncheon. We thought he was going to batter us with it. Needless to say, he didn't but gave us a last severe scowl, said goodbye to Mam and left and that was that. Our first 'job' and we had got away with it.

Dad came home from prison yet again. I liked it better when Dad was away although life was harder. But when Dad was home, things happened. He was always angry with someone, whether it was with Mam or one of us kids and it always meant trouble. Well, he was back. We still had the mad dog Laddie, so mad by this time he had to be kept in the outhouse which was really a brick-built shed opposite the back door. When Mam fed him she would put the food on a shovel and poke it through the window. Laddie would even attack the shovel! Stupid dog, talk about biting the hand that feeds you. We kids were not allowed to go into the outhouse *ever*! Mam said Laddie would kill us. That was enough for me; I never liked him anyway.

Dad really liked this dog; it was as mad as he was. It was good for his hard man image I suppose. He decided Laddie could be trusted and he was let out of the outhouse. Well, one afternoon Laddie was in the garden, Dad had gone into the house and Kenny was in the garden with Laddie. The next thing we knew, Mam was screaming, "The dog's got the baby." Dad ran out, we followed; Dad grabbed an axe from the outhouse and ran up the garden. Laddie by this time had grabbed Kenny by the head and dragged him to the ground and was standing over him, stiff-legged, guarding his kill. Dad was telling Kenny to be quiet, which was difficult for the poor little fellow as he had been badly bitten about his head by this mad creature. Dad was talking to the dog in his sotto voice. Laddie, his legs rigid, his eyes staring, kept growling, keeping one eye on Kenny and the other on Dad.

We all stood silently watching as Dad swung the axe and hit Laddie on the side of his head. The dog just dropped to the floor. Dad whacked Laddie once again then grabbed Kenny. Mam rushed Kenny off to the hospital; he was covered in blood and looked terrible. We were all worried that he would die but in fact he only needed eight stitches to his forehead. He was really shaken up by the whole thing—so were we come to that. Laddie wasn't looking too good either. Dad had thought he had killed the wretched thing, so he dug a hole in the garden to bury him. John and I watched silently as Dad threw the dog into the hole. We both jumped as Laddie opened one eye and growled. We were scared witless. Dad on the other hand was quite pleased. It looked like this dog was invincible.

Dad took off his belt and tied it around Laddie's muzzle so that he couldn't bite him and lifted this once pure white, now completely scarlet, dog out of his grave. He took it into the house and we scurried behind him, keen to know what would happen next. He pushed all the stuff off the draining board and laid this beast down. We watched as he washed the dog's wounds. Dad had chopped great big holes in his head; now, here he was, trying to mend him. He got a needle and thread and sewed the dog's head up. We watched, all feeling quite sick. The dog, still dazed but not unconscious, was not happy about what Dad was doing to it and growled continuously while attempting to get back up on his feet. Thank goodness he couldn't.

When Dad had finished tending the dog's wounds, he lifted it off the draining board and carried it to the outhouse. We trotted on behind and watched through the window as he laid it down. We wondered what it would be like now? Probably madder than ever and what would Mam say when she got back from the hospital? Plenty, believe me. She went mad! "Get rid of it. I am not having that dog near my kids. It could have killed Kenny." But Dad, as always, talked and bullied her and the dog stayed.

Laddie grew stronger and stronger. Dad had such a weird way with him when it came to his dogs. They had the best. He would buy steak for the dog while we ate bread and jam. Anyway, Laddie got better. It turned out that Dad had a bit of a scam with him. He sold the dog to some bloke in the pub who liked to fight dogs and was impressed with Laddie. He thought he was buying a pedigree bull terrier. Instead he got a pedigree crazy beast that wanted to fight anything that moved and, sometimes, it didn't even have to move. It was a savage killing machine and it had a real attitude problem to say the least.

Mam was thrilled. Dad came home with money and no dog. Then a couple of days later Mam went to the outhouse to get some sticks to lay on the fire first thing in the morning and came face to face with Laddie. She nearly died. She rushed back into the house yelling, "The f*****g dog is back. You said you sold it."

Dad yelling back, "I did, woman, I did." The poor bloke had brought him back in the middle of the night.

This happened a lot. Sometimes they would leave a note saying that they had changed their mind, they didn't want the dog but we could keep the money. One bloke who bought it was pinned up against the wall for hours by the mad beast. He dared not move, the dog petrified him, so when Laddie finally let him move, he muzzled him and brought him back under cover of darkness. He left a note saying he didn't want the dog or his money and that Dad could keep it as long as he kept the dog.

Moving South

DAD KEPT PROMISING MAM that he wouldn't go to prison again but trouble seemed to follow him. He was constantly fighting. Then one afternoon he came home with news that he had been offered a job in Crawley in Sussex, as a Ganger man on a building site. Crawley New Town was being built. He explained to Mam that he would get a gang of his mates together, go down to Crawley and make a fortune and he would send money to Mam every week. She was won over by the last statement.

He persuaded all his drinking cronies that this was a good idea and they all left, including Laddie, for Crawley. He worked on building Furnace Green, Gossips Green, Langley Green and various other areas for about two years. During this time he lived in a caravan with Laddie. Both were as mad as each other. Dad spent his evenings drinking and fighting so it didn't take long before the Sussex Police knew all about him.

Dad used to come home every month for a weekend when he would tell Mam all about Sussex. She liked the sound of it, though I remember when Dad got drunk and Nack would come around, we would hear about the seedier side of Sussex. I remember hearing Dad talk about a café called The Blue Pencil where he and his lads would set about the Sussex lads. There would be pitched battles; there were broken noses, ears bitten off and stabbings, the lot! Dad was crazy and he loved it all but his mates were not so keen. They all skulked off in the middle of the night back to Mexborough. They came and told Mam that Dad had completely flipped. He would work like a mad thing and make his men do the same. Up at dawn and they were working till dusk. They were made to live in a hut with bunks. Dad, being the Ganger man, was the only one with a caravan which he shared with Laddie. The men were all terrified of them both.

Laddie was attacking anything that moved. One morning a little girl was walking her dog—Dad said it was a small poodle. Laddie got out of the caravan, ran over to the fence, found a hole, grabbed the poodle, shook it like a rag and then ate it! Dad was shocked. He realised what was happening but it was too late to stop it. He ran over and grabbed Laddie. The horrified little girl was left holding the lead with no dog. Dad realised after this that Laddie was a real danger; it could so easily have been the little girl that Laddie had attacked. Laddie had to go.

He took him up to the woods one Sunday afternoon, put a gun to the dog's head and shot him. Dad said that just as he pulled the trigger, Laddie turned and looked defiantly up at him and growled. Mad to the end!

Dad was mad too, living the way he was, drinking, fighting and driving the men so hard that no one would work for him. He was crazy. He was also as strong as an ox and when men couldn't do what he could do, lift as many slabs, carry as many lintels, then he would attack them calling them idle gits and worse. So, as I said, all his men left and even the Sussex men were scared of him.

He came home one Thursday saying he had jacked it in as he couldn't get the men. Mam wasn't having any of that. All the time he had been working down south he had sent money regularly and she liked that. He went on a drinking binge on Thursday night and didn't come home till Sunday evening. Mam had him up bright and early Monday morning and on the train south with instructions to find us digs, she wanted to move south.

A few days later Mam went up to the phone box. Dad would phone at specific times each evening. When she came back she was all excited. She told us that Dad had found us lodgings with one of the men from the site and we could move south as soon as we were packed. That didn't take long. She sold, or gave away, every stick of furniture we had, packed a couple of suitcases with what bits we had and we were ready. It was all a bit scary; we were leaving Gran and Grandad. I didn't want to do that, they were my safe haven. We were also leaving Phil. I didn't want to do that either but we did.

I remember vividly standing in Gran's kitchen saying goodbye to everyone; Gran was saying we could all come back if we didn't like it. We were excited to be going yet sad to be leaving Gran, Grandad and Phil. The taxi arrived and we all piled in. At the station I watched as Mam got the tickets. This was all new to me, I had never been on a train before. When the train came into the station, it frightened us half to death, the noise and the steam. It was an awesome sight and sound. We were on the train for what seemed like an eternity. John and I spent our time looking out of the window, watching the world go by and what a big world it was. My world had consisted of Mexborough up until today and now look—the world was enormous.

Mam had made sandwiches for lunch. We ate them, had a drink and, tired of looking out of the window, John and Kenny settled down on the seat for a sleep. I continued watching the world. I remember thinking when houses would appear, who lived there, what kind of life they had? Strange, the things I remember!

When we arrived at Kings Cross Station, Mam told us to all hold hands and stay close. She poked her head out of the window and was scanning the sea of faces looking for Dad. He was coming to meet us and then all of a sudden she yelled, "KEN, KEN! We're here!" We all jumped up and were peering out of the window. There was what seemed like millions of people out there. Dad would never be able to find us but before that thought had time to panic me, Dad's face appeared at the window. This was one time when I was very pleased to see him! He gathered us all up and Mam was so excited, Dad was kissing her, he kissed us all, then picked up Kenny and the cases and we all held on to each other and followed Dad.

We came out of the station and got into a taxi. "Victoria Station," said Dad. I took it all in. Dad pointed out things to us all as we made our way across London and it seemed *so* big! We passed Buckingham Palace. "That's where the Queen lives," said Dad. We were spellbound. This was nothing like Mexborough.

We arrived at Victoria Station and had to catch another train to a place called Haywards Heath. We were all so tired; John and Kenny gave in and fell asleep. Not me, I wanted to see it all, even though my eyes felt like they were on fire. I was determined not to go to sleep. When we arrived at Haywards Heath it was late and dark so we couldn't see much. Dad was carrying John and the cases, Mam was carrying Kenny and we got into yet another taxi. "Bentswood Avenue" was our destination. I thought it sounded so posh.

When we arrived, Mr and Mrs Rice were waiting for us. They seemed really nice. It was a three-bedroomed council house, very clean and tidy. Dad introduced everyone, then Mrs Rice showed Mam our room—we were all in together. Mam put us kids to bed and we all slept like the dead, we were so tired.

We stayed with the Rices for a few weeks, then Mam found an old lady who took in lodgers and we moved in with her. We rented two rooms which meant we kids had our own room. The atmosphere in this house was very different to the Rices. The old lady (I can't remember her name) was nasty and always telling us off. We were not allowed to go into the garden and once we were downstairs we weren't allowed back up. She was constantly on at John and Kenny, saying they made too much noise. This meant that Mam was on at us too. She was scared we would be kicked out.

Dad was still working in Crawley, though things were different now because he was living with us so he wasn't out drinking every night with his mates and that in itself caused rows. Life was quite miserable living with this old lady. Mam was always on the lookout for somewhere else to live and it finally paid off. We moved yet again to live with Mr Henew. He had a prefab bungalow—temporary housing built after the war. Anyway, it was lovely. He was a really nice man and he liked kids. What a relief, even though he was a bit scary. He suffered terribly with asthma and had to have an oxygen cylinder with a mask which he would wear whenever he had difficulty breathing. He sounded scary and Kenny would run to Mam or me, whoever was nearest, and cling on like a limpet. I think Mr Henew was divorced; he had two sons who often came to stay.

I started school yet again. I was eight. New England Road Primary. I didn't like it at all. I had missed quite a lot of school and had fallen behind. I also had a very broad Yorkshire accent so the other kids would take the mickey out of me. I didn't make any friends here and felt very isolated. I couldn't wait for the bell to go so that I could be home with John and Kenny who thought I was the bee's knees.

While we were living here Mam put our name on the council list. Meanwhile she had found a privately-owned house to rent, 28 Delney Avenue. It even had a name, 'Silva Lining'. We were all excited about yet another move but this time we had our own bedrooms. It also had the biggest garden we had ever seen. John said, "We've got our own field." We had no furniture, bedding or anything but we were used to roughing it. Mam got stuff from jumble sales and second-hand shops. We had mattresses on the floor for ages which we liked because Mam couldn't hear us get out of bed.

Dad was working as a painter and decorator with a friend of his called John Potten. He was good for Dad; a real craftsman who taught Dad all he knew. Dad also had some friends who were not so good for him. I think having us all with him cramped his style but he was still thieving and Mam didn't mind as long as she got the proceeds and Dad didn't get caught.

Moving here meant I had to move schools again. Not that I was too bothered because I hated the last school. Well my new school was St Wilfred's Primary and it was at the bottom of our road. I was in Mr Spires' class. He was very nice, even explaining to the class that the reason I spoke differently was because I came from a different county and that if anyone of them went to my county they would sound as strange as I did. Everyone wanted to talk. I felt like a celebrity.

John's first day at school was somewhat fraught. I was in the juniors and John was to be in Mrs Brown's class in the infants. I took him to his classroom and left him. He apparently started screaming and kicking Mrs Brown's shins as soon as I left. He didn't want to be separated from me. Poor old John had a real problem with people he loved leaving him, ever since Dad first went to prison when he was little. He thought they wouldn't come back. Anyway, Mrs Brown's legs were red raw. John had weed himself and I was called from my class to calm him down. His little face was all swollen and red and he had his usual snotty nose.

As soon as he saw me, he came rushing across the classroom, wrapped his arms tightly around me and sobbed, "Don't leave me, Faydee. Please don't leave me." Mrs Brown said I could take him home and change his trousers which I did and calmed him down. When I took him back to school, Mrs Brown said I could stay with him for the rest of the morning. Poor little fellow, he was so insecure. Neither of us fitted in very well, everyone seemed so posh. They dressed posh and talked posh. We, on the other hand, certainly didn't dress posh—our clothes were jumble sale stuff. I'm not knocking jumble sales, I love them, but my Mam wasn't very selective. "Owt would do," she'd say, so we looked right sights, plus our broad accents didn't help. We were sitting targets. Playtimes were a nightmare. Kids can be so cruel and they were.

We had been in school for about four weeks and Mam had got herself a job working in Macfisheries as a shop assistant. We were given a note to take home saying there was a school trip to Brighton to see the ballet *Swan Lake* and it cost £2 each. Dad read the note and said I could go. I was ecstatic. I'd never been to the cinema before let alone the ballet. It was the first time I had been allowed to do anything that had cost money. Well, apparently they were oversubscribed by four names and decided that the fairest way was to put everyone's name in a hat and pull out four names who wouldn't be able to go. I remember standing in the school hall as the headmaster drew the names out.

As he did, I crossed everything I had to cross. I so wanted to go. I kept saying over and over in my head, "Please don't let my name come out." I cried buckets when he read my name out. The first thing I'd been allowed to do and now I couldn't go. I felt sick. I should have known. I was sobbing my heart out. I remember Mr Adcock putting his arm around me and saying how sorry he was but there would be other things I could go to. He didn't understand. Dad had been in a good mood when I asked him this time. Who knew when his next good mood would be? I was shattered.

Running Away

MAM WAS WORKING, so on Saturdays she would leave me to look after John and Kenny. I was eight, John five and Kenny two. Well, one Saturday I thought to myself, *I've had enough of this*, so I packed a little green and black plaid bag with clean knickers and a frock. Mam always left the rent money on Saturday and John, Kenny and I would walk down to Mr Snell, the bakers, (he was our landlord) and pay the rent. Well, this Saturday was different. I told the boys I was going back to Mexborough. I hated living in Sussex and I was off back to Gran's and did they want to come? John said he wanted to stay with Mam and Dad so I went next door to Mrs Bakers and asked her if she would keep an eye on the boys while I went out. She agreed, no problem, so I gave them both a kiss and told them to be good boys and off I went with the rent money.

I caught the bus to the station. It passed Macfisheries and I saw Mam. She didn't see me thank goodness. I thought, "That's the last I'll see of you." I got to the railway station and asked the man in the booth for "a half to Victoria please." It never occurred to me for one minute that he wouldn't give it to me. I was very cocky. He handed me the ticket. I recognised him as he lived at the end of our road. "Thank you." I was on my way.

The man on the gate punched my ticket and told me which platform to wait on. The train pulled in. My belly was full of butterflies as I climbed onto the train. I could feel my heart beating in my throat and I thought it would burst! I was SO scared. I found a seat and put my bag down next to me so no one could sit there. I stared out of the window all the way to Victoria and when the train finally drew into the station, everyone rushed off. I followed the throng and found the taxi rank.

I remembered when we came down from Mexborough as I had taken it all in. So I thought I just had to do everything backwards. I got into the taxi. The driver looked at me rather quizzically. "Kings Cross please." Here I was, in London, better than any old ballet anyway. We pulled into the station. I had butterflies the size of blackbirds in my stomach. Here we go again. The taxi man told me the fare was two and sixpence. I gave him the money. Then he said, "It's usual to give a shilling tip."

Cheeky swine, I thought. "Well," I said, "I'm only little so here's sixpence," and off I strode.

In the station I had no idea where to go. I must have looked a sad little sight. A porter came up to me and asked me where I was going. I told him I needed a ticket to Doncaster and he took me to the ticket office. I could barely see over the counter. "A half to Doncaster please."

He looked at me in a quizzical manner and said, "How old are you?" Quick as a flash I said, "I'm ten sir. I've been sent home from boarding school." He called over a porter and asked him to see me to the platform. He gave me my ticket and I gave him the money. I still had some money left. The porter took me through the station and I noticed a stall selling newspapers. I asked the porter if I could go in as I wanted to buy some comics for the train journey. I chose the *Beano*, *Dandy*, *Bunty* and *Judy* and I felt so flash. The porter took me to my train. There was a queue of people waiting to get on.

He asked a little old lady if she was going to Doncaster by train. She was, so he asked her if she would keep an eye on me. She said she would love to. We finally got on the train, found seats and made ourselves comfortable. We introduced ourselves and settled down for the mammoth journey ahead. I waited for the train to start before I started reading my comics as I didn't want to waste them by reading them in the station.

I felt like the Queen of Sheba. I knew also that once the train was moving I was safe. I sat across the table from my little old lady and the porter came round, asking if anyone wanted tea or coffee. I asked my lady if she wanted a drink. She smiled at me and said she would buy her own. I bought myself a bottle of pop and a chocolate bar. "This is the life," I thought. We chatted for ages. I told her the biggest load of twaddle and she seemed to believe it all, bless her. My Mam was at home and Dad was meeting me at Doncaster as I'd been crying myself to sleep at boarding school so they decided it was best all round if I go home to be with my beloved mother! What a load of old cobblers.

I settled back to read my comics again and she read her newspaper. The train rumbled on when I caught myself listening to it. It seemed to be saying, "You're going to get caught. You're going to get caught." It made my heart jump in my chest as I listened to it. I tried not to listen but there it was all the time rumbling on. I got back to my comic but I couldn't concentrate. "You're going to get caught. You're going to get caught."

I started to wonder what was happening at home as Mam would be back by now. She would know I had pinched the rent money. She'll have gone spare, I thought. She would also be mad that I had left the boys. She would probably ask John where I'd gone and when he told her she more than likely wouldn't believe him. I think I'd rather listen to the train!

Finally, we arrived at Doncaster. I collected all my bits together and said goodbye to my little old lady. I went up the white tiled stairs to the bus stop outside the station. No, I'll take a taxi. I've still got some money left, I thought. "30 Hawthorn Crescent please."

I arrived at Gran's. I knocked and Phil answered the door. He looked shocked to see me. "Is Gran in?" I asked.

"Yeah," he said. Then he shouted to Gran, "It's our Faydee."

Gran's face appeared around the kitchen door. She looked shocked. "What are you doing here? Where's your Mam?" She ran out of the house, past me and into the street, looking up and down. No Mam or Dad.

"I've run away, Gran, I don't like it down south."

"Eee lass," she said and then she hugged me.

"Oh I've missed you, Gran."

She took off my coat and shouted upstairs to Grandad Ned. "Our Faydee's here. She says she's run away and by the colour of her neck, she's telling the truth."

Granddad Ned came running down the stairs. "What the… well …. I'll be." He burst through the door; wearing only his trousers and a vest with his braces hanging down. "Well I'll be," was all he could say. Then he scooped me up in his arms and kissed me with his bristly face. He made me laugh and I loved him lots. It was good to be back.

Gran made me something to eat then ran me a bath. Everyone was asking me questions. "Where did you get the money? How did you cross London? How did you know where to go?" I felt SO clever. Phil said he could have done it too. He couldn't. Gran and Grandad kept looking at me, laughing and saying, "Well, bugger me. She came all that way on her own."

Two days later a policeman knocked on the door and I answered. "Is your name Fay Lancaster?"

"No," I said.

Gran came into the kitchen. "What do you want?" she asked. The policeman said that police all over the country were looking for me. My little brother John had told them that I said I was going back to Mexborough but apparently, the police had said that I was too young to make such a journey. They had spent the previous day looking for me in Sussex, in sheds and parks and places like that. Mam said if I was going to run away it would be to go somewhere specific, not someone's shed. Both Mam and Dad thought I'd have probably gone to Gran's but it was hard convincing the police that I was capable of making the journey. They eventually phoned the Mexborough police and asked them to send a copper round and they found me. The policeman said I could stay and that Mam and Dad would be up in a week to pick me up.

The taxi pulled up outside my Gran's house. "Don't let them hit me, Gran," I said.

"Don't you worry, lass. He'll not hit you while I am around," she replied. Mam and Dad and the boys walked in. I sat on the horsehair sofa by the window. I was concentrating on the prickly bits that were sticking into the backs of my legs. Mam looked over at me, I kept looking at the ground and then she said, "Do you realise we are a week in arrears with the rent because of you, you little bleeder."

That was it! That was all she was going to say. I couldn't believe it. I didn't get a thrashing, not even a slap up the chops. In fact Mam and Dad were positively nice to me. It was worse than a good hiding because I kept thinking they were just biding their time so I was on tenterhooks all the time. It was terrible.

When I recall that time, I remember thinking it was quite funny that when they arrived at Gran's, Mam was wearing a huge brown fur coat and Dad was dressed to the nines. Mam had said that when she went back to Mexborough she'd show 'em! Well, she certainly did. They stayed for a week and were out every night, Mam dressed to kill in her fur. They lived in the affluent south now, don't you know, and it showed. They never said anything to their mates about being in arrears with the rent.

Back to Sussex

WE SAID GOODBYE ONCE AGAIN to Gran and Grandad and headed south. After a long tedious journey, we arrived in Haywards Heath. I really didn't want to be here, that's for sure. Gran and Grandad had said that I could stay with them during the long summer holidays. Mam was all for that—if she could palm us off on someone else, she would. Anyway, Monday morning and back to school. Mr Spires was really nice to me. He said that if ever I needed to talk he would always be there for me. The kids in my class were all being nice to me and kept asking where I'd been and what I'd done. I was a celebrity in my own classroom, though it soon wore off and the mickey started being taken yet again.

Also I remember Dad asking me if there was anything I really wanted. I couldn't believe my ears! Not one to miss an opportunity or take advantage of the situation I asked for a record player. They only got it for me. I couldn't believe my luck. Dad was working with a young lad who gave him masses of records for me. I was chuffed to bits. There was Frank Ifield's *I remember you* and another one I liked called *When my little girl is smiling*. We played with this little red Dansette record player whenever we were allowed. I loved it and felt very grown up. John would say he was going to run away and then he would ask Dad for a bike.

I also remember going into town with Mam. There was a second-hand shop called 'Jolie Shoes' or something like that. Anyway, in the window was the most beautiful dress I had ever seen. "Ooh Mam, isn't that pretty?"

"Do you like it," she said. Is the grass green! Of course I liked it. We looked in the window at the dress. It was pale blue, made of a kind of stiff material with little flowers in a sort of raised velvet. 'It's exquisite', I thought and I willed Mam to buy it for me. It was two shillings, which was quite expensive for a second-hand frock, especially when you got frocks for a penny each at a good jumble. We stood at the window for ages. Mam got out her purse and my heart was pounding. She's going to get it for me. I couldn't believe it.

"Come on," she said and in we went. Mam asked the lady if I could try it on. I was so excited. She got the dress out of the window. I stripped off quicker than ever, never mind the changing room. I was down to my knickers in the middle of the shop. I didn't want her to change her mind. The lady slipped this dream dress over my head and buttoned it up, tied the lovely big bow at the back and led me to the mirror. I looked fabulous! Wonderful! Like a princess! Never in all my life had I ever worn anything so beautiful. "Do you like it?" Mam asked me.

"Do I like it, I love it, I never want to take it off!"

She bought it for me. I was overwhelmed. I couldn't believe it. "Thank you, thank you," I kept saying as I carried it home, one hand holding the bag, the other *in* the bag feeling the little velvet flowers. They felt wonderful. It was the first dress, or anything for that matter, that I had bought from a shop. It didn't matter that it was a second-hand shop.

When we got back, Mam said Dad would be home soon and I could put on my dress to show him. I was so excited. I took great pleasure in changing into my princess dress. I pranced around the bedroom, swirling round and round, making it stick way out. It was gorgeous! Dad came home; I ran downstairs shouting, "DAD, LOOK AT ME. LOOK WHAT MAM BOUGHT MEEEE." I was standing in front of him grinning from ear to ear. "Isn't it beautiful?"

He looked me up and down, made me turn around and said, "It most certainly is lovely; you look a picture, you really do." I knew I did. Mam made Dad a cup of tea and they were chatting in the kitchen when John asked Mam if he could have an orange. (We had lots of fruit because Mam was allowed to bring home anything from the shop that was bruised or damaged. Needless to say she would 'damage' whatever she fancied.) Well, sometimes oranges are easy to peel and sometimes they are hard. John got a hard one.

"Peel it for me please, Faydee." I took it off him and headed for the kitchen for a knife but Mam and Dad were in there talking. I went into the dining room but could only find a Stanley knife. 'That'll do', I thought. I held the orange in my left hand and started cutting. Suddenly, I felt a sharp pain in my hand and then a flash of blood spurted across the front of my beautiful dress. I felt sick. I didn't care about my hand, I could have cut it off. It was my dress I was worried about. John ran to the kitchen. "Mam, Faydee's bleeding."

They both came into the dining room. Mam took one look at me and said, "I don't believe it. You've only had it five minutes. You don't deserve anything nice, you little mare. I've wasted my money. Well, I won't do it again and that's for sure, you ungrateful little bitch." I stood there, knowing everything she was saying was true. I felt wretched. I was desperately trying to stop my hand from bleeding. I was fighting a losing battle as it was pouring onto my beautiful dress. I sobbed as Dad pushed me into the kitchen and held my hand under the tap. Inside, I was screaming but I said nothing. I had cut a deep flap of skin from my hand. Dad pressed hard on the flap, squashing it in and then he taped it up. Mam told me to go upstairs.

I went into the bedroom, threw myself on the bed and sobbed. John and Kenny came up and they both cuddled me without saying a word. John went to the bathroom and wet some toilet paper for me to me to try to rub the blood off. It only seemed to make it worse. I sobbed some more. I stayed in the bedroom all evening and I felt sick every time I looked down. When Mam came up to put the boys to bed, I started to get undressed when she walloped me. "Don't you dare take that off. You wanted it and you'll bloody well wear it." She made me wear it to bed. I hated her. I climbed into bed and I cried myself to sleep that night.

Next morning I woke and looked down at my dress. The blood had dried and it now looked black. It was all creased up. I cried again. I brushed it down but it made no difference. When the boys woke up, they were trying to cheer me up. They were play wrestling and messing about. It did make me laugh but then I caught sight of my dress and bang, I was back in the pit of despair.

Mam got up and we all went downstairs. I went and got the boys' breakfast. Mam didn't say a word. After breakfast I got the boys dressed, all the time wondering if she would let me take off the dress. I daren't take it off without her say-so. She told me to wash up and make her a cup of tea. I did as she said yet she still didn't say anything about the dress.

We went out in the garden to play and I sat on the wall watching the boys. I remember feeling so sad. Dad came home at lunchtime. He took one look at me and said, "Go and take it off." I rushed upstairs and took it off. I brought it down to the kitchen where Mam snatched it off me. I watched her screw it up and throw it in the dustbin. I couldn't believe she could be so cruel and she seemed to enjoy it. My hand was hurting but not nearly as much as my heart.

28 Delney Avenue was a lovely house and it even had a cellar. Dad put up a light down there and would work down there in the evenings. To get into it there was a trap-door in the dining room floor just in front of the patio doors. Well, one evening Dad had been down the cellar and when he came up for a cuppa he

obviously left the trap-door open. While he was on his tea break Mam noticed that the curtain was coming off the rail in the dining room. She pointed it out to Dad. "No problem," he said, striding towards the window, looking up at the curtain rail. The next thing we knew Dad went straight down the hole! He was jammed up to his armpits and had taken off all the skin from his waist up to his armpits. We were all dying to laugh but we daren't, not until Mam did, then we fell about. Dad didn't see the funny side for ages.

This house was lovely. It had three rooms downstairs: the front room that we never sat in, a dining room and a kitchen. The dining room had a table pushed up against the wall and a tatty three piece suite. The window was lovely big glass doors that opened onto this huge long garden. Dad actually made the boys a see-saw from a scaffolding plank. I remember that where he joined the plank onto the base in the middle, were two long screw things with nuts on, but the screw things poked up a good four inches. Dad kept saying he was going to saw them off but he never did.

John fell on one of the screws when he and Ken were playing pirates and he was walking the plank. When he fell the screw went into his calf and he screamed. Mam came out and was so angry. She yanked John off the screw not realising just how far it was into his leg! He was bleeding like a stuck pig, bless him. She took him into the kitchen, wrapped a mucky tea towel around his leg and told him to stop crying. He sat in the garden holding his leg for most of the afternoon. No antiseptic cream or trip to the hospital for a stitch—just a mucky tea towel!

Since we had lived down south, Mam had invited people from Mexborough to stay, so we had lots of Dad's friends staying with us. Mam wanted to buy nice stuff for the front room. I never understood why, because we never went in there, but she bought a red moquette three-piece suite. She was so proud of it. I remember Graham Hully, Nack's son. He had run away from the navy and he came to us. He even got married from our house. I think it was when he was with us, Mam invited Mr and Mrs Rice round with some other mates of Dad's. Well, Mrs Rice got so drunk that she weed on Mam's new moquette settee!

Mam was furious. "Dirty cow," she said. The thing was, she had never had a new suite before. She had just got this one on the 'never' and it was in the front room. We weren't even allowed to sit on it and here she was, her first party with her new gear, and Mrs Rice weed on it.

I also remember the dog we had at the time, a Welsh terrier. Mam had now banned fighting dogs in the new house. Dad would pick this dog up by its tail and hold it inches from the ground. It would chomp its teeth for all it was worth. We thought it was funny. We called it Fred Flintstone's grass cutter. Poor old dog, he came to a sticky end. Dad hated it, so one night he took it out, killed it and threw its body over into the graveyard just down the road. Next morning we asked where the dog was and Dad cracked on he didn't know. We all looked for him, Dad even helped to look, he hadn't bargained on helpful neighbours.

Someone came round and told us they had seen our dog in the graveyard. They said it looked like someone had hit it with a car, realised they had killed it and slung it over the railings. Very nearly true! Anyway, Dad had to go and fetch this dead dog back home and bury it in the back garden. We were all sad; he was a sweet little dog. We all thought Dad was sad too as it was his dog. It was years later that I learnt the truth.

Granny, Grandad and Phil came down to stay. We were all excited; it was SO good to see them again. They loved Haywards Heath. We also took them to Brighton to look around the shops and sit on the seafront and eat an ice cream. Granddad thought it funny that it was supposed to be posh down south but the beach was pebbles, not lovely sand like Cleethorpes.

Dad didn't have a car. He had a motorbike and sidecar. So when Gran and Grandad were down we had to go everywhere by bus. Gran and Grandad loved Sussex and as we rode through all the lovely green countryside Grandad would tell us what this tree was and point out things of interest. He would say such eloquent things about the rolling downs. Gran would just light up a fag, smile and raise her eyebrows as if she was fed up with him, but she wasn't, she took it all in.

Phil was such a show-off but it was nice to have a big brother again. I had made a friend called Janice who lived round the corner from us. I had told her that I had a big brother who lived in Yorkshire but she didn't believe me. Well, now she would have to believe me because here he was. At first we were polite to each other but that soon wore off and we were brother and sister again. We had a great time and played out lots. We went over into the woods and made camps. We fought then made up. I loved having three brothers but time flew far too quickly and Gran, Grandad and Phil were going back to Yorkshire. It was very hard to say goodbye to them again and when they went home they took Kenny too. I don't know why. John and I missed them both very much. I went from having three brothers to only one. Our house seemed empty with just the two of us and no Gran and Grandad either.

The long summer holidays arrived and Mam said I could go stay with granny. Fantastic! Granddad came down on the train and took me back with him, though I did tell him I could have done it on my own. He just laughed and said, "Yes pet, I know you could." I was so excited; the train journey back was wonderful, I was with my Grandad and I felt safe, cuddled up to him as the train rumbled on. I looked out of the window. We were hurtling towards my granny and my tummy was full of giant butterflies.

We arrived at Gran's at nine in the evening. She was so pleased to see us that her face was beaming as she opened the door. She scooped me up in her little skinny arms and planted a big kiss on my cheek. I loved her so much. "Hello flower," she said. It was great to be back, the house was always warm and homely and I loved the smell of it. It was a safe smell and you could relax there. It was great to be back with Phil and Kenny. We played the whole summer, went pea picking and earned some pocket money. Also at the end of the day you were allowed to pick a bucketful of peas to take home. Gran would enthuse about these peas. I really thought I was helping her out when, in truth, she was probably sick to death of bloomin' peas but she never let on. She always acted as if I had brought her the best present ever. Bless her little heart.

When it was time to go back I was inconsolable. I really didn't want to go. I vividly remember kissing Gran and Phil on Mexborough station. Granddad was taking Kenny and me back. I was waving to Gran and Phil as the train started pulling out of the station. I was sobbing. I didn't want to go. I wanted to stay with my granny. I got hold of the door handle. The train wasn't moving very fast and I could jump off. I wouldn't hurt myself too much. Granddad took my hand. "Come on pet," he said and I was away from the door, the moment gone. The train built up speed and I just melted into my Grandad's arms sobbing. "There, there pet, you just cry." I did, all the way to Peterborough.

Back in Haywards Heath, Mr Snell, the landlord of 'Silva Lining', asked us to move out as his son was getting married and he wanted the house for him. Mam found us a new home, back down Hanbury Lane in the prefabs, number 13. I remember our first night there. Nothing was unpacked and we had a mattress on the floor. It was very late when Dad brought the final load of stuff in. We were all exhausted. We three kids all cuddled up together on a mattress and we slept like logs. John weed on us again, bless him. Still, he couldn't help it.

We got ourselves settled. It was a lovely little place with a big garden, backing onto a huge field. In effect, we had a massive playing field all to ourselves, apart from all the other kids who lived on our lane. But the way we saw it, it was ours!

Phil in Trouble

MAM READ OUT THE LETTER TO DAD just before we left for school. It was from Gran and Grandad. They said Phil had been in trouble with the police and Gran said she just couldn't cope with him any more and she thought it best if he came back to live with us. We just stared at Dad to see what his reaction would be. "Well, the little swine, I'll sort him out. Write and tell 'em we'll have him back", and with that he was out of the door and off to work.

We chatted on the way to school, wondering what Phil had actually done and why Gran didn't want him anymore. He must have been very, very naughty. The letter also said that Gran and Grandad would bring him down and stay for a bit of a holiday. We managed to get the prefab in some kind of order before they arrived. I remember coming home from school and they were there. It was lovely to see them all again. Phil was very subdued; I think he was worried about Dad. To be honest, I didn't blame him. Dad was not best pleased with the way Phil had behaved and here we were waiting for Dad to come in from work. When he finally did arrive I was laying the table ready for tea, Mam and Gran were busy in the kitchen and Grandad was in the garden with the boys.

Dad shouted for Phil. He came into the kitchen. "Hello Dad."

"Never mind hello Dad. What have you been up to?"

"Nothing much," said Phil. I got really nervous for Phil at that point. He hadn't been around Dad for a long time and he didn't seem to realise that you didn't talk to Dad like that unless you were sick of living. Dad gave him 'the look' that said 'DON'T YOU DARE TALK TO ME LIKE THAT'. But Phil didn't seem to recognise the look.

"If you haven't done anything much why have your Gran and Grandad asked us to have you?"

Phil looked him square in the eyes. "Well, I dunno, do I. Ask them." I knew what was coming even before Phil finished his sentence. Dad lunged at him, gave him a whack across his face and grabbed him by the front of his jumper.

"You are NOT dealing with your granny now, boy! Don't you get cocky with me, UNDERSTAND!" As he said this he was about an inch from Phil's face. Phil looked as if he understood only too well. *Welcome home Phil*, I thought. Poor Phil, he had to learn that in our house children NEVER answer back. They should be seen and not heard. Mam would tell us that all the time. I often wished I were invisible and then I would have been her perfect child, 'not seen and not heard'. Mam said tea was ready and we all sat round the table in silence. Phil was sulking and we were scared. He didn't realise we weren't allowed to sulk either, he'd find out soon enough. Gran started chatting to Mam and broke the silence. 'Thank goodness for Gran', I thought.

Gran and Grandad stayed for a couple of weeks. It seemed to fly by. Then the morning came for them to leave. We were all very sad. Phil had an air of indifference about him, "Bye then," he said and went out, off to school. We ran up the lane and caught up with him. "Aren't you bothered, Phil? Don't you want to go back with them?"

"Nah, they don't want me. I don't want them! Anyway I belong here." That was that. When we got home from school, Gran and Grandad had gone. It was quiet without them; Grandad was always full of chatter and laughter, such a gentle man in every sense of the word.

Dad came in from work and called us all into the living room. Whenever Dad called for us all to see him it usually meant someone was in trouble and we were expected to stand in line like soldiers. John and Ken were perfect little soldiers, straight back, chin up, arms down by your sides, tummy in. I wasn't so good and Phil followed suit. Dad gave us all a lecture. He said, "Your Gran and Grandad have gone now. It's back to normal and Philip, you will learn what normal is around here. You will do as you are told, *when* you are told to, not when *you* decide to. You will NOT answer back. You will have jobs to do and you had better do them and do them well. If I ask you to do something you do not ask why, you just do it, understand?"

"Yes Dad," we all answered, knowing that he was talking to Phil but we didn't like to not answer him in case we got clouted.

Bedtime came and we were all in the same room. This was the first time Phil had shared a room properly for years, it must have been very hard for him. He had to wait for the bathroom; he wouldn't go in with us and he was shy. Kenny and Johnny were running about starkers. Not Phil, he even got undressed in the bathroom. We all piled into bed and the light went out. We weren't allowed to talk after lights out, but we did, we whispered. Kenny was never very good at whispering and Mam would shout, "If I hear one more word out of you, I'll be in there and tan your hides."

Anyway, Phil was saying he hated Dad and all his rules. You'll get used to it, we told him. "NO I won't," he said as he turned over. We all settled down for the night, I could hear sobbing.

"Are you alright Phil?"

He blew his nose on the blanket. "Yeah, nowt wrong with me."

"I missed Gran and Grandad when we first came down here too. You'll get used to it," I said.

"I'm OK, leave me alone," he said. I knew he wasn't OK and I felt really sorry for him.

The weeks went by. Phil seemed to be in trouble with Dad all the time and he was always getting a good hiding for something. I remember one particular time. Dad had been riding to work on a pushbike for ages. He looked really funny sometimes with ladders strapped to the bike, buckets and paint tins hanging off the ladders. Anyway, he had seen a moped he liked—a Tina—and was going to buy it. It was a pale lavender colour and very nice, like a Lambretta scooter. Anyway, he got it. He was thrilled with it and we all had to go out when he arrived home with it and OOOH and AHHH over it to keep him happy. Mam had a ride on the back and we all laughed when Dad braked and nearly shot her off. We had a little shed in the garden, a small Nissan hut with a round corrugated tin roof, and Dad put his Tina in there.

One night we had tea and played for a bit. Then Mam and Dad said they were going to The Pilgrim, the local pub, for a drink. Off they went. Phil was in the hut before they were out of sight. He'd got Dad's keys from the hook in the kitchen. "Don't touch it Phil. He'll kill you," I said.

"Nah, he'll never know," and with that he started it up. We were watching him drive it round the garden, thinking, 'He's going to get killed'. Then he took it into the field. As soon as it was out of the garden, we all seemed to forget that it belonged to Dad.

"Let's have a go Phil," I yelled.

"Get on the back then." I did and we went flying around the field, laughing and giggling.

"Now me," shouted John. The field was so bumpy that John fell off. He cried for a bit but soon stopped and wanted another go. Then Kenny. We tore around this field for ages, it was such fun. Phil thought he was Evil Knievel. We realised that we had been playing for ages and they might be home soon so we all charged back to the prefab. Phil cleaned off the Tina and put it back in the hut. We went indoors. I got the little ones ready for bed, got myself ready and we went to bed. Phil wouldn't get ready; he said he would wait till they were coming down the lane before he would go to bed. He made my stomach turn over when he did things like that.

Next morning we were eating porridge when Dad went to get his Tina out of the hut. We heard him start it, then there was a crashing sound and Dad was swearing. We jumped up and looked out of the door. Dad was coming out of the hut, his shins bleeding. We couldn't see what had happened in the hut but Dad was evil mad! "Philip, have you touched my scooter?"

"NO Dad, honest!"

"You bleedin liar. I'm going to kill you, come here." Phil was off, over into the field and Dad was chasing after him. We watched, knowing that he couldn't escape Dad's wrath. Dad caught him, punched him all the way back to the prefab, took him inside and punched him some more. Phil was crying and telling Dad he was sorry but Dad wasn't listening. Phil had taken his scooter and Dad was going to make sure he didn't do it again. While we were waiting for Dad to finish hitting Phil, we went outside to see what had happened in the hut. It seemed that Phil had left the scooter in gear and as soon as Dad switched it on, it shot off its stand straight into the wall. Dad had cuts all down his shins and the scooter was all battered at the front. It had lost that brand new look.

Phil finally emerged, his eyes red and swollen and his legs red with welts where he had been hit. He showed us his back too. Poor old Phil, he wasn't used to this. "I hate that bastard," he said. We understood. He wiped his face, blew his nose and we went to school, though we all finished up laughing at the thought of Dad flying through the shed wall. We all said we would have liked to see his face as he hit the wall. He must have been so surprised. We thought it was good that Dad had hurt his legs. Good old Phil! Phil felt better now as he was our hero. He was also learning that living with us was no picnic. He had had life so easy at Gran's. It was different here, but he was learning.

When we came home from school Mam said we had to tidy up the hut and when Dad came home he made Phil clean the scooter. Dad kept coming out and glaring at Phil. I thought for sure he was going to hit him again. He would grab his belt buckle and we would all breathe in, thinking he was going to thrash him with his belt. He didn't, he just kept saying things like, "You little swine, I ought to…" and then he would go back inside. It made us all very nervous.

Phil kept his head down for the next few days until Dad had calmed down a bit. We all kept out of his way. I noticed Mam was also trying to 'sweeten him up' too; he made life very unpleasant for everyone when he wasn't happy. Phil was a quick learner. He learnt never to speak when Dad was speaking or you got a smack up the chops. And when Dad made us stand like soldiers—arms down by your sides, chin up, chest out, tummy in—someone was going to get a thrashing, that was for sure. Something had happened and he was going to get to the bottom of it or we would all get a thrashing. He was such a bully. Well, as I said, Phil soon learned, even though he was much mouthier than we were, that Dad wouldn't have that; he'd soon knock that out of him. No kid would get the better of him! That was his view. Phil was only 10 but he had such a strong will. If anyone would get the better of Dad, it would be Phil!

Phil soon learned if Dad had been drinking you should keep well away from him and try to be invisible. Don't speak, don't move, don't do anything because he would grab you and try to make you say or do something that would justify him hitting you. Mam would never try to stop him either. I thought that was because when he was hitting us, he wasn't hitting her.

Cuckfield

I WAS NINE OR TEN when we were given our first proper house. It was a three-bedroomed council house in Cuckfield Village with a lovely big garden which backed onto fields. It was great. We moved in and Dad started painting and decorating. My room was the smallest, the box room. I didn't care how small it was as it was my own room for the first time ever and I loved it. The boys' room was opposite. They had a pair of black metal bunk beds for John and Ken and a single bed for Phil by the window. It had a built-in cupboard for their clothes, next to the fireplace—a nice big room. Mam and Dad's room was next to mine—a big room too. The bathroom was at the other side of mine. It was *very* small with only a bath when we first moved in. Dad put in a toilet and a washbasin much later, but until then we would all just wee in the bath if we needed the loo in the night, except for Mam and Dad who had a chamber pot or a po as they are more commonly known. We all thought they were disgusting but it wasn't at all disgusting to wee in the bath! We did have a toilet downstairs but we were all too idle to walk down.

That summer Dad was drinking heavily. He had made friends with an Irishman who lived up the road from us called Mossy. We liked Uncle Mossy. He was a navvy and typically red-headed. When he was drunk, he was very funny. Not only did he have red hair on his head but all over his chest and back. His 'party piece' was to set fire to his chest. We kids loved it. "Set fire to yourself Uncle Mossy," we would beg. Sure enough, if he was drunk enough, he would strip off his shirt and vest, get out his lighter and WHOOSH! His arms would be going fifty to the dozen as he tried to put himself out. We would laugh and applaud him as we thought he was brilliant. But he was no good for my Dad and I'm sure Dad was no good for him; they just encouraged each other's bad habit. Drinking.

Phil and I started at the secondary school in Cuckfield. It was a lovely school but we felt out of place. We were supposed to have school uniforms but Mam

50

wouldn't buy them. "I haven't got the money for flash uniforms." So that was that, we didn't have it. We felt such prunes in the assembly hall as we were the only ones not in uniform. I had made friends with two girls up my road, Pam and Penny. They were nice girls and they knew my Mam and Dad. Pam had seen Dad hitting me on a couple of occasions and she was scared of him too, so when other kids would take the mickey Pam would stick up for me. I liked having a friend like her. She had been in my house too and she didn't say anything about it being mucky, neither did Penny.

They both understood when I couldn't do stuff with them because we didn't have any money or Mam wouldn't let me. They were still my friends, it was great. When we did get together after school, we would have a laugh. We would go over the 'roly poly', which was just a field with a slight slope at the end. We would lay on our side and roll down the slope. Then we would have a fag and swear at each other. We thought we were so cool but it was good to have friends.

That summer Gran and Grandad came down for a holiday. It was brilliant to see them. We had a great time and they decided that they wanted to live down here. I was ecstatic! We spent days looking in estate agencies for a house or flat to rent. We eventually found one in Haywards Heath. It was a ground floor flat in an old Victorian house and it was massive. They loved it. The rooms were easily 20 feet square and it had a huge garden. Granddad was a great gardener so he was thrilled. They moved in to 'Pontrasena', Perrymount Road. I was so excited; they were going to be around and part of our lives again. I loved my granny and Grandad so much.

By this time Phil was in BIG trouble with the police. He went to court and was sent to an approved school in South Godstone called 'Court Lees'. I was really shocked as he was only 12 and I didn't think they could send you away at such a young age. Mind you, I don't think I was half as shocked as Phil, poor old thing. We had been getting on really well too; it was nice to have a big brother. I missed him a lot and looked forward to the visits. Mam and Dad never visited him. Granddad Ned would take me with him when Phil was allowed visits. It was a huge imposing building with playing fields and a farm attached to the school. Phil had been mouthy to one of the teachers and his punishment was to scrub the pigs with a nailbrush. Poor old Phil, no sooner had he scrubbed one clean than it rolled in the mud and he had to start all over again.

I remember it was around that time that I started to have bad tummy pains. I remember Mam saying, "It's probably your periods. Stay away from boys."

That was it, my sex education. What a ridiculous thing to say to me. I lived with two boys. I kept saying, "Keep away from me", although I hadn't the slightest idea why.

They thought it was a joke and took great delight in chasing me. "Why can't we be near you then?"

"Cos I've got bellyache, that's why, stupid," I replied.

"That's stupid," they would say. They were right.

I was in the first year at school and enjoying having friends. I'd never really had friends before, only my brothers, because people didn't like their kids associating with a convict's kids. I wasn't going to have the mickey taken out of me any more I decided, so if anyone said anything I didn't like I would just punch them. End of problem! Perhaps Dad's way was right after all, it worked anyway. Soon everyone knew not to say anything to me unless they were looking for a fight.

I remember P.E. was always an ordeal. I loved it and I was good at it but Mam wouldn't buy me a P.E. kit and everyone else wore proper little girl's knickers. Mam never bought me any knickers, I had to wear hers. I was the only 11-year-old doing P.E. in black see-through drawers. I hated her. So I decided the only way I would ever get a proper P.E. kit would be to nick it. So I did! A skirt from one locker, a t-shirt from another, socks from another. The only thing I couldn't nick were knickers—nobody took them off and they were the things I really wanted!

When I look back on my life at 22 Glebe Road, it was the place we all grew up from children into men and women. I have some funny, some happy and some very unhappy memories of life there. Here are just a few.

John was about seven and still desperately insecure. He still didn't like anyone to leave him and would sit very close to whoever was next to him. He needed contact to feel secure so if Mam was sitting in a chair John would sit on the floor by her feet and just stroke her leg. Dad would go mental with him. He would make Phil or me put the boxing gloves on with John and we would have to give him a 'good hiding'. Dad was convinced that John would be 'queer' if he was left to do that. Stupid man! His answer was, knock that out of him and stop him doing that.

Poor old John, he was always eager to please. If Mam wanted something from the shop John would always volunteer. We never volunteered. We would call John a little martyr, so it came as such a shock to all of us when John had been to the shop for Mam, she gave him a £5 note and he came home with change for a £1 note. John said that was all that Mr Paine had given him. "Honest Mam." He hadn't thought it through enough.

He should have known she'd phone the shop. "Mr Paine, I sent John with a £5 note and you've only given him change for a £1 note."

"NO, NO, NO, Mrs Lancaster, I gave John change for a £5 note." Mam went crackers. She had taken to keeping a riding crop. It stood by the side of the fire and if any of us got lippy or wound her up in any way, she would lash us with her crop. Well, poor John, she grabbed the crop, "Where's my bloody money, you devious little git?" John didn't deny nicking it, bless him. He thought she had only given him £1 note. So when Mr Paine gave him all that change, he thought all his birthdays had come at once, poor little fella.

Anyway, it turned out he had buried his money in the twitten. "Well, fetch it NOW," she said. Poor old John scuttled off in tears to dig up his treasure. He came in the door, handed her the money and then she went crazy. She picked up the riding crop and lunged at him. She whipped his legs, his bottom, his face, his back. He was screaming but so was she, in temper. "Don't you think you can get the better of me, John Lancaster, because you bloody well won't." Her face was distorted with rage as she whipped this defenceless little boy. Ken and I were terrified she would kill him. Ken was crying too.

I pleaded with her. "Please don't hit him any more Mam, please," I begged. Then she stopped. John was a crumpled heap in the corner. He had weals all over him and he looked frightful. His face was red and swollen, his usual snotty nose was streaked with blood, he had black streaks down his tear-stained little face. When we got a good look at him, he was covered in raised red stripes. They looked awful and his little legs were covered. I remember helping him up and wiping his face. He was beaten in more ways than one.

Mam went in the kitchen, lit a fag and shouted at me to make her a cup of tea. I scuttled into the kitchen. I hated her! She was breathless, *poor thing*, she had just beaten a seven-year-old half to death with a horsewhip and it took it out of her! The cow, I thought. I made her tea and I spat in it! It gave me such satisfaction to see her drink it. She sat in the sitting room and said to me, "The little swine took my money. That'll teach him. He'll not do that again in a hurry." I didn't know why she was telling me. I said nothing.

When she had finished her fag and calmed down, she came through to the other room. It was supposed to be a dining room but it wasn't, we had another settee in there and a fold-up table up against the wall but we hardly ever used it. We kids were trying to comfort John whose sobs had subsided somewhat by this time. When she saw what she had done to him, she was visibly shocked, so much so that she kept him off school for two weeks until he looked better. We hated her yet she was all we had.

She was really handy with that horsewhip until Phil came home on leave one weekend and Mam whipped me across the face for answering her back. Phil asked me afterwards how long she'd been using the whip. "Ages," I said. He took the whip when she'd gone to bingo and buried it over the field.

She was furious when she went for it and it wasn't there. "Where's it gone, what have you done with it?" she said, as if we would bring that thing back. No way. We were so pleased to see the back of that hateful thing, even though she reverted to her favourite hairbrush or pan. She was so sadistic. If she was trying to hit you in the face and you put your hands up to protect yourself, she would scream "PUT YOUR F***ING HANDS DOWN." Well, you can't, it's a natural reaction to cover your face, so she would call one of the others and if it was me she was hitting, she would call John and say, "Hold her hands down" and he had to do it. If he didn't she would hit him too. Sick woman, I hated her so very much!

I remember coming home from Gran and granddads in Haywards Heath. Kenny and I had been up the fields and collected bucketfuls of sheep poo. Granddad had said he would pay us for it, so we set too and collected loads. The only trouble was transport. How would we get it to him? I worked it out. We needed a go-cart or a 'buggy' as we called it. We took the wheels off an old pram, got some wood from Dad's shed and worked for two days building our 'transporter'. It was brilliant.

We put the two small wheels at the front and the large wheels at the back. John was the designer. He drew a picture and told us what we needed to do. He always knew how to make stuff. He told us to connect them with a long piece of wood which we put a bolt through to enable us to steer with our feet. Wonderful, we thought. We were so clever! In fact it was all John's idea and handiwork, although he wasn't interested in collecting the poo. His loss we said! We then nailed an orange box onto the wood and filled it with sheep poo. Excellent. All we needed now was a lid. We soon found wood and made one and we set off to Grandad's. It was four miles to Haywards Heath from Cuckfield. Kenny's legs soon got tired so I sat him on the lid of the orange box. With our piece of washing line tied to the front I pulled the buggy, Kenny and our precious poo. We got to the Hilton Park corner where I was running and we had built up quite a speed but as we turned the corner the buggy tipped over slightly. Ken, trying to stay on, grabbed hold of the box and the whole thing went over.

The box came completely off the buggy. Ken went flying and the poo seemed to follow him. It all seemed to happen in slow motion. When everything stopped moving Ken was on the floor covered in sheep's poo. I thought this was so funny and couldn't stop laughing. Kenny on the other hand couldn't see the funny side. When I could control myself I picked Ken up and picked up the box. We hadn't thought to bring any tools with us so I took off my shoe and banged the nails back in with it. Then we had to pick up all our sheep poo. That done we continued on. I decided this buggy wasn't built for speed and walked the rest of the way. Kenny still rode on top of the cart.

When we arrived at Grandad's, he laughed at us and said we stunk. We told him that the price of this poo had gone up to 2/6d because it had been hand-picked twice. He gave us the money. We were thrilled. He made us wash and gave us a sandwich—he said we'd earned it.

We went up the town, spent some of our hard-earned cash on sweets and decided we would catch the bus back home. We could afford it, so why not. I remember sitting behind a lady with two little girls of about nine and ten. They were laughing together. The lady stroked the hair of one little girl, laughed and told her she was sweet. She meant it too; you could tell by the way she was with them that she loved them. As I listened to their conversation, it was obvious they were going to visit a relative. The girls asked if they looked nice.

"You look beautiful, both of you", she answered. It struck me that nobody had ever said that to me. Mam had told me I was an ugly little bugger, a grunt, built like a Suffolk punch. I didn't know what a Suffolk punch was but I knew it wasn't nice and an ugly swine was one of her favourite things to call me, but never beautiful or pretty. I wondered why and thought it must be because I was neither beautiful nor pretty and I was jealous of the two little girls who were and their lovely Mam.

Aiding and Abetting

IT WAS COMING UP TO CHRISTMAS. Dad was home but didn't have much work or much money so he was thieving again. John and I had seen a cottage in the woods. We had never noticed it before and anyway we mentioned it to Dad. We couldn't understand why Dad wanted us to take him to the cottage. We did and Dad had a good look round and there didn't seem to be anyone there. He looked through the windows; it was furnished but no one was home.

Two days later, after midnight, Dad woke me up. "Get dressed, I need your help," he said. I did as I was told. When I got downstairs Dad was drinking a cuppa. He handed me a cup of tea too as he said, "Get that down you." I wondered what he needed me to do. Dad put his coat on and got two big bags. "Get your coat on and put your wellies on, it's been snowing," he said. I did, wondering where in the world we were going at this time of night. "Come on then, let's be off," he said.

"Where are we going Dad?"

"You'll see, come on and be quiet," he said as he pulled his hat down and his collar up. We went through the woods; it was very quiet, very still and very scary. The only thing it wasn't very, was dark! Because it had snowed it seemed like daytime, it was very bright. We made our way through the woods and I had worked out by now where we were going and I instinctively knew what for.

We arrived at the cottage which was all in darkness. Dad beckoned me to follow him. We walked all around the cottage and Dad was looking at the windows. We came full circle back to what seemed to be a pantry window where the catch wasn't very strong. Dad had it open in a flash. The trouble was, the opening was only about a foot square. Dad bent down and with his face inches from mine whispered, "I'm going to push you through there and when you get inside you go to the back door and open it. Don't make a sound, understand?"

I understood all right. He lifted me up and I was halfway through the window with Dad holding my ankles. I was frantically trying to feel what was below me.

"Let go of one leg, Dad," I whispered. I pulled my leg in and managed to twist round, holding onto the window and pull myself upright. "Now the other leg." I was in and standing up. So far I hadn't made a noise. Dad gently shut the window. My eyes had accustomed themselves to the darkness of the cottage and I could make out the shapes of the chairs. I felt my way across the room, wondering if anyone was upstairs sleeping. That made my heart jump. *Don't think about that*, I told myself. *Just get that door opened.*

In the kitchen I could see the door and Dad's outline through the glass. He had squashed his face up against it in an attempt to see me. I remember thinking he looked stupid and I wanted to laugh but I didn't. I tried to turn the key. It was a big and old-fashioned, very stiff. I could hear Dad whispering, "That's it, turn it, go on, a bit more." I did it! Dad opened the door. "Good girl," he said. He put his bags on the kitchen table. There were horse brasses everywhere. Dad motioned to me to collect them up and put them into the bag and I did as he said. He was busy with the lovely brass oil lamps that seemed to be all over the place. Dad would point at something and I would put it into the bag.

This was exciting. The bags filled up. Then Dad spied the horse's hames collar—that's what he said it was called. It's the big collar that goes around a carthorse's neck. It had brass horns on it and chains hanging off. It was SO heavy, but Dad was desperate to have it. He took off his coat and put this huge thing around his neck. Then he put his coat back on top of it, the brass horns poked out above his head so that he looked like a demon!

We gathered everything together and let ourselves out of the back door, closing it very carefully. Outside it was snowing. Dad said that was good, it would cover our footprints. We hurried through the woods. Coming back through the churchyard we were making a bit of a racket with all the brass in the bags clanking together and the chains from the collar. I had a duffel bag full of stuff too and this was all exciting. Dad was being nice to me. He was on a high, he had a good haul and we were nearly home and dry. There were benches in the churchyard and the odd dosser would spend the night curled up for the night.

Well, imagine the poor fellow. We are walking through the gravestones and in the moonlight and the snow, coming towards him was this horned beast with clanking chains. We just saw him run off. It wasn't till later that we realised what he must have seen and it made us both laugh. Halfway across the churchyard, Dad's trilby blew off. "Quick get it," he yelled. I chased after it but couldn't catch it and then it was gone. "Come on then, leave it." We hurried home.

When we got home we were like kids at Christmas. "OOOH look at this, isn't it lovely, look at this." Then Mam came downstairs. Dad took everything out of the bags and there was so much stuff. "We'll take it down to Brighton tomorrow and get rid of it," said Dad. He then told Mam how good I'd been. He said I could have the day off school tomorrow and go with them to get rid of the stuff. Excellent! Then he said I would have to go early in the morning and find his hat. We all had a cuppa and went off to bed.

I was up early. I could hardly sleep and it had been an unusual evening to say the least. Wait till I tell the boys! Dad said to go find his hat even before I'd had a drink or anything, huh! "And don't come back without it," he shouted after me. I went all over the graveyard and couldn't find it. It had snowed very heavily and was probably full of snow and covered up somewhere. I thought I'd have to stay in the blinking churchyard till it thawed. I walked round and round, looking over every grave and kicking at the snow. Then I thought it might have blown over the wall. I was getting desperate and I needed a wee badly. I walked all around the wall, kicking the snow. I thought I saw something brown, just the very tip of his trilby maybe. I hoped it was, ran to look and there it was! I grabbed it and pulled it out of the snow. YES! I had found it. I ran home with a big grin on my face as I went into the house with the trilby on my head. Dad was thrilled. I'd pleased him at last. "Was there anybody about?" he asked.

"No, I didn't see anyone."

"Good," he said. I rushed to the loo and as I sat there I felt so good about myself. I had been good last night—Dad said so himself—and now I had been good again today. I smiled to myself and felt very pleased.

Mam got herself all dolled up and we were off to Brighton. Dad said if we got a good price for our stuff I could have a pair of boots. *YES!* I thought. In the back of the van I was so excited; I'd never had new boots. I always had jumble sale wellies. The 'in' look at that time was white PVC boots, so that was what I wanted. We arrived in Brighton. Mam said I had to wait in the van—she was in a mood 'cos Dad said I could have the boots. I sat in the back of the bloomin' van and, boy, was it cold. I was getting myself all excited, hoping they got a good price. I had been good so I should get those lovely boots.

Two hours later they arrived back. They had obviously got a good price. Great I thought, I'll get my boots. Then Mam chucked a bag at me. "Here you are, here's your new boots." I opened the bag and my heart sank. They were brown moulded boots, like wellies only about an inch down from the top of each boot was a window with brown gingham in it. They were revolting!

Dad turned and looked at me, "Mam said they were what you wanted," he said.

Mam was glowering at me. "Yes, they are lovely," I lied. I hated her so much. I can only remember wearing those rotten boots once and everyone laughed at me. I hated her some more. I think she got some kind of thrill out of it. She saw how disappointed I was and made a big thing of how ungrateful I was and that these boots were much more serviceable. Who gives a stuff about serviceable…*COW!* I thought. When I look back I think Mam was jealous. If Dad was nice to us kids then she would be nasty, it was as if she was competing with us. I think because Dad had said I had done well on the burglary she saw that as something to be jealous about. He said to buy the boots, she was jealous. She bought ugly brown ones when she knew well which ones I wanted. She was a very cruel, sick woman!

That was the winter of the 'fur hat'. They were lovely, they were a bonnet type hat with long leather ties and they had fur bobbles on the end. They were the thing to wear. I put the 'feelers' out to see if there was any chance that I would be allowed one. Dad decided that I could have a fur hat BUT a fur hat with a difference. He was going to make it. (Please don't let it be true, I thought!) Mam had bought a manky old fur coat from a jumble sale so Dad cut it up and made my hat. It was gross! Everyone else had the fur on the outside but not me, mine was on the inside.

"To keep me warm," he said. "What's the point of having the fur on the outside?"

I wanted to say, "Because it's cool and trendy and it's the fashion and I'd like just once to be like everyone else," but I didn't dare, so I was stuck with that hideous hat that had the skin on the outside and all Dad's stitching. I looked such a plonker. Needless to say, I only wore it until I was out of sight of the house then it was stuffed into my school bag until home time. When I got to the bottom of Glebe Road, I would fish the stupid thing out again and put it on. I hated it so much.

Dad Cuts My Hair

MY FRIEND PAM HAD HAD HER HAIR CUT INTO A CILLA BLACK BOB and it looked fabulous. I had hair down to my waist and I wasn't allowed to have it cut as Dad had a thing about long hair. Well, he was wallpapering the front room when I thought this might be a good time to ask if I could get my hair cut. He was in a good mood and Mam was out. "Dad," I said. "Please, please can I have my hair cut?" I had my hair in a high ponytail at the time of asking.

"No," was the reply. In for a penny, in for a pound, I thought. He was definitely in a good mood, I could tell by the tone of his voice.

So I pressed on. "PLEASE DAD." As I said the words he cut a piece of wallpaper and it happened to be wrong. OH BOY! I wanted to be invisible! It was my fault—I had distracted him, I'm in for a thrashing now. "YOU WANT YOUR HAIRCUT, DO YOU? WELL, COME HERE," he yelled. I could do nothing but obey. As I stood in front of him, he had a huge pair of paperhanging scissors in his hand. He grabbed hold of my ponytail, pulled it straight up in the air and chopped it off! "There," he said, "you've got your haircut. Now piss off!"

I ran upstairs and looked in the bathroom mirror. I couldn't believe what he'd done to me. I looked SO ridiculous. I had long bits at the front and around the sides with short stubby bits on the top. I looked stupid. Why couldn't he be like other people? Why did he do this? I got a pair of scissors and tried to tidy it up a bit but there wasn't much you could do. I lay on my bed and cried. I don't know why I cried, I think it was a feeling of helplessness that just overwhelmed me. I hated him.

When Mam came in she thought I'd done it to myself. As if! Anyway she called me all the stupid names under the sun. When she stopped yelling long enough for me to tell her that Dad had done it she looked at me, laughed and said, "Well then. You asked for it and you got it. Serves you right." And that was that.

John and Kenny laughed at me and told me I looked like a coconut! Then later they said it didn't look too bad and tried to make me feel better about it, but that was impossible, I figured it would grow and I just pretended to everyone, except my friends Pam and Penny, that this was the way I wanted it.

This was also the year of the mice! Mam was allergic to housework so our house was filthy. Whatever housework was done, us kids did and not very well either. No point, no one cared. Mam just didn't see the need. Dad would go spare every now and again and belt Mam because this wasn't done or that was mouldy. We had dogs fighting in the living room regularly. Dad would bring home a dog he had 'found' and after tea all the furniture would be pushed to the sides of the room and Taurus and the poor mutt Dad had brought home would be brought into the living room and held by Dad and Phil in opposite corners.

On Dad's command they were released and the dogs would start fighting. It didn't stop until Taurus had the mutt by its throat and Dad would have to strangle Taurus off and be declared the winner. So blood, snot and all sorts were spilled on the carpets, not to mention fag ash, tea and anything else that you can think of. The carpets rarely got swept and I can't ever remember us having a Hoover. One of mum's favourite things was, if a carpet got too mucky and stained she would go off to a jumble sale and get another one. She had this 'thing' about underlay, so we never took up the old, mucky carpet, we just put the 'new' one on top of it! Mam reckoned it was better for the new carpet to have underlay and by leaving the old carpet down she was saving money because it acted as a sort of underlay.

This process of Mam's had been done several times so we must have had at least four carpets down. We even had to plane off the bottoms of the doors because they wouldn't open over the pile of carpets! We would take the mickey by saying we'd all be hunchbacks if she kept it up because the floor was getting closer and closer to the ceiling! She also insisted that we didn't cut the carpet to fit the room. She said that if we cut it we couldn't move it to another room if ever we wanted to. The fact that we had never moved a carpet once it was down was immaterial, so every carpet lapped up the walls. It looked delightful!

We had coal fires at that time too and the coal bunker was just outside the back door under the kitchen window. It was a very hard winter so Dad decided to knock a hole through the wall under the sink into the back of the coal bunker. This was to save anyone having to go outside to fetch coal in. So when you opened the cupboard under the sink there, along with the washing powder and

61

washing up liquid was the coal, tumbling through the hole in the wall. We had all the 'mod cons'.

As I said, it was a very cold winter and the mice had found their way up from the field at the bottom of our garden and into the coal bunker. Once in the bunker they were home and dry, straight into the kitchen. They thought they were in paradise. So they invited all their friends and relatives to come to 'PARTY'! Believe me they did, hundreds of them.

Another of Mam's foibles was washing. Doing it, we didn't even have a laundry basket or anything to put dirty clothes into but we did have an airing cupboard and it was in the kitchen. Above the tank in the airing cupboard was all the clean stuff; sheets and towels and stuff like that, and below, stuffed all around the tank, was all the dirty washing. We were into lagging our tank even before it was trendy! The drawback was that it stunk. But we got used to it. Anyway the smell didn't put the mice off, they loved it. They made nests in the mucky washing. When I had to do the washing I would pull all the dirty stuff out, and mice would scuttle all around my feet, making me jump. The dog would go crazy and would catch and eat them. If there were nests with little pink babies he would eat them as though they were jelly babies!

We were overrun by mice and they chewed holes in the clothes, they got into all the cupboards, they chewed their way into flour, sugar, cereal—there were mouse droppings in everything. We would laugh because you could see the scratch marks in the butter. They were everywhere. Mam would leave the frying pan with fat in it on top of the cooker overnight and the next morning there would be tiny footprints in the fat and, funnily enough, there were always little black bits in everything she cooked. "It's all right," she would say as she flicked the black bits off. I like to think she was building up our immune system!

The mice got so cheeky that they came into the living room. They would run across the back of the settee and up the curtains while we were watching telly. The dog would go mad trying to catch them. If he did manage to catch one he would swallow it whole, which made us all laugh. Then the mice discovered the 'run' around the edge of the room where the carpet lapped up the walls. This was perfect for the mice; we could hear them scurrying around the room. Taurus (the dog) would go crazy. He knew where they were but he couldn't get at them. We were completely overrun by mice.

One night we woke to a crashing sound downstairs. We all rushed down to see what was going on. The kitchen was alive with mice. Taurus had jumped onto the draining board but with his front legs and, like a cartoon character, was skimming plates across the kitchen in an attempt to stay on the draining board and catch the mouse. Needless to say the mouse scampered, Taurus fell off and we all laughed.

Dad, being the way he was, and our family, being the way it was, the neighbours didn't like us, or the trouble that followed us. They got up a petition to get us out. Dad took great exception to this and thought up ways to annoy them. Our immediate neighbours to the right were the Polstocks and they hated us all. They bred all different kinds of rabbits; lop-eared, dwarf and others. Well, Dad had been to Haywards Heath and in the pet shop he saw a rabbit that was the same breed and colouring as one of their rabbits so he bought it. That night he and Phil blacked up their faces and crept into their garden. They undid all the rabbit cages and let them all go free. They came back into the house laughing their heads off. Then Dad killed and skinned the rabbit he had bought and hung its pelt on our washing line for them to see.

The next morning there was pandemonium! Mrs Polstock was screaming, "Those animals next door have murdered our rabbits," at the top of her voice. Dad and Phil were in hysterics. Mr Polstock came round (that was a very brave thing for him to do as he was terrified of Dad).

Dad opened the door. "What do you think you are doing?" he said in a very wobbly voice.

Dad loved every minute of this. "What are you talking about, man?"

"You know what I am talking about, my rabbits!" With that, Dad just slammed the door in his face.

The next thing we knew there was a policeman at the door. "Mr Lancaster, could I have a word with you about the disappearance of Mr Polstock's rabbits and the pelt on your washing line?"

Dad looked so cocky, Phil too. "I don't know what you are talking about officer. I know NOTHING about their bloody rabbits but the pelt on the line is one I bought yesterday, look here's the receipt."

The policeman knew something devious was going on but what could he say apart from, "Sorry to bother you, Mr Lancaster, and thank you for your help."

Dad added insult to injury by saying, "If you need any help officer, don't hesitate to ask." When Dad shut the door we all fell about laughing. He had shown 'em! They had to get up very early in the morning to catch him, he said.

Another time they had annoyed him he took their cat and tied it to a tree miles away from home and let Taurus go at it. Luckily, it managed to get away from the dog and climbed the tree, so he left it there. For weeks Mrs Polstock was heard shouting, "Candy," morning, noon and night. Then the cat appeared, very thin but she was alive. Mrs Polstock was thrilled and told Mam and I as we were in the garden, "But," she said, "the funny thing is, whenever she hears Ken cough (Dad had a habit of coughing all the time), she leaps on top of the telly, spits and arches her back."

"Well now, I wonder why she does that," said Mam.

Gimpy and the Cats

I HAD WANTED A CAT FOR AGES and since we were overrun with mice Dad said I could get one. I was so excited. We got it from a farm; it would be a good mouser the lady said. It had better be I thought. It was only a kitten and so small and sweet. It had a bit of a gammy leg so I called it 'Gimpy'. It was a lovely tortoiseshell and she was very pretty. I couldn't believe Dad would really let me have a cat but he did and I was over the moon.

It stayed about six weeks I suppose. Taurus, who had always been encouraged to chase and kill cats, was being driven mad by this playful kitten. "Don't let him kill Gimpy, please Dad," I asked. Taurus was the most obedient dog ever. If Dad told him to leave the kitten alone, even though every fibre of his being wanted to kill it, he would leave it alone, though every time he saw Gimpy he would shake with self-restraint. Dad trained his dogs really well. He treated them like he treated us and if they displeased him he beat them. Now he was teaching Taurus *not* to bite the kitten. The poor old dog would sit with Dad yelling "leave it" at him. The kitten would be climbing all over him; his eyes would be bulging and he would be shaking with restraint but he didn't touch the kitten.

I came home from school one day and called, "Gimpy. Where are you?" No Gimpy. I searched high and low but no cat. "Where's Gimpy, Dad? Has the dog had her?" I asked.

"NO, he hasn't. What do you think I am? You know I taught that dog not to touch her. She must have wandered off." I searched everywhere for her. I waited weeks, thinking she might come back. Every time I went out I was looking for her. It wasn't until years later that Dad told me he had chopped her head off. He said he couldn't stand it so he killed it.

I should have known when I think back to our entertainment evenings. These were when Phil or Dad would go out and catch a cat and put it in a bag. Then we would all troop up the road to Dad's garage by the Rose & Crown. I never really understood why he rented this garage because he never put the car in it although he kept a lot of other stuff there. Anyway, when we were all inside Dad would wind the dog up by holding him by his collar, letting him sniff the bag and all the while he would be saying, "Cats, get it, kill Taurus," and pulling him away from the bag. The dog would be squealing with desire to kill the cat. At that point he would let the cat out of the bag. Once out the dog would go wild and chase the cat. This was our entertainment! We were all encouraged to hate cats and this was supposed to be 'fun', even more so when the dog eventually caught and killed the cat.

One evening Phil came in saying he'd got a 'beaut' cat so Dad said, "Come on kids. Let's have some sport." We all grabbed a coat and ran up to the garage. Phil shook the bag and out of it came the biggest cat I have ever seen. It was enormous! It looked like a small tiger and it was even bigger than Taurus. When it was eventually let out of the bag Taurus ran at the cat but it turned and ran straight up Dad's back and on to his head. Taurus was jumping up and down, barking in frustration. The cat was terrified. It was hissing and spitting and sunk its claws deep into Dad's head. He said later they were like needles.

Every time he put his hand up to get it off it lacerated his hands. "GET THE EFFING THING OFF ME!" he was yelling. The dog was still going crazy, desperate to get his plaything, squealing and so wound up. We were trying to calm the dog down but he wouldn't be calmed, he wanted that cat. Phil didn't know what to do. The dog was jumping up and barking which made the cat spit and claw Dad's head. John, Ken and I were laughing as it looked so funny.

Then Phil had a brainwave. Dad had a 12-bore shotgun which he kept in the garage. Phil got the gun, loaded it and pointed it straight at Dad's head. "Go on Phil, shoot, kill him." I wasn't meaning the cat.

Dad's face went grey. "Put the gun down Phil. DON'T SHOOT." We waited. It seemed an eternity. Was he going to shoot him? We all wanted him to. Dad glared at Phil and he put the gun down. The cat meanwhile had seen the rafters of the garage roof and jumped. She ran along the rafters and disappeared into the next garage. Dad, lacerated and bleeding but very relieved, screamed at Phil, "DON'T YOU EVER POINT A GUN AT ME AGAIN, DO YOU UNDERSTAND?" We were disappointed with Phil. He could have done it but he didn't, though he was wishing he had now. We would have to get rid of Dad another way!

I really hated Dad. He'd started to act really funny with me. I'd never felt safe around him because he was either drunk and angry or sober and angry and I had constant butterflies in my stomach whenever he was around.

I would spend all day Saturday doing housework or shopping; generally doing whatever Mam wanted done, which would put her in a good mood. Then I could ask if I could go and stay at Gran's and, if I had played my cards right, she would say yes. I had got this down to a fine art. I always made her a cuppa, spat in it, got her fags and put the telly on. I then made sure there was nothing left undone in her line of vision, such as an empty coal bucket or dirty cups. I had learnt that anything like that could jeopardise my mission! When I was given permission to go, I would very quickly shove a nighty and a clean pair of knickers in a carrier bag and I was off. I had learnt to my cost not to take too long getting ready as all it took for Mam to change her mind was to decide there was washing to do and that was my job.

I had to walk to Haywards Heath as I had also learnt not to ask for the bus fare—that would be a good reason for me not being allowed to go. So I would walk the four miles. Gran and Grandad were always pleased to see me. I loved them so much. I could do whatever I wanted at Gran's and I just loved being there. I would help Grandad with his garden and we would sit on the bench at the bottom of the garden surveying his estate!

He would tell me what he was going to plant and point out where it would go. I would nod in all the right places as he lit his pipe. He would puff away and chatter to me. I can close my eyes and see him now and smell his pipe. Gran would shout us in when dinner was ready. I loved Sunday dinner at Gran's. She would make Yorkshire puddings the size of dinner plates. We would have one each filled with gravy and a generous dollop of mint sauce. They were lovely, and then we would have meat and veg. When we had finished our pudding I remember asking Gran why she did that and she told me it was to fill you up so you didn't eat so much meat or veg. Apparently they did it during the war because of rationing and it had become a tradition. It worked too. I could never eat much dinner after that as I was always stuffed with lovely Yorkshire pudding.

In the afternoon we would wash up, Grandad would put on the telly and read out to us what was on. It was a little ritual. We would always watch the film, whatever it was, and Gran would bake apple pies, jam tarts and sponge cakes. She would always make extra so that I could take some home. Her sponge cakes were lovely but her pastry was like lead. We would eat it anyway as you could soften it up with a dollop of custard!

When six o'clock came I would get myself ready to leave. Gran would put the pies into a bag ready for me to take home, I would collect all my bits, say goodbye and kiss them both. They always stood on the doorstep to wave me off. Granddad would give me two shillings which would pay for me to catch the bus and have some money for sweets. Good old Grandad!

Abuse

I WAS IN BED FAST ASLEEP when I was woken up by Dad. He was drunk—I could smell his beery breath. He was pulling my vest up and I was frightened. "What are you doing Dad?" I asked. He made a SHHHH sound. I was trying to pull my vest back down as he was feeling my chest. I didn't understand what he was doing but I knew I didn't want him to do this. He leant down towards me and kissed me on my mouth! It was a horrible, wet, sloppy kiss. I felt sick. I squeezed my lips tight shut. I wanted to scream, LEAVE ME ALONE! He stopped, looked at me and then went. I was in shock. Why did he do that? I lay awake for ages in case he came back but thankfully he didn't.

I didn't want to look at him the next morning, I was so nervous of him. I tried not to have eye contact with him He could say lots with his eyes and I didn't want to see, or hear any of it! I tried even harder than before to be invisible. I didn't want him to notice me at all. But of course, he did.

Quite often Mam would cook Dad his dinner and have it all ready. He insisted that his dinner MUST be ready and on the table as he walked through the door. NO WAITING! Well, as I said, she would have it ready and he would be late so she would put his meal onto a plate and put the plate on top of a pan of boiling water to keep it warm. I used to go down to his shed where he had all kinds of bottles and potions, knotting, paint stain, thinners, meths, mouse and rat poisons. I would take a bit from this bottle, a drop from that one, some of this powder, and take it up to the house. When Mam wasn't in the kitchen I would mix my potion into his potatoes and gravy so it wasn't visible in the hope that it would kill him.

Quite often, after he had eaten and gone to bed, we would sneak into his room to see if he was still breathing! When he went to bed he would empty all his 'smash' (loose change) onto his bedside table. Well, several times, when we thought we'd mixed in a particularly potent mix, we would take most of his money and split it between ourselves. We would get such a shock when he came down for his tea! He never seemed to notice that he'd been robbed.

Other times when Dad was so drunk he couldn't get up the stairs he shouted for John and me to help him. We got either side of him, which was quite difficult on our narrow stairs. Anyway, we got him almost to the top when John lost his grip, Dad staggered backwards so I just let go and he went crashing down the stairs. John looked at me and whispered, "You let him go on purpose, didn't you?" I just nodded. We both followed Dad down the stairs. "Is he dead?" John asked.

I put my face close to his, I could feel his breath. "No, he's still alive." We left him there until he woke up.

We persevered with this for quite a few years. A few times we thought we had succeeded, like the time I went up into his bedroom to see if he was still asleep. I had been doing some ironing and was putting the iron away but I was still holding it in my hand when I went upstairs. Dad was fast asleep. I held the iron up above his head and smashed it down as hard as I could, pointy end first! It made a thud sort of noise. He didn't move! I lifted up the iron. There was a triangular hole in his head with white spots in it—then suddenly it gushed with blood. That must have killed him, I thought. I went downstairs and told the boys I had definitely killed him.

We were in a bit of a panic. We hadn't got a clue what to do with his body and at one point we decided we would put him under the compost heap. We didn't know what we would tell Mam. In the end we decided we'd leave him and she would find him dead.

We nearly died when he came downstairs holding his head, saying he felt like he'd had a kicking! "What the f*** happened to me?" he said.

Quick as a flash I said, "You've been fighting Dad."

"Oh," he said as he walked into the kitchen for a wash. Foiled again! We didn't kill him, not through lack of trying, but I feel sure that because of all the stuff we mixed in his dinners, he suffered the rest of his life with terrible stomach ulcers!

It was around this time that Mam had a miscarriage. I remember being in the front room. A single bed had been brought downstairs and Mam was lying on it. I didn't understand what was going on at all. Then the doctor arrived. He and Dad were talking and I just kept making tea for everyone. I worked out through 'ear wigging' that all was not well with the pregnancy. When the doctor left he said that if anything else happened to call him straight away. Well, it was late afternoon. I was in the kitchen and Dad was in with Mam. She was groaning and making weird noises. I remember that I was quite scared. The next thing I knew Dad was standing in the kitchen with a four-inch-long baby in his hand, showing me my brother! He was fascinated. "Look, it's even got fingernails and eyelids," he said. Mam stayed in bed for a few days so I stayed off school to look after her.

Dad was quite nice to Mam at that time, though she didn't know he had taken the baby down to his shed and put it into pickling fluid in a jar! He kept it in there for quite a long time. I remember thinking it was sick to keep your dead baby in a jar, but I was fascinated by this tiny little baby. I would go down the shed and look at this tiny little thing from all angles. It looked so perfect, yet it died. Strange, I thought, as I looked at him. We're related, he's my brother and it all seemed very weird. I nearly told Pam about my baby brother in the shed but something told me this wasn't something to share.

Life was pretty difficult at home. Mam was very depressed after losing the baby, Dad was working on and off, also doing the odd 'job', but money was still scarce. This caused many rows between Mam and Dad. We all tried to keep our heads down but we got it in the neck from both of them. We couldn't win.

As time went by Mam seemed to be feeling a bit better. Dad had given her some money to go to bingo with and she was chuffed to be going out. I was told to get the boys ready for bed at 8 o'clock and they both went out, Mam to the bingo, Dad to the boozer. We watched telly, then at eight I said, "Come on you two, bed." They were very good and usually did what I said. We all trooped upstairs, into bed and lights out. I made myself a cuppa and went up to bed myself.

I had been in bed for about an hour when Dad came in. At first I thought it was Mam but wild horses wouldn't drag her from the bingo. I listened intently, trying to work out where in the house he was. I heard him on the stairs and my heart started pounding. I was so frightened. I'd pretend to be asleep and then he would leave me alone. I knew that the boys were asleep so there was no one to save me. He came into my room and quietly closed the door. My heart was pounding so loud I thought he could hear it. He pulled the blankets off me and I turned to him. "PLEASE DON'T, DAD."

"Shhhush," he said and in the half-light he gave me the look that said, 'Do as I say or else!'

He was feeling my chest. I didn't like the feel of his hand on my skin. I was trying to move away from his touch. He kissed me, the wet horrible kiss. I clenched my lips tightly together. He lay down next to me, then in a flash he was on top of me. I was scared. *What's he doing?* I thought. I could feel him so heavy on top of me. He was kissing me again and then I felt something poking me in my tummy, then between my legs. He was moving up and down, he was hurting me and he kept kissing me. They were wet horrible kisses. I wanted to cry. It seemed to go on for ages and then suddenly, he jumped up and went. I lay in my bed so scared he would come back. I cried, but I cried quietly. I didn't want anyone to come in. I couldn't work out what was going on. I'd rather he thrashed me than do that.

With Gran and Grandad living in Haywards Heath I was still allowed to stay with them for the weekend, IF I had done everything Mam could think of to make me do. Anyway, this particular weekend Mam had said I could go. I loved staying with them; life was so easy and you weren't constantly nervous like at home. She never shouted at me, she was lovely and kind. Granddad was as soft as a brush and I loved them both so much. I loved to help Grandad in his garden and go shopping with granny. Well, this weekend we did all of that. We had a lovely day on Saturday and on the Sunday we had a lovely roast dinner. Granddad had gone for his nap and we were going to dig over the veggie plot when he woke.

Gran and I were washing up when in walked Dad and he was so drunk. He had been sat in the park, drinking meths with a tramp. He looked terrible and smelt worse. I was very nervous of him. He was shouting at granny and then I heard, "AND SHE'S COMING HOME WITH ME NOW AND I'M GOING TO HAVE HER!" I knew what he meant and I felt sick and frightened all in one. Granny won't let him take me, I'm sure she won't. But she did, she couldn't stop him. "Get your coat," he said. I looked at Gran but she was powerless against him, she wouldn't have eye contact with me. I was screaming inside. I wanted her to save me, to stop this hateful man taking me but she couldn't, she was scared of him too.

My heart was beating fit to burst! I did as I was told. We had to walk up to the bus stop in Boltro Road. He held onto my shoulder as we walked. I couldn't speak, I was so frightened of what he was going to do to me. When the bus finally came, my friend Pam was already on. I rushed to sit next to her and Dad sat behind us. Dad kept shouting and insulting the people who got on the bus. I wanted to die. Pam thought it was funny, him being drunk. I couldn't tell her how unfunny it was!

At Butler's Green a very butch-looking lady got on. Dad called out that she was a lesbian. I had no idea what a lesbian was. Dad leaned into us and asked Pam and I if we knew anything about lesbians? Pam said, "No" and I shook my head. He then went into great detail as to what a lesbian was and what they did. I was so embarrassed. Poor Pam, I thought. She was embarrassed too.

We all got off the bus at the Wheatsheaf and walked together, Dad hanging onto my shoulder. I wanted to run away, I wanted to push him under every car that passed us, I wanted to tell Pam what he was going to do to me but I couldn't do anything. I didn't have the courage. In no time at all we were home. *Please, please be home, Mam*, I thought. We went indoors and Dad shouted, "Anybody home?" *Please answer, someone.* No one did! "Upstairs you, NOW," and he pushed me through to the hall.

I couldn't breathe, let alone talk. We had a handrail at that time that ran halfway up the stairs. I put my arm through the rails and around the banister. "NO," I said, "PLEEEASE don't Dad. I'm not going upstairs."

He grabbed my hair and pulled. "Let go you little cow," he yelled at me. I held on for dear life as he tried to pry me from the banister but I wasn't budging. By this time I was crying, begging and pleading with him not to do this terrible thing. I don't know where I got my strength from but he couldn't pry me off the banister. "I will have you!" was the last thing he said to me and then the back door went. Quick as a flash, he said, "Tell her you're crying because I won't let you stay with your granny."

Mam appeared at the hall door. I was red-faced, sobbing and snotty. "What's the matter with you?" she asked.

"Dad won't let me stay at granny's."

"Well, shut up and make a cuppa," she said. I rushed into the kitchen while Dad went into the sitting room, sat and chatted to Mam. I was shaking, my heart pounding in my ears. I was so relieved. I felt weak and my legs felt wobbly. I made them both a cuppa and took it into the sitting room. Dad drank his tea and then took Mam to bed, and I went and sat under the hedge. He wasn't half as drunk as he was making out to be, the BASTARD. I hated him so much. I had never been so pleased to see Mam.

For some reason Dad always washed in the kitchen. He would move all the dirty dishes out of the sink, fill it with hot water and proceed to scrub himself. It was fascinating to watch because he would cup his hands and scoop water and throw it at his face. He would have water all over the kitchen floor and all up the walls. Mind you, that was the only water the kitchen floor ever saw, it was never washed! Then he would get his toothbrush, dip it into his Smokers Eucryl tooth powder and brush vigorously for ages. Sometimes I would go into the kitchen when no one was home and dip his toothbrush into the powder and brush my teeth with it. I loved the feeling of clean teeth and I couldn't wait to be a grown-up and be able to clean my teeth every day. I didn't realise that children could clean their teeth; we weren't even worth a toothbrush.

Colin Wolf

ONE TIME I WAITED AT THE BUS STOP FOR AGES. The last bus was six thirty and I waited till ten to seven, then thought I had better start walking or Mam would go ballistic. I walked from one bus stop to the next, convinced that the bus would come. I was just kidding myself. By the time I got to Tyler's Green it had started to get dusky. I could hear footsteps behind me but I couldn't see anyone and it made me a little nervous. I quickened my step. I was just rounding the corner coming into Cuckfield when I was aware that someone was close behind me.

I turned round and saw Colin Wolf, a 19-year-old boy who lived down our road. His Dad was on speaking terms with my Dad but I had nothing to do with Colin. I don't think I had ever spoken to him before. I was really startled to find him so close to me. "Hello Fay," he said. Something in his voice made me scared.

"Hello. I've got to rush, my Dad is waiting for me at the bus stop," I said. (He wasn't but I thought it might scare him.) We had walked round the corner, when suddenly Colin said, "Let's see what you're made of!" and pushed me through a gap in a big hedge.

We were in the garden of a posh house. I was so scared! Why did he do that? What did he mean? My mind went crazy but it was like a dream. He grabbed hold of me and started pulling at my coat. My buttons popped off and then he was pulling at my dress and trying to kiss me. I was fighting him but I had no strength. This was different to fighting with John and Ken; he meant to hurt me. I had to fight him! He put his hand up my dress and pulled my knickers. He pulled them so hard he ripped the crotch completely out at the front. My heart was pounding so hard in my chest. I felt dizzy.

Then from nowhere came a sudden burst of strength. Throughout this whole ordeal I had held on to Gran's pies! I swung the bag with such force. I hit him in the face and he let go of me. I couldn't get past him, so I ran to the house and banged on the door. "PLEASE OPEN THE DOOR!" No one came. I turned and he was grabbing me again, calling me a stupid bitch. His hands were all over me. He said he would teach me a lesson.

I felt sick. His breath was on my face and his hands were on my skin! His nails were digging into me. I was scratching and hitting him but it had no effect. Then I saw his willy! He was pulling me close, lifting up my clothes and I could feel his willy on my leg. "PLEASE DON'T," I begged him. He laughed and continued pulling and poking me. I was terrified. He was trying to get me onto the floor. I was doing everything in my power to stay upright. He almost got me to the floor when it dawned on me to bite him. Why hadn't I thought of that before? I sunk my teeth deep into his shoulder, trying to make my teeth meet!

Now he was trying to get me to let go of him! He was yelling, "LET GO, YOU EFFING BITCH!" I did and ran to the gap in the hedge. He wasn't behind me and I just kept on running all the way home. Halfway up London Lane I realised my dress was all open at the front, my knickers were hanging off and I had only one shoe on. I pulled my dress together, still running and hugging myself and I ran in the back door.

Mam yelled, "Where the bloody hell have you been till this time?" Then I burst into the living room. Everyone turned to look at me, the shock on their faces scared me. "What happened?" Mam said as she got out of her chair and came towards me.

I couldn't speak for sobbing. "Co- Co- Colin, sob sob, W- W- Wolf, sob, sniff." I looked up.

Dad was sitting in the armchair, clutching the wooden arms so tight that his knuckles were completely white. "Colin Wolf what?" said Dad.

I started to tell what had happened when Phil jumped up and shouted, "THE BASTARD!" I thought Dad would kill him for saying that but he didn't say a word. When I had finished telling them what had happened Mam picked up the poker and said "right" and walked out of the house. I wondered where she had gone. Dad never moved. He just sat with his white knuckles in the chair. John, bless him, made me a cup of tea while I tried to calm down. But I just couldn't, the sobs wouldn't stop. John and Ken kept rubbing me, telling me I would be all right.

Suddenly, the door burst open and in flew Colin Wolf followed by Mam wielding the poker. "Get in there, you little shit," she was saying. I just stared at Mam; she kept prodding him with the poker. Apparently, she had knocked on his front door, he answered and she dragged him out and kicked and poked him all the way round to our house.

Dad looked up at him. Dad was clenching his teeth and he didn't unclench them all the time he was speaking to Colin. He was really mad. Colin stood looking terrified. Dad said, "What do you think you were doing, messing with a 12-year-old girl?"

Colin Wolf swallowed hard, then said, "I don't know what came over me. I'm so sorry, Mr Lancaster."

Then Dad said, "If you want to drag someone behind a hedge and mess about with them, take him," pointing to Phil. He then said, "Phil, take him outside and give him a good hiding." Phil jumped up, pushed Wolf outside and proceeded to knock him senseless. He was bleeding and begging Phil to stop. Then Dad stepped in and stopped it. Wolfie was crying He looked pathetic. Dad said, "You're not such a big fella now are you, you dirty little bastard?"

Mam jumped in and threatened him that if he so much as look at me again she would have his eyes out. As she said that she poked the air with the poker to emphasise her point. Dad dragged him to the gate and threw him out of the garden.

When Colin Wolf had gone Mam took me in the kitchen and asked me what exactly he had done to me. "Did he take his willy out?"

"YES," I replied.

"What did he do with it?" she asked.

"He touched me with it!"

"Where?"

"Up my frock," I answered. She was trying to find out if he had raped me but my answers weren't very clear. She just swore a lot and told Phil to give that Wolfie git another good hiding next time he saw him. Phil was in his element. He was the hero of the day.

"Nobody messes with my sister and gets away with it." I went and had a bath. It was the first chance I had to look at what he had done to me. I took off my dress; all the buttons were missing and the buttonholes were ripped. I remember being cross about that. I liked that dress and he had spoiled it. I looked in the mirror. I felt sick when I saw what he had done to me. I didn't have any breasts, they hadn't begun to develop yet, but Colin Wolf hadn't known that. He had groped around inside my dress and when he realised I didn't have what he was looking for, he dug his nails so deep into my chest. It looked as if he had tried to pull my nipples off. The nail marks seemed to be in a perfect circle.

I took off my knickers, or what was left of them! I remember looking down at them. The crotch was only attached at the back; he had ripped it off at the front. The tops of my legs had deep scratches and felt so sore. When I turned around and looked at my back, it was as though I had been whipped. There were long weals across my back. I knew he was hurting me but I didn't realise quite how much.

I climbed into the bath. I remember how the cuts stung as the water washed over them but it felt good, warm and comforting. I lay in the bath for ages looking at the scratches and thinking why? He didn't know me. What was it in me that made him do all that stuff to me? As I thought about what had happened I remembered Gran's pies and how I was glad she made pastry like lead. I smiled to myself as I thought, 'I bet he thought I'd got a brick in the bag when I hit him with it.' He would never in a million years guess it was apple pies! Good old Gran!

Mam came up to the bathroom. I was out of the bath and into my nighty. I remember it so vividly. I didn't want her to see what he had done to me. She put her arms around me and cuddled me. I was so taken aback; it was the only time I ever remember her doing it. It felt awkward but I liked it and then she said I should go to bed and put it all out of my mind. She had taken care of 'him' and Phil would keep him in check from now on. He wouldn't dare to lay so much as a finger on me or Phil would kill him.

I lay in bed for ages. I couldn't get to sleep. I remembered Colin Wolf saying, "Please Mr Lancaster, don't report me to the police and please don't tell my Dad." He didn't tell his parents or the police and I always wondered why. I think now as an adult, he was scared if the police were called I might say what he was doing to me. I found out years later that Colin Wolf had gone on to rape a girl he picked up at a bus stop and then raped another girl at knifepoint. If only they had reported him maybe he would have been stopped. Who knows?

When Dad had been out drinking we could tell by the way that he walked what kind of mood he was in. Often we would keep a lookout for him coming home. As soon as we saw him we knew what to expect. If 'the walk' told us he was in a bad mood we knew someone was going to get a thrashing so whoever had been 'lookout' would come running. "Quick, he's coming and he's mad!" We would all run out of the back door, through the hedge at the bottom of the garden into the safety of the field. There was quite a drop from our garden to the field so you couldn't see us. We would sit under the hedge come rain, hail or snow until he had eaten his dinner and taken Mam to bed. Dad was drinking so much at this time he was hardly ever sober.

Ferrets

I WOULD SPEND AS MUCH TIME OUT OF THE HOUSE as I could. I had a ferret called Freda and she was lovely. I would take her to school with me inside my jumper. Once Kenny was helping me clean out the ferrets and he shoved Freda up *his* jumper. She must have tickled his tummy with her claws. Anyway, he squealed and she was out of the neck of his jumper and had sunk her teeth into his chin in a flash. He screamed like a stuck pig. It took ages to get her off. Funny thing was, Kenny never wanted to help me anymore. Freda was so tame and she was an excellent rabbiter—she put food on our table many a time.

Dad had a polecat at that time called Freddy. He was a huge, mean fellow and I was scared of him. He would bite you as soon as look at you. Well, I had mated him with Freda and she had 14 babies! They were lovely but we had to take Freddy out of the hutch as soon as the babies were born or he would have eaten them, so Dad told me. Dad put a bale of hay in his shed and said Freddy could run loose there until he made a hutch for Freddy. So when I fed Freda Dad asked me if I would do the same for Freddy. I didn't like doing it because I had to open the shed door and grab Freddy. He would rush to get out so you had to grab him at the back of his neck, pick him up, put his food down and then throw him into the bale of hay and quickly shut the door, giving the bottom of the door a kick because it stuck. I never liked feeding him; he was too stroppy for my liking.

On this particular day, I had fed him and Freda. I let Freda and the babies out into the garden. They were so sweet and they played in a small hedge near the shed. They would jump onto each other, wrestling and play-fighting. John, Kenny and I loved watching them play. The boys would catch a couple of babies and lay on the floor and let the babies climb all over them; they loved them too. Freda was such a good mum, always on the lookout for danger. They tired themselves and poor old Freda out, so we would spend ages trying to catch them all and back into the hutch they went.

Next morning, after laying the fire in the sitting room, John would light it and make sure it didn't go out, and I put the pan on for porridge. I headed down the garden to feed Freda and her family. I was standing by the hutch when Dad came down the garden on his way to feed Freddy. I didn't see Dad open the shed door, I just heard him! He came out of the shed like a lunatic and in his hand he was wielding a dead, stiff Freddy! "YOU KILLED HIM! YOU STUPID BITCH! YOU BROKE HIS NECK." Dad was holding the deceased Freddy like a sword, with Freddy's head in his hand and his body pointing at me. I was scared.

What's he going to do to me?' I thought. "I'm so sorry Dad. I didn't mean to. He must have rushed at the door when I shut it." I had obviously broken his neck as I kicked the door closed. The next thing I knew I was being thrashed with a dead polecat! He was stiff and, boy, did it hurt. Even so I thought this was a bizarre situation and I wanted to laugh. I had been hit with everything from a hairbrush to a clothes prop but this was definitely the first time I'd been hit with a dead polecat!

After the babies had been sold and Freda was back to full health a friend of Dad's called round. He was a gypsy called Trevor and he asked Dad if he could borrow a ferret. He wanted to go rabbiting and didn't have a good rabbiter so Dad lent him Freda. I was upset; he didn't consider asking me if I minded. I minded! But that made no difference. I guess Dad knew that so he didn't bother asking me, he just told me to go get her. Trevor put her in a bag. I knew not to question Dad too much but I did ask how long he was borrowing her for. "Till he's finished with her," he said and that was the end of that. I was gutted, she was my pet and I loved her.

Weeks went by and I kept asking Dad when Trevor was bringing Freda back. "It's only a bleedin' ferret, now don't ask me again." It was a Sunday evening when Trevor arrived. "I put the ferret in the old copper boiler outside," he said.

Our back garden was always full of scrap metal bits. Dad had been given an old copper boiler to weigh in for scrap and poor old Freda was in it. I went straight out, lifted her out and cuddled her. I was so pleased to see her but shocked to see how thin she was. I took her into the kitchen and into the light. She looked ill. I poured some milk into a bowl and put it on the floor for her to drink but she just fell over, she couldn't stand up. I wanted to cry. I went into the living room. Dad and Trevor were off to the pub. I asked Dad to have a look at

Freda. "She can't stand up, Dad." Trevor said he thought she'd eaten a dodgy rabbit but she'd be OK.

"It's nature's way," he said. I wanted to punch him. He didn't care about Freda, she was just an old ferret to him, but she was mine and I really loved her. I took her up to my bedroom and kept her with me all night. I kept trying to feed her; she was trying to drink but didn't seem able to.

Next morning I asked Dad if I could take her to the vets. "If you can pay for it," he said. I had earned three shillings helping Grandad in the garden so I set off and walked to Haywards Heath with Freda up my jumper. When I got to the vets I explained how she had been borrowed by a friend of my Dad's and this was the state she was in when he brought her back to me. He examined her and when he tried to open her mouth he couldn't. A good look revealed that she had a rabbit's vertebrae stuck between her top and bottom teeth. After a bit of a struggle he got it out but the vet said he didn't hold out much hope for her as he thought she must have had it stuck in there for a couple of weeks. She had in fact been starving to death and was very weak.

I was gutted but thought if I took her home and fed her she would recover. I put her up my jumper to keep her warm but she was past saving and died on the way home. I was devastated. What a way to die! Poor Freda. I cried for ages as I carried her thin lifeless little body home and buried her. I was filled with hatred towards Trevor for starving her to death and to Dad for lending her to him.

A few weeks later Dad decided to get himself another ferret. He said he would get me one too, so he and Phil went off to buy ferrets. They came back with three, one for me and two for Dad, but on the way they decided to let the dog have Dad's ferrets to see how long it would take the dog to kill them!

They came back all hyper. "Come down the field for a bit of sport," said Phil. "We're going to see how long it takes the dog to kill the ferrets." So we all traipsed over the field. The dog was so excited. He had done this before so he knew what the crack was. Dad was winding him up on the way so as soon as the ferret was released Taurus was on it in a flash and in a second it was dead. "OH, that was too quick. Let him calm down a bit," Dad said. Taurus was an excellent ratter so this was sport to him and he loved it, almost as much as Dad did. The next ferret was released and SNAP, he had it in his jaw before we even realised that Dad had let go of it. "That was disappointing. Go get yours Fay. It might have a bit more fight in it than those two," said Dad.

"Oh please don't kill mine Dad."

"Phil go get it," he replied. So Phil ran home and got my ferret. He arrived back and I was still pleading with Dad not to kill it as Phil released it. Taurus was taken by surprise. The ferret bit his lip and hung on literally for dear life with Taurus trying to shake her off. It didn't take long until Taurus had grabbed her, sunk his teeth into her and she was dead. "Good boy," said Dad to the dog. Phil loved all the dog fighting. John, Ken and I weren't keen but we had to go to watch. If we said we didn't want to we would have been in trouble and mocked for being soft…and we weren't allowed to be soft, particularly the boys! Tough was what we had to be and if we weren't, Dad would toughen 'em up!

Poor Taurus was bleeding. I was glad she bit his lip and I was mad at Taurus. Even so I realised that he only did what he was told to do. Just like us he too was scared of Dad and so I couldn't be mad with him for long.

It wasn't just ferrets that Dad took over the field to kill. He would take Taurus and anything, including ferrets, cats or dogs. It was Phil's quest to find a dog that would beat Taurus, not because he hated the dog but if he could beat Taurus it was a way of beating Dad and we all wanted to do that.

With that in mind he rang a dog rescue centre and after much toing and froing and telling many porkies, went to collect this dog. I came home from school and Phil was there. He was all excited. "Look what I've got," he said and pointed towards the outhouse, a brick-built shed attached to the house. It had a small window three-quarters of the way up the door and looking out of that window was what looked like a donkey!

"What's that?" I said.

"It's an Irish wolfhound and it'll do Taurus, you wait and see."

Dad arrived home and when he saw what we called the donkey he laughed and said "No chance. Taurus will eat it." So over the field we all go with both dogs. We all wanted to see what would happen. Both Dad and Phil were winding their dogs up as we walked across the field. They faced the dogs towards each other and, after egging them both on, let them go. Taurus went straight for the donkey's throat and hung on; his feet didn't even touch the ground. The poor wolfhound was trying desperately to shake him off but Taurus wasn't having any of that so after what seemed like ages of the wolfhound trying to shake Taurus off, Dad and Phil intervened and strangled Taurus off. Both dogs were tired so Dad said we would go home, let them both rest and do it again tomorrow!

When we got home Dad sewed up the wolfhound's wounds, fed him and put him back in the outhouse. Phil was saying that his dog would kill Taurus tomorrow, you just wait and see. But the following night when Dad was home from work again we all traipsed over the field. Again they faced the dogs and let go. This time the wolfhound just ran and ran and ran in the opposite direction to Taurus. Taurus ran after him for a little while but Dad whistled him back. That wolfhound wasn't nearly as daft as it looked, it just kept on running. We were all laughing, we never saw it again. Poor Phil, he was gutted. Dad had won yet again.

I remember Dad going out. He had a three-wheeler and he was going on a bender, we knew that much. He and Mam had had a row and that always gave him an excuse to go really mad. Anyway, Mam went off to her bingo, she loved it. We were left to get ourselves to bed which we did without much ado. Next morning I made the fire, fed my ferrets, put the pan on for porridge but Dad didn't appear to make the porridge. He had this thing that no one could make it like him. John loved it and would eat often eat the panful. I sent Ken upstairs to look in to Mam and Dad's bedroom and see if Dad was still asleep. He came back down with the news that Mam was fast asleep but Dad wasn't there. John went out to see if the car was there. No, it wasn't. This meant trouble.

Hard Times

I GOT THE BOYS OFF TO SCHOOL, washed up and then Mam came down. "Where's your father?" she asked.

"I don't know, he didn't come down and do the porridge this morning," I said.

She looked shocked. "Where the hell can he be?" she said, not really wanting an answer. "Make me a cuppa." I did, she lit a fag and took a long drag. "He'll come home Mam, don't worry," I said.

It was about then that we realised that the dog was missing too; Dad must have taken Taurus with him. I went off to school, leaving Mam in a state. When I got home a policeman was at the front door. Apparently, Dad was arrested in the early hours of the morning in Brighton at the Seven Dials. He was so drunk he had stopped the car and got out to try to read the road sign. A policeman saw him and asked him what he was doing. Dad was incensed that this copper dare question his judgement, so he hit him. Then several other policemen became involved. Anyway, he was in Brighton nick. Here we go again! He was done for GBH, got 18 months and went to Wandsworth Prison.

Mam was so upset that I felt quite sorry for her. We told the boys that Dad was working away. John was particularly upset. He really loved Dad and was sad that he hadn't said goodbye. I, on the other hand, was thrilled. I breathed a sigh of relief when Mam said he'd got 18 months. 'Brilliant', I thought; he couldn't mess about with me from there.

Taurus was still missing. It seemed that when Dad was fighting the policemen, Taurus had got out of the car so when Dad was arrested and the car impounded the dog was left to wander the streets. About a week later we heard a whining noise at the back door. We opened it and in rushed a very thin Taurus! We were all so pleased to see him, even Mam. We were full of praise for him and how had he found his way home. We gave him a rabbit we had caught earlier and he wolfed it down. He drank gallons of water too, then he settled in front of the fire and slept. He made us all laugh because after eating a whole rabbit he spent the rest of the evening farting. He was so stinky but we didn't mind. We loved him.

We struggled on. I don't think there were such things as 'benefits' then. All I know is that life was hard. Mam had cleaning jobs and John and I would go rabbiting—we ate a lot of rabbit. It was a very harsh winter and the snow lay thick on the ground. My feet were so cold I couldn't wait to get home and warm them in front of the fire.

When I got home one day the house was dark and cold. Mam was sat in the living room in her coat, smoking a fag. "They've cut off the electric," she said.

"What about the fire?" I asked, my feet tingling with cold.

"We've got no coal," she said. The boys came in and they were cold too. 'What are we going to do?' I thought. Then Mam said, "Right, we'll not bloody freeze. John, go and get the hatchet." John did as he was told. "Help me with this chair, Fay," said Mam.

"What are we doing with it Mam?" I asked.

"Burning the bugger," she said and laughed. We all started chopping and pulling the chair to bits. Mam laid the newspaper in but we didn't have any kindling wood so John pulled out some stuffing from the chair.

"That'll do," I said. Then on went some wood from the arm of the chair. We soon had a grand fire going. We did toast on long bits of wire held close to the fire. Kenny kept whining, his hands were burning so he couldn't toast his bread. Still, all in all it was quite a good evening. We were warm, our bellies were full and we had loads more furniture to burn.

On one of our rabbiting expeditions John and I discovered the back way into the coal yard. It was quite difficult but we did it! I took the rabbits out of the bag, tied them together with my shoelace and slung them around my neck. We then proceeded to fill the bag and our pockets with coal. It was very heavy but we managed to get it over the wall, across the fields and home. Mam was thrilled when she saw what we had got and, what's more, we could always go back for more, which we did regularly. Things were looking up.

We also found an orchard with loads of pigs in it. There were styes, sheds and all sorts of wooden buildings. We were very quiet as we searched through these buildings, finding all sorts of things. We took some strange-looking brass things which turned out to be old-fashioned stirrup pumps. We had fun with those, squirting each other. We made our way into the orchard where we had to climb the trees to get any apples because as soon as they fell to the ground the pigs had them. Once we had collected enough apples we turned our attention to the pigs. We thought they were great, the piglets were lovely but the big ones were a bit scary. John got on to the back of one and was pretending to be a rodeo cowboy. Well, that gave us all a laugh and we all tried. We fell off, got trodden on and the muck that we fell into was really stinky but we didn't care, it was fun. These pigs could be really nasty sometimes. They would try to squash you up against the wall and try to bite you, but it all added to the excitement. This was fun, we would come here again. We did, often. Mam was pleased with our spoils too, so everyone was happy.

Phil was still in Court Lees. When he behaved himself he would come home on leave and tell us how awful it was. He hated going back and I felt so sorry for him. One night about three o'clock I was woken by tapping on my bedroom window. I got up, looked out and there was Phil. I couldn't believe my eyes. "What are you doing here?" I whispered.

"I've run away and I'm not going back." Poor old Phil. He looked exhausted as he climbed in through my window.

Gran and Grandad had gone on holiday to Durham and had given me the key to their flat. I was looking after Grandad's plants. "Here's the key to granny's. Go there. I promise I won't tell anyone where you are. You'd better go if you want to get to Haywards Heath before it gets light."

"Thanks Faydee. Better get moving," and he was off, out of the window and away. I had difficulty getting back to sleep, wondering if Phil had made it to granny's. I imagined policemen and dogs tracking him down. The truth of it was they wouldn't even realise he was missing until breakfast.

I went down to granny's to see to the plants. Phil was there, like Lord Muck. He sat watching telly, eating peaches out of a tin. "Have the law been round?" he asked.

"Not that I know of and Mam would have said something but she hasn't so you're OK." I saw to the plants and we watched telly for a bit. "I'd better be off, do you need anything?"

He looked thoughtful for a moment and then said, "Naaa. Gran's got plenty of grub in, though if you can get me some money that would be handy."

"OK, I'll try," I said and off I went. By the time I got home the police had been.

"Phil's run away," Mam said. "Where the hell can he be?" She looked at me.

"I don't know Mam," I said rather indignantly.

"Make a cuppa," she said. I went through to the kitchen. John and Ken were telling me that 'the coppers came'. I made the tea and we all sat in front of the fire. We had discovered that old shoes burn really well and they last a long time. Needless to say we had burnt all but one pair each—even Dad's shoes had gone on the fire.

I guess Phil had been at granny's for about a week. I remember the headmaster of Court Lees coming to our house and asking me if I knew where Phil was. I looked him dead in the eye. "No sir, I don't know where he can be; I'm so worried about him." *Silly old git*, I thought. *You won't find him if I've got owt to do with it.*

"Good girl," he said. "Don't you worry, we'll find him."

No you won't, I thought, but they did, two days later and dragged him back to Court Lees. Mind you, I got a good hiding from Mam when she realised the only way Phil could have got into Gran's flat was if I had given him the key and I must have seen him when I watered the plants. No amount of protestation on my part would convince her I was innocent. I thought it was worth a try!

John and Kenny were playing in the garden. The next thing Mam and I knew, John came running in, tears falling down his face. "It's not true, is it Mam?"

"What are you talking about, love?" she said. Mrs Grange, our next-door neighbour, had told the boys off. They had been throwing mud at each other and some had gone over into her garden.

She shouted, "You little swines. You should be locked in a cell like your father; you're not fit to run loose!" Mam was out in the garden quick as a flash and I was behind her. I wasn't going to miss this for anything.

Mam was over the fence and grabbed hold of Mrs Grange. "HOW DARE YOU! DO YOU GET SOME KIND OF KICK UPSETTING CHILDREN? YOU OLD COW, DON'T YOU SO MUCH AS SPEAK TO MY KIDS AGAIN OR I'LL MURDER YOU, YOU BITCH!" We just stood there, our mouths open. Brilliant, good old Mam, she was our heroine. She climbed back over the fence and back indoors we went.

"That told her Mam, old cow." Then we realised that John wasn't entering into the 'after punch-up banter'. Mam called him, poor little man, he looked so sad. "Is it true Mam, is Dad locked up in jail?"

"Yes love, he is, but he'll be home soon, don't you worry about that and don't let that old cow next door upset you, she knows nothing." I thought that was a daft thing to say cos she did know that Dad was in nick, but it seemed to help John. He was full of questions: Where is the jail? How long will he be there? When will he be home? Are you sure he's going to come home? Mam answered them all and John seemed calmer but he just sat in the garden all afternoon and irritated Kenny because he didn't want to play. Kenny had taken it all in his stride, bless him; he was only little, I thought.

Winter Blues

WINTER CONTINUED AND IT WAS AWFUL. I remember it so clearly only because I suffered terribly with chilblains; they were SO, SO painful. I used to take off my wellies, hold my feet in front of the fire till they tingled and then I would just rub my feet on the carpet. They itched so much, but when I stopped rubbing them it was agony so I would keep on rubbing, knowing that if I stopped I was in for some serious pain. I rubbed some more until I realised they were bleeding. That was a painful winter. Mam would tell me off and say it was my own fault, I shouldn't put them in front of the fire but I couldn't help myself.

I also remember Christmas. We had no money and no illusions that Father Christmas would bring us toys. We learnt that lesson long ago. In fact, the first Christmas I remember Dad was in prison, it was Christmas Eve and, as always, no money. Mam was looking out of the window and called us over. "Look, there's the North Star. That's yours, that's all I can give you," she said. We all looked at the star. It was lovely and twinkled beautifully and I'm sure, at that time, we were the only kids to own a star. But, you can't play with it, you can't eat it and when we woke up on Christmas morning it was gone. So when Mam said she gave us a star it sounded so romantic and lovely but in reality it was crap!

I remember another Christmas when Dad was in the nick again and Mam had no money as usual, but she did have a doll. It was *her* doll. It was made of celluloid, he was called Jimmy and she had had him since she was a little girl and she kept him in a cupboard. Well, here we were on Christmas Day and no toys, so she gave Jimmy to me! I was thrilled, she had never let me play with him and I had always wanted a doll. Well, play with him I did. I made a bed out of tea towels and put him to bed. Kenny had other ideas and went to pick him up. In the scuffle I fell on top of Jimmy. He had a funny sort of body and anyway it now had a big dent in it. Mam went mad, she walloped me and told me I didn't deserve anything nice and took Jimmy off me. I never saw him again until years later in Mam's cupboard which brought this memory tumbling back.

Winter was a long time going that year but spring arrived on time. It was lovely to see the spring flowers. One old lady friend of Mam's (we called her 'The Old Mort') was particularly glad to see them. She was a gypsy and her sons were drinking pals of dads. She was a sweet old lady and would call in on us at least once a week. Quite often she had been into the village shops where they would give her the stale bread and bacon pieces. She, bless her heart, would come to our house and give Mam the best bits of bread, bacon or whatever else she had. "You got to feed them their chevies," she would say. She was a sight to behold. No more than five foot tall, her face had more lines on it than a road map, she had brown weathered skin and the most beautiful piercing blue eyes. Her hands were rough and always dirty; they looked like a navvy's from all the hard work she did. She seemed to be the only one in her family who actually worked and she did plenty of that.

She was lovely. She always wore skirts down to her ankles and she seemed to wear loads of skirts at once and on top of them she wore an apron. She always seemed to have several jumpers too and on top of all that she wore a beige raincoat that hadn't been beige for a long time.

Well, in the spring she would pick primroses and bunch them up until she had a basketful. Her basket was enormous, like an old baker's basket, and she would walk into Haywards Heath, stand outside Woolworths and sell her flowers. Quite often, if she'd had a good day, on her way back home she would call in to us with some grub. She was so kind; she understood what it was like to go without. Her sons were all big drinkers like my Dad and she knew all the consequences of that. Also she had seen my Dad blind drunk and he scared her. Anyway, she was the main provider for her family and, bless her, she even provided for us whenever she could.

Money being tight yet again, Mam decided that the Old Mort's flower selling was a good idea so she said I wasn't going to school and to plait my hair, put on one of her skirts and a pinny. I looked like a little gypsy, which was the plan. We walked to Haywards Heath on the side of the road. In people's gardens there were hundreds of daffodils, so we just picked as many as we could carry. We wrapped them into bunches, carted them into the Heath, parked ourselves outside Woolies and sold our stolen spring flowers. We made a few quid and Mam was chuffed. We did it a few times. I remember one time selling a bunch to my art teacher who didn't recognise me, thank goodness! We were sad to see the end of spring and those lovely flowers.

The weeks came and went and Mam was getting all excited because Dad would be home soon. John was thrilled and was counting the days. I, on the other hand, was dreading his return. It had been bliss while he was away: no butterfly in my tummy, no looking for him coming in drunk and no being scared of him. I had slept at night, not lay awake wondering if he would come in. Now he was coming back.

John, bless him, had never stopped wetting the bed since he was little. Mam did what she always did and hit him for doing it, poor old thing, I remember one time Mam got an alarm thing that went on his bed and as soon as it got the slightest bit damp it would sound the alarm. Well, we were all in bed and all of a sudden this alarm went off. Everybody woke up except John; he slept through the whole thing. Mam disconnected it in the end. I have a picture in my mind of John, head bowed and Mam yelling at him, telling him what a disgusting little bleeder he was. She seemed to take delight in making him feel dirty and ashamed and then she said he had to wash his own sheets when he wet the bed, so he had to wash them in the bath in cold water. Sometimes, if we were up late, he wouldn't have time to do them and would sleep in wet sheets the next night.

Well, the day arrived when Dad came home. Mam was like a schoolgirl, all giggly and silly. She was all over him. We were sent out to play and they went to bed. When they got up Dad said he was going up the Rose and Crown. Mam wasn't best pleased. He'd only been home five minutes and he wanted to be off drinking. She wasn't going to be left out so she dolled herself up and went with him. He settled back into home life and was soon ruling the roost again. It took a while before he had any work, so, as usual, money was tight.

It was summer and at school we had changed into summer uniform—a white short-sleeved blouse, a blue and white striped cotton skirt and a blue cardigan. That is, all except me! Mam, as usual, wouldn't get it for me. My friend Pam had made her own skirt. It was lovely; a mini skirt with huge belt loops and she said you didn't need much material. So, the next time Dad came in drunk, I waited for him to go to bed, checked that he was asleep, went into his bedroom and pinched £1. Having done that I made a point of telling Mam that Pam was going to give me some material that she hadn't used and I would be able to make myself a school skirt. So, Monday morning I didn't go to school. Pam and I caught the bus to the Heath, straight to Baldwin's, the material shop. I got all that I needed, plus cotton as Mam didn't have any. I was so excited. We messed about in the Heath all morning, then at lunchtime we went into school. I couldn't wait to get home and get started on my skirt.

As soon as I got home I showed Mam the material and asked if I could get started on my skirt. "When you've helped me with tea."

"Great, let's get cracking then." Tea ready, eaten and washed up and I was up to my room like a flash. I had never made anything on my own before. I had been ignored for years in the sewing class at school by Mrs Ward. She had caught me eating chestnuts in her lesson. I was so hungry, having had no breakfast, but she went mental, called me a little guttersnipe and told me to go and stand outside the door. I was insulted, even though I didn't know what a guttersnipe was, so instead of standing outside the classroom door, I walked out of school and went home. I told Mam what had been said.

She was narked and marched me back down to school, into the sewing class and yelled, "How dare you call my daughter a guttersnipe, you old cow!" Mrs Ward was so shocked and so were all the girls. I thought Mam was going to hit her but she just swore and bad-mouthed her. Miss McConnacky arrived just in time and defused Mam! Took us both down to her office and promised Mam she would do something about Mrs Ward and that seemed to pacify Mam. I was allowed to go home with Mam.

The next time I had needlework Mrs Ward completely ignored me and continued to do so for the rest of my school life. I think she thought it was safer that way. So, needless to say, I learned diddly squat about sewing.

So there I was, material, cotton, scissors, needle and a hand full of pins. Pam had sort of explained how to make it. I measured my waist, hips and how long I wanted it to be, then added a bit to allow for seams and hem, then I cut it out. My heart was in my mouth, I wanted this skirt so bad. I hoped I'd cut it right, it took me ages to sew it all by hand. I had to fetch the iron up to my room. Then I cleared a space on the floor and kept pressing this or that. I had such difficulty making the belt loops and then I realised I hadn't bought a zip. Not to be defeated, I took the zip out of a pair of Phil's trousers, he'd never notice.

Voila. I put it on and it was fabulous! It fitted and I was so thrilled with it. I actually had a skirt that fitted me. I went downstairs to show off my creation. "Look Mam, Dad, look what I've made." I was in the middle of the sitting room, twirling round.

Dad looked at me and said, "Come here." The butterflies arrived!

"What Dad?" I said as I walked over to where he was sitting. I stood in front of him.

"Turn around," he said. I did as I was told, then he put his hand in the top of my lovely skirt at the back and yanked. He ripped it completely off me. "If you want to show your arse, go to school like that." Mam and he laughed at me. I was numb. How could he! I ran upstairs and lay on my bed crying for ages. I hated him so much. I felt powerless against him and I hated that feeling.

The summer was long and hot and we spent as much time as we could out of the house. The summer holidays were here so we wanted to go play. Mam and Dad had other ideas; we had to work in the garden. We didn't mind if Dad wasn't there, he would tell us what had to be done and we had to make sure it was done. Then at least we could have a laugh with each other, but if Dad was there, it was nerve-racking; someone always did something wrong and finished up getting a thrashing. John and Kenny asked Dad if they could build a camp over the fields and sleep the night. "OK," he said. "YES!"

They were off. They took bits of wood, dust sheets, bits of plastic—all sorts of rubbish. It took them the best part of the day to make this den. They took jam sandwiches and a bottle of water and off they went. Dad went over the field at about 10 o'clock, taking Taurus with him. He came back laughing. Apparently the boys were asleep but were woken by Taurus sniffing and scratching outside the den. They were both terrified, thinking it was a badger and Dad had told them how strong badgers were. They were sure they were about to die. Dad whistled Taurus and left. The boys said they were awake most of the night terrified the 'badger' would return.

Then Phil came home. He had changed quite a bit; he looked so much older and his manner was different. He wasn't so stroppy which was a good thing for him as Dad always thrashed us for being stroppy, but he did seem angry all the time. I think he had a really bad time in Court Lees. Sometimes he would say what had happened to him there, but not often. Anyway, it was great having him back.

Gun Fun Summer

DAD HAD DONE A JOB and brought home a bag full of air rifles, .22s and .177s. Great, he gave us each one. We would go down the fields and play cowboys and Indians! It was great fun. We would actually try to kill each other! I remember once John hit Phil on the hand. John only had a .177, so it just stung a bit when he hit you. Phil, on the other hand, had a .22 and was out for blood, preferably John's! Poor old John, he was crapping himself as Phil meant business! He chased him around trees and through bushes, shooting all the time so John was panicking. We were shouting at John to shoot Phil again but he didn't dare stop and aim. Then Dad shouted us all in. John had a big grin on his face—saved to fight another day. Next time we played we all remembered, 'Don't shoot Phil, he doesn't like it!'

Phil decided we would shoot at targets so we would pin them to pieces of wood, stab the wood into the ground, stand back, take aim and fire. More often than not we would all miss, or the piece of wood would snap. Phil did his John Wayne impersonation. He started shooting at my feet, saying, "Dance little lady." Dance I would, all the time protesting but scared to stop in case he shot me in the foot, which he did on a couple of occasions. "Get those knees higher," he would shout. I would be screaming for him to stop and he would just laugh. Then he would make me hold the targets at arm's length, one in either hand, John shooting at the left, Phil at the right. How I still have both eyes is a miracle!

That was a fun summer. It was also the summer the cornfield caught fire. It was the same time as Kenny nicked some of Mam's fags and matches and disappeared over the field. He came rushing back in looking very worried. Then we saw the fire brigade trying to put the fire out, but to no avail! I often wondered whether the two incidents were connected!

Now Phil was home, when Dad needed a labourer he would keep Phil off school and take him to work with him. I used to feel sorry for Phil; Dad would make him do all the grotty jobs. If Dad was wallpapering Phil would have to make sure there were no bits of off-cut left on the floor and that there was enough paste. Dad would make whoever was helping him mix the paste. The name of that paste is imprinted on my memory: Rex's Cold-Water Paste. And there were to be no lumps!

When I had helped him I would come home with my pockets stuck together. I would fish out the lumps and put them in my pocket rather than get slapped with the pasting brush for mixing it wrong! Also, he had a thing about not getting paste on the paper hanging table. "Get your paper to the edge and put the paste on in a herringbone fashion," he would say. We had to learn how to do things properly or not at all. I always wanted to say, "Not at all for me then if you please," but I never had the bottle. Anyway, now Phil was home I didn't have to go to work with him which was great for me, not so hot for Phil.

"Come on Fay, you're coming with me today, Phil's not coming." My heart sank. I got dressed, and as we had to wear overalls, I got Phil's and put them on. I had a woolly hat and had to stuff all my hair up into it to make me look like a boy.

"Where are we working Dad?" I asked. "Is it a long job?" That was all I cared about.

"Never you mind, just get going." He went down the shed, collected the wallpaper, paste, brushes, scissors and table and loaded them into the van. We were off; we hadn't gone far when he pulled up. I knew the crack. He went and spoke to 'the lady' and I unloaded the van. It was a bedroom he was papering He had been there a couple of days doing the paintwork and preparing the walls. I set up the table, mixed the paste, put the lumps in my pocket, then laid out the brush, scissors and cloth. Dad came up. "Good girl," he said and then set about measuring and cutting the paper.

I suppose he had hung about four drops of paper when he looked at me. I began to panic. I was picking up the off-cuts. I looked up and Dad was locking the door. He'd always been drunk when he did anything 'rude' to me before. Well, here he was stone cold sober. He pushed me up against the wall and kissed me on the mouth. I tightened my mouth and screwed up my face. He was pulling at my clothes and feeling at my chest. I HATED HIM SO MUCH! I felt powerless and scared. He made me lay on the floor. He lay on top of me, kissing and touching me as he was writhing up and down on me, rubbing himself up against me. I started to cry and he shouted at me to "SHUT IT." Then he stopped, got up, unlocked the door and went to the toilet. I got up, put myself back together, wiped my eyes and nose. He came back into the room and continued working as if nothing had happened. He even tried to make me laugh by flicking paste at me.

When we got home, I was in the kitchen cleaning the brushes. Mam came in. "What have you done today, did you get it finished?" I so wanted to tell her what he'd done.

Dad's voice came from the back garden, "She's been a little treasure. I wouldn't have got done without her."

How true, I was thinking. *You bastard. "She's a good little worker." I HATE YOU! I WANT YOU TO DIE*! was what was going through my mind.

As the weekend loomed, I dreaded Mam going off to bingo and leaving me with Dad. I decided to tell Mam what Dad was doing to me. I started by asking her if I could go and live with Gran and Grandad for good. "Why?" she asked.

I took a deep breath to help me get the words out, "Because Dad keeps touching me and kissing me and doing rude stuff to me…and I don't like it. PLEASE MAM." She looked at me for what seemed like ages, then she slapped me across my face. She hit me so hard I thought she had broken my teeth.

"YOU LYING LITTLE BITCH. GET OUT OF MY SIGHT!" I ran over the field. I felt gutted and empty inside. I should have known she wouldn't believe me. What do I do now? She'll tell Dad and he'll thrash me. What have I done? I should have kept my mouth shut. It was dark when I went back home. I had long since stopped crying but the bruise on my face was to last a few more days. I went into the kitchen to get a drink. "Oh, you decided to come home did you?" said Mam.

"Yes Mam," I said.

"Better get yourself to bed before your father gets in. He's going to kill you, you little liar. I asked him if he had ever touched you and he went mad! What a thing to say about your own father!" What was the point of saying anything? I went up to bed. I half expected a 'visit' so I couldn't sleep. Thankfully, I was wrong and so was Mam.

Next morning Mam was in a strange mood. I had made a cup of tea, Dad was in the back garden organising stuff for work when out of the blue, Mam said, "So you want to go live with your granny do you?" looking not at me but at Dad. I felt sick, I didn't answer. Dad had been kneeling down.

He straightened up and said, "YOU ARE NOT GOING ANYWHERE, UNDERSTAND?" Only too well! I still hadn't said anything. I was expecting a good hiding and by the looks of things Mam was looking forward to me getting one, but I didn't get one. Dad went off to work without saying goodbye to Mam and she didn't like that. As it was my fault for upsetting the applecart, as she described it, she promptly hit me round the head with the hairbrush.

I realised it was a mistake telling Mam because she now had a weapon to wield over me and wield it she did. Whenever she wanted me to do something that I wasn't keen to do she would say, "Well, if you don't do it I'll have to leave you at home with your Dad," knowing full well I would do anything rather than be on my own with him. She was as bad as him. I hated them both and I didn't feel safe around either of them.

It was a few months after this that Mam told us she was pregnant again. Dad said we would all have to help a little more. Mam took this as meaning she did nothing and we did everything. As I said Mam was never keen on housework, washing or ironing, so they became my jobs. We had to take it in turns and since Phil came home he had to do his share. We were still having to light the fire every morning. I hated to do it because it either went out and I got walloped or I put a piece of newspaper across the front of the fire to 'draw' it up and I would always manage to set fire to the paper.

Once I discovered that a few squirts of Dad's lighter fluid and the fire was away, I didn't mind so much. John and Kenny had jobs too. They had to make sure there were enough sticks (kindling wood) and they both loved chopping that up. The worst job was picking up the dog poo in the garden and they would fight over who did that! They had to collect up all the dirty cups and empty the ashtrays which was a disgusting job. Mam and Dad had ashtrays next to their bed, which is disgusting, but it was the norm for our house!

Mam would quite often say, "It's a nice drying day. You're not going to school today, Fay, you can do some washing." We had a manky old twin tub and I would be on all day with it. I didn't mind doing it because I wasn't keen on school as I had missed so much schooling. I would go into classes and have no idea what we were doing. The teachers would get cross with me for not doing homework or not having the relevant books so I would mess about to cover my embarrassment. Staying at home was preferable, except I was Mam's slave!

When the washing was done the ironing piled up and I would stay off school to do it, or the shopping needed doing. The funny thing was, Dad had a car but he never took us shopping in it. We had to walk into Haywards Heath and catch the bus back with all the shopping. It occurred to me that he could have made life so much easier by driving us there and back but that would have been inconvenient for him and he liked to have a kip on the settee while we were out. It was nice and quiet for him, selfish git.

Although we had a bit of a scam going on. When we got back Mam would say, "Put it away Fay, and make me a cuppa," so I would unpack the shopping and take a bag of sugar, a packet of tea and anything else that we had two of, give them to John and he would sneak it upstairs and put it in the little bedside cabinet in my bedroom, while I gave Mam her cuppa. Then, when we ran out of sugar, tea or whatever we had stashed upstairs, Mam would send either of us with the money to Mr Paine's shop. We would go to Mr Paine's, ask him to change the £1 note or whatever she had given us, ask the price of whatever we were supposed to be getting, then pocket that amount, give Mam the change and pop upstairs to collect the sugar or whatever. Hey presto. Money for nowt! We never got caught so this scam went on for ages!

Anyway, I was hardly at school at all during Mam's pregnancy. I remember the truant officer coming round and as soon as we saw him coming down the steps Mam would say, "Quick Fay, on the settee." I would grab Dad's blanket, cover myself up and put on a pained expression. The truant bloke would come in and Mam would say, "As you can see, she suffers terribly with her monthlies!" He would ask me how I felt and I would give him such a performance that when he'd gone I didn't want to get up, I was that poorly. The thing was I hadn't even started my periods, and he had never known anyone so young to have so much trouble.

The day arrived. Mam was in labour and the midwife, Sister Drew, lived directly over the road from us. She was very nice, came over and told Mam she was doing well and to call her when the contractions were closer. Dad came home. He was all excited and sterilised cotton wool balls in a tin in the oven! What for, I was never sure. He had kettles boiling and all sorts. We had brought a single bed down into the sitting room. Mam was pacing up and down, puffing and panting. He had old sheets ripped up in a pile and towels, while Mam was smoking like a chimney. It seemed to go on for ages. I put the boys to bed and asked Dad if I could stay up until the baby was born. He was so taken up with the whole thing, if I had asked if I could paint him with petrol and set light to him, he would have said yes. Darn, missed my chance!

Comings and Goings

DAD SENT ME FOR SISTER DREW. She came over straight away, all dressed up in her uniform. She made you feel safe; she knew what she was doing. We sighed with relief when she walked through the door. I was sent out of the room while she examined Mam. "It will not be long now," she said. I wasn't allowed back into the room so I sat at the bottom of the stairs where I could hear Mam. She seemed to be in a lot of pain. I had always thought childbirth was a painless experience so this all came as a shock. I thought at one point she was dying, she was making so much noise. Then suddenly everything went quiet and I was listening as hard as I could. What was happening?

Then out of the silence I heard a baby's cry! "IT'S HERE. IT'S BORN!" I could hear Dad's voice and Mam's. What's going on? What is it? I sat on the stairs for ages. It was one o'clock in the morning on 18 December 1964 and I didn't know whether I had a new baby brother or sister! Then the door opened. Dad stood there with tears in his eyes. "You've got a baby sister, come and see her." I was in the room quick as a flash.

Mam was sitting up in the bed and she looked exhausted. She was holding my sister. I looked at her and she was beautiful. So tiny. I looked at her lovely little face; she was a true peaches and cream baby. Her little hand and little, tiny nails, she was sleeping so peacefully and I loved her instantly. I had always wanted a sister and now here she was. I was over the moon. "What are we going to call her Mam?" I asked.

"I've decided on Kayla." I looked at my sister Kayla again and she was lovely. Dad was in a state. Apparently he was in the room at the birth and he'd never experienced anything like it. It had really had an impact on him. Sister Drew had delivered Kayla and sorted Mam out.

Dad was overwhelmed by the whole thing and kept saying, "THANK YOU, THANK YOU." Sister Drew said she was just doing her job, there was a 'higher force' at work here and they should thank him. Dad was all in favour so they all sat together and gave thanks to God for the safe delivery of Kayla Lancaster.

I went to bed but I couldn't get to sleep. I kept thinking about little Kayla downstairs. Wait till the boys wake up! They were sure it was a boy! HA! They were wrong. Now there were two girls and I liked the sound of that. I had just had my 13th birthday and this was the best present ever—a sister! Next morning Dad woke us all up. We had to be quiet because both mother and baby were sleeping. Dad let the boys sneak in to look at the baby as they were excited too. We all went off to school telling everyone we met that we had a new baby sister. Dad stayed home to look after both Mam and Kayla. He was like a kid with a new toy!

Mam loved her new little girl too but the novelty soon wore off and it wasn't long before I was changing, bathing and generally looking after her. I loved it. I stayed home from school more and more but I didn't mind one bit. She was lovely and she loved me. She would smile and kick her legs when she saw me and if she was crying I was the only one who could shut her up. I loved it! It made me feel loved and special. Also, when she started to sleep through the night, Mam moved her cot into my room so quite often I would lift her into bed with me and she would snuggle up. I loved her so much.

When she started to talk, she called me mammy! That gave me such a kick. I wanted people to think she was mine. I loved dressing her and making her look pretty; not that she had many pretty things. Occasionally, Dad would come home with a dress for her that he'd seen in a shop—all frills and flouncy—but she was so gorgeous she would look beautiful in anything.

Gran and Grandad had a visit from Grandad's long-lost sister. They had had a falling out some 20 years ago and never seen or spoken to each other in all that time. Auntie Mary and her husband stayed for two weeks. It was lovely to see Grandad so happy. When it was time for them to leave Mary asked them to go back with them for a while, so after much toing and froing they decided to go. When they came back, Grandad was full of stories and Gran had so enjoyed it they decided to go and live in Willington, Co. Durham. That was where Grandad originally came from.

They packed everything up, a removal van arrived and they stacked all their belongings in the back. I was heartbroken. It had been wonderful having them back in our lives and they were my haven. Somewhere I felt safe and now they were leaving. Granddad had explained to me how he and his sister Mary had been so close and now that he had found her again, he didn't want to lose her. I understood. I just didn't want them to leave us.

The morning they left was terrible. I was SO tempted to hide myself in the back of the van and go with them. The van pulled off, Gran and Grandad checked the flat, then we walked down to the station. I went up onto the platform but wished I hadn't because when the train came I started crying and couldn't stop. They both kissed me, told me I could go and stay with them anytime and they were gone. I felt empty. The rest of the day I just cried.

The saddest thing was that Gran and Grandad had been living in Willington for just three weeks when Aunty Mary had a heart attack and died. Granddad was devastated, but at least he'd had those few weeks with her. I thought they would come back to Sussex after that but they had bought a little cottage and were happy there so they stayed.

Winter is always a bad time for painters and decorators because no one wants the disruption in cold grotty weather, so, as always, Dad had no work and no money. Mum and Dad were rowing lots and always about money, or rather the lack of it. I have a vivid memory of Dad sharpening the axe. I didn't know why he was doing it and then Mam was saying things like, "If you're going to do it, do it. Stop poncing about!" She said this a couple of times. Dad kept coming indoors, having a fag and then going outside, pick up the axe and stand there for a bit, then come back indoors again. Mam was getting agitated.

What's going on? I thought. I went upstairs to my bedroom so I could watch Dad and see what he was up to without him seeing me. I had just hung a line full of nappies on the washing line. Dad went out again. I watched him pick up the axe, put his finger onto the corner of the coal bunker then CHOP! I was shocked. "He's chopped his bloomin' finger off," I said out loud. The next thing I knew, he had grabbed a nappy off the line and wrapped his hand in it and there was blood everywhere. Mam was saying he should get himself up to the hospital. "But don't take the finger. I don't think it counts if they sew it back on!" I ran downstairs and went outside; my line of nappies had a streak of blood right across them.

It turned out that Mam and Dad had looked at the insurance policies and if Dad broke his leg, he would get £60, so he tried to break his own leg. He smashed down on his shin with a sledgehammer but it didn't break. "It just bounced and hurt like hell," were his words. So the policy also said, I think, that if you lost a finger, they would pay £30. He decided he could live without the index finger on his left hand. Hence the axe sharpening; he wanted a clean cut. Mam just wanted the money. Well, he came back from the hospital. They had sewn up the end (he had cut off his finger just below his knuckle) and it was all bandaged up. He told us all the gory details of what they did to him.

The boys were fascinated. "Did it hurt, Dad?" Silly question! Dad didn't even answer that one; he just gave Kenny 'the look'. After Dad had had a cuppa, he went outside and came rushing back in. "Look, I've found my finger," he shouted. We came from all over the house to see this. He had too. It looked weird, not being connected to his hand. We all had a good look at it. The boys wanted to hold it and squeeze it to see if it would bleed. Then Dad took it down the shed, put it in a jar of pickling fluid and kept it for years. He was a very odd man. The sad thing about that whole story was that the insurance took ages to come through by which time he had some work. He had chopped it off for nowt. Silly berk!

Kayla was walking and talking now. She was a delight and we all loved her; she was such a little doll. I had to take her everywhere with me as Mam had got a cleaning job so my schooling came to a virtual standstill. It was ironic that Mam's work was cleaning! It was for a family with three kids and she used to buy things to take into work for them!

One of the kids must have had a record player, because she bought an LP for him. I can even remember the record: *Little children, why don't you come outside* by Billy J Kramer. How odd that she would buy *them* gifts… and never us. And she never cleaned our house!

I stayed at home and looked after Kayla and did whatever jobs Mam decided I should do as well. Dad had been up to no good and had been thieving again. Anyway, one Sunday afternoon I was up in my room reading to Kayla as Dad had come home from the pub drunk. I was keeping well out of his way and Kayla too. I didn't want him shouting and frightening her.

He was just eating his dinner when there was a knock on the back door. My bedroom window was directly above so I looked out to see who was there. It was two policemen. Dad opened the door. "What do you want?" I heard him say. "We would like to talk to you regarding such and such" (I can't remember the words exactly). "I'm eating my dinner," he said. They were two young policemen who obviously didn't know who they were dealing with. "Never mind your dinner, we need to talk to you now," said one of the policemen and tried to push his way into the house.

The next thing I saw was the policeman come flying backwards out of the house and land on his back in the garden. I called the boys to come and see. We were all peering out of the window, only to see the other one run out of the garden. "What's all this about?" asked Kenny. "Why are these policemen in the garden?" He had no sooner asked the question when the garden seemed to be full of policemen, all trying to get hold of Dad.

I could hear Mam shouting, "Stop it Ken." All to no avail. Dad had lost it and policemen were flying out of our back door left and right and were all lying knocked out in the garden. More and more policemen seemed to come round the corner into the back door then come flying backwards. Dad had really flipped.

Then this older man in plain clothes started talking to Dad. He seemed to know him. Dad seemed to calm down a bit. "Just come with us to the station, Ken, we really do need to talk to you."

Mam was saying, "What about all this?" pointing to the dazed policemen on the garden.

"We'll say nothing about this, Ken. Just you come with us." Dad made them wait until he finished his dinner then he got his coat. We rushed through to Mam's bedroom window, opened it and waited. It overlooked the front garden and the road. Dad walked up the steps. All the neighbours were out watching. They all hated us as a family so this was just what they wanted. Anyway, Dad went to get into the police car when a young policeman gave him a helpful push. Dad went stiff, he reminded me of Laddie! Anyway he wouldn't get in the car. They were pushing and pulling him. I found myself shouting, "HIT HIM, BASH HIM!" Then I realised Mam could hear me so I shut up. Finally they all stopped and he got in. He was proving a point; no one could make him do something he didn't want to do.

Well, Mam was in a blind panic, John and Kenny were crying. I don't remember if Phil was there. Kayla was oblivious to it all and was her cheery little self. I was thrilled. They would definitely lock him up and it served him right.

Prison Again

THEY LOCKED DAD UP FOR 18 MONTHS. The thing was, he didn't go to prison for thieving, which was what the police came to talk to him about, but for GBH to all those policemen he punched in our garden! "No, Mrs Lancaster, we'll say nothing about this!" I heard them say it myself! Still, I would have said the same thing if it meant he would go with them quietly but it made me a bit unsure of policemen. I always thought they told the truth.

Dad went to Wandsworth Prison. He had it cushy really; three meals a day, warm and clean sheets every week and no worries about bills or anything. Mam, on the other hand, had all those things to worry about. This made her unbearable to live with; she would bite your head off for the slightest thing. John was old enough to understand now; he and Kenny knew where Dad was. They would get teased at school and John would invariably come home crying. The kids had got him in a circle and were shouting, "YOUR DAD'S A CONVICT!" over and over again. Little swines. Phil said he would sort them out. He'd give em all a good hiding. That was his answer. Mind you, we all agreed with him at the time.

Mam was acting strangely at this time; she was fed up with Dad and his behaviour. She asked us all what we thought of what had happened to Dad, and how we were feeling, which was a real turn-up for the books. She had never asked us how we felt about anything before! She asked for our opinions—something else that had never happened before.

Dad had been terrible over the last year. He was extremely violent towards all of us, Mam included. It was like walking on eggshells being around him; you never knew what would set him off. He beat us all and he was very scary. He would get us to stand in a line like little soldiers, chest out, tummy in, arms straight down by your side, head up. He would question us if he was trying to find out who did what. After ages of not getting the answers he wanted he would thrash us all saying that he had got the guilty one anyway. He was also drinking more and that was frightening. Even Mam got scared because he would hit her when he was drunk.

He had a horrible way with him too, he would get so close to your face and scream and growl at you. It sounds stupid but when all the veins in his face and neck were standing out and he was yelling and his spit was hitting your face as he said, "I'M GOING TO KILL YOU, YOU STUPID LITTLE SHIT," sometimes I thought my heart would burst with fear. He took delight in humiliating the boys in particular, telling them they were useless articles, couldn't do anything right, were no good to man or beast. Even John was sick of him. Dad had brought in a huge drawer from the shed filled with nails of all sizes, screws, nuts, bolts, tacks, roofing nails…and much more. "Sort them into kinds," he said to John.

Now John always loved Dad, even though he was scared of him, he so wanted Dad to love him and be pleased with whatever he did. He spent hours doing it, putting each kind into boxes, tobacco tins and biscuit tins in the drawer. When Dad came in, John was thrilled to show him what he had done, a big grin on his face. "I've done it, Dad," he said, holding up the drawer to show him.

Dad yelled at him, "Don't interrupt me when I'm busy," and with that, he took the drawer off John and tipped it all over the floor! John was gutted, his face just crumpled. "Now do it again, and don't interrupt me!" I think this was the straw that broke the camel's back. John was deeply hurt, he was always the more sensitive of my brothers, and it was the first time I had seen anyone cry silently. Kenny and I and even Kayla helped him sort them, but his little spirit was broken.

So when Mam asked us what we were feeling, we said, "Please don't have him back."

Phil really wanted Dad to come home as Dad had said that when Phil was a bit bigger he would take him with him on jobs. He already took him when he was fighting the dogs for money so Phil wanted him home for all the wrong reasons. Though even he had to admit Dad was a nutter and we would be better off without him. We talked it over with her which was a first because, like I said, she had never asked our opinion on anything before, though I think she didn't want him back herself but couldn't say it. When we said it I'm sure it was a relief to her. So she wrote to Dad, telling him that we didn't want him to come back to us. It was a great feeling. I remember thinking that was the end of him and I liked that thought.

Kayla had been given a three-wheeled tricycle but she was too young to ride it, so John, who was at least ten, had taken to putting one foot between the two back wheels, leaning over, holding the handlebars and scooting himself along. He went everywhere on his baby bike. Then he got himself an old ironing board, took the tricycle to bits and bolted the ironing board where the crossbar would be and attached the back wheels on too. It looked like a rocket on wheels. If only he had patented it then, it was the first skateboard! He would go to the shop and pile all his goodies on the back, he loved it and it was the first of many of John's inventions.

Life continued and Mam had a letter from Dad saying that it was fine. The marriage was over and he understood that. Mam was a bit shocked; I think she wanted him to beg her not to do it but he didn't. Apparently he was quite relieved to get the letter. He felt trapped by family life and responsibility. So now he was free to do what he wanted. He had met some pretty dodgy characters inside, in fact someone had approached him about killing a man when he got out. They would provide the gun and pay him so many thousand pounds. Now that he was free he said yes, he would do it!

It was round about that time that a little old lady started calling at our house; she was a Jehovah's Witness. I was never allowed in the room, only to take a cup of tea in to them. My curiosity would get the better of me so I would open the serving hatch from the kitchen slightly and earwig. I was so surprised as they were talking about God! What a let-down. Mam told her all about Dad and this silly lady told Mam that she shouldn't end the marriage like that; she should give it another go. I couldn't believe my ears. "No, don't do that!" I wanted to shout, but I couldn't as I wasn't even supposed to be listening. She didn't say anything to us kids. I was desperate to ask her whether she was going to have him back but I daren't, she'd clout me for earwigging.

I got myself a Saturday job at a dry cleaners in Haywards Heath. I got fifteen shillings for that which I gave to Mam, it all helped. Phil had left school and was working full time on a building site. He also gave Mam his wages and, with the National Assistance, we seemed to manage.

Anyway, Christmas was here again, Dad was away again and there was no money again. Phil had taken on the role of provider for the family, bless him. He was working on a building site at this time and always came home filthy and tired. He would often fall asleep in the chair, exhausted after his dinner. He came home this one evening with what we thought was the best Christmas tree ever, in fact it was the top of a leylandii. But bless him, he had been working near a wood, saw this tree that he thought was a Christmas tree, climbed to the top and chopped off four feet. We were so excited; we had never had a Christmas tree before. Phil put it in a bucket and we set to decorating it with milk bottle tops. Mam showed us how to make bells with them and we cut up bits of paper into star shapes and snowflakes—it was great fun. Phil looked so chuffed with himself and we were pretty pleased with him too.

Mam had been in touch with the WRVS and Dr Barnardos because Dad had been a Barnardos kid. She thought they might help us. She also got in touch with every other voluntary service she could think of to see if anyone would help. Then, bless them, a man from Barnardos arrived on Christmas Eve with a box of toys! It was fabulous. They weren't new but they were new to us. It was wonderful; we were beginning to think there really was a Father Christmas after all!

Miss McConnachie, who was the deputy head teacher at school, had asked me what we were doing at Christmas. "Not much," I said. She knew all about us. She was a very brusque woman but very kind, quite often she would take me into her office when I was looking particularly scruffy. She had given up asking me to tell my Mam to buy me a school uniform, which she realised was never going to happen. So she would take me into her office, get out the box with second-hand uniforms and give me a new shirt or whatever it was that was the scruffiest. Sometimes I'd be wearing Dad's shirt and Mam's skirt. I would roll it up at the waist; this was the era of the 'mini' after all. So I would finish up with the biggest midriff bulge you ever saw in my attempt to be trendy! What a joke.

Anyway, that was Miss McConnachie. Well, she arrived at our door. "Come and help me Fay. You too boys," she said. We followed her to her car, all very bemused by this. Well, she opened the boot of her car where there were two sacks of coal. "Come on, you boys, you can manage them surely," she boomed. They did. Then she opened the back door of the car and on the seat were two big boxes of groceries. "Come on, Fay, we can manage these."

I picked up a box; it was heavy and full to the brim with nice things. I could see biscuits—we never had biscuits—and fruit. *This is great*, I thought, it was like Christmas. IT WAS CHRISTMAS! Miss McConnachie came into the house, said, "Merry Christmas" to us all and then went. We were all gobsmacked! Mam couldn't believe it, none of us could. We dived into the boxes. There was a Christmas pudding, crackers, tinned fruit as well as fresh fruit, veg, sugared almonds, bread, jam, potted meats, mince pies, butter, you name it and it was probably in those boxes. Bless her heart, we were all laughing hysterically and the boys were jumping up and down. This was going to be the best Christmas ever.

As we had all the makings of a brilliant Christmas, all I needed now was to buy everyone a Christmas present. The only trouble was, I didn't have two pennies to rub together so this called for desperate action. When Mam wanted a new lipstick, she would take me into Woolworths and pick up the one she wanted. She would make sure I had seen which one it was and then she would go out of the shop, leaving me to 'do my thing'. I would mess about with all the lipsticks and stick the one Mam wanted up my sleeve and then make my way out of the shop, making sure no one was following me. Job done. Mam would be chuffed with me.

I did it for all sorts of things for her, so now I was going to do it for me. Woolworths, here I come. I mooched about the shop looking at everything, trying to sort out my shopping list. I got Dinky cars for John and Kenny and for Mam and Gran these lovely bracelets (well, I thought they were anyway). The irony of it was that it had the Ten Commandments on little discs and a tiny Bible hanging from a mock gold chain. It didn't strike me as hypocritical that one of the discs said 'thou shalt not steal' and I had just stolen it. I managed to get presents for everyone; I was well pleased with myself.

We did have the best Christmas ever. There were presents for everyone, the best grub we had ever had and it would see us through the holidays. This was really living.

Phil Takes Charge

PHIL WAS THE HEAD OF THE HOUSE NOW. He was only 14 but he took his responsibilities very seriously and was always telling us off. I thought he was getting too big for his boots and I would tell him so. We would yell and fight all the time. I remember one time he had some of his mates round and they were waiting for him to get ready. He started to get mouthy with me. Then as I walked past him, he grabbed hold of my skirt and yanked it up, showing all the boys my knickers. I was incensed. He was too big for me to hurt him by hitting him now so I went outside and got a shovel. They were all still laughing when I came back into the room. Phil had his back to me. I picked up the shovel and swung it. It hit him at the back of the head. He just dropped like a stone to the ground.

All the boys had gone silent and didn't know where to look, whether at me wielding the shovel or Phil unconscious on the ground. I knew what goes down must get up. I certainly didn't want to be in the room when he got up so I threw the shovel outside, ran up to my room and barricaded myself in. I didn't have to wait very long before he came bounding up the stairs. "You little cow! I am going to get you. You've had it, you're dead meat," he yelled. But try as he might he couldn't get in. He said he would set the door on fire if I didn't open it.

Am I really that stupid…not! He went out with his mates, swearing he would get me when he came back. By the time he got in, Mam was back from Bingo and I had told her my side of the story and she told him to leave me alone. HA! One to me, I think.

Phil was very particular about his clothes so when I pinched one of his shirts and cut the tail off to make it into a blouse, he went ballistic. I was wearing this blouse when he came in. He gave me a sideways look and then said, "Is that my shirt?" I was stuck; well he never wore it so I thought I might as well have it. Phil's face was purple with rage. "RIGHT," he said. I was expecting him to hit me and I braced myself but no, he just ran upstairs. I was shocked but I liked it.

Let him sulk I thought, that doesn't hurt me one little bit. How wrong could I have been?

It was much later when I went upstairs. Phil had gone out with a big grin on his face and he didn't say a word to me. When I went to take Kayla to bed there on my bed were all my trousers with the legs cut off and all my blouses with the arms cut off. I couldn't believe it. I marched straight into his room. Stupid pig; he hadn't thought this through at all. All my clothes came from jumble sales, his didn't; he had bought some of them new. I set to work with the scissors. All the sleeves off his shirts, all the legs off his trousers. Two can play at that game.

I was in bed when he came in. I heard him go into his bedroom and then I heard a low growl. "She's dead this time for sure." I was out of bed and halfway down the stairs before he came out of his room. "Come here you," he yelled.

"Get lost. Mam, our Phil's going to hit me," I yelled as I ran down the stairs and into the living room. We both burst into the room.

"What's going on here?" Mam said. We explained the whole saga, both wanting her to be on our side. She looked at us both and said, "Don't you think I've got enough on my plate without you two buggering about. No more cutting people's clothes up. OK."

"Yes Mam," we said and turned around, back up the stairs.

Phil gave me a mighty clout. "You little shit; you're going to pay for this."

"And who's going to make me, pea-brain," I said as I shut my door.

That was how we were with each other. We fought all the time but I loved him. If anyone said anything about him, I would punch them but I could call him worse than muck and I did frequently. John and Kenny too. I had always been able to control them; they were scared of me. I used to wallop them if they were naughty. I was like their Mam but they were both growing and were getting bigger than me, John in particular. I remember one time when John had done something that I wasn't happy about and he was being mouthy to me.

Little swine, I thought, *I'll teach him*. So I gave Kenny Mam's hairbrush, it was like a hedgehog with a handle but the bristles were steel spikes, and told him to stand by the door. Our house had internal doors in a circle, so that you could run round and round through all the rooms. I said something insulting to John and, as planned, he started to chase me through all the doors. As I ran through the dining room, I said to Ken, "When John comes through, hit him."

Kenny daren't disobey me and belted John on the back of his hand as he came through the door. I heard John yell. Mission accomplished I thought. I stopped running and went back into the dining room. Kenny was standing staring at John's hand. No one spoke and the hairbrush was buried deep in John's hand. It looked funny just sitting on the back of his hand like that. John looked at me and said, "He hit me."

I wanted to laugh again. When I told Kenny to hit him with the hairbrush, I meant the flat wooden back of the brush, not the spiky side. We all went into the kitchen. "Pull it out, John," I said. It looked very painful. He pulled and the spikes popped out one by one. The back of his hand looked like a ladybird and little red spots appeared. We washed it and rubbed some antiseptic cream into the holes. The hairbrush had never seen water so I figured it would have germs on it. That done, John wanted to kill Kenny. After explaining that I had told him to do it and that I would always get the better of him no matter how big he got, I still held the power and he must obey me. He seemed to accept my little explanation. Good lad. You know it makes sense!

Another time for some reason we were burning baling twine on the living room fire. Kenny had this long length of burning twine and the silly wally started swinging it round so there was melted plastic flying all over the room. "Stop it Ken," I said.

"Shut it you!" he said and flicked this burning twine in my direction and laughed. I was mad with him now and it was my duty to get the twine off him and punch him really hard! Cheeky swine! I was demanding that he give me the twine as I walked back towards him. He just laughed, egged on by John who was telling him not to give it to me. I lunged at him and he whacked me on the hand with the burning twine. "OUCH." It was burning hot and as it hit my hand, the melted plastic set. When I peeled it off, my skin came off too. John and Kenny wet themselves laughing; they thought this was hilarious. They didn't think it was so funny when we looked around the room and there was melted orange plastic on everything, even the ceiling and I wouldn't help them get it off! That'll teach 'em.

John was into fitness and bodybuilding, and he was as strong as an ox. He had a chest expander that he got from a jumble sale which he used all the time. He would say, "Feel my muscles," every time he saw me. Boring! He would be out in the garden doing one arm press ups. Kenny would do a couple and collapse in a heap laughing, but John took this all very seriously and would walk around with no shirt on, flexing his muscles.

We had a row about something. I can't even remember what we argued about, but I hit him and ran into the house. He was after me as quick as a flash and caught me in the passage by the back door. He wanted to punch me, but he knew he would really hurt me, so he pushed me up against the wall and put his back against my front, put his feet on the passage wall and pushed every bit of breath out of me until I fainted! This was to become the thing he did instead of punching me and I hated it. The roles were changing; he was bigger than me now and he had the power. Well, he thought he had!

So life was much better without Dad. Phil had a girlfriend called Maggy Balchin. She was a nice girl and spent a lot of time at our house. We had gone to school together. She was very quiet and I liked her. I had met a boy at the youth club. He was very sweet and his name was Barry Blake. Mam was not bothered if we went out as long as she could go to her Bingo so I would look after Kayla and the boys for her and in return she let me go to the youth club.

I really looked forward to Thursday nights. I remember Barry asking me out. I was so excited; I was only 14 and he was 16 and had already left school. I couldn't believe it when he eventually asked me out. I had no confidence in myself. I would try to make everyone laugh so that they would like me. It came as a complete shock when this handsome boy liked me. I was so nervous; I was sure that after one date he would finish with me. But he didn't. I was over the moon. He was so sweet. He was tall, blonde and blue-eyed and I thought he was gorgeous. He also had a really good sense of humour which was essential, but the very best thing about him was he liked me. We went out with each other for about eighteen months. We were in love and it was wonderful. He bought me a lovely heart-shaped crystal necklace for Valentine's Day and I was thrilled. I'd never been loved like this before and I liked it a lot! He was kind and funny to be around.

The first time he came to my house I was so worried. What would he think of our mucky house? I spent the day cleaning but it didn't make much difference. He came and Mam wanted to know all about his family—I was so embarrassed. When we finally got out of the house I was full of apologies about the state of it and my Mam, etc. He just laughed and told me not to be silly. He didn't care about those things, he just cared about me. I loved him! He did ask me where my Dad was though and I had been dreading that one. I told him he was in Wandsworth Prison and he laughed and told me to stop messing about. After swearing and promising that I wasn't lying he finally believed me. I was worried he would finish with me because of Dad but he said he was going out with me, not my Dad, though he did say when we went to his house not to tell his mum and Dad where my Dad was!

Our first Christmas together was lovely. Barry's family had a party and I was invited. I'd never been to a party before. What would I wear? I hadn't got any really nice clothes but Pam had. She lent me her mini kilt and a jumper to match and I looked the business. I had bought a navy blue reefer jacket off the catalogue but the sleeves were too short. Mrs Tester, a lovely lady who was one of the few neighbours who spoke to us, was clever at sewing and said she would let the sleeves down for me.

Bless her, she did a grand job. I looked lovely—well, I thought I did. Barry arrived to pick me up on his bike. In those days, if you were a passenger you didn't have to wear a helmet, so here we were, me in my new coat and my borrowed clothes. It was winter and we had a ride from Cuckfield to Pease Pottage. What with the wind in my hair and many other places I wouldn't care to mention, by the time we got to his house I was blue with cold and I looked like the wicked witch of the west! My hair was so tangled and there was me wanting to make a good impression.

His mum and Dad were lovely and made me feel very welcome. His cousin David was there and we all got slowly drunk. I remember Barry being sick over his cousin's head in the downstairs loo. I thought Barry's mum would go mad but she didn't, she was really sweet. Also, because it had snowed Barry said he couldn't take me home and I would have to stay the night. I was so nervous; I'd never stayed anywhere but my Gran's before.

His mum loaned me a nightie and I slept in this really nice bedroom. Next morning Mrs Blake brought me breakfast in bed. I felt like royalty. This was so nice. Barry came and sat on my bed and shared my breakfast and I liked this. We spent the rest of the day together and then he took me home. We were saying goodnight and kissing when I felt him trying to put his hand up my jumper. I was so shocked. "What are you doing?" I asked him. He said that he loved me and that touching one another was part of loving. I was horrified. Not in my book it's not! "If you love me," I told him, "you'll never do that again."

I couldn't understand why he would want to do something so awful to me and he couldn't understand why I wouldn't want to show my love for him in that way. He was really perplexed. Poor boy, he wasn't to know what had gone before to put me off anything to do with sex but, bless him, he never tried it again.

We continued to go out. A whole crowd of us who hung around together. Phil and Maggy, Pam and Charlie, Christine (Pam's elder sister) with Acca, Helen and Tim, Jackie and Dave and there were other unattached boys and girls as well. Mick who lived opposite us would hang around with us too. There were some twins, Kenny and Colin, who were quite mad! They tore around in odd vehicles and bikes. We would meet up at youth club and decide what we were doing, usually something stupid.

Barry had bought a car. It was a bubble car, and it looked so sweet. I loved it. It meant we could snog in warmth and almost comfort! One evening Barry took me indoors to ask Phil something. Phil wasn't home but was due in any time so Barry decided to wait. Phil came in full of laughter. When Barry left, Phil rushed to the window and told us all to look out. Poor Barry, Phil and his mates had turned his bubble car upside down on our front garden. We all laughed, even Barry. Then the boys turned it right side up and after a bit of engine trouble it finally started and off he went.

The Prodigal Son

AFTER MUCH PERSUASION FROM THE LITTLE OLD JW LADY, Mam had decided that she would have Dad back after all. I was gutted; I couldn't believe she could be so stupid. She said she had written to him and explained that the little old lady who had been coming every week had said that marriage was for life. After much thought and discussion and many tears she was willing to give him another chance, so she wrote to him telling him just that—if he wanted it. We all waited with bated breath for his letter to come. I was hoping and praying he would say, 'Thanks, but no thanks', but to my dismay and Mam's joy he didn't. He wrote saying he would love another chance and she wouldn't regret her decision. He promised he had changed. *OH, well that's OK then...NOT*, I thought.

But no one asked me what I thought!

We kids sat in the dining room and talked about Dad coming home, Phil was all for it, John had mellowed and said Dad might be better. Kenny didn't want him back and I certainly didn't. Kayla, bless her heart, had no clue what all this was about. I was sitting in the dining room, smoking a cigarette, when he walked in. He just walked up to me, snatched the cigarette from my hand and said, "You can pack that in for a start." He was home! Mam had gone to the station to meet him and they had come from Haywards Heath in a taxi. I hadn't expected them so soon. The boys were nervous and excited at the same time, yet apprehensive about him being home.

"Hello Dad," I said.

"Hello love," he replied, "it's good to be home. Pop the kettle on, there's a good lass."

He was home and I was nervous. He called us all into the living room. "Things are going to be different around here from now on," he said.

Here we go, I thought. We all sat down ready to listen to the new 'rules'. "Something happened to me in prison," he said and he went on to tell us how he had been in his cell on Christmas Eve. There was a service in the prison chapel

116

and lots of the inmates had gone. When a screw had gone into his cell and asked him if he wanted to go, Dad said NO and that the chapel would fall on him if he went in. The screw replied, "If anyone needs God it's you Lancaster." But he stayed in his cell. He said he was lying on his bunk and he could hear singing. He knew all the prisoners who wanted to had gone to church and they would be singing, but this singing didn't sound like a bunch of convicts, it sounded wonderful.

He lay on his bunk listening to what he said sounded like angels. He said that as this singing continued he felt he needed to get onto his knees and as he knelt on the cell floor, his head on his bunk, he felt an overwhelming sense of his sin! He said the words he heard being sung were, 'The Lord is my shepherd, I shall not want, he maketh me to lie down in green pastures, He leads me beside the still waters, He restores my soul.' He thought of what the screw had said. "If anyone needs God, it's you Lancaster." In that moment, he said, he knew there was a God and he knew he was a sinner.

He knelt there on the cell floor sobbing. He said he poured out his heart to God, asking for forgiveness for all the terrible things he had done and, just as he knew there was a God, he knew he was forgiven. The tears he shed were a mix of repentance, sadness, remorse and joy, all rolled into one. He went on to tell us how, when his cellmate came back from church Dad asked him about the song they were singing, 'The Lord is my Shepherd'.

His cellmate said, "We didn't sing that." But he knew the words came from the Bible. Dad didn't believe him, so the next day his cellmate pinched the Bible from the church to show him. Dad said he couldn't put it down and he felt like he had been given a second chance from God while he was in prison and wanted us all to start again! 'OH YEAH, we believe you', I thought. 'This is just another scam.' But what could I say? Mam was falling over herself to tell Dad about the old lady who had been coming every week and talking to her about God. Dad was weird. This wasn't how I expected him to be and he scared me. What was he up to?

We spent an uncomfortable evening with him and all he kept talking about was how different things were going to be from now on. We were all surprised as the evening wore on that he didn't get his coat on and head for the Rose & Crown with his mate Mossy. I think Mam was too, though she never mentioned it. Phil was thrilled he was home but just as puzzled by this new behaviour as I was. He had looked forward to going out drinking with Dad and this was a bit of a let-down. John and Ken seemed thrilled to have him home; they were full of questions about prison. "What was it like Dad? Did you just get bread and water? Did you have to wear a ball and chain?" and to my amazement, instead of telling them to P off, he explained what prison was like in all its gory details. We were all spellbound. Mam looked like the cat that had got the cream. She sat next to him on the settee and they cuddled up together. And he wasn't even drunk!

Something strange was going on here and I am not sure I liked it; it unnerved me. While Dad had been inside Phil had been going up to the local Baptist chapel. Don't misunderstand me. He hadn't gone all religious on us but had been passing the chapel one Sunday evening and noticed there were lots of pretty young girls coming out, so he figured he would go in and see what was what. So, when Dad said he would like to go to church, Phil said that the chapel was alright so Dad sent Mam on the first Sunday to test it out. She came back saying that it seemed OK and there was a bloke sat at the front of the church who sang like he was fit to burst and really believed what he was singing about. That was good enough for Dad. He said we would all go next Sunday. I wanted to laugh. I didn't want to go to blooming chapel but I didn't have the bottle to say so.

The first week with him home was very odd. We all expected him to be off boozing. He was still the same Dad but there was something different and I couldn't work it out. I hadn't slept properly since he had been home because I half expected a night time visit from him and that hadn't happened. I put that down to the fact that he hadn't been drinking and was dreading him heading for the pub. I was still on my guard.

We soon got back into a routine of sorts. Dad would get up first and make the porridge. I would get Kayla up and dressed while the boys would be either chopping sticks for the fire or clearing the grate and laying the fire. Phil would be getting ready for work and Mam would be lying in bed. Dad would take her a cuppa and a fag—that was her breakfast. Meanwhile Dad had dished up four bowls of porridge which only John liked, so while Dad was upstairs with Mam John would eat all four bowls, he loved the stuff! Dad made it with water and salt for some strange reason known only to him and it was truly revolting. The only way the rest of us could possibly eat it was to add huge spoonfuls of sugar when he wasn't looking, but if he caught us he went mental and battered us and then made us eat a big bowlful with no sugar.

The week passed and Sunday arrived. Dad was up early, making tea and porridge and shouting to us all to, "Get a move on because we are going to church and it starts at eleven, so come on!" Kayla was sat in bed with me. "Come on love, better get you dressed." She was such a sweetie and was out of bed and dressed in no time. I got myself ready. I remember being nervous. I couldn't remember going to church before and didn't know what would be expected of me. We had breakfast and were all ready. Dad led us like a line of elephants, him at the front carrying a huge Bible under one arm, and Kayla on the other arm, then Mam, Phil, me, John and Kenny. We walked up Glebe Road, through the twitten and cut out into the car park of the chapel. We went in and all squashed into one pew. It was a quaint little chapel and it smelled of damp. There was a man playing an organ at the front and he had to pump it with his feet. I remember thinking it looked like hard work; it made a funny asthmatic wheezing sound.

After a little while a man went up into the pulpit and welcomed everyone and then we sang a hymn. Mam was right. There was a man who sat directly underneath the pulpit and he really did sing as if he would burst. His name was Mr Stanley Hogwood. The preacher was a man called Errol Hulse, a South African, and that morning he preached on 'The Prodigal Son'. I remember it so well because as he preached about the son and how he had gone so far away from his father and sunk into sin but when he came to his senses and returned to his father. He was waiting for him, looking out for him, forgave him and welcomed him with open arms.

Dad shouted out, "That's me, that's what happened to me!" Well I was mortified, we all were. *What on earth is he doing?* I thought. He was standing up and shouting this to the preacher! How embarrassing. He's gone nutty! The preacher smiled at Dad, and Mam pulled him down and whispered for him to shut up. What on earth was the matter with him? But he wasn't listening to her and as the preacher went on, Dad kept on interjecting with, "That's how I feel" or "Yes, that's right"; we were all SO embarrassed and by the end of the service we couldn't wait to get out.

I am never coming back here, I thought, but as we got to the door the preacher was standing there, shaking everyone's hand as they left. Now Dad was face to face with this poor bloke he had been shouting at throughout his sermon. I thought he would be really narked with Dad but he wasn't. Dad was trying to tell him what he had told us, about how he felt God had forgiven him and given him and us a second chance, just like the prodigal son. He asked Dad if he could visit him sometime during the week. Dad said yes and gave him our address. He went on to tell Dad that there was a prayer meeting on Wednesday night at 8.00 and would he like to come. "Yes," he said, "I would." I was thinking that if he thinks I'm going, he's very much mistaken!

When we got home, he couldn't sit still. He kept on about God and how it was amazing that the preacher knew all about him and how he had spoken about him in his sermon. Then he dropped the bombshell. "We'll all go tonight and Wednesday night to the prayer meeting." We all looked at each other and our hearts sank. Was this how it was going to be from now on? We hoped not.

But life at 22 Glebe Road changed out of all proportion. Everything was different; Dad had changed so much. We *did* go to chapel every week, three times on Sunday, because we kids had to go to Sunday School in the afternoon. This was non-negotiable. Mind you, nothing much was negotiable in those days—not that anything ever was!

Turning Over Leaves

THE PASTOR HAD EXPLAINED TO DAD that what had happened to him in prison was what is called 'conversion', which meant he had become a Christian and now he had to live a Christian life. He told Dad that the Bible was God's handbook for living, rather like when you buy a new car, the garage gives you a manual which tells you what you need to put into the car to make it run properly. Well, he explained that the Bible was our manual and everything Dad needed to know about living the Christian life was in there, so he needed to read it.

No sooner said than done. Dad would sit reading his Bible at every opportunity. He would enthuse over this passage or that psalm. He loved reading his Bible and would read out passages that had touched him. Whatever Dad learned on Sunday it was put into practice by the Monday. Like the time the pastor said that we should 'be in the world but not of it'. The following day we had the television on and one of the adverts said 'we bring the world into your home' so Dad got up, unplugged the telly, took it out into the garden and burnt it! We were all shell-shocked. Dad said, "We don't want the world in our home," and that was that, we didn't have a telly. But Dad would read us Bible stories every night so we all learned about Samson and Delilah, David and Goliath, Jonah and the whale, David's mighty men and lots more.

I found the stories fascinating but most of all I liked the fact that Dad was reading stories to us. No one had ever read to us before and there was a side to Dad that we hadn't seen before. He would act out the stories and be very dramatic; becoming the character he was telling us about. He could make us laugh or cry and we loved it. Things were most certainly different but we kind of liked it. We had never been read to before. I would read to Kayla, but this was different and I think the fact that Dad was not shouting at us, hitting us, being angry with us, we just soaked up this attention.

Dad would meet with a bloke from chapel. They would spend hours studying the Bible and praying. We were all watching and waiting with bated breath for

121

him to go back to being the Dad we knew but that didn't seem to be happening. Don't misunderstand me. He was still a very angry man with a temper that would scare Superman but he was trying to keep it under control. Also he would *ask* us to do something instead of telling us to. We still jumped and did exactly as he asked. We were still terrified to upset him.

I was very wary of Dad. He had been home a few weeks and he hadn't 'visited' me, which I was *very* thankful for, but it was like living on a knife edge. I would lie in bed, listening to him downstairs with Mam off at her bingo and I would wonder…. if he comes, what will I do? But thankfully, he never came to my room again.

We started to eat together as a family which was odd because we kids had always eaten separately to Mam and Dad. This new arrangement meant we couldn't give John all the stuff we didn't like. Also Dad had started to say grace before meals. We thought this was very strange. Why was he thanking God when Mam cooked it? Mam was a bit puzzled by all this religious stuff too but she went along with it because it meant Dad was sat at home with her most nights and was not up at the Rose & Crown, and he was trying to stop swearing too!

Mind you, this was a turn-up for the books, because if swearing was an Olympic event he would have won a gold medal hands down. He knew swear words no one else had ever heard of and used them at every opportunity, so when he said that now he was a Christian he wasn't going to swear. Phil took this as a challenge. "Bet you I can make him swear," he said.

"Don't do it, Phil," we said, but Phil, being Phil, had to push it. He had been working with Dad on a painting job. The routine was the same. When they got home Phil had to bring in the dirty brushes and rollers, wash them in the kitchen sink and put them in the airing cupboard to dry ready for the next day. He also had to shake out all the dirty dust sheets and fold them and put them back in the van.

Well, Phil didn't wash the brushes; he just left them in the paint kettle. This would have been OK if there had been paint in it or white spirit but there wasn't a drop of either, so by the next morning the brushes were stiff as a board! Dad went mental. "What do you think you are playing at, you pillock," he said to Phil, who looked gormlessly at Dad. "You know we need these for today." As he said that, he jabbed Phil in the chest with the brushes. "I could knock your stupid head off. NOW GET THEM WASHED!" he screamed as he punched Phil in the chest. Phil turned towards the sink and started washing the brushes. We were well impressed. He only punched him once and he didn't swear! Such control! Phil had such a smirk on his face as he washed the brushes. Challenge accepted!

The week went on. Dad had changed out of all recognition. Going to chapel was very much part of our lives. Bible reading and prayers were the order of the day and, strange though it sounds, we quite liked this new way of life, apart from having to go to chapel so much! Though Dad had changed he still hit us but not quite so much and he always tried to tell us *why* he was hitting us. Now that was a turn-up for the books. It sounds odd but before he became a Christian quite often we didn't know why we were being thrashed, now it was explained to us. This was a much better system. We thought it was anyway.

The pastor came round to our house to talk to Dad about being baptised. He explained to Dad that it was what he needed to do as an outward sign of what had happened to him on the inside, and it was a great witness to other people. They talked for ages, then prayed together and a date was set for Dad's baptism. Dad invited everyone he met to come and watch him being baptised. The chapel was full to overflowing with friends, old drinking pals and neighbours, along with all the chapel's regular congregation. Dad stood up at the front and gave his testimony. It was the second time I had heard it and it fascinated me that God was interested in him and our family.

Dad finished speaking and Mam was crying. The pastor invited him to step down into the water. I remember feeling sort of proud of him and that was definitely a first! I had never felt proud of him before but things had changed, he had changed.

Christmas was approaching and this was to be our first Christmas together for a long time. Dad was home and working so we had money. Christmases in the past had just been awful (apart from last Christmas when Phil brought the Christmas tree). Dad just spent the whole time drinking, arguing with Mam and fighting and we all tried to become invisible because if we were caught in his line of vision he would take great delight in humiliating us and then thrashing whoever he decided had annoyed him the most. So, as you can imagine, we were a little apprehensive to say the least.

We were sitting in the living room, all but Phil who was out with his mates. Dad had his Bible out and told us all to sit and listen. He said he would tell us the Christmas story, which he did. He read from the book of Luke all about how the angel went to Mary and told her she would have a baby. Dad did his usual dramatics and brought this wonderful story to life for us. I had never heard this story before. I had seen nativity scenes in shop windows and knew it was 'Baby Jesus' but I had no idea who he was and to learn that he was God's Son was quite something. I was fascinated.

After the story, Mam and Dad asked us what we would like for Christmas. We all just looked at them. They had never asked us before. "Well, come on, you must want something," said Dad.

John was first. "A bike, I want a bike, please Dad."

"We'll see. You, Frowser (he always called me that when he was pleased with me). What do you want?"

"I'd like a doll please."

He looked at me and smirked. "Aren't you a bit old for dolls?" I was 14.

"But I've always wanted one Dad so please, can I have one?"

"We'll see," he said. Kenny had a list as long as your arm of the things he wanted and they both laughed.

When Christmas morning arrived we were all excited. This was a whole new experience for all of us. When I woke up, at the bottom of my bed was a parcel all wrapped up in pretty paper! Kayla had a parcel under her cot. I ran into the boys' bedroom. They had parcels too! "Do you think we are allowed to open them?" We were all squeaking. Dad's door opened. "Are these for us, Dad?" we asked, pointing at the parcels.

"Whose name is on them?" he said. We looked and our names were written on the paper. "Well, you'd better open them then." So we tore into the paper and when Kenny opened his, it was a doll in a red dress with white lace trim. It stood about two foot six tall and had lovely black hair pulled back off its face. Kenny looked sooooo disappointed. I opened mine and it was a lorry with stuff in the back. Dad laughed and said perhaps we would like to swap! We did.

Ken was zooming around the bedroom and unloading his stuff. I took my doll into my bedroom. She was beautiful, just what I wanted. I took her out of the box and held her for a bit then put her back into the box. I didn't want to play with her. I just wanted to own a doll and now I did. I was thrilled.

Kayla tore into her parcel. It was a monkey called Jacko, a sort of chimp. She was petrified of it to start with, but after much persuasion she laughed and liked him. John didn't get a bike but was equally thrilled with his present. Kayla, bless her little heart, found my doll, took it out of the box and painted nail varnish on her eyes and fingernails. I was cross when I went upstairs and found what she'd done. I did yell at her and she just cried and said she was sorry, bless her. She was only little. I gave it to her in the end. She loved it and, anyway, it was a bit daft to want a doll at my age!

We all went off to chapel for our first Christmas service. We thought it was a bit of a bind to have to leave our presents and go to chapel and it wasn't even Sunday! But it was OK and in no time at all we were back home and getting organised for Christmas dinner. I was peeling potatoes and doing the veg, Mam had already put the meat in the oven. This was like a proper family and it was nice. I would be able to tell people that I got a present for Christmas and we had a proper dinner. This was the life!

After dinner, John and Kenny got a balloon and were bashing it over a streamer that we had put up. We all joined in and played this for hours. This is the only memory I have of us all actually playing a proper game in the house. It was fabulous fun. We all laughed and giggled together and all remember that time and playing the game.

It was almost the end of term and I would leave school at Easter. I had got myself a Saturday job at Harlequin Cleaners in Haywards Heath. They said I could work full time when I left school. I liked working there. Phil would give me a lift to work on the back of his motorbike and then pick me up on his way home. He used to terrify me. He would go so fast I couldn't breathe and when he went round corners he nearly took the skin off my knees many times, but it was cheaper than catching the bus and I liked being picked up by my big brother.

Phil decided he was going to add a sidecar to his bike. That way he could drive a bike with a bigger engine. So he got himself a really big old motorbike and made a sidecar out of scaffolding poles. It was just a triangle with a wheel on one point of the triangle and then somehow attached it to his bike.

Mam had run out of milk. It was a Sunday afternoon and the shop was closed but up at Cuckfield Hospital you could buy a carton of milk from a vending machine so she told us to go and get some. We had to be sneaky because Dad was against shopping on a Sunday. It was the Lord's Day and a day of rest so we had to go when Dad was having his kip. Phil said I could go along for the ride but he made me sit on the triangle and hold on and, like a fool, I did. As we rounded a corner the triangle went up in the air with me on it, then as it came down and the wheel hit the road I bounced and my bum went through the triangle and onto the road. It soon came up again I can tell you! I was shouting at Phil to stop but he just laughed and carried on to the hospital. When he finally stopped I got off to look at my backside, which all the world could see. The road had ripped a huge hole in my jeans and the skin off my bum! Phil suggested I go into casualty but I was too embarrassed. II should have done so because I had loads of bits of tarmac embedded in my behind which took lots of soaking in the bath to get them out. Needless to say I didn't take up his many offers to ride in his sidecar again. Once bitten twice shy.

With Phil being into bikes, John and Ken were also bike mad. I don't remember where they came from, but the odd motorbike would appear in the back garden and the boys would take it down the field. They would take it in turn to tear around like mad men on the thing, until it ran out of petrol. Then they would be looking for money or they would syphon petrol out of Dad's car! I also remember them frantically digging a great hole in the garden and burying a bike! I think we can safely say the bike had been nicked and whoever they nicked it from suspected them. Anyway, several bikes were buried in the garden at 22 over the years!

Dad had bought himself a Reliant Robin van. It turned out that he had never taken a driving test. He had been driving for years illegally but now he was a Christian he had to do things right and you could drive a three-wheeler with a provisional licence. Phil would panic me so much because when Dad had gone to a prayer meeting or up to his pal Ian's house, Phil would take the keys and be off driving the Reliant with all his mates. He would drive up to Handcross to see his girlfriend Maggy. I would be in such a state at home, worried that he wouldn't get back in time. He always did though.

Dad would often say things like, "I thought I turned the van round last night" when Phil had parked it pointing the wrong way, or, "I thought these Reliants were supposed to be easy on the petrol. Well this one isn't," and we would give each other a sideways glance. One time Dad went out in the morning to load up the van and it wasn't there. Phil had brought it back and in his haste to get out of it and into the house before Dad returned he forgot to put the handbrake on. When we looked down the road it had rolled down Glebe Road and right across London Lane and was stuck in the hedge on the other side. That could have been so nasty if anything had been coming down London Lane. Thankfully, Dad just assumed he had left the handbrake off.

Youth Club

I HAD STARTED GOING TO THE LOCAL YOUTH CLUB. Lots of the boys from Handcross would come on their motorbikes and all the Cuckfield girls would flirt with these boys. It was great fun. I first met Barry at the youth club and we continued to meet there every week. Dad didn't like me going out with Barry and would stop me going to the youth club for the slightest thing and I would be sent to my room. Well, this Thursday I had been sent up to my room so I decided he wasn't going to stop me and I climbed out of my bedroom window onto the concrete canopy above the back door and then down onto the coal bunker and I was away over the field and into the youth club. "He'll have to be up very early in the morning to get the better of me," I thought.

I was sitting on a settee watching *Top of the Pops*. Barry next to me with his arm around me and I was smoking a fag when all of a sudden I was lifted over the back of the settee by my hair! Dad was screaming at me. "Thought you could disobey me, did you, well you can't." With that he threw me across the room. Everyone was dumbstruck and just stared at us. I remember feeling so embarrassed.

Here I was, trying to be all grown-up and he has to do this to me. I didn't mind the girls seeing me battered, Pam and Penny had seen that happen before, but Barry and all the boys, this was too much. I was heading for the door followed closely by Dad's foot as he kicked me all the way home. Poor Barry, he didn't know what to do or say and very wisely, he did neither. When we got home Dad said I had to learn that what he said he meant and I had better be a fast learner or life would be very unpleasant. I just assumed this sort of behaviour was finished with now that he was a Christian, but no, this was still very much part of our lives, though he would always justify beating us now.

I was banned from the youth club for weeks after that. Dad said I had to be punished for my disobedience so I didn't see Barry for ages. Then, one evening he came round, which was very brave of him after seeing Dad in action. He wasn't allowed in so we talked on the doorstep. He asked me when I would be allowed out again. I didn't know. I just had to wait and hope he would relent and let me out soon. I walked out to the gate and we were standing by the gate kissing when WHOOSH, we were covered in freezing cold water. Dad was standing, empty bucket in hand.

"Get indoors, you," he said. Both Barry and I were gasping for breath. That was such a shock. "And as for you, CLEAR OFF HOME," he said, glaring at Barry. Poor Barry was wet through.

"But Mr Lancaster, we weren't doing anything wrong," said Barry.

"Never mind all that claptrap, just get on that bike and GO." Poor Barry did as he was told. I imagined he would have pneumonia by the time he got home, bless him. I went indoors.

Mam looked at me and laughed. "What happened to you?" she said. Just then Dad came in, the bucket still in hand.

"What do you think you are playing at?" he said, looking straight at me.

"I wasn't playing at anything. I was just saying goodnight to Barry, that's all. Why did you throw water on us?" I questioned him. I had never done that before. With that he just whacked me with the bucket and told me to go to bed. I remember lying on my bed feeling so angry and powerless and I hated those feelings.

One Sunday after chapel a lady called Corby spoke to me. She was a founder and head of Mill Hall School for the Deaf up on Whitemans Green. Her full name was Miss Mary Stephens Corbishley but everyone called her Corby. She asked me if I would like to go to tea with her. I was shocked, I had never been invited to tea before but said yes, I would love to. So Sunday afternoon I walked up to her cottage and 'took tea' with Corby. She asked me all sorts of questions about our family as we sat and ate sandwiches in her posh front room. She had brought in a tray with a plate of sandwiches and a plate with a cake on. Also on the tray were two little plates and Corby handed one to me. I had no idea what I was supposed to do with it. When we had sandwiches at home there was a plate full of sandwiches and you just took one and ate it, no problem, so this little plate was very worrying to me. I watched as Corby took a sandwich, bit it then put in onto her little plate. Sussed it, I thought and did the same. This is how posh people eat sandwiches.

After tea she took me up to the school and showed me around. Some of the kids were in one of the rooms playing games. I joined in with them and played for a while. Corby said afterwards that they needed someone to work weekends and would I like to do it. YES I would, I said, so as well as working at Harlequin Cleaners in the week I worked at Mill Hall at weekends which I loved, and it got me out of home and away from Mam and Dad. I thought if I was working on Sunday I wouldn't have to go to chapel but it turned out that if I was working on a Sunday I had to go to chapel with the kids and Corby. No escape!

Poor little Kayla was so confused when I went off to work and she was left at home with Mam. She missed me a lot, because as soon as I walked in the door she was on me like a limpet! I think she was just left to her own devices when everyone was out at school and work, bless her. When I was home I would take her up to the park and actually play with her. Mam never played with any of us and had no intention of starting now!

With my first big wage from the two jobs I decided to take Kayla into Crawley and buy her some new clothes, so on my day off we caught the bus. I loved taking her out, she was so cute and I would tell her to call me mammy. She more often than not did anyway, but on the bus people were looking at us and I so wanted them to think I was her Mam. We went into the shopping centre and I found several little outfits and she tried them all on but the one I liked best was a little powder blue coat, hat and trousers, edged in navy. She looked like a little dolly so I bought it for her. I paid for it then put it on her. I felt so pleased with myself. She wasn't going to look like we had done; she would have nice clothes from shops. When we got onto the bus to come home a lady said what a little darling she was. My chest swelled with pride and even Mam said she looked a picture, which she did.

Life was very busy for me, what with doing two jobs and life at home had changed. Dad was *very* different. He had been invited to give his testimony at various churches which he did regularly. He was studying the Bible more and trying to serve his God, though his temper still got the better of him, but I could see that something had indeed happened to him in that prison cell and he was a changed man.

He was trying to be a proper Dad to us and even when he lost his temper and belted us he would try to explain why he had to discipline us. He said the Bible said spare the rod and spoil the child. Absolutely no chance of us being spoilt then I thought! But the truth of it was, I liked it. I liked what had happened to him. I liked the fact that he didn't drink any more. He had even stopped swearing at us which was weird because every other word had been effing this, so his vocabulary had increased and so had ours. We had to look words up in the dictionary to find out what he was calling us now! *And* he worked and paid the bills. Also Kayla had never seen him rolling drunk and battering us since he came home. I loved that he hadn't visited me at night and that Mam was easier to live with too. She had found it all a bit too much at first but then she went to a chapel over in Barcombe when a visiting speaker called Bill Summers was preaching and she said that she had realised that she too was a sinner and had asked God to forgive her too. Since then our house was definitely a nicer place to be. Don't get me wrong, I am not talking clean, I am talking atmosphere and I wanted to be part of that.

Dad was always telling us that all we had to do was repent and ask Jesus into our hearts, so I knew what was expected of me. I told Dad I had done it and Jesus was my Saviour. He was thrilled and hugged me. It wasn't like the other hugs, this was different and I liked it. I wanted him to like me and be pleased with me and now he was! I hadn't thought this thing through at all. Dad told the pastor and the elders and I had to meet with them and tell them how I had become a Christian. That would have been OK if I really had become a Christian but I hadn't. I just wanted to be part of what was happening to our family and I wanted to be loved and figured this was the way to do it. I would just make it up. I was a liar. I had been taught to lie about stuff so now I would do it about this. So I told the pastor exactly what Dad said I needed to do. I said I had read I was a sinner. I repented and asked Jesus to be my saviour and he had come into my life and I was changed.

Well, they asked me one or two questions and then they said how thrilled they were that I had been saved and now I would need to be baptised. Yes, I realised that as I had been to Dad's baptism and that was a fantastic evening. The chapel was packed and it was after that night that we all came to the conclusion that Dad really had changed, so I knew what to expect and figured I could do it, no bother! So it was arranged for the Sunday evening and I would be baptised. I was very nervous. I remember Dad being so thrilled when he was telling his pals that I had become a Christian and was being baptised.

The Sunday I was to be baptised arrived. I was a little nervous but I was also the centre of attention and it was for something good, at least in their eyes, and I liked it. The chapel was full. I was called to the front and I gave my 'testimony' and walked down into the water. Errol said, "Fay, I baptise you in the name of the Father, Son and Holy Spirit," and with that he plunged me under the water.

As I emerged from the water the look on my Dad's face said it all; he was thrilled. I had pleased him, I knew that. It didn't occur to me that I was doing something wrong. After I was baptised I went into the back room of the chapel to dry and change clothes. I remember thinking they would love me now because I was part of Christianity. God didn't even enter into my thinking.

The midweek prayer meeting was at eight o'clock on Wednesday night. Dad yelled upstairs, "Come on, Frowser, or we'll be late." I hadn't realised that I would have to go to that but I figured it would be OK so I got myself ready and off we went.

I had no interest in the prayer meeting whatsoever so to me it was the most boring thing I had ever been to and on the way home Dad was telling me how the prayer meeting was the most important meeting of all. It was the heart of the church. I had to feign enthusiasm and to think I would have to do this every week. *What have I done?* I thought, but this was my lot now, I knew that much. My only hope was to leave home!

Corby came around to see me at home. "Fay," she said, "I know you work at the dry-cleaners during the week and I feel that you are wasted there. I am so pleased with the way you work at the weekends and I am wondering if you would like to come and work for me full time."

Without hesitation I said, "YES PLEASE."

"Wonderful," she said. "You do realise this will mean living in, don't you?" I hadn't realised that at all but I thought this would be the answer to my problem.

"I will have to give a week's notice and can start straight after that." So it was decided and I moved my meagre bits into the attic room I was to share with a girl called Gwen.

There were two other girls who I would be working with, Marion and Anne. They were great girls. Leaving home was hard. Kayla was like my own baby. She was only two and up to now I had done virtually everything for her. Her little face dropped when I left the house and she would cry. When I came in, she would beam; she loved me and I loved her. Mam loved her, but in truth she had no patience with kids at all, and the idea of her playing with Kayla was crazy— she just wouldn't. Dad, on the other hand, would tease her and make her laugh. He loved her but he too was out all day. Poor Kayla, I couldn't take her with me or I would have done.

Part of my job was to help with the kids; getting them up in the mornings, helping at meal times with the little ones and at bedtime putting them to bed.

During the day I would help in the nursery. I loved it. I would volunteer to work on Wednesday nights so that I had a genuine excuse for not going to the prayer meeting. I couldn't get out of going to chapel on Sunday morning because we had to take all the children to chapel who didn't go home at weekends, and Sunday School was held at Mill Hall so I couldn't get out of that. But I could skive out of Sunday evenings sometimes which I thought was wonderful and I didn't have Dad going on at me because I didn't see him. I didn't live at home anymore.

Poor Kenny was having a miserable time of it. He was a bright kid but he couldn't keep his mouth shut. He was constantly in trouble with Dad for answering him back. Dad would often lose his temper with Kenny. I would go home to visit and Kenny would be full of woe. He was grounded or he had to do some job or other before Dad got back. If it wasn't done he would get a good hiding. He really hated Dad and Mam was very cruel to Kenny too. It was as if she took delight in his misery. She had always been like that with us but looking back, it seemed worse for poor old Kenny.

Mam was still a terrible cook and we had all suffered her cauliflower cheese. It was the most revolting mess. It looked and smelled for all the world like vomit and she knew that we all, without exception, hated it, so whenever she was feeling spiteful she would make it. The thing was, her and Dad never ate it. That pleasure was reserved just for us kids and the rule was whatever was on your plate you *had* to eat it. Nothing could be left.

Well, I had dropped in on this particular day to visit and the unmistakable aroma of cauliflower cheese hit me as I walked in through the back door. It was teatime and Kenny, John and Kayla were sat at the table with a huge pile of what we referred to as cheesy vomit on their plates. John, bless him, ploughed through his and Kayla spread hers all over her plate and the table but poor Kenny was having such trouble even swallowing his. His throat just wouldn't let him swallow it. Mam kept shouting at him to, "eat it or else...." Lots of things you could feed to the dog but even Taurus wouldn't eat this. I was wearing a pink shirt dress with huge pockets and a navy reefer jacket. I walked into the dining room, held open the pocket on my dress and pointed at his dinner and then my pocket as I continued to talk to Mam who was in the sitting room. Kenny poured this revolting mess into my pocket. I didn't stay very long; I could feel this gunge seeping through my pocket onto my leg. I made it to Glebe Twitten and turned my pocket inside out and poured this foul mixture onto the grass. She is the only person I know that makes *grey* cauliflower cheese and it doesn't sound nearly as revolting as it tastes!

The Truth is Out

JOHN HAD BEEN AT CUCKFIELD SECONDARY SCHOOL FOR A TERM. He loved it and made lots of friends. He was such a gregarious boy and very bright. He didn't have a school uniform and there was no likelihood of him getting one; my heart ached for him, but he said he wasn't bothered! I knew he was because that's exactly what I used to say. I went into Crawley and got him a school shirt, trousers and a jumper, he was so chuffed. Then we all went to a jumble sale in the Queens Hall on the Saturday afternoon and found a school tie and blazer. We were thrilled; he look like any other schoolboy, which is exactly what he wanted to look like! Fabulous!

John was earning money now. He had got a job doing a bit of clearing up in the garden for a chap who lived near the Wheatsheaf. He would go every Saturday and mow lawns, dig the veg patch and generally tidy up. He was paid ten shillings for the whole day and he would give the money to Mam who said she would save it for him. He wanted to buy a bike and worked for many months but when he asked Mam for his money, she just laughed at him. "What money?" she said. He was gutted. When he told us, we hated her more than ever. She had had no intention of saving it for him.

John asked Dad if he and Ken could go with him the next time he went to the scrapyard and he took them. They got broken bikes, spare wheels and chains, piled them into the back of the van and worked and worked on them for days. Finally, they were both mobile. Brilliant! They would disappear for hours on their bikes. Freedom!

Kenny was now starting Cuckfield Secondary School and didn't have a school uniform. Dad would make him wear one of his shirts and a pair of old brown cord trousers that he got from a jumble sale. They were too big for Dad so poor old Kenny, who was a skinny little fella, looked ridiculous in them. Dad seemed to take delight in humiliating Kenny too, so when I got paid I went off to Crawley and bought him trousers, shirt, tie and blazer. He was thrilled with it all, though he did tell me that the trousers were itchy! But he looked the business in his new gear. I was so pleased for him, knowing just how embarrassing it was wearing your parents cast-offs.

We all hated Saturday mornings because we had to work in the garden. Poor Kenny hated it far more than any of us. Dad had a real problem with Kenny, or should I say Kenny had a problem with Dad. He just hated him and all he stood for. So it was always daggers drawn. Well, this particular Saturday, Kenny wanted to go out as soon as the jobs were finished and Dad knew that, so was doing all in his power to keep Kenny working. So much so that he would tell Kenny to move bags of cement from place A to place B, then back again, just to keep him occupied.

Well, Kenny had had enough so while moving the cement for the umpteenth time he asked Dad where he wanted it. Dad was busy doing something and just pointed and said, "Put them over there." Right where he was pointing was a puddle. So Kenny put eight bags of cement in the puddle. We were all shaking our heads and gesturing to him not to do it but he had reached the end of his tether with Dad so he just ignored us and did it. We were all waiting for Dad to notice what Ken had done but he didn't. Finally, we were all finished and could go out.

It was Sunday afternoon when Dad finally noticed the cement. We had been home from chapel, had dinner and Dad went down the shed to get something when he saw the cement. Kenny was in the kitchen. Dad called him and we all froze. Ken went out into the garden. Dad just pointed at the cement and looked at Kenny. "You told me to put 'em there," said Kenny. With that Dad just lunged at Kenny and started battering him. Kenny figured he'd rather be hung for a sheep than a lamb so he started fighting back. This was a first. None of us would dare to do that so we were in awe of Kenny.

Dad had been laying a path from the house to the shed and there was just rubble down so they were slipping on this uneven ground and Dad fell. The look Kenny's face was one of pure joy but on Dad's, of total disbelief. Dad jumped up, grabbed Kenny by the neck and forced him backwards into the rain barrel so Kenny's head was completely submerged by the rainwater and the look on Dad's face said he wasn't going to let him go! We were screaming "LET HIM GO DAD PLEASE" but he wasn't listening.

John ran into the house. "Mam, stop him. He's going to drown our Kenny." Mam ran into the garden and tried to pull Dad off Kenny who had gone floppy by this time. She was shouting at Dad to let go but it was like he couldn't hear her. She was pulling at his clothes but she couldn't budge him so she picked up the shovel, swung it as hard as she could and belted Dad up the side of his head. He let go and Kenny fell to the ground, coughing and spluttering. Dad was dazed and he looked shocked. I was never sure whether he was shocked by what he had done or what Mam did to him but boy, did he have a cauliflower ear, swollen face and a black eye for quite a few days after. He didn't say a word. He just went into the house and Mam followed.

We stayed in the garden to look after poor old Kenny. He looked terrible. His neck was badly bruised and he said he had a bad headache. We were full of sympathy and made Kenny laugh by saying that the cement had gone rock hard and Dad wouldn't be able to use it. Serves him right for trying to drown you!

Dad was doing well as a painter and decorator. Corby asked him to give her an estimate for painting the whole exterior of Mill Hall. This would be a big job. It was a huge place and would take him quite a while to complete but it would mean regular work for a long time. Corby accepted his estimate and he started work which was great for him, not so great for me. I had not been going to Wednesday prayer meetings and Sunday nights. On Monday morning Dad would be painting a window and would shout to me, "Why weren't you at chapel last night, or the prayer meeting. You make sure you don't miss next week." There was no escaping him and this went on for months. I would be sneaking around the school looking out of the windows, trying to work out where he was painting so I could avoid him. It was awful. I had been pretending to be a Christian and been baptised to make him happy and to make him like me and all it was doing was making him angry and upset with me because I wasn't living the Christian life. Well, I couldn't because I wasn't a Christian. It wasn't real to me.

It was a Saturday night and I decided I would tell them the truth that I wasn't a Christian and then perhaps Dad would stop hassling me to go to chapel. I went around to Glebe Road. Dad was sat reading his Bible and Mam was in the kitchen. I went and sat with Dad. "Hello love," he said. My heart was pounding in my throat. I have got to tell him quickly or I will lose my bottle, I thought.

"Dad, I've got something to tell you," I said.

"Go on then," he said.

"I'm not a real Christian, Dad. I only said that so that you would like me. Jesus isn't my saviour and I don't want to go to chapel anymore."

He just stared into the distance for what seemed like ages and then he looked at me. "Of course you are a Christian love, this is just Satan speaking and we don't listen to him do we."

"No Dad, it's not Satan, it's me."

But he wouldn't have it. "We all go through times when we feel low love, but we must press on towards the mark of our high calling. Let me pray for you." And he did. I felt sick; he wouldn't believe me. I went back to Mill Hall that night wondering how this mess was going to sort itself out. It didn't.

Dad came to work on Monday and he was up a ladder painting a window singing, "A sunbeam, a sunbeam, Jesus wants me for a sunbeam," at the top of his voice. I tried to avoid him all day and managed it until just before he went home for the night. "Hello love, how are you feeling? I've been praying for you, any better?"

"No Dad, I'm not a Christian, NOT born again and I don't want to go to chapel anymore." There, I had said it all. He just picked up his paint kettle, brushes and bits and walked to the car. He said nothing, just got in the car and drove away. Half of me was pleased. *Finally it had sunk in*, I thought, and the other half of me felt sad that I had disappointed him. The weird thing was, since he had been a Christian all I wanted to do was please him and win his approval. That was why I had said I was a Christian in the first place, to please him and now it had all backfired on me. I walked back inside to the staffroom. I could have cried, I felt so bad.

One of the girls I worked with, Anne, had applied for a job at Great Walstead School in Lindfield. She was a great girl and I was going to miss her. All four of us girls got on really well but Anne was more on my wavelength. We both had a stupid sense of humour and would find the funny side of most things. She was a Christian as were all the other girls and they thought I was too. I really had made a mess of this; I would have to tell them too, but not yet.

Sunday came round very quickly. I was on duty so I had to go to chapel with the kids. So much for my great speech about not going to chapel anymore! Dad was in his usual pew but he ignored me as I walked past him. Kayla shouted, "Hello Faydee." I smiled and whispered hello to her and we all marched up to the front pew. Because the children were deaf and lip-read, they needed to be as close to the front as possible so no skulking in the back row for me, OH NO! Up on the very front pew, and I could feel Dad's eyes burning into the back of my neck. This was going to be a long service! The final hymn was *And can it be*. I could hear Dad singing. This was his favourite hymn and as we sang the verse 'my chains fell off, my heart was free, I rose, went forth and followed thee'. I knew exactly what he was doing without turning round. He was leaning backwards punching the air with every word, his arm high above his head, every vein on his neck swollen as if they were about to burst, his face as red as beetroot and tears running down his face as he bellowed out the verse with every fibre of his being. The joy on his face was evident to a blind man. He loved that hymn; he said he knew how the bloke who wrote it felt because *his* chains had fallen off too.

After the service was over everyone congregated outside chatting. I came out with the kids from Mill Hall. I saw Dad chatting to the pastor and they both looked over at me. I felt embarrassed and ashamed all at the same time. I knew what Dad was telling him and I wanted to run away. I had let him down too. I thought that everyone would hate me.

We walked back to Mill Hall. I felt terrible, I wished with all my heart that I hadn't done it, that I hadn't told Dad I had been saved, that I hadn't been baptised, that I hadn't lied to the elders of the church, but I had and now I didn't know what to do. I spent the afternoon with the kids physically but my mind was elsewhere. Monday morning came and so did Dad. He was painting the first window I passed on my way to wake the little ones. He gave me a look and shook his head. He didn't have to say anything, his look said it all. I went about my duties and got the children dressed and ready for school but first breakfast. I looked out of the dining room window and there he was again. I couldn't escape his disapproving looks. It's difficult to explain just how awful I felt, I so wanted his approval. What had I done? He would never love me now.

I stopped going to chapel except when I had to with the Mill Hall kids. I just felt too embarrassed and ashamed. I also tried to stop going home to visit quite so often because Dad would give me the third degree about what I had been doing and how I was a disgrace to God, the church and him and Mam, but I missed seeing the boys and Kayla so I would ride my pushbike through the twitten and look down Glebe Road to see if Dad's car was there. If it wasn't, I would go home.

I knew Mam wouldn't give me the third degree. She didn't care whether I was saved or not. She never talked to me about God which I found a bit odd, but I liked it. She never changed. She was still the same old Mam except she would go all holy when she was around Christians, same as I had, only she hadn't been found out yet. She still swore but not around Dad. She was still as sneaky, still as nasty, still as devious but she was careful not to let Dad see that side of her but we kids didn't count so we saw it all. Living at Mill Hall was fabulous, but I missed having Kayla around me and watching her grow and I missed the boys.

Phil was working for Crawford and Crane, digging. Dad's pal Mossy worked with him. It was hard work but good money. His relationship with Maggy was going strong. She was a very sweet girl, very quiet. She loved Phil and he so needed to be loved; he was such a damaged boy and so angry most of the time. Maggy lived in Handcross. Phil had a motorbike and would drive over and pick her up and bring her back to our house, or to the youth club if it was on.

Mam Runs Away

MAM MUST HAVE GOT FED UP WITH ALL THE PRETENCE because on Sunday morning she said she wasn't going to chapel. After Dad tried to persuade her to go, all to no avail, he took the boys and Kayla. I saw them at the chapel and asked John where Mam was. He told me Mam and Dad had had a barny about coming to chapel and Mam said she wasn't coming. I decided to go home after I finished work to see what had happened. How would Dad handle her not wanting to go to chapel? But when I got home, things were worse than I thought. Mam wasn't there.

Apparently, as soon as Dad left for chapel, she left for Durham! She borrowed some money from a dear lady, Mrs Tester, who lived at the bottom of our road and she had gone up to stay with Gran and Grandad. Dad was in a state. He said I would have to stay at home and help with the kids so I rang Corby and explained what had happened. She said I could live at home and go into work as soon as the kids had gone to school and finish in time to pick Kayla up from school at four o'clock. Once Dad was home I could go up to Mill Hall and do the late shift until Mam came back. That was great and Dad seemed to calm down a bit when I told him what Corby had said.

Apparently, Mam was having some sort of mental breakdown and had seen a doctor up in Willington who suggested that she go into hospital for a few weeks so she admitted herself into Sedgfield Mental Hospital. I think she thought it would be restful; in fact it was anything but. She was put into a ward with very mentally ill people and it scared her witless. They were screaming and shouting, with very odd behaviour. She wanted out but she had to convince the doctors she was OK, which took some doing. After a few days she discharged herself and went back to stay with Gran and Grandad.

Dad rang and spoke to her. She said she couldn't cope with all the changes in their lives and that Dad expected too much from her. All the chapel stuff was difficult for her and she hated the way the pastor told Dad what he should be doing and Dad did it. After much toing and froing, she said she would come home. Dad was chuffed and said we all had to be good and help Mam.

Dad picked her up from Haywards Heath station. When she came in she had her 'I'm poorly' face on and when she had that face on it meant she wasn't going to do a thing. We had to do everything! Dad told me to make them a cuppa which I did. We all said 'hello Mam' and when she spoke she had her poorly voice too, which was bad news. She sat in the chair and drank her tea and lit a fag, took a long drag and settled back. Dad called us all into the living room. "Now, your Mam is not very well and we need to be helping her more. I don't want to hear any of you giving her any lip or there will be trouble. Frowser, on your days off you come home and help. You can do the washing and stuff like that." So that was that; she was back and we were her slaves, at least that's how it felt.

We all soon worked out that there was nothing much wrong with Mam because as soon as Dad had gone to work she changed from this poorly creature who could barely walk or talk to the Mam we all knew. She would yell at us to get a move on, telling us all that she would tell Dad we hadn't done as we were told if we didn't hurry up.

I hated it. On my days off I would get home at about ten o'clock and she would be sat in a chair puffing on a fag. "Better get on with the washing first." I hated that word 'first'. It told me that she had a list of things lined up for me to do while she sat like lady muck, dishing out the orders. I would get out our old twin tub. It was such hard work and there was always so much to do. But I would get it done and out on the line to dry. Then it would be, "tidy up in here, do the washing up and sort out the kitchen," which was an endless task because it was always such a mess. But then again, the whole house was a mess. "Go make my bed" was next and then the whole day would be peppered with, "Fay, make me a cuppa—make me a sandwich—nip to Mr Paines (the corner shop) and get me some fags" and so on until she couldn't think of anything else for me to do. The sad thing was, even after I had done it all it didn't look any different.

As soon as Dad came home she was back being the poorly Mam with the weak voice. She would tell Dad how she could barely lift her legs to walk when she had been running up and down stairs all day with no trouble. He would make a fuss of her, which she loved, but it didn't take Dad long to suss out that she was fannying and there was nothing wrong with her.

I don't think he knew what to do with her. She wasn't a child that he could punish and since he had been saved and had stopped hitting her she had got really

141

cocky. She had run away once and, if he upset her, what was to stop her doing it again? But he couldn't have her behaving like this. She was doing nothing in the house, she didn't read her Bible or pray with him, she wasn't going to chapel and he didn't like the fact that she 'thought' she was getting one over on him. The Pastor came to see Mam. He talked to her for a while and prayed with her before leaving. I had been in the kitchen 'earwigging' through the service hatch. Dad would go mad if he knew what she was saying about him. She told him that Dad was a bully and he pressured her to go to meetings which she didn't want to attend and she couldn't take it anymore. She said she couldn't cope with other people knowing her business and she didn't want him coming round anymore and she would go to chapel when she was good and ready, not when he or anyone else said she had to! *Well you've got to give it to her*, I thought. *That told him.*

Dad had made a good friend at chapel; a bloke called Ian Randall. He was a Christian too and they would spend evenings together studying the Bible and praying and I'm sure Dad shared his worries about Mam with Ian. I remember Dad taking Kayla up to Ian's house one evening. They had been praying for some time with Kayla sitting on quite a high stool. Then, bless her, she fell asleep and fell off the stool but they continued praying as she lay on the floor fast asleep. We laughed when he told us about it but it shows just how fervent they were in prayer, nothing would distract them. Also, I think, he drew strength to cope with Mam from his times of prayer with Ian, and boy did he need strength to deal with her!

I had had enough of looking after Mam of being a complete slave to her and of being a complete disappointment to Dad. Someone left a *Lady* magazine in the staffroom. I was flicking through it and saw an ad. It said 'Nanny needed, for a three-year-old and a nine-month-old baby, both boys.' I applied and had a letter saying they were interviewing at the Birch Hotel, so I duly went. They were a very odd couple. She was German and about 38, he was Swiss I think and around late 60s early 70s. The boys were very sweet. We all had lunch together and they asked me a million questions. After lunch they said they would let me know as they had a couple more to interview.

Well, the letter arrived. Before I opened it, I thought 'Didn't get it', but actually it said they were very pleased to offer me the job! I was elated. I gave in my notice and would start the job in two weeks. When I told Mam that I had got a job in Sandy in Bedfordshire, her face was a picture. "But who's going to help me look after Kayla and do the washing?"

I took great delight in saying, "You'll have to do it yourself! I start in two weeks."

I didn't like leaving Kayla who was just about to start school, so I spent my last two weeks packing and any free time I had I went home and spent it with Kayla, though Mam had a list of stuff she wanted me to do. I took Kayla to Crawley and bought her some school shoes and some cardigans. Mam had said she didn't have to wear uniform. She had a few pretty dresses but only tatty cardigans, so now she was ready for school.

I caught the train to Sandy and the man I was to work for was there to meet me. I liked him. We arrived at the house and I was shown to my room—lovely. Then around the house—beautiful. Then his wife arrived holding the baby, who was screaming, and just handed him to me. No hello, welcome, nothing. Then she came back and said, "Put on the uniform that's in your room."

Great, I thought, *This is going to be a bundle of fun!* The baby was teething, bless him, and the three-year-old was a little sweetie. Uniform on, I went into the nursery. I loved these two little boys; they were just lovely and we got on like a house on fire. On my day off, the man would drive me over to my uncle and aunt's house in Old Warden. It was lovely to have somewhere to go, and my cousins Angela, Marcia and Sandra were there too. I got to know them better and spent some lovely days with them all.

I remember being there babysitting for Uncle Bill and Aunty Kath once. Angela was being very lippy and wouldn't do as I told her. Having only dealt with stroppy brothers, I did what I would do to them and punched her! Poor Angie was very shocked. When I think about it now I'm ashamed. Sorry Angie! I had been there for a couple of months, when the mum came into the nursery to tell me she was going to Germany, taking the boy and leaving the baby with me. *Great*, I thought. I didn't like her at all.

The following day off she went and I loved her not being around. To be honest, I think the Dad did too! He cooked dinner for us both and we had steak and eggs—fabulous! He told me I didn't have to wear the uniform while his wife was away. After dinner, when I had put the baby to bed, I would usually go to my room. He said if I wanted to join him in the lounge I would be most welcome. I did and we chatted and watched telly—such a nice fella. He asked me if I would mind on my day off taking the baby with me. He bunged me a few extra quid and drove us both over to Old Warden.

The saddest thing was that while she was away, Mam called and said Phil and Mags were getting married. I couldn't go! I was gutted. It was only a small affair she said, registry office, but it didn't matter. My big brother was getting married and I couldn't be there! They were both so young, Phil was 19 and Mags 17, but they were happy, though I did feel sorry for Mags because they lived with Mam and Dad for the first few months. I am sure Mam would have made Mags her personal slave too!

I had been working there for six months, but really it wasn't what I wanted to do. I gave my notice and she went mad. "You can't leave!"

"I can and I am," I said. I worked the week and on Saturday I ordered a taxi. She stood back against the door. "You can't!"

Her husband came through, pulled her away from the door, and said, "Thank you Fay for all that you have done. We are sorry you are leaving and the boys and I will miss you, but you be happy in your life." I thanked him and was off.

I arrived home and the house was full. It was weird Phil being a married man and Mags had fitted into life at 22 really well. John had got himself a girlfriend, Sharon Sands. We had all gone to school together and she had been head girl. The first time she came to the house and I was there, she said, "I remember you, you punched me."

"Sorry Sharon." Kenny was his usual daft self. He could make us all fall about laughing, though he didn't make Dad laugh much—a very fraught relationship! I slotted back into my bedroom with Kayla and the routine of chapel on Sundays, prayers at every meal and Bible study whenever Dad thought we would benefit! I needed to get out of here. I wondered where I would get another job!

Great Walstead

ANNE HAD LEFT MILL HALL and I met up with her in Haywards Heath for coffee. She told me there was a job going at Great Walstead for an assistant matron. She said it was great fun working there and she would put in a good word for me. Well, that would be the answer to my prayers, except for the fact I didn't pray. But you know what I mean. I would be away from Cuckfield, wouldn't have to go to chapel anymore, wouldn't see Dad daily and wouldn't have him breathing down my neck. "Wonderful, please do it," I said and within a week I had an interview.

Mrs Parkes was waiting for me. "Do come up to the flat," she said and proceeded to lead me through a maze of corridors and upstairs. I remember thinking, I hope she brings me back down or I will be lost forever in here. "Please sit down, Fay," she said, so I sat on the settee. She made us coffee and just chatted to me about what the job entailed. She was so sweet and it was soon obvious that she thought I was a Christian. After all, this was a Christian school which was run on Christian principles. If I told her the truth I wouldn't get the job and I needed to get away from Dad so I led her to believe I *was* a Christian and I got the job.

The weirdest thing happened while I was sat on the settee. I felt something touching me. It felt like an arm sliding around my waist. I looked down and to my horror a snake was curling around me! I nearly died of shock. Mrs Parkes saw my face and very matter-of-factly said, "Oh there he is. He's been missing for a few days." With that she just unravelled this snake from around me and put it into a tank as if this was the most normal thing, and just kept talking all the while she was doing it. I was in shock, but trying to hold myself together; not easy!

Apparently, it was her son Andrew's pet boa constrictor. He had brought it up to the flat and 'lost it' a few days earlier. I had only ever seen snakes on the telly and, believe me, after this encounter, that was where I preferred to see them.

145

I was to start the following month but could move my stuff in whenever I wanted. She took me up some more stairs and showed me my room. It was a lovely sunny room. I thought I would enjoy living here. I was so excited about moving to Walstead. I had given my month's-notice to Corby. She was quite cross with me I think, but accepted it and wished me well.

Because Walstead was in the middle of country lanes I decided I would need to buy a moped so that on my days off I wouldn't be stuck there, so I went into Haywards Heath and tried one out. This was fun. I ordered it, a Honda Graduate, and before the week was out I had my little moped. I loved it and the freedom it gave me.

I moved into Walstead with my few belongings and immediately felt at home. The atmosphere was great, the boys were great and the staff were great. I was going to enjoy working and living here. It was so much more relaxed than at Mill Hall and I was soon used to it all. I loved it in the summer because if it was a lovely day we matrons would stick a notice on our sitting room door saying 'Matron's in the swimming pool' or 'Matron's on the terrace'. Fantastic! We would take a load of clothes that needed repairing—buttons on shirts, hems on trousers etc—and sit on the terrace sunbathing as we did the mending and nattering as we sewed. It was lovely.

The business of chapel wasn't an issue here. I didn't have to go to Cuckfield *but* the school had its own chapel which the boys had to attend every morning for assembly and on Sunday mornings and evenings. We were expected to attend too, which I did. In fact I grew to enjoy going, partly because I loved to hear the boys singing. It was wonderful, partly because it was easier to understand than Cuckfield as it was aimed at the boys. Also, a big bonus was, it was *much* shorter than Cuckfield and, as a non-Christian pretending to be a Christian, this was a big bonus.

There were lots of flats in the grounds that were often rented out to people who didn't work at the school. I asked if Phil and Mags could rent one. Yes, they could. Mags was thrilled and they moved in fairly swiftly! They didn't have much furniture but I am sure getting their own place was all they wanted. They had moved out of 22 and were living in one room at Sister Smith's house, a really lovely lady who was the Sister on the children's ward at Cuckfield Hospital. She had a little girl called Jeanie, the same age as Kayla, and Mam would look after her when Sister Smith was on duty, so Kayla and Jeanie became very great playmates.

146

Phil was now working with Dad, so he did still get to see him on a daily basis. They were both working for Graham Slegg who was a builder and a member of Cuckfield Baptist Chapel. He took Dad on when no one else would and taught him so many things. He was an amazing Christian and showed both Dad and Phil how to give a good measure well pressed down—in other words, never short change people with your time, your skill or your money. Dad never forgot that although I'm not sure it stuck in Phil's mind!

I remember one evening at Walstead looking out onto the playing fields to see Phil on his motorbike tearing round the fields. 'Pillock!' I thought. 'He'll get me the sack and he and Mags will be kicked out of the flat.' I have odd memories of them living there. Phil had done a burglary and nicked a car. I remember going down to the flat and Phil had a motorbike in bits on the floor in the kitchen. Poor Mags! I'm sure she hadn't bargained on this when she married him. Mags was from a normal family and was shocked rigid at some of the things that went on in our family, bless her.

I remember the police saying they were looking for some 17th century wall hangings that had been stolen. And then I remember thinking that Phil and Mags had very odd taste in carpets. Phil had put the wall hangings on the floor!

Anne's parents had moved to Eastbourne and she decided she would like to move down there too. She got a job in a girls' college in Eastbourne and left Walstead. I was sad to see her go as we worked well together and were good mates too. Mrs Parkes told me there was a new girl starting soon; her name was Rachel Cox.

She arrived on the Sunday evening ready to start work on the Monday morning. We hit it off straight away. She was lovely, 17, quite tall, with blonde shoulder length wavy hair with the broadest grin I had ever seen. She was so friendly. She came from Tunbridge Wells and she too had a moped. We would go off to Haywards Heath in our time off, racing along the country lanes on our bikes. We thought we were flying along but in reality our bikes didn't do more than 40 mph! But we felt like speed demons.

It was a really beautiful hot summer's day, we had been swimming in the pool and I was wearing a bikini. For some reason, I decided to drive into Haywards Heath on my moped in my bikini! Well, I got a great reaction. I must have looked a sight with my long hair flowing in the wind behind me. Blokes were whistling and shouting comments. I thought I looked the business. Anyway,

I had stopped at the roundabout by the Sussex pub at the bottom of the High Street when all of a sudden I was pulled off my moped by my Dad.

He was holding the back of my bikini bottoms with one hand and my hair and the skin between my shoulder blades with the other. He lifted me up off my bike and threw me into the back of his Landrover. I was in shock. The back of his Landrover was just a mass of tools and so I was being stabbed in very painful parts with screwdrivers, hammer handles and a host of other implements. Also, my bikini bottom had been pulled so tightly up my bottom I thought I would never be able to get it out. Then, to top it all, he threw my moped on top of me. All the while he was shouting that I was a 'scarlet harlot' and should be ashamed of myself, parading around town near naked! He drove me back to Walstead and screamed at me the whole journey, telling me how I had let him down, let mum down, let God down. I was a disgrace.

We arrived at Walstead and I climbed out of the Landrover. He dragged my bike out, threw it on the ground and drove off. I stood there for a few moments looking down the drive after him when one of the boys brought me back to reality. "Miss Lancaster, are you alright?"

"Yes," I said, "I'm fine."

"You don't look it, Miss. Did you have an accident?" I looked down at myself. I looked a mess. I had a huge burn on my leg, blood was running down the back of my leg and I was covered with red welts. The burn was from the exhaust pipe. As Dad threw the bike on top of me, it had landed on my leg. I hadn't felt it burn me at the time because I was in shock. The blood was from being stabbed by tools and the welts were where I had been manhandled and landed on all the tools. Also, my head felt very tender and as I ran my fingers through my hair a great chunk of hair just came away in my fingers. I burst into tears. I had done it again. I was a disgrace and it had all gone terribly wrong. All I had wanted to do was please him and everything I did *displeased* him. This poor little boy was so bewildered. "No, I didn't have an accident. It was just my Dad, don't worry," I said. I picked up my bike and pushed it up the drive.

Rachel was very sweet as I explained what had happened. I can't imagine what she must have thought of us but she didn't say anything. Before long we were great mates and spent most of our time off shopping in Haywards Heath and Lindfield or visiting my home or hers though there was a big difference! Our council house was a complete mess while hers was a beautiful town house with umpteen bedrooms and very posh. I remember the first time I went home with her, her mum was so lovely and made me feel like one of the family. We stayed for the weekend and I went to chapel with them and afterwards home for lunch. It was such a treat to be included in a normal family. Everyone was so nice to me and Rachel was treated with such love and respect by everyone, it made me realise just how abnormal my family was. I often wonder what Rachel's first impression of my family was. Bless her, she never said anything about our house and the mess it was in.

We enjoyed working at Walstead. It was such a great place; the staff were such a lovely bunch. The Latin teacher was so eccentric. I would often be riding up the drive on my moped and almost have a heart attack at the sight of Mr Maddox, pushbike on its side, on his back with his legs up a tree! The first time I came upon him like this I stopped and ran over to him, thinking he was hurt only to have him tell me he was resting his legs!

Life was good. I was having a great time. I was enjoying my job, being away from home, I had a place to stay, good food, good friends and I wasn't having to go to Cuckfield chapel. This was the life and not having Dad breathing hellfire and brimstone down my neck through every window was the icing on the cake!

It was a Saturday morning and I saw Dad's car in the car park. 'What's he doing here?' was my first thought and then I saw him with Mrs Parkes. What's going on? I watched as they walked round the entire school. I realised what was going on and my heart sank. He was giving her an estimate for painting the school. I couldn't believe it and blow me down if he didn't get the job. It was a couple of weeks later on a Monday morning. There he was again with the "why haven't you been to chapel" and every time I saw him we had a row about my lack of interest in God. I couldn't believe it and the school was huge and would take him weeks to paint. This was going to be a long summer.

The sports master, Ted Hanley, was great fun. We became good friends and often after work Rachel, Ted and I would walk up to the Snowdrop pub for a glass of cider. This was fine in the light summer evenings but on a dark winter night walking down country lanes with no lighting and cars hurtling round corners at us was a bit scary to say the least.

It was the summer of '69. Rachel was only at Walstead until she was old enough to do her nursing training and was applying to London hospitals. I so admired her. I so wanted to be a nurse but because of my lack of education felt I just wouldn't be able to cope. There were huge gaps in my basic knowledge and I felt I was too stupid to even attempt the exam. Seeing Rachel planning her future made me realise you could actually do that. I just let life happen to me, the thought of planning life was quite alien. Mam and Dad never talked about our future or what we wanted to do with our lives.

It seems weird to think I have three brothers who are all exceedingly talented. Phil is a brilliant artist and sculptor and should have been encouraged to go to Art College. John is a brilliant businessman, always full of ideas, and had the propensity to be an architect but wasn't encouraged. Ken was picked out of hundreds of boys for a fantastic job at Gatwick airport, working as an engineer, but Mam and Dad said it was a waste of time and too expensive to get him there, so they all finished up working on building sites and with Dad.

Then there was me and my desire to be a nurse. What a dreadful shame that none of us ever had a conversation with Mam and Dad about our dreams. None of us felt we were cheated; it was just the way it was. Like I said, it didn't come into our thinking that we could plan a future or achieve goals, it was a matter of surviving. My sister Kayla actually went to do her nursing training and passed, only to show Mam and Dad that she could achieve something. In fact she didn't want to be a nurse at all, she just wanted them to be proud of her. I think they were. I know I certainly was.

I was living at Walstead but would pop home to see everyone. I did miss the boys and Kayla. I called in one day to see John lying on the sofa very battered and bruised. He told me he had been to a party in Haywards Heath and had got drunk. Someone rang Dad and he went to pick him up. He was furious. Apparently, John was so drunk he couldn't stand up. He was in the front garden of whoever's party it was, lying on the floor, having been sick in a bird bath. His friends were very worried about him and, as he couldn't talk, they called Dad. When Dad arrived, he walked into the garden, picked John up by his arms, threw him over his shoulder and then threw him into the back of the van. John's mates were in shock; they didn't expect that.

On arriving home Dad opened the van door, dragged John out by his legs and dragged him down the steps, scraping the skin off his back and arms and into the house where he was sick on the floor. Dad lifted him upright, half carried half dragged him upstairs, filled the bath with cold water and threw John in fully clothed. He then proceeded to punch John everywhere, he really lost it! He lifted John out of the bath and punched him. John was only 16 whereas Dad had been a professional boxer who prided himself of being fitter than most and he never held back when he was punching any of us. Well he battered John so much that he wore himself out!

He then dragged John into his bedroom, threw him on the floor and left him there. Next morning he told John if he ever saw him in that state again, he would kill him. I think if John hadn't been so strong, young and fit, he probably would have killed him that night! He looked dreadful, but instead of being angry with Dad John was ashamed of himself. He said he would never drink to excess again and he thought Dad had beaten him to stop him becoming dependent on drink. Maybe he was right but I think Dad just lost it. When he saw what he had done to John the next morning, I think he was shocked and ashamed of himself. John had broken ribs, bruises everywhere, black eyes, split lip and difficulty breathing deeply. It took ages for him to recover.

Dad justified doing it because the Bible says spare the rod, spoil the child. Well, there was no chance of any of us being spoilt ever! And he said it was for his own good! Maggy said she used to hate the sound that Dad punching the boys made. The thud of fist on flesh made her feel quite sick and scared for them. I don't think John ever got drunk again. Not because he got beaten, but because he was ashamed of himself.

When Rachel was leaving to start her training, I was desperately sad. Mrs Parkes was keen for me to do something with my life, not just bumble through doing menial jobs. I had fallen in love with Ted Hanley but he was engaged to someone else and had no love for me at all. I felt I needed to get away from Sussex and have a fresh start, so I wrote to my Gran and Grandad in Durham and asked if I could stay with them for a while.

Smelly When Wet

GRAN, BLESS HER, WROTE AND SAID I COULD STAY AS LONG AS I LIKED so at the end of the summer term, I left Walstead and headed for Willington, County Durham.

I arrived nursing a broken heart but knowing this was a new beginning for me. Willington was a small mining village with a high street consisting of maybe 16 shops, five pubs and a bingo hall. The heart had been taken out of the village with the closure of the pit. Men would sit in what was known as 'The old men's shed' which was like a huge bus shelter in the centre of the high street because they were used to going out to work. Now there was no work they congregated in this shed and talked and smoked the day away rather than be at home all day.

It was a sad sight because these were men who wanted to work and believed that it was a man's place to provide for his family. They had worked in the pit since leaving school and here they were in their 50s and the chance of getting any other work was slim, if not impossible. The only other main source of work for men was the brickworks but since the pits closure they had taken on all the young men so these middle-aged men were, in effect, on the scrap heap and they knew it. My great uncle was one of these men and he never got used to not earning his living.

Off the high street were rows of back-to-back houses. At the top of the high street was a council estate, in the middle was another and at the very bottom of the village was yet another. Willington was once a thriving little place where there was plenty of work and plenty of housing.

My grandparents had bought a little cottage in Sunny Brow, a suburb of Willington; a one-up one-down terrace house with an outside toilet. It was a lovely, homely little place but because it had no bathroom they were put to the top of the council housing list and were allocated a three-bedroomed house in the estate at the top of the high street. It was lovely. In fact it had two toilets! How flash was that! So my arrival was timely. It needed decorating and with all my training from Dad I was the one for the job. It was great fun. Granddad and I had such an easy relationship. He was such a gentle man; he never shouted or got cross with me and I loved him. So this time decorating brought us close together again. We splashed paint and paste on each other while Gran told us off and made endless cups of tea for her workers.

When we wallpapered the hall and landing I nearly killed us both. I was balancing with one foot on the banister at the top of the stairs and the other on the windowsill opposite, straddling the stairs with a length of pasted wallpaper in my hands. I slipped and fell. Granddad was standing halfway up the stairs ready to hand me the scissors when I came crashing down on top of him. He broke my fall; we both rolled to the bottom of the stairs, the length of wallpaper wrapped around us both and paste everywhere. How I didn't break his neck or how he didn't stab me with the scissors, I don't know, but we were both laughing hysterically once we realised neither of us were injured. Gran made us laugh even more when she came in to see what had happened by saying, "Well you two daft buggers, we'll have to buy another roll of wallpaper now."

At the weekend Gran and Grandad would get all dolled up and go up to the pub for a few drinks so I got dolled up too and went with them. We went to The Market in the middle of the high street, a very friendly pub though it did have a 'men only' bar which I thought was outdated. No one seemed to think it strange and the men wanted to keep this private domain. I found that out when I walked in there by mistake. Boy, did I get some filthy looks! I was told in no uncertain manner that I had to leave!

There were two other rooms aside from the men's bar; one where the middle-aged to elderly drank and the other where the younger crowd gathered. Being with Gran and Grandad I sat with them. The barmaid introduced herself to me as Pat. She was the landlord's daughter. She was tiny, really tiny, but what she lacked in height she made up for in personality. She was fun. She took me into the back room and introduced me to the younger group, about eight people my age and among them was a tall blond boy named Ronnie. He was very sweet and bought me a drink. I had a great evening. I met some lovely people and thought living in Willington was going to be all right. Gran, Grandad and I walked home.

Granddad was a little tipsy and started telling me how, as a young man, he had stood on the corner of the street preaching the gospel in his Salvation Army uniform and how happy he was then. But he went on to tell me that at that time in his life he was also a socialist and his captain had told him he couldn't be both.

It was a choice he had to make, either a Christian or a socialist. He couldn't understand why he had to choose but chose socialism and, bless him, he had never felt right about that choice since. We had some wonderful conversations about his life and the choices he made when he was tipsy. I found out so much more about him on our walks home from the pub than I ever knew before. It was great. Gran would just tell him to "Shut your rattle, you're drunk." He would look at her, smile, tell her he loved her, she would shove him and call him a daft bugger, but you could tell she loved it and she loved him.

We settled into Luxmore Avenue and although I loved being with my Gran and Grandad I missed my family. I felt sort of disjointed. I would go over to the phone box and ring home only for Dad to answer. His first question when he realised it was me on the other end was, "Are you going to church?" When I said no he would sigh and hand the phone to Mam. Even three hundred miles away and I am still making him sigh with disappointment.

I would chat to Mam and she would ask what I was doing, if I was working and so on, then she would put John, Kenny or Kayla and we would natter on, feeding coins into the phone. It was like feeding a donkey strawberries. It just gobbled them up, but it would make me feel part of them again. When I walked back over to Gran's a wave of sadness would often wash over me and I would cry. I missed them so much but once in with Gran and Grandad I would tell them all the news from home. If I was upset Gran would say, "I don't know why you bother with him (meaning Dad). He's a religious nutter and you are best well shot of him." She really didn't like him!

John told me he was working as he had been expelled from school. That was such a shame because he really was a very bright boy, but just messed about at school, something he came to regret much later in life. He went to work at Hiltons, bricklaying. He could turn his hand to anything actually, a very practical boy! While he was working there he met up with a girl he had gone to school with, in fact she had been head girl, Sharon Sands, and she asked him out! He said yes, but actually thought it was a wind-up so he asked his mate Mick Lawrence to go with him. Once John realised it wasn't a wind-up, he spent all evening trying to get rid of Mick! He fell headlong in love with Sharon and loved her until the day he died, bless him. She really was the love of his life.

Gran's sister Beatrice lived in Blackpool with her husband. They had run a bed and breakfast place for many years before retiring. Her husband was a heavy drinker and poor Beatie had a hard life. She wrote to Gran saying she would like to visit so it was arranged that she would come on the coach and stay for a couple of weeks. Beatie was to arrive on the Monday afternoon. Gran had cleaned the house from top to bottom. It was immaculate. Gran was so house proud, something I had to adjust to as Mam was the complete opposite! It struck me that even though the house had three bedrooms, there were only two beds, Gran and Grandad's and mine. The third bedroom was used as a sort of store room. It was small enough for a single bed but it didn't have one.

We were eating dinner when I asked Gran where Auntie Beatie would be sleeping and nearly choked on my pork chop when she answered, "With thee, lass."

"NO she's not," I spluttered! But as Gran pointed out, there was nowhere else for her to sleep. I hadn't actually seen Auntie Beaty since I was three years old and so felt very awkward at having to share my bed with a stranger. She was a very sweet lady and I liked her, very like Gran except Gran had blond hair and Beatie was very dark. She had a very broad Yorkshire accent just like Gran too and it was lovely to hear them chatter. I swear they got broader as the week went by.

Well, bedtime inevitably arrived and I went up first to get into my nighty and claimed my side of the bed. Beatie followed me up and I felt very uncomfortable as she undressed right next to me. She was in her seventies and was extremely thin but I hadn't realised how thin until she undressed. Bless her, she was tiny, she also had VERY dry skin and as she slipped into her nighty, then into bed, I scooted over so I was on the very edge. She was asleep in no time. I spent the entire night trying to avoid contact with her as she snored, wriggled, tossed and turned.

At one point she threw her arm right over my face and I lay there willing her to move it. In the end I wriggled down underneath it. It was an exhausting night and to top it all, she suffered terribly with wind! Well, I was the one suffering, she was oblivious to it. I was so pleased when the morning arrived and I could get up.

Grandad was downstairs and asked if I slept well. I told him about Beatie's night-time antics and how I hadn't slept a wink and he laughed. "It's not funny Grandad," I said, "I'm not sleeping with her anymore and that's that!" When Gran got up, I told her too and said I would sleep on the sofa as from tonight and Beatie could toss and turn to her heart's content, but not with me as a bed buddy!

Beatie came down to breakfast and I went up to the bedroom to get my clothes. Beatie had thrown the bedclothes right back and I was shocked to see that the bed was full of dry skin! That did it; I was definitely not sleeping in there ever again. I told Gran that Beatie should be known as Flaky Beatie from now on. Bless her, she was too, but not to her face. When she went home and the sheets were changed and the room hoovered, I asked Gran if we should post the hoover bag on to Beatie because there was more of her in the bag than actually went home on the bus. Needless to say Gran clouted me and called me a cheeky bugger, but she laughed too.

I was going regularly up to the Market pub and got to know quite a few regulars. I had noticed a boy called Ronnie and had been introduced to him by Pat, the landlord's daughter. Ronnie asked me out on a date. I was so excited. He was gorgeous; a printer by trade but a footballer for fun. He played in the pub team and he asked me if I would like to watch him play. I hated football but I liked him so I said I would go.

It was a freezing cold Sunday morning and I was up early deciding what to wear. I had bought lots of new clothes with my last wages ready for my new life. I had two or three pairs of south sea bubble loons in various colours with polo neck jumpers to match which I loved. I had also bought a maxi coat and an Afghan collar which was fine as long as it didn't get wet, when it would stink to high heaven, a couple of long skirts and several pairs of platform shoes. I felt very modern and with it, particularly in Willington where it took a while before London fashion reached. The people in the pub would call me 'the lass from down London' and they thought I was really hip-hop and happening! I had only been to London a handful of times and we lived nowhere near London but as far as they were concerned that's where I was from.

I met Ronnie and stood on the side-lines and watched him play. Other girls were there watching their boyfriends playing too, along with some friends, parents and one or two fans. It was freezing cold and it started to rain. I hadn't thought to bring a brolly and anyway it was very un-cool to hold one, so I stood in my Afghan coat getting slowly soaked and this game seemed to go on forever.

The game was over and they won! All back to the pub for celebratory drinks. Ronnie was man of the match having scored! We were sat in the pub, all the blokes dissecting the game saying what should have been done, who should have been sent off and what a pillock the ref was, when Ronnie gave me a sidelong look. I said, "What is it?"

"Nothing," he said. We sat and chatted more. It was getting very warm in this little room when Ronnie looked at me strangely again.

"What is it?" I said.

He looked very embarrassed and said, "What's that smell?" It was at that moment that I realised that my Afghan coat reverted back to its former life as a stinky camel, or whatever revolting creature the fur was taken from, as soon as it got wet! I was mortified with embarrassment and made a mental note never to wear it if it looked in the slightest bit damp outside. We laughed but it struck me that he had initially thought I was making that revolting smell and there was I thinking it was a combination of wet footballers and smelly feet when all the time it was my trendy coat.

Meeting Greg

RONNIE INTRODUCED ME TO HIS MATE GREG who looked like a cross between a tramp and a Mexican bandit. He was really scruffy, about six feet tall with shoulder length black wavy hair and a droopy moustache, but he was really funny and I liked him. He was on the dole too so Ronnie asked him to show me around during the day if I was bored. Greg, being a friendly bloke, called for me the following afternoon and asked me if I would like to play a game of crazy golf. I had never played it before but thought it would be fun so we went round to the Miners Welfare Club which was the hall where we signed on the dole.

In the grounds was a children's playground and the crazy golf area. We collected our clubs and balls and started playing this stupid game. Greg took it so seriously but was making jokes the whole time. I hit my ball under a hedge and Greg scrambled under it to retrieve my ball. As he came out from under it he ripped his jacket. I felt awful but he made light of it. I kept looking at his jacket. It was obviously very old and it was very shiny. Under the jacket he was wearing a bright yellow jumper. Well I say jumper, apparently it was a cardigan in the summer and a jumper in the winter. How, you might ask. Well he just cut it down the front in the summer and sewed it back up for the winter! Easy peasy. Hence the cross between a tramp and a Mexican description. Also Ronnie, who was six foot six, had given Greg his old coat. That was very kind of him but on Ronnie the coat came down to his calves while with Greg, being six inches shorter, it actually touched the ground. When he fastened it up you couldn't see his feet. But what he lacked in dress sense he more than made up for in personality and humour and hey, who am I to start being picky about what people wear. I have worn some dreadful stuff in my time but the difference being, he chose this himself!

We would all meet up in The Market in the evenings and then Greg and I would meet up during the day. The thing was, I was enjoying the days more than the evenings and began to realise I was actually falling for Greg. We laughed so easily together, we had fun and took the mickey out of each other. I didn't have to try with him. He seemed to like me too and I loved the way he didn't care what he looked like. We could talk about anything and everything and did lots of that, much more so than I did with Ronnie. So in the end I told Ronnie that I liked him, he was a lovely bloke, but I fancied Greg and hoped he wouldn't be too hurt. He wasn't, in fact, he fancied another girl called Lynne whom he went on to marry, so all was well there.

I knew Greg would never ask me out because with all his mouth and bravado he was in fact very shy around girls. As a mate he was great but as a boyfriend, that was a whole new ballgame, so with my heart in my mouth I asked him out. He looked stunned and I told him I had finished with Ronnie because I liked him and hoped he liked me. He looked awkward and told me he did in fact like me and would love to go out on a date. We would meet at the Black Horse at 8.00 that night for a drink and a chat. I was thrilled. I went home and told Gran I was going on my first date with Greg. She looked at me like I was mad. "That scruffy bugger with the tash?" she said.

"Yes Gran, he's really nice, you would like him. You WILL like him; he is really sweet and very funny. Well, I like him and that's all that matters," I said.

She was rolling out some pastry as I was telling her and as I finished, she took a handful of flour and chucked it on the pastry, banged down the rolling pin and said very quietly, "We'll see, lass, we'll see."

I went up to my room. I only had four hours to decide what to wear! I walked down to the Black Horse having tried on every article of clothing I possessed. Quite why I was making all this effort for a man who wears a yellow cardie/jumper I don't know but I wanted him to see I had made an effort for him because he was important to me. I arrived ten minutes early. He wasn't there. I bought a drink and sat myself around a corner so he wouldn't see me straight away when he entered the pub. Eight o'clock on the dot and I heard the door open. I was nervous. I smelt him before I saw him. This waft of Brut hit me and then there he was, like I had never seen him before!

What a vision, he was positively shining! His hair was brushed back and had so much Brylcreem on it that it looked wet. He looked like he had scrubbed his face with a scrubbing brush and he must have poured a whole bottle of Brut over himself. He was wearing a suit with a white shirt and a tie. Admittedly, the suit was his brother's, and he was at least three stone heavier than him and much broader, so he looked like a bag of coal tied in the middle. The jacket positively hung off him but, bless him, he had gone to so much trouble for me and I was very touched. He wanted to make a good impression on me too. I would definitely NEVER forget this moment.

We had a lovely evening, just talking and drinking, though he did seem a little nervous and at one point my hand was by my side as we sat side by side. He went to hold my hand just as I reached for my drink and there was this awkward clash of hands. We both went a lovely scarlet colour, but the evening went well. Greg walked me home and I half expected him to hold my hand. He didn't, in the end I reached out for his hand. He seemed really relieved that I did and was very comfortable with me doing it. We talked all the way to my Gran's where I was expecting him to kiss me goodnight. What I actually got was my hand shaken and a "Thank you for a lovely evening."

I was gobsmacked. That had never happened to me before but I said, "Thank you. I had a lovely evening too," and he went. I watched him walk up the path.

He turned and said, "Shall I see you tomorrow?"

"Yes," I said.

"Pick you up from here at eight?"

"Fine," I shouted back and in I went. Gran and Grandad were in bed, no one to talk to. I made a Horlicks and went up to bed. I sat in bed for ages, going over the whole evening in my head. How sweet he looked, he had made such a huge effort, no yellow jumper/cardie. But I hoped he didn't do it again tomorrow and easy on the Brut, it had given me a headache.

Grandad and I had finished all the decorating. I needed to get a job. I had signed on the dole and had to go to collect my benefits and see if there was anything job-wise I was capable of doing. The only thing going was a job as a machinist in a dress factory in Crook so I went for an interview. "Have you any experience in this line of work?"

"No," was my reply.

"Start on Monday." That was it, I had got the job! Full training would be given they said and so my foray into the fashion world was about to start.

A bus picked us up in Willington ready for an 8.00 start. We had to clock on. I was taken into the factory which was huge with row upon row of sewing machines all doing different tasks. The noise when everyone was at their machines was incredible. At the far end of the factory were about ten training machines where I was assigned one. The only sewing I had done before this was at school and I was kicked out of the sewing class, so this was going to be a challenge!

There were other girls on these machines at various stages of training. I was given a piece of material and told just how to use the machine. How to thread it, change the bobbin and then place my material under the foot, then press the pedal. My foot was supposed to gently depress but whoosh! She was not impressed. After many pieces of material I finally got the hang of it and progressed from bits of material to pieces of clothing. Learning to do darts, seams, put on cuffs, collars, sleeves, put in linings and do hems. It seems that after just six weeks I was ready for the assembly line! Now I could earn real money.

The way it worked was that rows of machinists sat either side of a conveyor belt and boxes containing dresses, all in pieces, were put onto each conveyor belt. The first person the box arrived at took the box off the belt. In each box was a piece of card with stickers on, each sticker denoting how many articles were in the box and itemised each part of the dress. I was sewing cuffs onto sleeves so I would take the cuffs sticker and stick it on my worksheet denoting at the end of the day just how many cuffs I had sewn on. If the required number in an hour was twenty, the aim would be to do twenty-five to earn a bonus. Some of the girls were brilliant and could earn masses of bonus. I wasn't that quick but would just manage to reach the hourly target which I was quite pleased about because six weeks ago I couldn't use a sewing machine to save my life and here I was earning my living sewing. To be truthful I didn't enjoy it. I didn't like the noise and being indoors all day. Also, if you needed the loo you had to stick your hand up and ask the supervisor if you could go. If she thought you just wanted a cigarette, which lots of the girls did, she wouldn't let you go. This was fine if you did just want a fag but if you really needed the loo it was very unpleasant.

The girls were very nice, all except one supervisor who took an instant dislike to me because she thought I was posh! Me posh, don't make me laugh! But it was because I came from 'down south' and didn't have a Geordie accent, so just as I had begun to make a little bonus on cuffs she moved me onto hems. That sounds easy but in fact I was using a hemming machine attachment and was sewing the lining hem on these very full skirts which was very difficult. I had all sorts of trouble with them. The idea was that when you finished your part of the dress you put your completed box back onto the conveyor belt. It went onto the next person to do their part and so on until it was a box of completed dresses.

Then the supervisor would go through the dresses checking every detail. If she found an error she would take it back to the person who had made the error and they would have to spend ages unpicking the mistake and re-doing them which was a real pain, because while you were doing that you weren't able to make any bonus. This bloomin' supervisor really had it in for me. She would pick on the slightest little thing and bring it back to me, insisting I unpick it and do it all over again. She really didn't like me and made no attempt to hide the fact. She would call me a snotty cow and I felt like I was back at school and being called names, but this time it was because she thought I was 'upper class'! That in itself made me want to laugh. If only she knew! But boy, could she make working unpleasant. I never made any bonus; she would make me practically beg to go to the loo. I had just about had enough of her stupid ways and I really didn't enjoy my work. It was just a means to an end and the end was pretty meagre.

I had been going to the dole office to see if there were any other jobs I could try and BINGO there was a job for a housemother in an approved school in a neighbouring town, so I went for an interview. It was in a castle, an actual castle, and to my amazement I got the job. I bounded into the factory the following morning, sat at my machine and began sewing those rotten hems. I just whizzed round the hems, not caring where I sewed, making a mess of them all, box after box until finally she came clutching what she didn't realise was the first of many boxes.

"What the hell do you call this?" she said. "You get this lot unpicked and sharpish." She slammed the box down next to my machine. I said nothing and she walked off back down the line with a smug look on her face. I, on the other hand, ignored the box and carried on sewing hem after hem as badly as I could. It wasn't long before she was back with another of the boxes. "I don't know what your game is, madam," she said, "but you had better get your act together and get this lot sorted NOW."

I just stopped sewing, stood up, took an armful of the badly sewn dresses from the box she had in her hands and threw them up in the air. "You, madam, can get stuffed, and YOU can unpick that little lot because I've had enough of you. You can stick your job as far up your arse as you can get it 'cos I'm off!" And with that I walked out of the factory. As I passed her, I said, "And by the way, there are a few more boxes for you to be working on." Her face was a picture and the girls on my line cheered and applauded me as I walked out. I felt euphoric.

As far as I was concerned, that was the first and the last time I would ever work in a factory. I had hated it, though I did learn to use a sewing machine. While working there, it had been my birthday and my Gran and Grandad had bought me, of all things, a sewing machine. In fact I used it to practise in the evenings making clothes for Kayla. One of the perks—what am I saying!—the ONLY perk of working at the factory was that you could buy remnants of material at really reduced prices. I would buy up loads and make Kayla little skirts, trousers and dresses which weren't too bad but my blouses left much to be desired! Poor little soul, they had really stiff collars. I hadn't quite perfected my collar attaching skills! But I just wanted her to be better dressed than I had been at her age. Mum was still getting her clothes from jumble sales and the ability to pick anything remotely nice seemed to have completely eluded her so I thought my homemade efforts were better than anything mum would be providing.

As I said, I would ring home regularly and I loved catching up with all the family news, some of it sad. Phil had been arrested and was sent down for five years, so poor Mags had moved in with Mam and Dad. I felt sorry for her because I knew exactly how Mam would exploit her. Mam was now fostering African children. Yes! I couldn't believe it. Intelligent people were trusting her with their babies! These people were training to be doctors and nurses in London hospitals. They had been to the house and *still* they left their precious babies with her! Actually she did love one of them, and in fact poor Kayla was very jealous of the attention Mam gave the little ones. Too sad that she had no time for her own kids; that's because she got *paid* for fostering these little ones.

Phil was in Albany Prison on the Isle of Wight and Mags would visit him every month. When you think she was only 17, bless her heart, and not married very long, and apparently Mam and Dad would tell her *not* to visit, to let him do his time. I rather think it was because she would leave early on the Saturday morning and not get home till late, so Mam would have to look after the kids all day by herself. Poor Mags had no support, bless her, but she loved Phil and faithfully visited him monthly for years. He had no idea how difficult it was for her.

The Castle School

I STARTED WORK AT THE CASTLE. It was a sad place for kids from broken homes who had got into trouble many times and eventually ended up in court only to be sent to approved school. It was a harsh regime but the kids were used to harsh, lots of them practically raised themselves, living off the streets and their wits. I could identify with lots of them. The school was divided into four houses, each with a housemaster and a housemother and we had around twenty-five boys in each house. Our job was to take over the care of the boys when the school day had finished. We would take them for hikes over the fells. We were supposed to walk, well hike, for at least five miles per night.

Stanhope is in the middle of some of the most spectacular countryside I had ever seen, rugged and harsh in winter, soft and beautiful in summer. The rolling hills were full of nature's secrets and we would be thrilled together as we discovered them one by one. We would walk by the river and watch the sea trout returning to spawn and be amazed as they leapt the waterfalls. The boys would try to catch them. Not allowed really, but they never caught any. We made a rope swing, also not allowed, but we did it anyway. I would let the boys play on the swing and swim in the river. They didn't have much fun in this dreadful place so when I took them out I would let them have a little freedom. I looked at them and I could see my brothers and they responded well to kindness, once they realised it wasn't weakness!

We would also play games. Pool, snooker, billiards and board games in the evening and then supervise their bed-time routine. Then in the morning their waking routine and be present at mealtimes, which were an ordeal as they had to be in complete silence. I used to feel sorry for them when they had a particular meal they didn't like; there was absolutely no choice and whatever was put before them they *had* to eat. One dish in particular was dreaded by lots of the boys. It was apple and liver casserole. It looked and smelt as revolting as it sounds. I love apples and I quite like liver, but together? No, thank you very much. But those poor boys had to eat it. I will never forget one dinner time one of the boys was sick onto his plate as he tried to eat this hateful concoction and the teacher on duty took great delight in making him eat everything on his plate, vomit included! What a bully. From that day on I would put a plastic bag in my overall pocket and stand with my back to the boy who was almost throwing up as he tried to eat and, keeping my eye on the teacher in charge, I would indicate to the boy to put in into my pocket, which they would do without being spotted by the teacher. I would do this several times a week for various boys and by doing this I had lots of very grateful and well-behaved house members!

One of the other housemothers was a girl called Athena and she was great fun. As I got to know her over the first few months of working at the castle I realised I had found a really good friend. She was half Greek and stunning looking. She had a son called Jason who was five or six whom she adored. She had a brilliant sense of humour which was essential in the work we were doing. We would laugh at the stupidity of the rules at the castle. It made it easier to cope with. She had a heart as big as a bucket and was as generous as the day is long. After work we would often go out together and boy, did we have fun. At that time she didn't have a boyfriend but I did, so I would meet Greg, go to the pub with him and he would walk me home.

Then I would get dolled up and Athena would pick me up at 11.00 and we would drive to Sunderland or Spennymoor to a nightclub and dance the night away. I wasn't interested in other blokes but it was just fun to be doing the nightclub thing and Greg wasn't into nightclubbing, or so he said! After the club closed we would get back to my house at 4.00, sleep for two hours and be up for work at 6.00. Poor Greg had no idea until one night he had walked me home, I ran upstairs, got into my glad rags, Athena arrived and off we went to the Top Hat club at Spennymoor.

I was dancing with some bloke when over his shoulder I saw what I thought was a bloke who looked just like Greg. After closer inspection I realised it was Greg! *The sneaky little swine*, I thought. *Fancy him going to a nightclub and not telling me, or asking me to go with him. What's he up to?* Athena and I spent the rest of the evening spying on him, without him seeing us. Not easy. In fact he was just with a bunch of his mates having a lads' night out. *The cheek of it*, I thought. It never occurred to me that I was a sneaky swine too!

The following evening when Greg met me from the bus after work we went into The Market for a drink. I asked him if he saw anyone after he left me at

Gran's last night. "No," he said. I was trying to see if he would tell me he had been to the Top Hat—not that I was going to tell him *I* had. Such a bloomin' hypocrite! I tried all ways to get him to tell me but he didn't. This was frustrating. I couldn't ask him outright because it would mean admitting that I had been there too.

When we walked down to Gran's house we stood on the doorstep and he kissed me goodnight. I opened the door and as he was walking back up the path he turned and said, "So did you and Athena enjoy yourselves last night at the Top Hat?"

I was shocked. "What did you say?" I whispered.

He kept walking and said, "You heard me, see you tomorrow," and he was gone. I couldn't sleep. How did he know we were there? He didn't see me, I was sure of that. In fact, he had seen me before I had seen him and took great delight in watching me trying to stay out of sight. I promised him after that that I wouldn't go to nightclubs without him or without telling him. I did, but was a bit sneakier about it! He, on the other hand, never went without me. I don't think!

Our relationship developed slowly and very gently. Greg wasn't and isn't a pushy man and I loved that about him. He was the total opposite of my Dad. I never felt afraid of Greg; he loved me and what I wanted was just as important to him as what *he* wanted. This was all so new to me. I can remember feeling dizzy when he kissed me and just longing for him to hold me. I would get butterflies in my tummy just thinking about him. I hadn't felt like this before. I wanted to be with him and we spent hours snogging till our lips hurt. When he would walk me home after an evening at The Market we would stop in a shop doorway. He had his long coat on and he would open it up and wrap me inside it and kiss me. He was everything I wanted, it was wonderful. I felt I wanted to stay there for ever, safe in the arms of the man I loved and who loved me back. I had never understood how people would *want* a sexual relationship before, but now, with Greg, I did! I realised it really was a part of love and I loved him.

Since Dad had become a Christian we had been taught that sex should be kept within marriage. It had been drummed into us all that it was wrong, wrong, wrong to have sex outside of that and I had been very happy with that because of my messed-up view on sex altogether. But now I felt differently because I was in love.

Our relationship did become sexual. I still had lots of 'hang-ups' regarding sex but I now understood it really was part of a loving relationship and not something you were forced to do against your will and made to feel used and dirty. I remember one time we were at Greg's mum's house for Sunday tea and Greg's brother Alan, his wife Susan and their little boy Darren had come too. We all sat chatting after tea, then Greg's mum went out and Alan and family went home. We were left on our own in the front room. The fire was roaring, the curtains closed and we were snuggled up on the settee.

Well, one thing led to another and we were laid on the floor, clothes everywhere, when we heard the key in the door! Greg jumped up, ran to the door and held it closed, at the same time putting on his clothes. His mum was pushing on the door, shouting that the door wouldn't open. I was in the front room having pulled on my dress, stuffed my underwear under the cushion, gathered myself together, straightened my hair and sat watching TV, my heart thumping, not with passion but with panic, trying to look as if nothing had been going on.

Finally, Greg let go of the door. His mum was in a spin about something she had forgotten and was now worried that the front door was sticking. She dashed into the room, took one look at me and got whatever she had returned for. As she left the room, she shouted, "I didn't notice earlier, Fay, but do you realise your dress is inside out?" I was mortified. She knew what was going on and I was so embarrassed. I thought I would never be able to look her in the eye ever again.

We decided that we wouldn't do that again. Too risky! So we would go up to the pub on a Sunday evening with Gran and Grandad. They would sit in the front room in The Market where people their age would drink. As soon as they were settled in there and we had bought them a drink, we would tell them we were going into the back room to be with the younger group. In fact, we would leave the pub, run home and go up to my room and afterwards run back to the pub and join Gran and Grandad for last orders. Very sneaky!

Greg was still on the dole and was quite resigned to the fact that he wasn't working and probably wouldn't get a job. I think he quite enjoyed staying in bed till lunchtime and when we went out anywhere I was the one who paid. Not that I minded. I loved him, but I was thinking long term. If we were to get married we both needed to be working to afford a house. A friend of Greg's said he was going over to a firm in Spennymoor called Smart and Browns, they were interviewing for several jobs. Greg's wardrobe was, well, non-existent, apart from the cardie/jumper and the trench coat, he had nothing else, bless him, so we went into Bishop Auckland and I bought him trousers, jacket, shirts, shoes and other bits and pieces and talked him into going for an interview.

Monday came and the interviews were at 11.00. Greg was up and ready in his new clobber. He looked the business! He was very nervous, having been unemployed for over a year. It was quite daunting. I told him he was brilliant and could do any job they were offering. So he and his mate caught the bus and off they went. I so wanted him to get a job and was thrilled to pieces when he arrived home with a grin like a Cheshire cat. I knew as soon as I looked at him, I knew he had got it. We went out to celebrate. He was working in the office and he loved it. His mate wasn't too pleased. He said if he hadn't mentioned the job interviews to Greg he would have got the job.

We were very much in love and in lust. We had never actually spent the night together till Greg's brother Peter said we could stay with him. It was New Year's Eve and the custom in Durham is for a tall dark person to be the first person to step over your threshold to bring you luck in the coming year. So with Greg being tall, dark and handsome, he was asked by several people to be their 'first foot'. As a first foot you would be given money and a drink, generally a spirit, so you can imagine after a few houses you were very merry. Well, Greg most certainly was! I was waiting for him at Peter's house. It was past two am and I was getting a little anxious so I decided to go look for him. I knew roughly where he had gone so I put on my coat.

It was freezing cold and snow was on the ground. I walked around the estate to where I thought he would be. No sign. I was walking back to Peter's house when I saw something under a hedge. At first I thought it was a dead dog but as I got closer I realised it was Greg! He was lying fast asleep under this hedge and he had frost on him! I couldn't believe it. I shook him, woke him and got him to his feet. He was so drunk. I had never seen him like this before and I was worried. The only drunk I had seen was my Dad and he was violent when he was drunk. I needn't have worried. Even drunk Greg was lovely, though the following morning he vowed he would never do that again, and he never has.

Conversion

MY BROTHER JOHN RANG to say he was coming to see me. He was only staying for the Friday night and going back on the Saturday night coach. He was all excited because he had something to tell me. I was very touched. Whatever it was he wanted to tell me face to face. I was intrigued.

He arrived at Durham bus station late Friday night. I was so pleased to see him, he looked so handsome and grown up. I hugged him and we were all chatter. We caught the bus to Willington. I was full of questions about home. How was everyone, Kenny, Phil, Kayla, Mam, Dad? He told me lots about everyone as we rode the bus back to Gran's. I made a sandwich and a cuppa and as we sat in the kitchen I asked him what this big thing was that he couldn't tell me about over the phone.

"Well Fay, I've been saved. Jesus is real." I was gobsmacked. He'd come all this way to tell me that. I certainly wasn't expecting that. "What do you want to do that for?"

"It's nothing I did Fay," he said. "I realised what Dad has been saying is true. Jesus is the Son of God, he does love us and he did die for us. For you Fay. It's true!" I didn't know what to say. In fact I was quite embarrassed but very touched that he had travelled all this way to tell me his big news. I said I was pleased for him but it wasn't for me just yet. That I would live my life to the full till I was 70. *Then* maybe, I would think about Christianity because as far as I could see the Christian life was restricting, boring and for old people, so until then I would sit on the fence. He said, "Well darling, that's OK but what if you die before then, and Fay, there is no fence, the Bible says you are either saved or you are damned." Then he said, "I want to pray for you Fay." I felt quite uncomfortable but closed my eyes while he prayed and his prayer was for me to find Jesus, his forgiveness and to know his peace and his love. I was very touched. After he prayed he said he loved me and wanted me to go to heaven when I did die and not to hell where I was bound if I didn't accept Jesus. He then asked me to promise him I would go to church at least once after he left. I said I would, just because I loved him and wanted to please him.

The following day he caught the coach back to London and was gone. I mulled over what he had said for a few days and told Greg what I had promised to do. He was not impressed. "You don't have to go to church, he won't know," he said.

"But I will and it was so important to him. I think I will go on Sunday. Will you come with me?"

"Not on your Nelly. I didn't promise anybody. If you want to go you go but don't think you're dragging me along with you!" I didn't say any more about it until the Saturday evening. We had been invited to a party that I didn't want to go to. Greg was getting stroppy and saying I should go, so I said I would go to the party if he would go to church with me on Sunday morning. He agreed, so we went to the party. It was awful but I stayed because it was a deal.

Sunday morning and we were up and ready for church, though I had no idea where the church was. Greg said there was an Anglican church down at the bottom of the village so we walked from the top of the high street and about a third of the way down was a shop with curtains in the window and a cross on the door. It was being used as a Methodist church and just because we were too lazy to walk all the way to the Anglican church and I had promised John I would go to church, this was a church and this would do! We went inside. It was very small with seats either side of the door in rows, maybe four rows of six at either side, a pulpit on the right at the front and an organ on the left. I think there was a banner on the wall facing the door. I can't remember what it said but it all worked together to make this little shop look and feel like a church. There were about ten old ladies, mostly in black with hats, and to be quite honest they looked like they were stuffed, kept in a cupboard and brought out every Sunday to make the church look full! Very rude I know but that's what I thought.

I know nothing about the Methodist Church but the preacher was a visiting preacher; apparently he preached in several churches on a circuit. So the organist started to play, we sang a hymn, then the preacher got up and his theme was 'The fence when it comes to Christianity' but that in fact there is no fence; you are either saved or you are damned! I nearly had apoplexy. This is what John had said to me and now some stranger, who doesn't know me, didn't know I was coming, is saying exactly the same thing. I would have to be really stupid not to realise God was speaking to me. Greg was fed up and kept huffing and puffing, shuffling in his seat. He kept whispering, "How much longer?" I just ignored him. I was transfixed; if this was God speaking to me I didn't want to miss a word. The preacher finished, the collection plate came round and I just emptied my purse onto it. I wanted God to know I was listening and he could have all that I had.

Greg, on the other hand, was shocked. "What are you doing?" he whispered and glared at me. "That's our beer money!"

I said, "I think God is speaking to me."

He gave me a look that said 'You've really lost it now' and said, "I'm off to the pub" and with that he left. I, on the other hand, was in a state. I wanted someone to help me, to pray with me, or to explain how I put this all into perspective. Was this God speaking or was it just coincidence that the preacher's theme was exactly what John had said to me? I looked for the preacher but he had left and the stuffed old ladies had been put back into the cupboard, or gone home. That left the organist, so I went up to him and said, "I think God is speaking to me and I don't know what to do."

He looked at me and blushed and said, "Where do you come from with that accent? You're not from around here."

"No I'm not but I need someone to pray with me." He just smiled and collected his music books together. I felt embarrassed, smiled at him and walked out of the church. Perhaps he wasn't a Christian and didn't know what to say to me. I was even more perplexed now.

I walked home and thought to myself, *If no one will pray with me then maybe I should just pray myself,* so I went up to my room and got out the Bible which Dad had given to me when I was baptised when I was fifteen and which I had kept. I didn't know what to read as this book was a mystery to me but I remembered one of the stories Dad had read and opened up to us one evening when everyone else was watching telly. We were not watching telly but were treated to Bible stories acted out by Dad himself. I looked up Job in the index, found it and read it. I thought Job was a brilliant bloke; he was tested beyond belief yet his faith in God never wavered. I thought that if I was going to be a Christian, I would want to be like Job.

After my disastrous pretence to be a Christian I wanted to be fully committed to it if it was real, so I sat on my bed and poured my heart out to God. I asked him to forgive me. I had done some terrible things and I told God all about them. I asked him to make me like Job so that I would be a faithful Christian, not a fake like I was before, but be a real one! I finished praying and felt—nothing! No different. I was deeply disappointed and went downstairs feeling dejected.

Greg came back from the pub. He was in a foul mood and kept saying I was mad and God wasn't even real. Why would I think he was talking to me? I got my Bible and tried to tell him about Job. He just snatched the Bible from my hand and threw it across the room saying, "That is a load of cobblers; I don't want to hear any more about this crap." I was stunned. He had never behaved like that before and it upset me. I asked him to go home and leave me alone. I cried when he had gone and wondered if I had got it all wrong—again! I went to my bed and prayed that I hadn't got it wrong.

I woke the next morning feeling very odd. I got out of bed, caught sight of myself in the dressing table mirror and did a double take. My arms and shoulders were covered in boils. I was in shock; my mind went all over the place and finished up at Job. I rushed downstairs and got my Bible, back up to my room, found Job, read through it again and was quite scared. Job lost everything; his wife, children, animals, home and finished up sat on an ash heap scraping his boils. He was covered in boils!

I freaked out. I thought God had answered my prayer to be like Job literally and that my family would die. I dressed quickly, ran across the road to the phone box and rang Mam and Dad. Mam answered and I garbled off the whole story about John, the fence, the church, Job, my prayer and now the boils. She said, "I'll get your Dad."

Dad came on and I repeated it all to him and said I thought they were all going to die. He laughed and said, "Don't be daft, love; I think God is just showing you he has heard your prayer."

I was relieved and said, "What should I do now, Dad?"

"Don't ask me love; ask God, he's the one you should be talking to, not me."

I went back up to my room and prayed. I asked God to show me what to do. I also thanked him for hearing me and for not killing my family. I wanted to make sure he understood that wasn't part of my being like Job.

Greg came round and I showed him my boils and explained what I had prayed and how this was God's way of showing me he had heard me and I needed a sign as I'm thick and God knows that about me. That's what Dad had said. Greg just laughed at me and I felt stupid. He said this was all too freaky. I couldn't cope with him being so unkind to me. I needed him to listen and be understanding and he was being so awful and very hurtful.

I knew that this was definitely a God thing and I had heard my Dad say so many times that whatever God starts he will finish, so I was kind of confident that he would show me what to do. My Gran was very confused by what was happening to me. My Grandad, bless his heart, had been in the Salvation Army as a young man and said, "Just keep praying lass." Very sweet but I needed to *do* something.

I wanted God to be real to me, to know it in my heart, to feel it in my soul, to know that I wasn't kidding myself just wanting it to be real. Gran was sat in her chair by the fire, Greg had just gone home and I was sat staring into space. "Why don't you go and stay with your Mam and Dad for a bit love?" I was taken aback by what she said because every time I had gone to visit Mam and Dad Gran would be very upset and say things like, "What do you want to go down there for. He's a religious nutter, you should stay away from him," meaning Dad. She loved having me live with them and was worried that if I went down south I might stay. Bless her. So here she was saying I should go and stay with Mam and Dad for a while. I thought this must be a God thing too so I said I would do that. The following day I packed a small bag and went to Durham bus station, found the right bus and said to the driver, "One to London please." You were supposed to book in advance but I got it into my mind that if this was a God thing, he would have saved a seat for me.

The driver just looked at me. "I'm full, lass," he said.

"You shouldn't be," I said, but he was. I felt puzzled and deflated. I thought this was God's plan for me and now it seemed it wasn't.

I stepped down off the bus and as I did, the man in the very front seat said, "Did you say this was the London bus?"

The driver said, "I did, sonny."

The bloke stood up, picked up his bag and said, "I'm on the wrong bus then" and off he got.

I was still standing at the bus doorway when the driver shouted to me. "Well, bonny lass, here's your seat" and pointed to the empty seat. I was stunned. God was in this! I got on, gave him my money and sat down feeling strangely elated. The bus pulled out of Durham station. I was on my way.

I took my Bible out of my bag. I had no idea what to read; I just opened it and read. I was hungry for God, I wanted to find him and I knew that the Bible was the place to look but didn't understand quite where to look. I finished up reading the Psalms, one after another. They were beautiful, lots of them were crying out to God asking him to 'lift up my soul'. Then I came to Psalm 51 and it was exactly what I needed to cry out to God. I read it through several times. It was my prayer and I sat with my eyes closed as we rode down the A1 and my heart cried out to God, "Forgive me Lord. Wash me, cleanse me from my sin, make me whiter than snow."

I poured it all out, the thieving, the lying, everything. I don't really know if anything physically happened to me but I felt as if I was lifted up, as if someone put their arms around me and loved me! It was an amazing feeling. I KNEW I was forgiven, I KNEW God loved me. I felt totally accepted; it was wonderful.

All my life I had wanted to be loved. I had been hurt and rejected by so many people. I would be whatever people wanted me to be in order for them to like me and in the hope that they might love me. In the end, even I didn't know who I was! But here I was totally open, absolutely laid bare before God, the real Fay Lancaster, and he not only liked me but he loved me! And in that moment I just felt whole. I cried but I wasn't sad, I was happier than I had ever been before in my life.

The journey was over before I knew it and we were in Victoria bus station. I couldn't wait to get home and tell Mam and Dad what had happened to me. I got my bag and walked to the railway station. My heart was bursting with excitement, I wanted to shout out, "God loves me" but I didn't, I just smiled a lot.

I walked into the house. Mam, Dad, Kayla, John, Kenny and Maggy were all pleased to see me. Hugs all round, then Maggy made a cuppa and Dad was all questions. They didn't know what had happened on the bus but they knew God was dealing with me and wanted an update.

I sat and just poured out exactly what had happened on my journey south. It was great to say it out loud and to see the expressions on their faces. When I got to the part where I was forgiven and felt as if God put his arms around me and loved me, Dad was crying. He put his arms around me, hugged me and cried. It was such an incredible feeling. Both God and my Dad loved me and the most wonderful thing was, it was nothing that I had done. God had done it all. Dad said God's hand was on our family. Then he said we should give thanks to God so we all sat and Dad started to pray, thanking God for all that he had done in all our lives, but particularly in mine. He thanked God for my salvation—mine, my salvation, I am saved! It sort of hit me. I prayed with all of my heart and everything in me. "Thank you so very much for saving me. I did nothing to deserve your love yet you loved me, love me. Help me all my life to love you, to serve you, to live my life for you. I really do want to be like Job; faithful to you, MY GOD."

We talked well into the night and when we eventually went to bed, I couldn't get to sleep, I was going over everything that had happened over the last week. My life changed forever and it was wonderful. I was a bit scared to go to sleep in case I didn't feel the same when I woke up. No worries, I woke up late, came down, the house was quiet. Maggy was making tea, not unusual as we all drank copious amounts of the stuff. If in doubt, make tea! I think it's a northern thing. Anyway, cuppa in hand I sat in the living room. Mam was yelling at Kayla for not doing as she was told, Dad was gardening, it was September and there was lots to do, he was always busy.

For years after he became a Christian, I don't think he ever sat and just relaxed, he was always doing something, or if he was sitting he was reading his Bible, studying or praying. He used to tell us that we should redeem the time; it was a commodity that shouldn't be wasted.

Moving Home

I WAS AT HOME WITH MY FAMILY and for the first time I felt I belonged and it felt like a proper family. Maggy was so sweet, she came and sat with me and asked me what I was going to do. I didn't really know, I hadn't thought about it but I realised I had lots of decisions to make but not just yet, I was enjoying being part of a family.

We all went to chapel on the Sunday, walking in a line, like elephants. Dad at the front, huge Bible under his arm, Mam behind, Maggy behind her and so on. We must have looked a funny sight but Dad used to say it was a witness to the whole road as we marched up. It was just brilliant being back and actually being a Christian. I had been a fake Christian and disappointed everyone and now I am not a fake. I really do know Jesus as my Saviour! It was a whole new world to me. I could understand the Bible, the preaching was so relevant to my life and I loved the worship.

Singing was wonderful. The hymns made sense to me now and I appreciated all these lovely people who had never stopped praying for me and welcomed me back in the church family.

John and Kenny were so lovely. I had missed them. John had changed jobs, after working with Graham Slegg who taught him so much. He was still going out with Sharon and he was crazy in love. Kenny was working for Dad, not quite so happily!

Kayla was growing up. She was all legs, teeth and glasses, but cute with it, though the boys wanted to strangle her a lot of the time. She wanted their attention as soon as they walked through the door. I guess she got none from Mam. I have a vivid image in my mind of Kayla standing with her back against the house wall outside, with a pair of old tights, both legs stuffed into one, and a tennis ball down in the toe end of the tight. She would swing it from side to side, above her head, and between her legs, as the ball bounced off the wall. She would go like lightning! There was a song that went with this action and she would be out there for hours playing this game. Dad built her an amazing little Wendy House and she played in it a lot. When she was in a strop, she would flounce out of the house and go and sit in her Wendy House, shut all the windows and the door and sulk to her heart's content!

As the weeks passed, I had a meeting with the pastor, Errol Hulse, who was a lovely man. I told him what had happened to me and that now I really was a Christian. I asked if I could be baptised because it was a commandment—believe on the Lord Jesus Christ and be baptised. But he said no, I had already been baptised and the Bible said One Lord, one faith, one baptism. I was devastated and argued that when I was baptised, I didn't have a faith and Jesus wasn't my Lord but he was now and I so wanted to be obedient to him. I had made such a mess of my life up to now and Jesus had washed me clean, given me a fresh start.

I so wanted to start my Christian walk by being obedient to God's word. Errol was adamant that I couldn't so, as disappointed as I was, I accepted what he said. He was my pastor but in my heart I felt sad. I could see what Errol was saying. He said he had to insist that if you had been baptised once, that was it or he would be re-baptising people left, right and centre. He didn't seem to understand that when he baptised me when I was 16 I wasn't a Christian at all, I was just pretending to be one. He seemed to think I had backslidden. Well, whatever he thought he wasn't about to baptise me again, so that was that.

I stayed in Cuckfield for a few weeks. I loved being at home with my family and I was learning more about God. I was finding my place in the church and I loved it. My big worry was Greg. I missed him so much. He phoned every night and we would talk for ages but it would always come back to my faith and his lack of faith. He just couldn't see why I had 'gone all religious' on him.

I went back up to Durham. We needed to talk. I loved him very much but couldn't understand how he could be so unkind about something that meant so much to me. Greg met me at Durham station. I was so excited to see him. My heart was racing as I got off the train. I saw him before he saw me and it gave me such a kick to see the look on his face when he found me in the crowd. It was a look that told me he loved me, that he had missed me. We hurried towards each other and he scooped me up in his arms and kissed me. It was wonderful to be back in his arms. We hugged and kissed for ages as we stood on the platform. Oh, how I loved this man.

We arrived at my Gran's house. I had written to tell her I was coming back so when we opened the door both Gran and Grandad were there. They were thrilled to see me and Gran had been busy cooking, bless her. She wasn't one for hugs and kisses; her way of showing you she cared for you was to cook for you and, boy oh boy, did she care for me! There were pies and cakes galore, it was great. I took my suitcase up to my room and when I came down the kettle had boiled and tea made. We all sat around the table. Gran wanted to know how everyone was and I told her.

Then Grandad said, "And what about you, lass? What's happening with you?" I poured out everything that had happened. They all sat and stared at me. I said that I knew that God loved me, that I was forgiven and I had to live my life differently now. Gran rolled her eyes and smiled. Granddad said he understood and went on to say how he wished he hadn't left the Salvation Army. Greg said nothing, just sat quietly. We all ate till we couldn't eat any more then Gran and Grandad went into the lounge. Greg and I stayed in the kitchen; I wanted to talk to him on my own, to find out exactly what he thought.

I asked him what he was thinking. He said, "I think you've taken this religion too far. It's all rubbish so far as I can see." I was upset by his remarks and tried to explain, but he just couldn't understand and said he didn't want to talk about it anymore. He came over to me, put his arms around me and kissed me. He held me for ages and was telling me how much he had missed me. He said he would stay till Gran and Grandad had gone to bed. I knew what he was hoping for.

I looked at him and said, "Darling, I'm afraid that sex is definitely out of the question now that I am a Christian. It's not that I don't love you, I do, but the Bible says you should only sleep together if you are married and we're not, so we can't."

The look on his face was of shock and disappointment. "You're kidding me. You really are taking this much too far. This is crazy." I wanted to cry. This was not at all how I imagined it would go. Greg just couldn't understand where I was coming from. I wanted him to say he could see what I was saying was true and he wanted it for himself but he certainly didn't and he made it very plain. He went home. I went to bed and I cried. Then I prayed that God would open his eyes like he had opened mine. I knew God could do it; it was just a question of when.

We met up the following night. Things were very strained and awkward. He was very sarcastic and mocking and it upset me, though I put on a brave face. He walked me home and as we kissed goodnight I realised that this wasn't going to work unless God did a miracle in Greg's life. I felt very much that I wanted to do what was right before God and I knew that I needed to be in a good church. I prayed that God would be in all my decisions which sounds a really strange thing to pray but I knew that I had made lots of wrong decisions all by myself and I didn't want to do that anymore. I wanted, needed, God to lead me.

I prayed so much that Greg would become a Christian, that he would realise that I wasn't a nutter and that Christianity was real, but he just didn't seem to get it. He was getting crosser and crosser with me every time we met. So, after much prayer and buckets of tears, I gave him back his ring and told him I couldn't marry him, that Christianity was vitally important to me and all we were doing since I had become a Christian was argue about it. I didn't want to live my life with a man so opposed to the Bible and Christianity and the Bible says that you shouldn't be unequally yoked to an unbeliever. Even though I loved him, I loved God more. He was shocked, upset and angry all in one. He looked so hurt, took my ring and said, "If that's what you want, fine," and walked out. I was numb. I cried.

I didn't sleep much that night but I felt I had done the right thing. I talked to God most of the night, pouring all my feelings out to him, telling him how much I loved Greg and if I shouldn't marry him then God would have to take away the love I had for him otherwise it would be too painful. I was asking him what I should do, where I should live, what church I needed to be in. It was so good to be able to pour it all out and to know God was hearing me, did love me and would answer me. I rang Mam and Dad to tell them what I had done and they were praying for us too.

It was an easy decision to make; I would move back to Sussex. My family was there, my church was there and Greg—wasn't there! That would be easier for both of us. I told Gran and Grandad what I had decided was best all round. They were sad I was leaving but they understood. I just wished they were moving south too. I would miss them dreadfully. I loved them very much but they were settled in Willington.

I rang Dad, told him what I had decided and how I was sure it was the right thing to do. He said he would drive up to collect me and my worldly goods. So I packed up my clobber. Dad arrived late, stayed the night and the following morning we packed up the van and said our goodbyes to Gran and Grandad. I promised to write often and visit often too. It was sad seeing Gran in her wraparound apron and Grandad looking smart in his shirt and tie, not his usual vest and dangling braces, standing on the doorstep waving to us. I cried as we left. I knew how this was hurting both of them and my heart hurt too. They had made my life so comfortable and easy. There was no fear in their house, just love, hard love, but love nonetheless. They were the best grandparents possible to me and I was very torn leaving them but I knew it was the right thing to do.

I didn't see Greg before I left. I toyed with the idea of saying goodbye but decided it would be too hard, so I wrote him a letter and posted it the day we left, just telling him that I had moved back home and that I hoped he would forgive me and that he would consider Christianity an option for his life.

We motored south down the A1. It was the longest Dad and I had been together for years. I was, to say the least, a little apprehensive but it was a great journey. We talked about Jesus and Christianity and how it was life-changing, about my life and what God was doing in it, and with me. About Greg and what I was praying for. About Dad and what God had done and was doing in his life. It sounds weird but it really wasn't weird at all. My eyes had been opened to Christ and all my priorities had changed. This must sound quite nutty and before I became a Christian I would have thought it nutty, but it's the most wonderful thing to have happened to me.

We stopped for a rest in a service station and I sat with my Dad, having a cuppa and it struck me that this was the first time I had ever been anywhere with him on my own, without being scared or on edge, apart from doing burglaries. I was 24.

We arrived home late. Mam was waiting for us and she made a cuppa and asked about the journey. We talked for a while. We were both very tired but Dad had to work the following day and I didn't, so we all went to bed. Dad said he would unpack the van in the morning. I was sharing a room with Kayla and Maggy. They were both asleep. I was in the single bed, damp and smelling of cigarettes, but it was a familiar smell, it was the smell of home. I settled in. I could hear Maggy and Kayla breathing. I lay there for quite a while just thinking about what I had done and how Greg was going to feel when he got my letter. I asked God to help him understand what I had done and why and that my letter wouldn't make him mad with me and with God. I wanted him to start looking for God himself because God has promised that if you seek you will find.

I must have drifted off to sleep because the next thing I knew was Kayla with a huge grin on her face. She must have woken me and was now cracking on she had only just noticed me. "Hello Faydee," she yelled and jumped on me, giving me a big hug. I am not at my best first thing in the morning at the best of times but having a nine-year-old leap on me, this was something different! I almost yelled at her to get off, but I didn't. Bless her, she really was pleased to see me.

"Hello to you too," I said.

"Are you going to live here now?" she asked.

"Yes I am," I said. "At least I hope I am, for a while anyway."

Hoping and Praying

IT WAS WEIRD FITTING BACK INTO OUR ODD FAMILY LIFE. Everything had changed beyond recognition since last I lived here. I needed to find my place in it. We had never been the sort of family who sat at the dinner table and talked, as you have probably gathered, but things had most definitely changed. When I dressed and went downstairs, Kayla had rushed down to tell everyone, "Our Fay is here."

Maggy, John, Kenny, Mam and Dad were sat around the table. That was different. I sat with them and poured a cuppa. Kenny was all smiles. "Hello Frowser, you're back then." Maggy was getting a move on, she was off to work. We were all sat around this table when Dad said, "Let's give thanks for journeying mercies!" I wasn't sure what he was on about but we finished eating and drinking, bowed our heads and Dad started praying, thanking God for our safe trip home and asking God to speak into my life, to make it clear what He wanted me to do. It was great. He also prayed for a good day's work for himself, John, Ken and Maggy. He asked that they would all give "a good measure well pressed down." I had no idea what it meant but I said a loud Amen. Here I was, back in my family home. It sounds so odd saying that, but it really was a family home now and I felt like a fish out of water.

I knew there were things I needed to do. Get a job for a start. Because my education virtually stopped when I was 14 I had no confidence in myself or my ability. All I had ever done was look after people, people of all ages, so as we lived near to Cuckfield Hospital I applied for a job there. I desperately wanted to be a nurse but hadn't the confidence to apply, knowing they would ask for my qualification. I had none. So I applied and got a job as a domestic, working on a geriatric ward.

I loved being in that sort of environment, it suited me. I got on well with all the nursing staff as well as the domestic staff, most of whom were Spanish. There were a few English girls working and living in the hospital accommodation. They had a bad reputation for being fast and loose! It took me quite a while to be accepted by the Spanish girls I was working with as they thought all English girls were tramps. I explained to them that I was different because I was a Christian. They were staunch Catholics so we kind of hit it off and I was included when gossip about one girl was being bandied about among the staff. They raised their eyebrows and tutted loudly about it and looked at me to do the same, so I did. That was it; we were mates now and on the same moral high ground! I am smiling as I write this because it seems a funny thing, me taking the moral high ground. I was to find it a very strange place to be but I was accepted and the Spanish girls treated me like an honorary Spaniard, quite an honour when I learned what they actually thought of the English girls!

It was a funny little hospital. The wards were converted Nissan huts and were joined by a range of covered walkways. It was quirky but lovely. I worked hard and was able to contribute to living at home. Mam was thrilled to have the extra income. I don't think she told Dad exactly how much I was contributing; she was a devious woman my Mam and she liked to keep the amount of money she had, or had access to, very close to her chest. Dad on the other hand was very generous. If he had money he would give it to anyone who asked him. This was a whole new Dad! He obviously gave Mam housekeeping but if he had extra cash she would go all out to get it off him before anyone else did!

Being back home I had found my place in the family again. This was weird. It was like living in our family but in a parallel universe. All the people were the same but different. Dad would now spend his time with the family! He would read to Kayla. I had never been read to in my life. The boys, John and Ken, weren't being beaten half as much. I say that because Dad still lost his temper when they had done something he disagreed with or didn't do something he had told them to do, but he explained to them why he was giving them a thrashing. Kayla had got Dad sussed. Whenever she did something wrong, Dad would say, "Right, I have to punish you," and Kayla would be on her knees in front of him, hands together in the praying position.

"Have mercy on me daddy, I am a sinner," she would say. The first time I saw her do this, I nearly burst out laughing. Dad made her go to her room and learn scripture verses. She wasn't daft, far better than getting a wallop! It was difficult to work out the rules now, but Maggy would explain things to me.

Mam found it all very difficult. I had never tried to see things from her perspective before but now, when I think of that time, all I remember of her was

183

that she was all things to all men. I think that sums her up perfectly. When Dad was around she was as godly as she could be and she was like that at chapel, but when we were at home and no one of importance was there, she was back to being the Mam we all knew. Not nice!

I was just finding my place in the church and in Christ too and I was thrilled to find out just how much He loved me, but it was always tempered with our/my responsibility and the fact that I had to work out my salvation with fear and trembling. God loved me but He was also angry with the wicked every day. It was here at Cuckfield Strict and Particular Baptist Chapel that the foundations of my Christian walk with Christ were laid down and I will be forever thankful to God and to Errol Hulse who was my pastor all through those years.

He taught me about my salvation and my justification. My place was secure in Heaven because Jesus bore my sins on the cross. That is the core of scripture but Errol unravelled the scriptures for me. I loved to sit under his preaching. Sometimes I didn't understand what he was saying because he used words I had never heard before, so when we got home I would ask Dad and he would explain it to me. The scales had fallen from my eyes and I loved to just read my Bible. It made my heart leap when I would come across a verse that leaped out at me. I loved the Psalms at that time. Still do, but back then they were special to me. I could understand David's fear and his delight in his God, his sadness when he felt God had abandoned him.

All the promises that are hidden in those precious pages, the joy I felt when something I hadn't understood suddenly became clear, as if God was opening things up to me slowly. I would spend hours praying and thanking God for all that he was doing in me and in my family and I was constantly bringing Greg before the throne of grace. That was one of the things Dad had to explain to me. Errol was always saying we were coming before the throne of grace. I had no idea what he was talking about. I thought maybe we were going on an outing as a church! I must confess I was a bit disappointed to find out it was just another way of saying, let's pray. I used to think God would be fed up with me, so I would try not to pray so much, but I really couldn't help it. I had found Him and He had found me and I didn't want to lose that relationship.

I would talk to Dad for ages about something I had read, but Mam was never enthusiastic and I felt that she was only going along with this Christianity because she was afraid she would lose Dad if she didn't. But she would push her luck with him. She would swear or answer him back and my heart would lurch.

She was just seeing how far she could push him and if he would respond in the old way and give her a back-hander. He didn't and she would give a little smirk as if to say, 'I've won'. It was like a game with her but you could see he was fighting to hold back his temper. It was something he would always fight with and sometimes lose, then that gave her ammunition to throw at him.

"Call yourself a Christian," she would say. "I don't think so. A Christian wouldn't do that." I would feel sorry for him when she did that but he seemed to cope with it and when I think now of all she had coped with over the years, he had caused her so much heartache and pain, I guess she thought this was payback time But to use Christianity as a weapon seemed harsh.

God had been faithful to me in answering my prayer to take away the love I had for Greg but I prayed constantly for him. He, bless him, would send me such wonderful love letters telling me I was the love of his life and wasn't Christianity about love so why couldn't we marry. I would write Dear Greg letters and tell him he needed to find Christ for himself and then he would understand what I was going on about. He asked if he could come down and see me. Mam and Dad said that was OK, he could doss down with John and Kenny. I think he had the notion that as soon as our eyes met it wouldn't be long before our loins would meet too and we would be back as we were. Not gonna happen! In fact, I asked Maggy not to leave us on our own at all and, bless her, she didn't.

Greg was working at that time for a firm called Smart and Brown. They sold electrical goods and he worked in the offices, so when he saw a delivery was to be made to Haywards Heath he got a lift down and stayed for the weekend. He did this several times so we saw quite a lot of each other over that year. It was always lovely to see him. He was so in love with me and I loved him like I loved my brothers but he was determined to make me realise just how much I loved him and this Christianity was just a phase!

Bless him, he would come to chapel with us all and never understand any of it, poor fella, but he kept coming and I kept praying! We would sit in the evenings and he would talk about what we had. I would try to be as kind as I could by saying that was in the past and if our future was to be together then he needed to be a Christian.

He would go home and call me most nights from the phone box outside his house. After a bit of chit chat, I would ask, "Are you a Christian yet?"

He would laugh and say, "No, not yet," which would give me hope. It sounded like he was looking.

Greg's Conversion

GREG'S BROTHER WAS GOING OUT WITH A GIRL WHO WAS A CHRISTIAN and he told Greg about this church in Durham and that it was a good church to try. So he went. He said it was an unassuming church, the preaching wasn't scintillating but at the end of the sermon the pastor said, "If Christ came back tomorrow, would you be ready?" Bless him, he knew he wasn't ready and he had been told so many times that he needed to repent of all his sins, believe in the Lord Jesus, ask Him into his life and he would be saved. That's what the Bible tells us.
He said he felt very self-conscious and tried to pray but felt a bit silly so he left the church, caught the bus home and went to his bedroom. He knelt on the floor and poured his heart out to God, asking Him to forgive his sin, cleanse his heart and make him a Christian. Give him fresh eyes to see and understand the Bible because he couldn't understand it at all. He said he didn't feel anything and was disappointed but God had heard his prayer!

He knew all that he had been told was true! Christ was his Saviour, he did die for him and he really knew it. He rang me that evening to tell me the wonderful news. "You'll never guess what has happened to me," he said. "No, tell me," I said. "I've been saved. I know it's true. Jesus is the Son of God and He did die for me." The excitement in his voice was contagious. "Tell me what happened," I said, barely able to speak. He went on to tell me the whole story and finished with how he had prayed and now he knew the truth! I was excited but sceptical. It had been almost a year since I had been saved and left Durham and in every letter I had received from Greg since then he had told me I was the love of his life and he wanted to marry me, so I was a little worried that he was just saying all this just to marry me. I needed it to be real, so I asked him to come down for the weekend.

He arrived about lunchtime on Saturday. I met him at the bottom of our road. The lorry he got a lift in passed the bottom of Glebe Road. He climbed down with a huge grin on his face. He wanted me to throw my arms around his neck and kiss him passionately but I was still wary. He put his arms around me and I hugged him and kissed his cheek. I felt his hurt and disappointment but I wanted to be sure what he was saying was true. I was holding my emotions firmly in hand!

We walked up to 22 and as soon as we were in the door everyone shouted, "Hello Greg." He had no sooner sat down, cuppa in hand, when the questions began.

"So you've been saved, have you?" said Dad. Poor Greg. As I think about this time it must have been terrifying for him, a little bit like the Spanish Inquisition! Questions fired at him from all directions and, bless him, he answered them as well as he could. He explained how he had been going to chapel in Durham for a few weeks. Also I had been sending him books to help him in his search to find the truth and he had read them. If you know Greg, you will realise that is a miracle in itself because he is no reader, the only book he reads is his Bible, even now! But I still wasn't sure if this was just a ruse. Anyway, after a long and gruelling evening, we all went to bed.

Sunday morning was a special morning in our house now. Before we walked up to chapel we would finish breakfast, generally a cuppa and a cigarette, then we would sit in a circle and each of us would pray. Greg had sat in this circle many times but always silently. He said he couldn't pray to a God he didn't know existed let alone had a personal relationship with. But this Sunday morning, all that changed. John had finished praying and Greg was sat next to him. I was at the other side of Greg and was just about to begin to pray when Greg started praying! It was wonderful; he was full of praise to God and we were all amazed.

When he finished praying I don't think any of us had a dry eye and the prayer I had prayed over a year ago that if Greg wasn't a Christian and I couldn't marry him, that God would take away the love I had for him—well, God now gave me back all the love I had ever felt for Greg and more. I knew he really was saved and did know Jesus as his Saviour and Lord. It was so exciting. We all walked up to chapel and it was such a special day; the first time Greg and I would worship our God together. It was August 1973.

Everything changed again. Now when Greg went back home I was aching for him to come back, which he did very regularly. I couldn't wait for him to return, but when he did come, life was very difficult for us because we had been in a sexual relationship. We both knew we had to wait until we were married before any hanky panky went on and we both wanted to obey God but we needed help. So, dear old Maggy to the rescue again. She, bless her heart, would sit up with us night after night so that we wouldn't give in to temptation and, believe me, it was very tempting.

Greg had no idea that I had asked Mags to stay with us at all costs and he would regularly say to her, "Why don't you get an early night, Maggy?"

She would say things like, "No thanks, I'm fine, thanks for asking," while her little eyes were closing all by themselves, she was so tired! He was always asking me what was wrong with Maggy. Didn't she realise we'd like some time alone? I didn't tell him until much later that I had asked her, that no matter what we said to her, myself included, DON'T LEAVE US ALONE! I owe Mags a lot.

Greg and I talked about our future together. We knew we wanted to get married but first Greg needed to be baptised, so he made an appointment with Erroll. It is, as I have said before, quite an ordeal to be baptised in a Baptist chapel. You have an interview with the pastor and the elders. You tell them why you want to be baptised and you give them your testimony. In other words you tell them exactly what happened to you and how God has become real to you. Once done, they ask you questions about your testimony. Once they are sure you really are saved you are given a date for your baptism, and so it was with Greg. He was given a date—September 1973. We were so excited.

The Sunday evening arrived and he had to stand at the front of the whole church and give his testimony. He was very nervous but he wanted to obey his God so he did it. It was a wonderful evening and God really blessed him. We both felt we were slap bang in the centre of God's will for our lives and it was a wonderful time.

We set about planning our wedding and looking for somewhere to live. A friend of ours, David Holden, worked in an estate agents and he phoned to say that a flat had just come in to his agency. It was at the bottom of Cuckfield High Street above the butchers. We were thrilled and we made an appointment to go and look at it. It was a period building so floors, walls and ceilings were all, well I think the word would be 'wobbly' but we agreed to rent it, so Greg moved in almost straight away and my brother John moved in with him to help with the bills and also to get away from home.

His girlfriend Sharon would come down to the flat. I was most embarrassed the first time he brought her to meet me. She looked at me and said, "I remember you. You beat me up at school!" I had lots of apologising to do now I was a Christian.

The same thing happened with a new couple who lived next door to Mam and Dad. They were a lovely couple and she was a hairdresser so Mam made me an appointment to get my hair done. I went round and she opened the door, looked at me and said, "Hello Fay, I remember you from school. You beat me up!" I had been such a hard-faced girl, but needs must and life had been hard and now it was hard being a Christian sometimes; your past needs to be dealt with but you can't do it all at once!

Maggy had been going to chapel and took it all in. She was at the Evangelical Church when David Coak was preaching. After the service he asked Maggy what was stopping her from becoming a Christian. She said she was waiting for a feeling. David told her that faith isn't a feeling. She told him she didn't know if she was sorry enough! She had said sorry to God many times, but always felt she needed to be sorrier! David said the Bible says repent and believe, but because Dad had such a Damascus Road type conversion Maggy was waiting for something like his. After David's chat she went home and said to God she was sorry. This was the last time she would say sorry. She had repented, she believed God and has lived the Christian life from that day to this, bless her.

A Flat and Two Weddings

THE FLAT HAD TWO BEDROOMS, a kitchen that had one floor cupboard and a sink unit. It had no window so, to borrow light from the room next to it, which was the bathroom, a window was put right next to the sink. While you were washing up you could open the window and chat to whoever was in the bath or on the loo—very friendly!

There was a long lounge but because it was a period place it was a strange shape, thin at one end and fatter at the other, and the undulating ceiling meant that the light was slightly off centre and right next to a 'wobble', so one end of the room was in the light, the other in darkness! So we had lots to do to make this flat our home. We bought wall lights. The landlord said he was happy for us to do anything we wanted, which was nice, so over the next few months we decorated the whole flat. Our John was a brickie at the time and I so wanted a stone fireplace. We took all the stones from Mam's rockery, scrubbed them up and we left John to build our nice square fireplace. I had seen some lovely fireplaces when we had been invited out for Sunday lunch at various friends from church. It was a 70s trend and I fancied being trendy for once.

We came back about three hours later and John had taken out the old fireplace, blocked up the hole and moved, what was loosely described as a fireplace, but what was ever after called 'a Neanderthal dwelling' to the corner of the room! It was a huge cave-like creation that went from floor to ceiling. We couldn't believe our eyes! John was so proud of his creation that we had to keep it, but we now had to buy an electric fire to go in the hole. More expense. We had hoped to have a real fire but because he relocated the dwelling place we now couldn't burn anything in it because it didn't have a chimney. We had to buy a fire so we found one that looked like a log fire, although it was a really naff plastic fake mess, but it was the best we could afford.

We had no carpets and Maggy told us of this bloke who did carpets cheap. He had done their flat for virtually nothing. So we got onto him, he came round and told us he could supply, or supply and fit the lounge carpet. Phil, my brother, said, "Don't bother getting him to fit it, that's a mug's game, any pillock can fit a carpet. I'll fit it, you just buy it." So that's exactly what we did. We bought the cheapest carpet he had in a very dark brown. It came in a roll and Phil came round to fit it. It was very thin and sort of nylon. We couldn't afford the underlay so we just put newspaper down. I made copious cups of tea for Phil and Greg as they set about fitting the carpet.

Remember that the Neanderthal dwelling held an electric fire, so the wire came from the fire around the edge of the hearth and into a plug. Phil rolled out the carpet so that it was lapping up the walls on all sides, then he just went around the room with a very sharp Stanley knife and as he went around the hearth, the fire went off! He had cut through the wire. We all laughed when we realised what had happened but I never understood how he wasn't electrocuted. We then had to get an electrician to put a new wire on the fire.

All the time Greg and John were living in the flat we were trying to buy bits of furniture second-hand and we saw a cottage suite advertised in *The Middy* so we rang up and went to see it. It looked fine and would fit into the lounge and still allow room for a dining table, when we could afford one, so we bought it. The man we bought it from delivered it for us as we didn't drive and couldn't afford to pay someone to pick it up. Our little home was taking shape.

John had made an archway in the hallway to borrow more light into the kitchen. He was working in a kitchen shop in Burgess Hill so when he was fitting a new kitchen he took out the old cupboards and the ones that weren't too bad and fitted them into our tiny kitchen. We were thrilled and it looked more like a kitchen and less like a corridor to the bathroom now. I was so looking forward to getting married and making this our home.

The wedding day was set for the 27th March 1976. We were so excited. Greg had been for an interview at two places in Burgess Hill. One was at a perfume factory called Charles of the Ritz who needed an office clerk. The other was at American Express, also as an office clerk. We prayed he would get one of them because we were so short of money and were thrilled when he got a letter from American Express saying he had got the job! His starting wage was £48 per week, which seemed an awful lot back then. We could start buying stuff for the wedding now. We were so in love and this was all so wonderful. God was blessing us and we were trying to honour him in the way we dealt with everyone and how we were with each other. Now Greg was living at the flat we were tempted to sleep together but I was determined that God had honoured me and answered my prayer to save Greg and that sex would wait till we were married but, boy, that was difficult sometimes!

We bought a dining table and four chairs from *The Middy* too, so our little home was becoming so cosy though I kept finding little pyramids of red stuff under the chairs and settee. It really puzzled me. I would sweep up this red dust until one day it dawned on me that the cushions were getting thinner. The foam inside the cushions was disintegrating! Still they had quite a way to go before they were uncomfortable so we just ignored it.

Mam and Dad were thrilled we were getting married. Greg had asked John to be his best man and Kayla was going to be my bridesmaid along with two little girls my mum minded, Tamzin and Nanna. So I was busy making bridesmaids dresses. My stint at the dressmaking factory came in very handy and the sewing machine Gran and Grandad had bought me was just the job. I had them made in no time. I also went to Brighton to look for a wedding dress. Maggy came with me and I tried several on but found the one I really liked. I paid a deposit and went down to Brighton weekly until I had paid it all off and brought my dress home. This was real. I really was getting married. I couldn't wait.

I tried on my wedding dress at home to show Mam. She seemed to like it. We spent evenings talking about the reception and what food we would have and the wedding cake and who would make it. Mam, as I have said before, was no cook, so a wedding cake was way out of her league. She had a friend called Jackie Farrell who was a brilliant cook and she said she would make our cake as a wedding present. We were thrilled. Also another friend, Kelvin Coomber, said he would do the photographs. This was just great. We were to be married at 12.00 at our chapel, then the reception would be a buffet in the halls of the Evangelical Church in Haywards Heath. We were ticking off the days and they seemed to drag.

Sharon went to Haywards Heath Evangelical Church and came from a lovely Christian family. She must have been shell-shocked when she first came to our house. Anyway, John had started going to her church too. It was a much younger congregation with a younger minister, Kingsley Coomber, who was really helpful to them both. John was working in Dibbens, a kitchen showroom in Burgess Hill, and enjoying a new challenge—he would soak up knowledge. He and Sharon were getting married in November and we were all very excited for them. The wedding was lovely; Sharon looked fabulous and John looked handsome. He grinned from ear to ear when he saw Sharon; they were so in love. Greg was best man and he felt very honoured to have been asked. It was a fabulous day.

Maggy had been on the council house list since she and Phil married and she was finally given a flat in Haywards Heath in 1971 which was lovely and they were thrilled with it. Phil would go through phases of being vegetarian and he invited Greg and me down for a meal. He cooked a casserole of veg and herbs. I swear he poured jars of herbs into this dish. Anyway, it was rank but we all ate it and said it was lovely! He was always wanting to make a few quid on the side, either thieving or some sort of car deal. He should never have been a criminal because he was rubbish at it and got captured 99 times out of a hundred! He would be arrested and sent down, usually for a long stretch. Poor old Phil.

Maggy would be at home for years by herself, faithfully visiting him. She would come and stay with us at the weekends and we would nip up the shops, mooch around Burgess Hill market and just enjoy being together. We did have some laughs and, bless her, she bought bits and made a lovely home for them both for when Phil came home from prison. When he finally did come home he was in a funny phase and decided they shouldn't have—stuff. So he gave all their furniture and all his clothes, except for what he was wearing, to Oxfam. This was just before our wedding and he realised, just after everything had been collected, that he would need a suit, so he went into the Oxfam shop in the High Street and explained that he had given everything he had to Oxfam and he needed a suit. Could he have one please? The lady said yes and he picked one. "That will be £4.50 please." He was incensed! He told her where she could shove that suit. Hence he wore his mucky white trousers and tee shirt to our wedding. We didn't care what he wore; we were just glad he was there.

Since John had moved out of the flat, Greg was there on his own, though I would spend most evenings with him. It was a cold little flat so Dad came up with the idea of double glazing the sash windows. We had no money for that so he made frames from wood and covered them with clear plastic. Once they were fitted it was definitely warmer as the old sash windows were very loose and when the wind blew they rattled like mad. Dad made us some WWWs (Willy Window Wedges), but when they were in place the wind howled through the gap. Our Heath Robinson double glazing worked a treat, the only drawback was, when you looked through them, everything was distorted, rather like the funny mirrors at a funfair! The cars coming down the hill looked all wobbly as did the passers-by but we were warmer and we could take them down for the summer.

Mam decided who would come to our wedding and began inviting people. She said that was the way it was done. We didn't want to fall out with her so we let her do it, but the sad thing was, there were lots of friends we would have loved to be at our wedding who weren't even asked and people we hardly knew but were friends of Mam's were there. We were so wrapped up in each other at the time that we didn't care; it's only in hindsight that we wish we had said something. As long as we were there, that's really all we cared about.

The week before the wedding I left off work. We were buying the food for the buffet and lots of people said they would help cook stuff. We bought potatoes by the ton. Well, it felt like it when we were carrying them home. They were for potato salad and we gave them to various people who were kind enough to cook them and take them to the hall on the morning of the wedding. At home we cooked a turkey, a huge ham and beef and sliced it all. It was all hard work but exciting. Flans and quiches by the dozen were cooked by us and friends. The cake looked fantastic; we were so touched by the way everyone was so keen to help us.

The morning of the 27th arrived and I was so nervous my tummy was all butterflies. We all smoked like chimneys back then, though we would all have a Polo mint before we went to church so that no one would know. The fact that we all stank of smoke might have been a giveaway but *we* couldn't smell it. So for breakfast I had a cuppa and several cigarettes. Lesley next door was doing my hair so I went round to hers. She was so sweet and she put my veil in place. I came back, went upstairs and put on my wedding dress. I felt like a princess.... I was a princess! The daughter of the King of Kings. What a morning, what a feeling.

John was at the flat helping Greg get ready. His Mam and his sister Brenda had come down and were staying with some friends of ours. We were both thrilled they had come down. Kayla was in her dress and looked lovely. Tammy arrived and put on her dress along with Nanna. I think Tammy's mum Lesley drove Mam and the bridesmaids up to chapel.

I remember coming downstairs. Dad was in the dining room smoking. He was wearing a pinstriped suit and looked all shiny and as I came through the door he looked at me and began to cry, took out his hanky, blew his nose and wiped his eyes. He would make a coughing noise but not really be coughing, to cover up the fact that he was crying and for the first time in my life he said, "You look beautiful, Frowser." My chest nearly burst with pride. I felt so good. He finished his cigarette and said, "Let's pray." He held my hand and asked God's blessing to be on our marriage today and always. He asked God to bless the day and all that would go on and then he asked God to bless me as I became a wife. I was holding back the tears; this really was going to be such a special day.

We didn't have wedding cars, they were an expense too far, so Dad was to drive me to chapel. I remember looking at the clock. It was 11.55 and Dad said, "Well Frow, we better get moving, he'll be thinking you're not coming." We both laughed and put in a Polo! I got into the back of the car and we arrived at chapel just a few moments late. Dad got out, opened the door for me to get out. My dress had quite a long train so Dad just rolled it all up as I was getting out. I was mortified when we got the photos back; he had rolled it so high everyone could see my knickers!

We sorted my dress out and my bridesmaids were all waiting just inside the door. The three of them looked so sweet but so nervous. I told them they looked beautiful and were doing a fabulous job and they beamed! Kayla was chief bridesmaid and was in charge of the two little ones, Tanny and Nanna, so they looked to her to tell them what to do. She was in her element! I put my arm through Dad's and we walked into the chapel. The organist began playing and everyone stood up. I felt my heart pounding in my chest. I looked to the front of the chapel. Greg was standing, looking forward. I willed him to turn round and he did. His face was beautiful. I loved him more than ever. He grinned at me and he was all shiny too. This was wonderful!

We walked down the aisle and in no time we were there. Dad was squeezing my arm and the organist stopped. I was standing next to Greg. I could see the vein pulsing in his neck. His arm was shaking, he was as nervous as me. When Erroll said, "Who gives this woman?," Dad said in such a loud voice, "I DO" and I wanted to laugh as he thrust my hand forward towards Greg, then stepped smartly back. I turned and gave Kayla my bouquet. She was so proud to be chief bridesmaid and gave the other two a very obvious smirk.

Erroll stood before us and we said our vows. When he said, "I now pronounce you man and wife," I started crying. I hadn't thought about how I would feel at this moment. I didn't have a tissue and I looked up at Greg. He didn't have one either. I looked past him to John who was also crying. He wiped his eyes then passed me the most disgusting looking hankie you have ever seen. That made me smile as I wiped my eyes with this filthy thing and I felt wonderful. I felt so loved, I couldn't be more blessed. God was certainly answering Dad's prayer already!

We went through to the vestry to sign the register. I was on cloud nine—we were married. I was Mrs Fay Summers!

We had lots of photos taken outside the chapel, then John drove us to Haywards Heath in his filthy cream Maxi but, bless him, he had put a ribbon on it. We arrived at the Evangelical Church and had photos taken outside there too. When we got the photos it looked like we had had two weddings as we were outside both church and chapel.

The reception went so quickly that I can hardly remember it. We didn't have any money left for a flash honeymoon but we were determined to go somewhere. Well, British Rail was doing an offer. Return tickets to Bournemouth and a weekend in a B&B for £14 each. We could just about manage that so we left the reception, went back to 22 where I got changed. Then John took us to the station. We were so excited!

We arrived in Bournemouth and found the B&B. It was a grotty place. The lady showed us to our room. It was a tiny room with a double bed, a cupboard and a sink. Not quite what we had expected. The bathroom was across the hall and was shared by the whole of that floor, but we didn't care, we were married and that was all that mattered. We had arrived too late for dinner but we weren't hungry anyway. It was 9 o'clock. We opened our suitcases and they were full of confetti. It went everywhere. Maggy had lent me a frilly nightie and negligee, very frilly at the top but sort of see-through. About 11 o'clock Greg needed the loo. He didn't have a dressing gown so he put my frilly negligee on. He looked so funny, I was laughing as he nipped across the hall. Just as he came out of the bathroom, the lift opened and a crowd of holidaymakers were dumbstruck at the sight of Greg in Maggy's negligee. Poor Greg was mortified.

At breakfast the next morning we were the talk of the dining room, Greg in particular. I think everyone had worked out we were newlyweds and Greg was the bloke in the see-through negligee!

We had to be out of the B&B by 10.00 so we asked where the nearest Baptist chapel was. Lansdowne Baptist Chapel wasn't too far away so we set off walking and found it in no time. We were given a warm welcome and sat through the service after which we walked through the town. We hadn't a penny between us so we just had to kill time until we were allowed back into the B&B at 6 o'clock.

It was a miserable March day; there was nothing open, so we wandered down to the beach. The sea was rough and choppy and we sat and watched it for a while. We talked about our future and how we were going to spend the rest of our lives together. This was wonderful.

We were so cold and hungry by the time we were allowed back into the B&B and we devoured the roast chicken dinner and jelly for pudding, as though we had never eaten before.

After breakfast the next day we caught the train back to Haywards Heath and then caught a bus to Cuckfield and our first home together. It was so lovely to be home. We decided we would have been better off just staying at home rather than going to that grotty place. We laugh about it now but back then it really was horrid and we said that once we had enough money we would have a proper honeymoon.

We both had the week off so we set about sorting out just what went where. We had been given some lovely wedding presents and enjoyed finding homes for them all. I also had stuff at 22 that needed bringing back to the flat. It was so cosy and we loved it.

We started our life together as Mr and Mrs Summers as we meant to go on. We wanted to be right before God in all that we did so we decided right from the start that we would pray together every day. We decided evenings were the best time for both of us, also it meant that if either of us were upset we could sort it out before we went to bed. We have tried to do this throughout our marriage and have mostly succeeded in 'never letting the sun go down on our anger'. Although we have had the odd exception!

Home Sweet Home

JOHN AND SHARON WERE LIVING IN A FLAT AT WALSTEAD, which was fine, but Sharon was pregnant and they were in the middle of nowhere. John wanted to buy a house, but in the south house prices were rising so he decided they would move up to Durham once the baby was born.

I remember being at 22 when John rang to say Sharon had gone into labour. We were all so excited and stayed there waiting for John to come from the hospital. We were praying for them all. It was quite late when John burst into the back door and we all jumped up. Well? John's face was beaming. "I have a son," he said. We all hugged him and gave huge congratulations. It was an amazing night; Mam and Dad's first grandchild and my first nephew. He was going to be called Paul which we all thought was a fabulous name. He was an enormous baby and poor Sharon was exhausted, bless her. John kept saying, "I can't believe it. I'm a Dad!" We couldn't believe it either and we all sat and gave thanks to God for the safe delivery of Paul James Lancaster on 27 May 1976.

I went into work early to the hospital next morning and because I was in my uniform I just walked into the maternity ward and no one stopped me. I looked into the nursery where they wheeled all the babies' cribs. I looked through the window to see rows of cribs with tiny little bundles in them but there was one baby who looked enormous. He had white hair about an inch long and it stood out from his head like a loo brush. *That must be Paul*, I thought. He looked just adorable. I went into the ward and there was Sharon, bless her, and her eyes were bloodshot! That scared me somewhat. "How are you, darling?" I said. "Well done, you clever girl! He's beautiful." I asked her what it was like, giving birth. She told me she couldn't believe how painful it was, but as soon as she held Paul it was worth every pain! *Yeah, right*, I thought.

Sharon stayed in hospital for two weeks. John was busy getting the flat all spick and span for them both to come home and we all bought baby clothes and stuff for mighty Paul. Even Dad was excited to have a grandson. They settled into family life and I have memories of Sharon, tall, beautiful, long flowing hair, in her maxi skirt and white top, pushing her pram through Haywards Heath. She looked like such a glamorous hippy! It was the summer of '76 and it was a scorcher. Paul would be laid in the pram in just a nappy as it was so hot. She had a sunshade to keep him safe and she was so thrilled to be a mummy and loved her baby so much. It was lovely to see them so bonded.

When John was home, he was such a proud peacock. He held his boy like a pro. I think lugging Kayla around and all the foster babies had stood him in good stead! They stayed in Walstead for a while. I have a vague memory of Paul being very chesty, and Sharon wondered if the flat was damp. It smelled funny and she was always spraying air freshener. She thought maybe that was causing Paul's chestiness. I remember Sharon crying because they had moved their bed and underneath it was the most enormous mushroom\fungi at least 18 inches across! They needed to move!

John got in touch with Gran and Grandad and asked if they could stay with them for a while until they found a house. Yes they could and they were off! We were all sad to see them go but it was the only way they would get on the housing ladder. John soon found a job in Bishop Auckland, working for a kitchen and bathroom company. He took many courses in design, did his apprenticeship and then bought a house in Shildon and bought into a business! Lighting and kitchens. He had lots of blokes working for him and opened up more shops. He was doing really well. The house they bought was a two-bed terrace but John moved the stairs, knocked walls down, moved the bathroom and made it into a three-bed terrace. He was so clever, he could turn his hand to anything.

I went up and stayed with them for a couple of weeks after Daniel was born. I had dreadful postnatal depression and Sharon said, "Come up for a break," so I did. I took the children with me and it was so lovely to see them and spend time with them both. They were so lovely to me, making me feel very loved and cared for. Paul, Ben and Naomi played so well together too.

They had joined a church in Darlington and were very involved and made some lovely friends. Sharon was happy in the church but in truth she didn't enjoy life in Shildon. Paul was growing up and was chatting away, the family was growing but the house wasn't! It was here that Ben Kenneth Lancaster was born and two years later Stephen John Lancaster. Life was great for John, he was in his element, but Sharon longed to be back in Sussex. They put the house on the market but no joy. They were on the mailing list of several estate agents in Sussex but nothing went right. Then they got a list advertising a shop with a flat above in Ringmer and fell in love with it. Within six weeks they had sold their house, loaded up the van and were in the flat in Ringmer. We were all overjoyed to have them back!

Kenny was not doing so well. He had been up to no good. I can't remember what he had done but he was arrested and sent to a Borstal near Ashford. He was shell shocked! It was a really harsh regime: up at 5.30 every morning, running everywhere on the double, marching for hours, scrubbing floors, officers had to be addressed with 'Yes Sir!' or 10 press-ups if you forgot.

Greg and I went to visit and we were both shocked when we saw him. He had his hair very short, back and sides. He had loved his long hair but now it was gone. As we sat in the visitors room waiting for him, we noticed tall boys who had trousers three inches too short, short boys who had trousers too long and that were baggy and rolled up. Jumpers were the same. They all looked ridiculous but I guess that was the idea. Ken asked us to bring chocolate as they were allowed to eat treats on the visit but were not allowed to take any back into the dorm. It was lovely to see him but it made me sad. He hated this place, but in all honesty he looked better than he had done for a while. He had been smoking a lot of weed, popping pills and not eating. Now here he was, working hard, running everywhere, up early, to bed early.

The thing he hated most was no sugar in anything so when we sat with him and took the chocolate out he devoured in no time. This was between telling us how he hated this place. It was a short sharp shock and he only had a month more to serve so hopefully he would behave himself and maybe this would be a good thing. He certainly didn't want to come back here! We chatted and Kenny ate, then a screw blew a whistle and visiting time was over. Big hugs and "We love you Kenny. Keep your head down and it will soon be over." He looked like he was going to cry. As we left the hall, boys were running to and fro out in a yard. Kenny was not one to move quickly and this was definitely difficult for him, bless him.

He *did* behave himself and was home for my wedding. It makes me smile when I look at the wedding photos, because Ken is trying to hide behind everyone because of the hair—all gone!

I loved being married, it was wonderful. I thought God was brilliant for thinking it up! We loved being together and we couldn't wait to get home from work, shut the door of our flat and just be us. It felt like we were playing house, but we weren't, it was for real! I had a lot to learn about being a housewife. I was a rubbish cook but I was a tryer. I remember our first roast. I had no clue what to do with the chicken so when I read in my shiny new cookery book to cook for 25 minutes per pound I just cooked it for 25 minutes! It was raw. Then brussels sprouts. We never had them at home so I didn't know what to do with them until I saw an advertisement on the telly. I think it was a gravy ad but the mum brought the sprouts in a serving dish with a great knob of butter on top and placed them on the table. "That's it," I thought. So I put raw sprouts in a dish, put a knob of butter on and popped them in the oven for 10 minutes or so. They were black little bullets when I took them out. This wasn't going to be easy I thought. I guess Greg thought that too though he was always very relieved when he cut into whatever I had cooked and it wasn't bleeding.

He also thought I was a bit of an odd bod about food. I was fanatical about buying lots of tinned food and always having a store cupboard. I needed to know that we always had food in the house. I think it stemmed from always being hungry as a kid and there never being anything to eat. I still have a store cupboard to this day.

We laughed a lot, which was great. I had changed my job and was working at a children's home in the village. The staff were friendly and the manager was a lovely woman called Mrs Shepherd. She was so kind to me. Some lovely people worked there and I made a couple of good friends. One was Susie Grant, a motorbike riding nutcase, but we got on like a house on fire. She was brilliant with the kids and everyone loved her. She came back to the flat a few times and met Kenny. This was a relationship that would blossom! Even when Susie left her job and went to work in Tonbridge, the romance continued.

I thought Susie would be good for Ken. She too was from a Christian family, and was a rebelling Christian herself. She was not into drugs, which was a definite bonus, and she wanted to go to church, which she did when work permitted. Ken would go with her occasionally. I was really happy that Kenny was going out with her. I thought she was a good influence on him though I'm not sure her parents were too pleased. Who could blame them; he was really into drugs at this time.

Mrs Shepherd had asked me to do extra work which was great as we needed the money and I enjoyed working there. I was still cleaning, sometimes helping with the children, sometimes cooking, wherever I was needed. I had been there a few months, it was August and very hot. I was going home, walking through the village and I felt very sick suddenly. I ran up the flat stairs and just made it to the toilet. Very odd, I thought, maybe a bug I had picked up from work? There was always a child with a cold or something, so I never gave it another thought.

The chapel was booked into Pilgrim Hall, a Christian conference centre, and we were going. We were both really looking forward to it. It was to be a week of teaching and fellowship—another funny phrase I didn't understand but it just meant being together, getting to know one another. There was a swimming pool and beautiful grounds. It was lovely but now, with me being sick, Greg suggested I go to the doctor. We didn't want me to bring the whole church family down with a sickness bug so I went up to the surgery.

Back then, we just went and waited. Sometimes you went straight in, other times you waited ages. This was a straight in day. Doctor Davies asked me a few questions and then said, "Could you be pregnant?" I hadn't thought of that but, yes, I guess I could. So he asked me to take a sample up to the hospital. I was so thick, I didn't know what he meant.

"A sample of what?" I asked him. He chuckled and said a urine sample and gave me a little bottle with my name on. He told me to do it first thing in the morning. I couldn't wait!

When Greg came home I told him what the doctor had said. We were both very excited but scared. I took my sample up to the hospital and the doctor told me it would take a week from then. That was when we would be at Pilgrim Hall. It was such a long week. The morning came when we could phone the surgery for the results. I so vividly remember standing by the phone and my tummy was doing summersaults, I was so nervous. When the doctor said, "Congratulations, Fay. You are having a baby," I burst into tears with joy. Greg and I just hugged each other.

Greg wiped my face and said, "We're having a baby!" We couldn't wait to tell people and everyone was excited for us.

We were very involved in the chapel and attended every service. Mid-week prayer meetings were wonderful and we loved them. Sundays were just great. We were being taught so much about our Bible and our God and we had such a good grounding at Cuckfield for which we will be forever grateful.

Greg was working for American Express in Burgess Hill, just a few miles from where we lived, but there were no buses and neither of us could drive so we bought a second-hand (I think it was probably more like tenth-hand) bike and, bless him, he would cycle to and from work. Come wind, rain, snow, there was Greg on this battered old bike. I loved being home first, putting on the fire, getting our dinner ready and as soon as he came in the door, especially if it was raining, I was there with a towel. I would make him take off his wet clothes and wrap a warm towel around him, make him sit in front of the fire all wrapped up. I would make him a cuppa and we would sit safe and warm. It was so lovely; I couldn't believe this was my life. I just loved being me! I don't think either of us could have been any happier had we been millionaires—though it would have made travelling a lot more comfortable!

Poor Greg came home late one night. He said he had been stopped by the police and told not to ride his bike as it wasn't roadworthy! He said he was riding down Ansty Hill when a police car passed him. Then about halfway down the hill the same policeman stepped out into the road and indicated to Greg to stop. He couldn't. He pulled on his brakes and nothing happened and he flew past the policeman. Greg put his feet down onto the ground to slow himself down and the policeman was running behind him, shouting for Greg to stop. There were sparks flying from the segs in his shoes as he tried to stop.

Finally, he did and the policeman caught up with him, looked him straight in the eye and said, "You are having a laugh aren't you? You can't possibly expect me to say carry on mate." He then told him to get off and push it the rest of the way and not to ride it again till he got new brake pads. Poor Greg. He did buy new brake pads, bless him. It was all a question of money and things were very tight. As I was to learn, Greg always leaves things till the very last moment. Dad helped him fix the bike and make it roadworthy again.

Things at 22 were getting fraught. Kenny and Dad weren't getting on at all. Kenny and his mates had discovered drugs and were popping all kinds of pills at every opportunity which caused all manner of strange things to happen to him. Dad wasn't sure what was going on at the time but the one thing he did know was that Kenny wasn't working. How did he know? Because he was supposed to be working for him and, as he wouldn't get up in the mornings, Dad went to work without him.

Dad had started working for himself as a painter and decorator when he had first come home from prison. A lovely man at chapel, Graham Slegg, had given Dad a job. He really helped Dad in so many ways but by giving him a job in his building firm and a fresh start as a Christian, he helped us all and Dad learned how to be honourable in the workplace. Graham gave Dad respect and Dad gave it back in bucketfuls. He loved Graham and had a great working relationship as well as a friendship and no one was more devastated when Graham died during an operation.

Well, Kenny was working, or should I say *not* working, for Dad and Dad was furious. He had told Mam and us not to feed Kenny. He said, "If a man doesn't work he doesn't eat." It said that in Proverbs apparently, so we weren't to let Kenny help himself to any food. Poor old Kenny. He was always in trouble with Dad. It seemed like every time we went round to visit, Dad had Kenny pinned up against some wall or other trying not to hit him. He would be holding him by his throat and screaming into his face what a useless article he was. Kenny would be white with rage and as soon as Dad let go of him Kenny would be off out the door with Dad yelling at him to come back. Well, Kenny never came back.

Kenny Moves In

KENNY CAME DOWN TO OUR FLAT LATE ONE NIGHT. He was in a terrible state. Dad had hit him and he said he wasn't having it any more. He hated Dad so much. My heart ached for him. He hadn't eaten for a couple of days and was starving so I made him some sarnies and we all had a cuppa. We had an old single bed in the second bedroom so we said he could stay the night. He finished up living with us for months.

We had a few altercations while he was with us. Dad still insisted that Kenny worked for him and would arrive at the flat at 7.30 every morning to pick him up. It was my job to get Kenny out of bed, into his work gear, sandwiches made and Kenny bright and breezy out the door. What a job! I would start at 6.45 by waking him. "Yeah, right. I'm on my way." Again at 7.00 and so on until 7.20 when I would go in with a cold flannel, pull all his blankets off, slap the cold flannel on his back and drag his blankets out of the bedroom with me. He would swear and shout at me but he would be dressed and ready for Dad, sandwiches in hand, by 7.30. Ken would annoy me because I would make sandwiches for him to take to work. Then he wouldn't go, so I stopped making them. Occasionally he would leave me funny notes saying, 'Please make me some sarnies'. He would do funny drawings which made me laugh.

He had some lovely mates and they would come round in the evening and sit in his bedroom drinking and smoking until one evening I went upstairs and could smell 'Wacky Backy'. I threw open his door. The room was thick with smoke. I clambered over all of them and slammed open the window. It was an old sash window in a very old frame and as I slammed it down the entire frame fell out and smashed on the roof below. They were all shocked but not as much as I was. I told the mates to leave and NEVER smoke that in our flat again. They all looked very sheepish and left. Kenny was very mellow on his bed by the window. I gave him a mouthful and left his room.

That night it poured with rain and when I went in to wake Kenny the next morning he was saturated. His entire bed, pillow, blankets, the lot. The stupid stoned boy hadn't the brains to move his bed away from the hole where the window should be. One good thing was, for the first time ever he got up at 6.45. We had blankets all over the flat drying. Dad came and fixed the window for us. I never told him how and why it happened.

We had lots of things happen while Kenny was living with us, some funny, some sad. The saddest was when one of Kenny's mates, Ian Birdett (nicknamed Birdie) was killed on his motorbike. He was a lovely lad and would come to the flat a lot. He was very polite to me and Greg and he, Ken and another friend of theirs, Kevin, were always together. Kenny was in shock as we all were; Birdie was only 18. Kenny was very depressed and was moping around a lot; he went out one evening and didn't come home. I was worried about him.

The following day I got home from work, still no Kenny. Later that evening I went up to his room, just to check he hadn't come home and gone to bed, he wasn't there. I noticed a letter addressed to Mam and Dad on the cupboard by the door. My heart did a flip. I picked up the letter just as the doorbell rang. I thought it was probably Kenny and he had forgotten his key. I ran down and opened the door. It was Dad. We went back upstairs and I told Dad the whole story and showed him the letter. He opened it. The letter began:

Dear Mam and Dad, by the time you read this, I will be dead.

We were gutted, shellshocked, sick, weak and we both burst into tears. We read on. The letter went on to say how he felt a failure and how he had never been the son Dad wanted. Dad was visibly shaken. We went down into the lounge. We didn't know when he had written this letter and if he was already dead. We both knelt on the floor and just cried out to God to keep him safe, not let him do this awful thing, bring him home. Dad asked for forgiveness for being so hard on him. We pleaded with God from the bottom of our hearts for God to save him from himself and bring him home.

We must have prayed for about half an hour. We didn't know what else to do, when suddenly the lounge door opened and Kenny stood in the doorway with a very perplexed look on his face. We leapt to our feet. "Kenny," I shouted.

"Son," said Dad.

We were all just looking at each other and then Kenny said, "What am I doing here? I thought I was in the squat." Dad and I looked at each other in absolute wonder and to this day we believe that God brought him home in answer to our prayers.

Dad changed in the way he was with Kenny and stopped screaming at him so much. Kenny would bring all kinds of lads back to the flat. One night he had found a guy sitting on the pavement. He didn't know him from Adam but invited him up to the flat. We were in bed, oblivious to this, but in fact this guy had just robbed the grocery store and the clock makers. He then proceeded to take every penny I had in my purse and my fags! The cheek of him! I realised what had happened when I went into the grocery store to get a few bits, went to pay and everything, even the tenner I shoved in the back of my purse for emergencies, was gone. Very embarrassed, I put everything back and went home.

Ken had never taken money from me before, so I was shocked that he had— or I thought he had. Very indignant, he said, "I didn't take your money!" Well, who else could it be? Certainly not Greg. "Oh," said Ken, "it could have been that bloke I brought home with me!"

Later that morning, the police were in the high street questioning people if they had seen anyone late last night as both shops had been broken into. I made Ken tell them about the bloke and told them he had pinched my money too. I felt odd being on the other side of crime! They did catch the man and Ken and I had to go to court as witnesses. In fact Ken had moved into a squat in Haywards Heath with a girl, and on the morning we were to be in court I had to go to the squat and drag him out of bed. He was off his head and trying to get him to talk sense was a bloomin' nightmare! Thankfully, the bloke pleaded guilty so we didn't have to speak!

My tummy was growing and I was feeling so wonderful about this little baby growing inside me. I couldn't wait to be a mummy. We talked about how we would love this little one and give it all we could possibly afford. We thought about living in the flat and how would I get the pram up all the stairs. It was a funny carry-on really. The shop below the flat was divided into two shops; the front a butchers shop and the back a greengrocers. Each had their own door and to get to our flat we had to walk through the greengrocery part. It was awkward when there was a shop full of people and you had to shove your way through them. The thought of pushing a pram through was worrying. Also, we didn't have a washing machine because there was nowhere for it to go. I had to do the washing in the bath.

There was a small flat roof just outside the bathroom window so I had put a clotheshorse out there and would climb onto the toilet, then up onto the sill and squeeze sideways through this narrow little window. It was a lovely little suntrap out there and the clothes dried nicely. That was fine until one day I had shoved out the washing basket, climbed out, hung the clothes on the clotheshorse and, as I stood up straight, I felt my baby turn over. It was a lovely feeling, very reassuring. My tummy had completely changed shape and it looked like a torpedo. I smiled as I rubbed it. I shoved the washing basket back into the bathroom, slipped one leg through the window onto the bathroom windowsill, sat on the outside sill and tried to slide myself through the window. My tummy wouldn't go. Try as I might I couldn't get my torpedo through the window!

I began panicking and imagining I would be giving birth to my baby on the rooftop. Greg wouldn't be home for hours; what was I to do? I prayed, please God help me to get back in. I sat for quite a while, then I saw the bottle of shampoo on the window ledge. I reached in and got it. I thought that if I stripped down to my bra and pants and rubbed shampoo onto my tummy it might help me to slip through the window. Still I couldn't get in. I poured it down my back and more on my tummy. I sat sideways, one leg in the bathroom the other on the roof and I breathed out, held my breath and pushed my tummy. Slip—we were in! I was never more relieved to be back in our little flat. That was the last time I went out there. We both realised I couldn't keep doing that and we needed a garden and, once the baby arrived, a washing machine. All those nappies!

We went to see David Holden, our estate agent friend and talked about buying a house. He said he would keep us in mind for a place in Burgess Hill if anything came his way. Mrs Shepherd's daughter Janice and I were friends and she could drive. She would take me to look at various houses that we liked the look of; none of which we could afford. Then a house on Fairfield Road came up. It had been empty for a while and we went to see it.

It seemed huge after the flat. It had three bedrooms, an outside toilet and coal house and a lovely garden. Downstairs it had a lounge, dining room and a fair-sized kitchen *but* it had a lot of damp, a hole in the roof, the kitchen hadn't been modernised, it had a sink, a brick-built boiler in the corner of the room and a black stove called a 'Bungalow Belle'. It was a Victorian terrace and we loved it. The price was £7,000.

We found out we could get grants to do the bathroom and Dad said he would do all the work. We would have to do all the labouring to bring the costs down, so we decided to go for it. We prayed that if this was the one for us that we would get a mortgage. David told us if we were to get a mortgage they would need to take my wage into consideration and if they saw that I was pregnant they would realise I would have to stop working for a while at least so, when we went to apply for a mortgage, I wore a huge coat. I was sweltering but I daren't take if off. We got our mortgage!

Just before we left the flat Phil popped round to see us. I think I explained how the flat was above a butchers and greengrocers; they were one big shop divided in half but you could walk through from one shop to the other. The shop was now closed so when Phil rang the bell I dashed down the stairs through the shop, opened the shop door to let Phil in and ran back upstairs as I was cooking, leaving Phil to shut the door and follow me upstairs. What he actually did was to wander through the greengrocers, helping himself to grapes, then wandered through to the butchers, opened the freezer and picked up a duck.

At this point the bloke who owned the shop and the flat poked his head out of the office and asked Phil what he was doing. Phil nearly had a heart attack, not realising he had been in the office all this time. He blurted out a load of excuses, put the duck back and made his way upstairs. When he told me what had happened, I was furious with him. "You can't nick from the shop, Phil. I've told you before, we'll get chucked out!" He thought it was funny. Plonker!

The following day the landlord had words with us, saying my brothers were not allowed in the flat anymore! I was very glad to be able to say, "We will give you a month's notice then!," as we were buying a house—but we didn't tell him that! Both Ken and Phil told me after we moved out, that every time they walked through the shop, they would help themselves to fruit and the occasional piece of meat or a few sausages! The rat bags!

Fairfield Road and Naomi

WE BOUGHT 97 FAIRFIELD ROAD BUT WE COULDN'T LIVE IN IT until Dad had sorted out the roof. We couldn't afford to pay the mortgage and rent on the flat so we asked Mam and Dad if we could stay with them until 97 was liveable in. Mam didn't want us to move in with her but Dad persuaded her that it wouldn't be for long, so we moved back to 22 Glebe Road. Greg and I were in the front bedroom and Mam and Dad were in the boys' old room. Kayla was in the back room and, if I remember rightly, Maggy too. Dad had converted the loft into a bedroom, Kenny slept up there for a while and couldn't be bothered to come down the ladder to the loo so he took one of Dad's wellies up there! He very carefully put an old bed spring in it to keep it upright. I will leave the rest to your imagination!

It was fine being back home but Mam thought I had moved back so that I could be her housekeeper. She figured if we weren't paying any board she would make me work for our keep. I was still working full time and I would come home and get dinner ready for Mam, Dad, Maggy and Kayla. We weren't allowed to eat with them because we weren't paying for anything so we had to buy our own food, which was fine. I would then cook for Greg and me and Dad would run us both over to 97 to work on the house. We would be ripping stuff up, taking out Bungalow Belle and knocking down the brick boiler while Dad set about the roof. He said we needed to be watertight first. There were more holes than a colander so lots of new slates.

Dad worked hard and so did we and we made the front room liveable. There were rotten floorboards and damp in the bay window but once that was sorted we could make it comfortable. We had the chimneys swept and made coal fires all through the house just to dry it out a bit. We had no electric so we had candles everywhere until the electrician got us sorted. All this cost money and we were both doing extra hours. I got a cleaning job in a factory on the industrial estate in the evenings. It was hard work but brought in much-needed cash.

Greg had taken lots of our stuff over to the house and things were piled into the dining room. We hadn't even looked at that but the lounge was looking good. Dad got us lots of magnolia paint cheap so we painted it—not to Dad's standard but this was *our* home and we could do it however we liked.

We were given a tatty old carpet. It was the foulest colours, brown and orange swirls, but it *was* carpet so we put it down in our lounge. We got our cottage suite from the dining room and put up a lampshade and some brown curtains we got from a jumble sale. Things were looking good. We had to boil water for a cuppa in a saucepan on the fire as we still hadn't got the electrics all done. At weekends we would sleep at the house and Maggy and Kayla would arrive on Saturday with Mam and Dad and a couple of the foster children Mam looked after, so the house was full of people, all working and helping us get our home ready for our baby's arrival which was only weeks away.

We were both exhausted. I had finished working full time at the children's home so I was able to work on the house all the hours I could. Dad was working full time on it too so lots of progress was being made. We were now living there, the electric was on and it was wonderful. We had no kitchen and an outside loo but it was great. Dad had come up with the idea of knocking down the wall between the downstairs toilet and coalhouse which would make the kitchen huge. He would halve the back bedroom, making a small nursery bedroom and the other half would become a bathroom. Wonderful, but we had to get planning permission and these things all take time. My brother John was working at the kitchen shop still and he knew a chap who would do plans cheaper for us. Good old John! He got our bathroom suite cheaper for us too.

Well, all that was almost finished. I was hugely pregnant and Dad had built the bathroom but nothing was plumbed in yet. Dad had knocked the walls down in the kitchen. It was a very cold winter, too cold to be going outside to the loo in the night. The loo was now right next to the kitchen sink—very hygienic—so for a little privacy we had put hooks into the ceiling and hung a candlewick bedspread in a sort of tube around the toilet so that when you were sat on the loo you could poke your face out of the tube and chat to whoever was doing the washing up or the cooking. It was a very friendly arrangement until one Saturday morning I had rushed down to the 'tube' completely starkers when the doorbell rang. Greg came down in his dressing gown to answer it. As he opened the door a huge gust of wind blew along the corridor into the kitchen and blew down the tube! There I was, hugely pregnant, starkers, sat on the toilet in the middle of the kitchen and the milkman was staring straight at me over Greg's shoulder. I was mortified and I told Greg we would have to change our milkman as I couldn't face him again. Greg said not to bother as he wouldn't recognise me if he saw me again because he wasn't looking at my face!

It was March 1977 and our baby was due on 14 April. I went for an appointment at Cuckfield Hospital and after my examination, the doctor asked me if twins were in my family. "Yes, my Mam is a twin," I answered.

"Well, I think you might be carrying twins." I was gobsmacked. TWINS! My head was in a spin. He said I would have to have an x-ray and booked me in for the following day. I was in shock. I told Greg when he got home. He was excited and thought it would be OK and we would manage but he wasn't the one who would have to give birth to two babies! I couldn't sleep, it was a long night. I arrived at the hospital looking dreadfully tired and went for my x-ray. I waited outside the x-ray room and the radiographer came out with my x-ray in her hand. "Excuse me, can you tell me if it's one or two babies in there please." She lifted up the x-ray and there, in my tummy, was this perfect little skeleton of ONE perfect little baby. I was elated but I think Greg was a little disappointed.

We got a lift to chapel with a lovely couple who also lived in Burgess Hill, Ebb and Rene Tingly. Rene was almost as excited as I was about our new baby's arrival. We were going to chapel one Sunday morning when Ebb said, "It's a shame your baby isn't due before 6 April because if it was you would get all that year's tax back." Neither Greg nor I had known that. Mam told me if I wanted to start my labour off I should drink cod-liver oil so on 28 March I drank two bottles of the wretched stuff and a bottle of liquid paraffin. I was on the loo virtually all day. I had gone to 22 to be near the hospital because neither of us could drive and I didn't fancy having my baby in the back of a taxi.

I was on the loo all night too and in the morning, sure enough, I went into labour. We waited till my contractions were every five minutes then went up to the hospital. I was taken into the labour ward and examined. Then I was told to have a bath. Then a nurse came and shaved me and I don't mean my chin. What an indignity! Men have it so easy! I was shown to a bed and told to time my contractions. It was around 2 am when they stopped. I slept really well and when the nurse came to see me after breakfast, she said the doctor was coming on her rounds later and would probably send me home. She can't do that, we need that tax money to pay for our kitchen to be done! When the doctor arrived at my bed, she had a trainee doctor with her. They stood and discussed me as if I wasn't there and then said, "You have two more weeks to go. It seems it was a false alarm so you can go home."

I said, "As I'm in here can't you just induce me and get it over with?"

The trainee jumped in saying, "I would love to induce her."

Thank you Lord and thank you lady, I thought.

So I was induced on 1 April. I didn't really want my baby to be born on April Fool's Day but beggars and all that! It wasn't a pleasant experience but at least now it wouldn't be long. How wrong can you be? I was in labour for the whole day and night and Naomi Louisa Summers was born on 2 April 1977 at 11.33 am. We were elated, she was beautiful and I loved her instantly. She was ours, no one would take her away from us. It seemed unreal. The midwife who delivered her was a trainee but was supervised by Faith Evans who was a friend from chapel, so it was such a lovely thing to be able to thank God for a safe delivery of our beautiful healthy baby despite what I realise now was a very stupid thing to do.

I was taken back to the ward with my baby in a little see-through crib which was wheeled next to me. I was so tired but I wanted to hold her. I picked her up and looked into the most beautiful little face I had ever seen. My heart was full of love for this tiny little bundle. I put her to my breast and she fed. I felt wonderful, I was a mummy and Greg was a daddy. I couldn't wait to go home so we could be a little family.

A whole new life began for all three of us that day, not just Naomi. We had to learn to be parents and we didn't have a clue what we were doing. That afternoon visiting time arrived. I was exhausted but everyone wanted to see this new little girl. Greg had gone back to Mam and Dad's and told everyone. He rang his Mam and Gran and Grandad; everyone was excited. I sat in my bed with my beautiful baby in my arms and everyone pressing in to look at her. I handed her to Greg. He looked so awkward as he held his daughter in his arms but his face was filled with love and pride as he showed off his baby. Everyone left except Greg; he sat by my bed holding Naomi and he looked up at me and said, "Isn't she beautiful. I can't believe she's ours." I was relieved to know he felt the same.

My locker was straining under the weight of flowers and cards. People were so kind and we had lots of pressies of clothes and stuff for Naomi. We all felt very loved.

My Gran and Grandad came down from Durham to see me and I just burst into tears. My Gran gave me the biggest hug—and she's not a hugger—so it meant so much. Granddad went straight to the cot. "Eee, she's a picture, lass," he said and then came to me and gave me the sloppiest kiss. I felt so proud.

We were kept in the hospital for a week and, to be honest, I was quite glad of the rest. When it came to leaving I was very nervous. I had looked after Kayla when she was a baby and I loved her but I hadn't even cuddled a baby since then, so taking this darling baby home and not having a nurse on hand to ask how to do this or why is she doing that, was worrying.

Greg made the front room so warm and cosy; he had lit the fire and been stoking it all day. He had bought a second-hand electric radiator and put it in our bedroom alongside the little crib we had been given. He had thought of everything, bless him.

It was lovely being a little family but it also felt weird. Naomi seemed to fit in perfectly; she was the most beautiful baby ever. We just sat and stared at her and when bedtime came we were all shattered. Such an emotional day, we all went up together. I fed Naomi and put her into her crib and we sat on the bed and just gave thanks to God for our little girl. We asked for wisdom, patience and love as we began this whole new life together as three. We were both worried we wouldn't hear her in the night but there was no need to worry. We heard her every time she moved, let alone cried.

We soon settled into a routine, my little girl and me. I loved being a mummy. I adored her and she was such a good baby, which was wonderful as we were still working on the house every time she slept. I was either painting, rubbing down or piling stuff into the skip. The health visitor would call regularly to check all was well with the pair of us. I used to pray she wouldn't ask to use the bathroom; I would have had to show her to the 'tube'. I was so relieved when the bathroom was finally finished.

Being a mother churned up all sorts of emotions and worries in me. I loved my little Naomi so much but I was scared; scared of being like my Mam. They say you learn to be a mummy by watching your mummy. Well, I certainly didn't want to do to my little Naomi what was done to me. I prayed so much that I wouldn't be like her. Also, now that I was a mummy, the feelings of love and protection towards Naomi that filled me was sometimes overwhelming. I would just watch her sleeping and I would be filled with such love for her I would cry.

I vividly remember the first time Greg changed Naomi's nappy—not disposable ones, proper terry towelling nappies. He had watched me do it many times, so I was confident he could do it. I laid her on the changing mat, folded the nappy for him and left him with her. I went into the kitchen as I thought I would make him nervous. I was getting on with dinner when I heard a piercing scream from Naomi! I ran into the lounge and saw Greg looking worried. "What happened?" I asked.

"I don't know," he said. Her little legs were pulled up and she was proper crying. I looked at the nappy and saw that the pin was in. I felt the nappy and tried to push my hand down behind the pin. I found I couldn't and took out the pin. He had pierced her belly! He hadn't put his finger behind the pin when he pushed it through the nappy! I was panicking and Greg was panicking, Naomi had stopped crying but she had two little pin holes in her belly! I was crying. I was terrified Greg had pierced her intestines.

So scared, I phoned my midwife who said to put a dab of antiseptic on the holes and she would be fine. "This happens a lot with new dads!" she said. Terrifying! So my Naomi had her belly pierced long before it became fashionable, bless her. Needless to say, Greg was terrified to try again, but he did and always remembered to put his fingers behind the pin!

It made me think about my childhood and I just couldn't understand how Mam could have treated us the way she did. Why didn't she protect me? Why was she so cruel and unkind? Why didn't she love me like I loved my baby? Didn't she ever feel that overwhelming love that I felt? I worried that I might be like her. I was aware that Mam and Dad's genes were in me but I was determined not to do as they had done.

I would pray morning and night that I, we, would be good parents and we did do our very best, learning as we went along. I would watch other people with their kids to see how 'normal' parents reacted. We learned as she grew that we could do this, we could be the best parents Naomi could ever need. We loved her and enjoyed just playing with her. Hearing her giggle was wonderful. We were a happy little family but becoming a mummy did something in me; it made me look back and I found it hard to deal with issues I had just pushed deep down inside me. I had never talked about my childhood to anyone. I had just touched on it with Greg but because Mam and Dad were Christians it seemed wrong of me to talk about it, dredging up the past but I had things that needed to be dealt with in me. When I became a Christian I had poured out my heart to God but there were things that I hadn't even spoken about to Him. I continued to push them down, unable to deal with them right now. I just needed to concentrate on my baby and my husband. There would come a time when I would be able to face it all, but not yet.

We started on the kitchen next. Dad said the whole floor needed to come up so he could put in a new damp proof course so Greg would work in the evenings with a sledgehammer smashing it up and the next day I would fill buckets with rubble and carry them outside. No taking it easy now the baby was here!

Well, the new floor was down, Dad painted this gooey black damp proof stuff all over it and halfway up the walls. He said it would be a waterproof membrane and we would be perfectly dry in the previously damp kitchen. When it was finished we went out of the back door, walked round to the front door to come in as this stuff had to be perfectly dry before it was walked on or the membrane would be broken and it would all have to be done again.

We were sat in the lounge when Greg walked in from work. "Hello darling, hiya da," he said. We both smiled and he bent and gave me a kiss, his face was cold.

"We didn't hear you come in," said Dad.

Greg said, "I came in the back door." He smiled and sat next to me.

Dad leapt to his feet. "You did what?" he screamed. Greg didn't know what he had done. We both went to the kitchen door and, sure enough, there were footprint-shaped holes in the membrane. I thought Dad was going to hit Greg, he was so mad. Greg kept saying he was sorry but Dad wasn't listening, he just kept shouting at Greg. "Didn't you see it was wet?"

But Greg hadn't and even if he had, he would have still walked on it I am sure because he just doesn't think in a practical way as I have learned over the years. He is the most impractical man I know and having all these practical brothers around me I found it very hard to believe he was that impractical—but he really is!

The membrane had to be done again. Dad did it the following day. I kept out of his way. Naomi was a good reason not to be on hand to be told over and over what a plonker Greg was.

It was such a difficult time for us, having Dad in our home every day. We knew he was there to help us get things done and was probably cheaper than having a building firm do all the work but he would have a go at us for not doing things as he wanted and it was like walking on eggshells a lot of the time. We would panic as to when he would put in his bill for money that we didn't have! When he finally finished we had to get a bank loan to pay him and the awful thing was he did lots of things the way *he* wanted, not the way we asked him to do them.

We had to get a plasterer in to do the kitchen walls because Dad couldn't plaster. The kitchen was just a shell now; floor all finished, walls all plastered but we didn't have any kitchen units and couldn't afford any. John got us a sink unit and one double floor unit and two wall units from an old kitchen he was replacing. He was still working for the kitchen shop and we were thrilled with them but they looked lost in this huge kitchen. Still, we thought in time we would be able to afford a proper fitted kitchen.

Burnt Chips

KAYLA HAD COME OVER TO STAY FOR A COUPLE OF DAYS. She loved playing with Naomi and she reminded me of how I was when she was born. It was lovely to watch them together. Well, Greg would normally get home at 5.30 from work. I was working in the evenings cleaning a factory and would start at 6.00 so Naomi would be fed and having a nap. We would be like ships passing in the night; he would walk in and I would walk out. It got to 5.45 and he still wasn't home. I knew if I didn't leave I would be late for work. As it was I would have to run all the way to the factory.

I said to Kayla, "Don't wake the baby and don't cook anything till Greg gets home. He should be home soon!" She promised. I just made it to work on time, got everything done and walked home. As soon as I walked into the house, I was greeted by a very dirty Kayla with a tear-streaked face crying, "I'm so sorry, Fay, I really am" and the terrible smell of burning.

My first thought was Naomi. "Where's Naomi?" I said, my heart pounding.

"She's asleep, she's fine," said Greg. He looked awful.

"What's happened?" I asked. Kayla sobbed and walked down the corridor to the kitchen. When she pushed open the door, my heart sank, it was soot-black from the floor to the ceiling. My cooker knobs were all melted, the kettle too. The kitchen units were completely black and all the Formica fronts were curling off. The worktop was lifted and bubbled, the windows were cracked, the paintwork on the frames and doors was black and blistered.

"What happened?" I asked. Through sobs and tears, Kayla told me that she thought she would surprise Greg and cook him some chips for when he got home so she put the chip pan on, turned it up high and went to the loo. On her way she picked up a magazine and she totally forgot about the chip pan! Greg had arrived home and opened the kitchen door just in time to take the empty chip pan off the cooker. It had burnt out. He opened the back door to let out the smoke and surveyed the damage. Even the light bulb had melted!

It was a terrible mess and everything was covered in a film of black grease. I wanted to scream at Kayla, "I told you not to do any cooking till Greg got home" but I didn't. She looked such a sad sight, her little face all tear-stained. I knew she didn't mean to do it but that's not to say I didn't want to strangle her!

I said, "As long as Naomi is OK. It could have been so much worse. We can clean this mess up. Stop crying."

She threw herself at me and wrapped her arms around me, sobbing some more. She just kept saying, "I really am sorry, Fay."

"I know," I kept saying. "Now let's get this place cleaned up." We started at 9.00 and went to bed at 3 am and we had hardly touched it. We just couldn't shift the grease. When Dad arrived the next morning, he couldn't believe his eyes. Poor Kayla thought she was going to get a thrashing but I told Dad I had dealt with it and to leave her alone. He ignored her all day. I felt so sorry for her and kept telling her it was OK but she kept going upstairs and crying.

We had to take our lovely kitchen units down to the tip and Dad replaced the glass in the windows. We had to throw out all the food that was in packets because they had black bits in. John got us two more units but, unlike the other two, they didn't match, but they were functional.

Dad gave us some stuff to put into the hot soapy water we were washing the walls with and it did seem to get the grease off but it took days. We worked day and night to get the kitchen back to square one before Gran and Grandad saw it. They were coming to stay with us and we wanted everything shipshape but we had so much to do. We got second-hand knobs from the tip and a new kettle. We had to get the electrician in to replace the melted wiring to the light bulb. It was a bloomin' nightmare! The walls looked disgusting with sort of mucky grey streaks. We had a huge tin of the brightest orange paint. We had been given it and never imagined using it but it was all we had that had any chance of covering the mess. It took four coats until finally we could no longer see the mucky grey grinning through but it was like being inside a tangerine! At least it was clean. Poor Kayla never forgave herself for this and would apologise every time she came over. "It's done darling", I would say. "It's gone and forgotten."

Kayla was 14 when she became a Christian. A visiting preacher came to Cuckfield and spoke about how Jesus loved each one of us. She thinks his name was Geoff Saunders. Anyway, what he said had a real impact on her and when she went home and went to bed she asked Jesus to forgive her and love her. She said there were no flashing lights, no fireworks; just a lovely sense of acceptance and peace. A lifelong relationship began and she was baptised in the Albermarle in Haywards Heath. Mam and Dad had started going there since Dad got stroppy with Errol for telling him he needed to come back to chapel instead of being off all over the place preaching and sharing his testimony. He needed to be built up, not giving out all the time. Errol could see this was not good for Dad; his ego was taking over. "How dare he tell me what to do," said Dad and they left. Wrong move!

Kayla got a job at 16 working at Mill Hall School too. She left home and lived in fabulous freedom, working there for a couple of years. Then she got a moped and a job in a nursing home, Compton House in Lingfield. She has such a caring heart and nothing fazes her. It was while she was working there that the matron recognised that she definitely had a gift for nursing and told her she should train to be a nurse. So as soon as she turned 18 she started training at St Francis Hospital and moved from living with mum and Dad into Linden House nurses' quarters and she loved it! Stuart got a job at the hospital too as a kitchen assistant and he lived with his drum kit in the men's quarters.

Mam was so jealous of Kayla. She had worked in nursing homes for many years but had never trained as a nurse, although she always told people she *was* a nurse. Once she went on a first aid course funded by the nursing home. We had popped in to see them just as she returned. "What have you been up to?" we asked.

"I've been on a training course and learned all about resuscitation."

"Oh," I said. "Tell us!"

She said, "When giving mouth to mouth, first you press three times really hard on their scrotum." We all fell about laughing!

Greg said, "Well, that would definitely make you take a sharp intake of breath!"

"Sternum. I mean Sternum."

"Too late, Mam," we said, but the worrying thing was she convinced herself she *was* a nurse and she would convince employers too.

Kayla was brilliant and passed her nurse's training. In truth, I think she only did it to prove she could. Mam and Dad were really proud of her, as we all were, and she worked as a staff nurse at St Francis Hospital for about a year.

We settled down again to family life at Fairfield Road. All the major work done, the cosmetic stuff could wait until we could afford it and now it was just the three of us. I loved it. I loved Greg and I loved our baby so life was wonderful. We were both working hard and any overtime was gratefully received. We were on a very tight budget so when Maggy asked to decorate her flat I jumped at it as she would pay me £10 per room. So I would catch the bus to Haywards Heath. She lived in Wilmington Way which was quite a way from the station. I would walk down, work all day hanging wallpaper or painting, pray Naomi would be good, (which, bless her, she usually was), get back home by 5.00 and get Naomi fed and organised. Greg would come in and I would go out to work. I started to ride his moped to work so that made life a little easier. It was all very tiring but we were young and strong and coped with it very well. We felt extremely blessed and were constantly thanking God for the way our lives were going. He was a great God and very good to us.

Maggy would come over and stay with us most weekends. She had a budgie called Jasper Carrot and an old Staffordshire bull terrier called Barney, a lovely old dog. Naomi was fascinated by him and would giggle and clap her hands every time she saw him.

Naomi was growing and we were enjoying every little thing she did. She had begun to crawl—a sort of commando crawl. It was so funny to watch her, it was like she was on a covert mission. We still didn't have carpet in the hall or on the stairs and, now Naomi was crawling, that was a priority. There was no way we could afford new carpet. But everything we had was second-hand so that wasn't a problem. But where do you get second-hand stair carpet?

We were at my brother John's church one Sunday evening when a chap came up to us and said, "John tells me you need a stair carpet."

"Yes," I said, "we do."

"Will you be in tomorrow at about 3.00?" he asked.

"Yes I will," I replied. His name was John Upton and he had a furniture shop in Haywards Heath. He came to our house with several carpet sample books. They were Axminster and about a yard square, just the width of our corridors and stairs. He gave us all these sample books which were great and we began sorting them into colours and shades. We started at the front door, went along to the kitchen and up the stairs. They were a perfect fit for one stair and one riser. We used ten tins of tacks nailing these lovely squares down and they looked brilliant.

Poor Naomi was always catching her tights on a tack but at least she wasn't getting splinters in her knees and, boy, it was much warmer, though the only really warm rooms were the sitting room where we had a coal fire and Naomi's room. We couldn't afford central heating and we would argue whose turn it was to light the fire. I hated doing it and it was so nice when Greg had made it to come down from the cold of the bedroom into the warmth of the lovely cosy sitting room.

Naomi was fifteen months old and had been walking for quite a while. She needed somewhere to run around. Our friends Jacky and Eddie lived just along the road and they had a daughter just slightly younger than Naomi called Victoria. They would quite often ask if we would like to go with them when they were going out in the car. I would jump at the chance to get out of Burgess Hill. On one of these outings I started to feel sick and Eddie had to stop the car to let me out. It dawned on me that I could be pregnant. I went to the doctor and I was! We were thrilled. I wanted lots of babies and I wanted them close together so this was perfect though extremely tiring.

Greg came home one evening and said, "You'll never guess what has happened at work. They have transferred me to Uckfield." I was stunned. We had bought our house in Burgess Hill because that was where Greg worked and now they were moving him! I didn't even know where Uckfield was. Greg said it was a bit more money and he was happy to drive there and back on his trusty little moped. That was fine in the summer but when autumn and then winter arrived, bless him, I was always praying for his safety and when he was late home I would be so worried that he had had an accident.

We started working in our little garden. It was just a tiny plot. Greg planted some vegetables and it was so exciting watching them grow. But now Naomi was on the move, there was nowhere for her to play so we decided once the veg had finished we would lay it to lawn. We were keen to get the garden sorted so she could play out there.

Then the semi-detached house across the road came up for sale. It was much bigger than our house with a huge garden. We thought if we could buy it then all the work would have already been done. It had a lovely kitchen and there was still quite a bit to do on ours. Well, we went to look at it and fell in love with it. We loved the garden and could just imagine Naomi and our new baby enjoying it as they grew up. We came home, looked at our finances, prayed about it and asked God to open the door for us if this was the right thing to do, or close it if it wasn't.

We put our house on the market and in the first week a couple who were in tied accommodation said they wanted it. Wonderful. We put an offer on the house over the road and it was accepted! We started to pack up our things and we waited for everything to happen but nothing did. It was January 1979 and I was now six months pregnant. I decided to pop over and see the chap who seemed to be holding everything up. He was very embarrassed and said he had changed his mind and didn't want to sell now! I was devastated. I rang Greg in floods of tears and told him. He was very calm and said, "Well, we asked God to close the door if it wasn't right. Looks like he has slammed it shut." The big problem was, the people who were buying our house had given in their notice on *their* house so we couldn't pull out, I felt dreadful and I cried a lot.

We had to find another house, and quickly. The people buying ours had to be out of their accommodation by the end of March. We rang lots of estate agents and they sent us details of several houses, none of which we liked the look of. Then Greg came home from work with details of a house in Uckfield. It hadn't even entered my head to move to Uckfield. We were settled in Burgess Hill, my family were local, our church was just two miles up the road and all our friends were here. We prayed that God would lead us.

Our friends Eddie and Jackie said they would take us to look at this house so we made an appointment with the agent and went. The house was on an estate; a three-bed semi-detached with a small garden back and front. Everything we saw we loved. It had a huge conservatory which would be great for a playroom for our growing family. We both knew right there that this was the house for us. We went straight to the estate agent and put in an offer. It was now late January. Everything went full steam ahead and we moved into 18 Nevill Road on 9 March 1979.

It was such a hectic day. Dad and John helped us move. John told us to hire a van and he would drive it, bless him, which we did. John picked it up and arrived at Fairfield Road where he and Greg loaded it up while I was cleaning. Maggy came over with Dad and helped clean too. It was pouring with rain! John, Dad and Greg had the van loaded—bish, bash, bosh as John kept saying. Then a cuppa, then a sweep through, making sure we had left nothing and that everything looked spick and span. All our worldly goods were stuffed in the van and we were off to our new home. It only took one trip as we didn't have very much stuff. John and Greg in the van and Mag, me and Naomi in Dad's Volvo.

The people who had bought our house asked us if we were leaving the carpets. Yes, we certainly were! We had put so many carpet tacks in them they were never going to come up! It was pouring with rain the day we moved but we didn't care, we were so excited. This was definitely the right house for us and we both felt we had come home.

Dad, John and Greg put everything in place and we all sat and had a cuppa. Then we gave thanks to God for the way he had brought us here and we prayed that our home would be blessed by Him and would be a place where our babies would grow happy and healthy and love would abound. I knew this would be the place where we would have the rest of our family and we wouldn't move. As a kid I had moved so many times, made and lost friends, gone to so many schools. Now I wanted my children to live in one place, to feel safe and secure, go to one school, make and keep friends, to call this place home and love it.

Putting Down Roots

WE SOON SETTLED INTO THIS LOVELY HOUSE. Naomi thought this through-lounge was brilliant. She would just run the length of the room, back and forth, giggling. We put all her toys in the conservatory, it was wonderful. And Greg was just ten minutes from work, brilliant. Our chapel had a sister church in Barcombe and we had been given the pastor's phone number. Greg rang him and asked the times of the services and also asked if anyone else came from Uckfield who could possibly give us all a lift. Praise the Lord! Yes. There was a man who lived just around the corner from us called Basil. Greg rang him and, bless him, he said he would be very pleased to take us and bring us home every week.

So the first Sunday after moving in, Basil stopped outside our house and we all piled into the back of his van. Not the most comfortable of rides when you are hugely pregnant but beggars can't be choosers and we were very grateful for this lovely man and his van. We arrived at this tiny chapel and when you first went in the smell of damp hit you. I had never seen or heard an organ like the one they had there. The man playing it had to pump it with his feet before a sound would come out so the notes were peppered with a wheezing sound as he peddled what I think were bellows. It sounded like it was having a musical asthma attack! We were made to feel so welcome. There were about thirty in the congregation and we were invited out to dinner the following Sunday by a lovely couple called Dick and Betty Cottingham.

We all came to love this dear couple and their family. They were a very big part of our new church family; the congregation made up of about ten families and their children and a few singles. We loved it and very soon felt like we belonged.

One Sunday Naomi was being rather noisy so I took her out into what was loosely called crèche. It was really just the porch as there was nowhere else to go except outside. There I met Simon Petit and his baby daughter Emily. He had the biggest grin and the loudest laugh I have ever heard. He was trying to change

Emily's nappy on the floor of the porch. She wriggled and giggled and it took him ages but finally he won. He picked her up, gave her a big kiss, plonked her on his knee, breathed a big loud sigh and said, "Boy, we don't want to do that again for a while" and gave a big laugh. I liked him instantly. He introduced us both to Emily and told us he was married to Lindsay and that he was a young teacher at the Community College. I thought he would be great fun as a teacher. After the service I met Lindsay and warmed to her instantly. They lived in one of the farm cottages in Barcombe and we were to become great friends.

On 19 April 1979, Daniel Edward Summers arrived. He was beautiful. We had both secretly wanted a son and here he was. We counted all his fingers and toes. He was perfect. How blessed we were. His little face looked up at mine and it was love at first sight. I had worried because I loved Naomi so much I didn't think I could possibly love another baby as much as I loved her, but I did. I didn't realise how a mother's love grows. It grows as your family grows and it's wonderful. God taught me so much about love through my little Danny. He really was the sweetest natured little man and Greg was as proud as a peacock of his growing family.

Naomi was such a darling. She came into hospital to see her new little brother. She sat on the bed next to me and I placed Daniel in her arms. She kissed his head and told him she loved him and she was his big sister. Greg and I were grinning from ear to ear. This was our family, these were our children, it was a dream come true. I felt so happy. We were inundated with cards, flowers and presents from family and friends and after just two days in hospital Danny and I were home.

I fed my tired little baby and Naomi and I took him upstairs and put him in his crib. He was a little grizzly but we both came downstairs in the hope he would soon nod off. I went into the kitchen and put the kettle on. Greg was fussing around telling me to sit down, he would make a cuppa, when we both realised Daniel had stopped grizzling. We smiled at each other, took our cuppa and headed for the lounge when Greg said, "Where's Naomi?"

Just at that moment, she shouted from upstairs, "He was crying, mummy." I was up and into the hall in a flash only to see Naomi standing on the top stair holding Daniel by his neck with his little floppy body dangling! My heart lurched into my mouth. I knew that if I sounded the slightest bit cross, she might drop him. "Good girl," I said in the calmest voice I could muster as I leapt up the stairs three at a time and scooped this floppy baby out of her hands. My heart was racing with panic.

Daniel took a huge gulp of air, then let out the loudest scream. It was music to our ears! We all came downstairs and had a cuddle. Both Greg and I were shaking with relief. We decided then that Daniel's crib would be wherever we were and told Naomi that only mummy and daddy could pick him up, at least until he was a bit more robust.

It's amazing just how much extra work one little baby is. I thought it would be much easier the second time around but I was wrong. Once we were home I just went under. I couldn't cope and I felt I was drowning. I didn't sleep well even though Daniel was a good baby. I found everything overwhelming. The midwife said it was baby blues but I knew different. I had been a bit weepy a few days after Naomi was born but that was nothing like this. I found everything difficult and I wanted to go to bed and just stay there. I didn't want to do anything. It was like someone had pulled my energy plug out.

Poor Greg didn't know what to do with me but he was brilliant with the children. He would come home at lunchtime and get Naomi's lunch ready only to find me sat in the same place I was when he left for work. I would be crying because I felt dreadfully guilty for feeling the way I did. When he got home at night he would bath Naomi and organise dinner. I am sure he was dreadfully worried about me. This went on for quite a few months. Poor little Daniel didn't get half the attention he should have got and Naomi was constantly asking me, "What's wrong, mummy? Why are you crying?"

Eventually, the doctor was called and he said I had postnatal depression and prescribed me some antidepressants. He explained that my body wasn't producing enough serotonin so I couldn't function properly and the antidepressants would put the balance right. I don't understand why it is but I felt I was a complete failure as a mummy, a wife and as a Christian. I felt I had let everyone down, God included. What a rubbish Christian I was. Aren't we supposed to be victorious? But here I was in such a mess having to take these pills.

The doctor looked at me and said, "If you were a diabetic you would have to take insulin and no one worries about taking insulin. Well, it's just the same sort of thing. Why people have such a problem with this is beyond me." As he said that it was as if a light had gone on in my head. He was right.

He left the prescription with Greg and explained that it wouldn't be an instant thing but would take up to four weeks for me to be feeling the benefit of the pills. Greg went straight down to the chemist, I started taking them as soon as he got back and within two weeks I was beginning to feel better. I began sleeping better and in just under a month I felt as if a black cloud had lifted off me and I had my life back. I thanked God so many times for those pills.

My dear little Daniel was such a good baby which was just as well because he hadn't had half the attention and love he should have had but, boy, I made up for lost time. We played and cuddled and bonded. It was wonderful and Naomi, bless her little heart, kept asking me, "Are you going to cry again mummy?" She would kiss and cuddle me and it was a while before she realised mummy was well again. Greg was so relieved. He told me he worried that it was all his fault for us moving to Uckfield and leaving all our friends, neighbours and family so close to giving birth. Poor man, he had coped all on his own with all of us and worked as well. He was wonderful. I felt so blessed to have this lovely man.

This was the last summer before Naomi would start school and I wanted it to be special. We had no money for holidays but we would make a picnic and take a carload of kids down to Treasure Island in Eastbourne, or have lovely long sunny days on the beach at Seaford. We would have the best times, the kids loved it, and it cost nothing. The kids were happy and healthy and it was fabulous.

We were so excited for Naomi as she was so looking forward to starting school. My babies were growing up and she was leaving playgroup. In the last week they had a party, a fancy dress party. Such things were really important to me because as kids we had never been to anything like that. No parties at all, let alone a fancy dress party! So I wanted my kids to do everything going! I thought about her fancy dress outfit. Naomi was such a tomboy, not at all a girly girl. I guess that was to do with having only Dan to play with until Becky came along. Anyway, I asked her what she wanted to be. "A punk rocker!" she said. "Do you really?" I asked. "Yes mummy I do. I really do." So I set to, sewing zips all over her jeans, attaching chains and a leopard skin bum flap, ripped tee shirt, and green food dye for her hair. I piled it all up and made it into a Mohican, sprayed it rigid with hair spray and food dye. She looked fabulous! We all went to the party. The fancy dress was to be judged by Bill Peters, the local vicar. There were ballerinas, lots of clowns, Cinderellas, pirates, cats, and then there was Naomi. She was thrilled when she won and so was I. My kids were going to have normal lives, do normal stuff, experience fun stuff, and not be the odd ones out!

The vicar gave her prize and said she looked fantastic. Then he laughed, saying he hoped I hadn't started something I would regret.

I couldn't wait to tell Greg but I had to keep my trap shut because Naomi was bursting to tell her daddy she was the winner! And that she was going to be famous because the local paper had been there and taken her photo. She was the first one in my family to be in the paper for something good! I was *so* proud of us.

I had been saving my pennies because it was so important to me that she had everything she should have for school: uniform, PE kit, shoes and plimsolls. We had been to buy it all and when she put it on she looked so tiny, far too small to be going to school! Her little face was a picture as she ran to look at herself in the mirror. She was tickled pink at how grown-up she looked.

Starting School

A SILLY THING THAT WAS AS IMPORTANT AS THE CLOTHES TO ME were the name tags. As a kid I always thought they were lovely. It was *your* name on *your* clothes. It meant you were somebody and you belonged to somebody. I used to rip them out of other people's clothes when I stole them. I always wanted my name on my clothes. It never happened but, by golly, it would for my kids. I took great delight in sewing Naomi's name on all her school clothes.

The morning of her first day at school arrived and we were up with the lark. She was so excited, jumping up and down and saying, "I'm a big girl. I'm going to school!" It was a bit of a rush to get us all dressed, fed and out of the door by 8.45—we would have to improve our routine—but we did manage it. We walked to Manor Park Primary School and made our way down into the playground. All the new reception children were carrying their new PE bags. Naomi's big girl song had stopped and she was holding onto my hand very tightly. Danny was in the buggy and when the whistle went and the teacher told us to take the children into the classroom, Naomi look at me with a worried look on her little face. 'Oh dear', I thought, 'she's going to cry'.

We all went in and found the peg with her name on it and we hung up her coat and PE bag. I gave her a big kiss and a hug, told her I loved her and we would be in the playground when it was time for her to go home. She bent and kissed Danny and, quite matter-of-factly, said, "You better go, mummy. Danny can't stay, only me. I'm your big girl." She was going to be fine. We came out and saw her sit herself on the mat. She was *so* ready for this. She was bright as a button, could write her name, knew her colours and could count to 20 by the time she was three. She loved drawing and being read to, she was eager to learn, and she would soak it all up like a sponge.

Both Danny and I were crying as we walked home. I realised this was a momentous day for both of us. Naomi was taking her first steps away from us and I was having to let go of her a little. No one had told me how difficult this was going to be. These children were mine, ours, and now I was handing her over to a teacher and this was all part of her growing up. This was going to be a painful process.

When she came out of school her little face lit up when she saw us and I felt a sort of warm feeling as I watched her. She didn't stand out, she was just like everyone else. No one was pointing or whispering about her; she just fitted in. This was how it should be and I felt like a proper mummy. I had made it right for her. She would fit in, have friends, love school, and be able to do everything everyone else did. This was a HUGE moment for me and when she saw me she ran and jumped into my arms, hugged me and said, "Don't cry mummy. I am here now and I like my school."

We walked home, stopping at the local shop for sweets. She chatted the whole way home about what she had done, who she played with, and what she was going to do tomorrow. She kept leaning into the buggy and tickling Danny. "Did he miss me, mummy? Was he OK without me?" She was such a little sweetie. He *had* missed her and was thrilled she was back. Naomi was his pal and they played so well together.

She couldn't wait for her daddy to get home so she could tell him about her day. She wouldn't take her school uniform off because she wanted daddy to see her in it as he had left for work before she had put it on. As soon as she heard his moped she rushed to the front door, so that he would get the full impact of his very big girl in her new school uniform! He was, of course, suitably impressed and made all the right noises. He sat in the chair, Daniel on his lap and Naomi jumping up and down in front of them both, telling her daddy all about her first day at school. Daniel had heard it several times but was also suitably impressed and made lots of noises too. This was a huge change for us all but, hopefully and prayerfully, it would be happy change.

Just before I gave birth to Rebecca Charlotte Summers on 27 May 1981, I had noticed a new couple who had moved in across the road. They lived at 18 Nevil Green and we lived at 18 Nevil Road. They were an odd-looking couple; he was extremely tall and thin, she was short and very round. I later realised that she too was pregnant! We called them little and large.

Here I was, three kids and just about coping. Lots of changes had taken place in our church. Several people were travelling to Barcombe from Uckfield so it was decided to plant a church in Uckfield. We started meeting in a hall at the bottom of the main car park. Simon Pettit was to be pastor and they duly moved from Barcombe to Uckfield. It felt very strange at first but very soon we were a church family again. Lots of young families joined us and it was great fun.

It was early September and as I hadn't seen little and large out and about, I assumed that their baby had arrived too. Wanting to be neighbourly, I popped over to say Hi. She was a very, very welcoming and bubbly American called Nancy Izzard and she asked me in. She was holding her baby, a beautiful little boy named Ben. She said that all she did all day was sit and pat his bottom and rock him! She was exhausted. I had a bouncy chair at home that I no longer used, so I ran over and got it for her. Ben loved it and so did Nancy! She was frazzled and looked so tired. Her mum had been over from the States to help with the baby but had now gone back and she was feeling very lonely. I knew that feeling.

Her husband was called Ray and the lovely thing was that they were Christians. We hit it off straight away. They had been going to the Baptist Church in Uckfield and they too were now going to join our little church. Yay! Another family. It was great to welcome them and to worship together too.

I had prayed for a friend and God had answered my prayer. The weird thing about this was Nancy had prayed for a friend too. I was the answer to *her* prayer! She was lovely, bubbly and so friendly. She was a few years older than me and we were polar opposites in our backgrounds. She was born in Indianapolis into a very middle-class family, had a wonderful childhood and was the apple of her parents' eye. She had everything a little girl could dream of including a beautiful pink bedroom (which I would sleep in many years later when we went on holiday together). Her parents just adored her and I loved hearing the stories of her childhood. I wanted to be her. I wished her parents were *my* parents, they were so lovely. Yet with all our differences we gelled. We would be in each other's houses most days, the kids grew together, and so did we. We would have days at the seaside together, eat dinners together, pray together and laugh such a lot together. I got her and she got me. I have such an odd sense of humour which few people understand but *she* did and does. We were friends and it was great.

As the church was new and growing, we were all keen to be involved. I would do soup lunches for all the mums and kids at our house. The fellowship and fun were great and we were all loving being part of God's family.

I had started work again because we needed extra money to make ends meet. I didn't mind what I did as long as it fitted in with family life. I found a job cleaning a factory every evening which worked because I could get dinner for the family and get the kids ready for bed. Then I would go to work, leaving Greg to get the kids to bed and look after them until I got back about 9.30 to 10.00. Nancy got a job supply teaching, so I would look after Ben when she needed me to and I loved him—we all did; he was such an easy child to love. I treated him just like one of my own kids. Ben and Becky were best friends and Daniel was the one they both looked up to and copied when Naomi was at school. All changed when she was home. She was most definitely the boss and they all looked to her for direction on games or what they were planning to do. Being the only one to go to school she knew everything about everything! Saying that, they all got on extremely well, apart from the odd hiccup!

Back at home we worried about getting to and from the chapel. Basil's van could only take so much. Lindsay came over one morning for coffee. "Why don't you learn to drive?" she said, "That would solve so many problems." I explained that we just didn't have the money to spare for that. "Well, let's pray for it. God knows your need," she said. So then and there we sat and prayed, asking God to help us. After all, he is our heavenly father and knows and understands our needs. We sat and chatted for a while and she left for home. I was getting things ready for lunch and sorting Daniel out. He was all over the place like a whirling dervish. He had been in the conservatory playing with his toys while we were praying and we could hear him but not see him. Bless him, he had tipped the plant pot over and the soil was everywhere; on the floor, in his mouth, in his hair, in his pockets and, later, when I opened the tumble dryer it was in there too. Little monkey.

The phone rang and it was Mam. She chatted on for a while then, out of the blue, she said, "Now that you are having another baby, you are going to find it difficult, especially doing the shopping with three of 'em, and those hills will kill you. What you should do is learn to drive. Well, I was thinking. I want to give you £60, that should be enough, but don't tell the others. I'm not handing money out willy nilly."

I nearly fell over. "Thank you so much, Mam, this is so kind of you. We prayed that God would help us and you are the answer to our prayers."

She was a bit shocked, and then she said, "Well, you might have asked God for it but I gave it to you!" She wasn't about to share her thanks with God.

"Well, bless you Mam," I said.

As soon as I put the phone down, I couldn't wait to tell Lindsey so rang her straight away and she was thrilled. God had heard us and answered our prayers in the oddest way I would ever have imagined. Mam was usually as tight as a drum skin, Dad was the generous one, so this was a little miracle getting Mam to part with money. It was a real boost to our faith. God WAS interested in the little things in our lives.

I rang round. I wanted to find a woman instructor. I found one, her name was Joan and she arrived with her little Mini. I was a little nervous as I explained that I only had £60 and needed to be ready for my test by the time the £60 ran out. She smiled and said, "Well, let's just see how you do shall we. Let's not run before we can walk." I was a quick learner but as my tummy grew it was more and more difficult to get in and out of this little Mini, but I managed. Joan told me I needed to swat up on my Highway Code. I did and got Greg to quiz me on it most nights. My £60 was used up and my test booked. Joan arrived. Greg had taken the day off work to look after the kids. I felt a little nervous so just before Joan was due to arrive, Greg prayed for my nerves to calm.

Greg kissed me and said, "You'll do it, don't worry." I ran out, or rather wobbled out, I was eight months pregnant and enormous. As I wedged myself in the car, Joan said, "Have you got your licence?" I hadn't. "Don't worry," she said smiling. "You'll only need it if you pass," she laughed. I wobbled back in and got it and then we were off.

She was asking me Highway Code questions all the way down to Eastbourne and I got them all right. All that swatting paid off and I felt quietly confident. When we arrived at the test centre, Joan said, "You want any examiner except the chief examiner. He's a rotter." We sat for a while and several people came out with clipboards and shouted out a name. That person would then go with their examiner. I began to feel a bit nervous. A stern-faced man with a clipboard came in. "That's the fella you don't want," Joan whispered.

"Fay Summers," he shouted. I looked at Joan and got up. I felt dreadful. Why was he a rotter? What made him one? Was he unfair? All these things were running through my head.

When we were outside he asked me to read a number plate that he pointed out. That done we walked to the car and got in. He looked at me and my big tummy and said, "Are you sure you want to go through with this?"

I wanted to make a joke and say, "It's too late to think about that option. It's due next month!" But looking at him, he wouldn't have seen the funny side. I said, "Yes I do." We drove off. I did everything he asked me to do and we arrived back at the test centre.

Joan was sitting on the wall as we pulled up. He then asked me several Highway Code questions which I knew and I answered correctly, thanks to Greg. Then he said, "Where do you put your foot when it's not on the clutch pedal?" I was baffled; I hadn't seen that question in the Highway Code book and Joan had never mentioned it. My mind was all over the place, trying to locate the right answer. Should I put it behind the other foot or hang it out the window? I gave up and said I didn't know.

He looked very sternly at me and said, "It should be on the floor. Yours has been hovering over the clutch pedal the whole of this test."

Quick as a flash, I said, "The baby is lying funny and I can't do that."

He smiled at me and said, "I am pleased to tell you, you have passed your test. Can I have your licence please?"

I was elated. "Thank you so much. I could kiss you," I said.

He looked horrified and said, "Well, restrain yourself please!"

I gave him my licence, he wrote out my pass certificate and we both got out of the car. Joan could tell by my smile I had passed. She was thrilled for me and as we drove home I told her about the foot-clutch question. She roared with laughter.

I walked up the path to the house looking dejected. Greg was at the door. He looked at me and said, "Never mind darling, you'll do it next time."

I beamed and said, "There'll be no next time, I passed!"

He hugged me and shouted, "Well done!" It was such a brilliant day and it struck me that it was the only exam I had ever passed! I was elated. Now all we needed was a car. Well, as God was so clearly involved with the money for the lessons, we thought we would pray about the money for a car.

I went into hospital on 26 May. I had started in labour, we had to call an ambulance and I was taken to Cuckfield Hospital. Greg came with me and my friend Val and her husband Mike looked after the kids. The contractions were coming thick and fast and then they just stopped. I couldn't believe it, but the labour suite was empty so they decided to induce me as I was two days over my due date. It was all systems go again in no time and Rebecca Charlotte Summers arrived kicking and screaming at 8.30 am on 27 May 1981.

She was beautiful. She had a shock of black hair; nothing like the other two who had been white blonde, but Rebecca had her daddy's colouring. We were thrilled with our little girl. We gave thanks to God for the safe delivery of our beautiful daughter. I cuddled her and Greg cuddled both of us, he was a very happy man. I was happy but tired. I was taken to the ward with my little Rebecca and at 12.00 was allowed to come home. Val arrived in her Mini Clubman with her two girls, my two and Greg. How we all fitted into that dear little car I don't know but we did.

When we all climbed out of the car and into our house, Naomi and Daniel were so excited to see their new baby sister. Naomi was squealing with delight. "I can teach her to be a big girl," she said. Daniel was more interested in me; he wanted a cuddle.

The midwife arrived just as I was trying to organise lunch. "You get up those stairs," she said sternly. I tried to explain what I was doing. "Let him do it," she said, pointing to Greg. "He hasn't just had a baby. Now get up those stairs and into bed. You need a couple of days to recover." I went meekly upstairs and Greg carried the crib up and put it beside the bed. Actually, I was exhausted and as soon as she had gone, I was out like a light.

When I woke, Naomi and Daniel climbed into bed with me, Greg sat at the other side of us and they all had a cuddle of this dear little girl. Naomi beamed as she held her sister. "I'm the biggest sister. I'm Daniel's big sister, so I must be Rebecca's biggest sister," she said. We explained that she was the big sister to both of them. She smiled the widest smile. It said she was very pleased with herself. It was such a lovely time. Everyone was so excited about our new arrival and she really was the easiest baby, such a little sweetie. We all fell madly in love with her.

My brother John and his wife and family were now living in Ringmer. John was such a clever man. He was very talented, as were all my brothers, but John was a real entrepreneur; so creative and extremely hard working. He had started a kitchen business in Ringmer and was doing quite well. I rang him to tell him I had passed my test and he was very pleased for me. He arrived at our house the following morning and handed me an envelope. "Put this towards your car darling," he said and then said, "Can't stop, see you soon." He kissed my cheek, smiled at me and ran back down the path to his van. I opened the envelope and there was £200! Bless his heart. I was choked up, how generous of him. I rang Greg at work and told him. He too was touched by John's generosity.

We spent the evening looking for a car for £200 as that was the only money we had. There were a few but as we knew nothing about cars I thought I would ask my friend Jill's husband Peter which would be the best. He was a mechanic and worked in a BMW garage. Peter said he would look for one for us. The following day he came round and told us that an old lady had gone to the garage and asked if they wanted to buy her car. She kept bashing into her gate post and figured it was time she quit driving as she was getting on in years. The garage wasn't interested but Peter asked her how much she wanted for her car. £200 was her answer so Peter very kindly got it for us. He looked it over and said it was in good nick apart from a couple of dents in the back. We didn't mind the dents. It was a mustard-coloured Datsun Cherry with almost a full year's tax. It was perfect. It was a hatchback which we would need for a pram and enough room for all of us. We were thrilled. Thank you John, thank you Peter and thank you God. Everything had worked together perfectly. We were now mobile! We had to get seat belts fitted for Naomi and Daniel and we bought some second-hand ones. The kids loved them. They were like racing driver's seat belts, so we never had any problem getting the kids in their belts!

Our little family was complete. I loved being a mummy and a wife. Greg loved being a daddy and a husband. This was wonderful. We didn't have much money but boy, were we happy! This darling baby was the easiest baby ever; she slept through the night in just six weeks. She was a darling and Naomi and Dan loved her and loved helping with her. We had more powder and cream on each other when it came to nappy change time but it didn't matter, they so wanted to be involved with their little sister.

Ben and Becky were around two and Daniel had just started playgroup. He loved it and had a great mate in David Cooke, Gill and Peter's middle child. They played well together. Gill and I would take it in turns to take and pick them up and it worked really well.

This morning, Ben and Becky were playing in the lounge and I went upstairs to the loo. When I came down, they were no longer in the lounge but in the kitchen and they were covered in washing powder and orange squash. They had emptied the massive box of powder onto the kitchen floor and proceeded to empty a two-litre bottle of orange squash into it! They were a sticky, messy little pair and as they both looked up at me, I could have strangled them both! Money was really tight, and I couldn't salvage any of the washing powder. It was well and truly mixed and smeared all over the floor and the two of them. The sticky slime was in their hair, all over their clothes and up their arms to their elbows. I shouted at them and told them that what they had done was very naughty and I smacked both their hands. I took them up to the bathroom, stripped them off and bathed them both. Ben was mortified that I had shouted at him, poor little man.

237

He was a very obedient child and this was a real shock to him. I felt really bad that I had upset him so much. Mind you, he was always so well behaved after that which I am sure was Becky's idea. She was gorgeous but there was a side to her that was stubborn, mischievous and cheeky!

We had to get bunk beds for the girls as they shared a bedroom and as Becky had outgrown her cot. She would stand up in it and throw herself over the side, hanging on to the top rail with one hand, then just let herself drop to the floor. She had done this since she was 16 months old. Then she would slide down the stairs on her tummy, legs first, and fall asleep in the hall by the front door. We would get such a shock when we were heading up to bed, to find this sleeping baby curled up in her Babygro.

It sounds terrible but in desperation I would tie the bedroom door to the banister to stop her coming down! I would check, open the bedroom door and find her asleep behind it. Then I would pick her up and put her back in her cot.

So bunk beds were the thing to get. Naomi was so excited. She was going to sleep on the top, as she was a big girl. We couldn't afford new ones, so in the local paper we found some brilliant second-hand ones. They looked great and the girls were thrilled when daddy and I put them up! We told Becky she was a big girl now and she should stay in her bed. Naomi was a bit put out and kept telling us, "She's not really a big girl, is she, mummy, because I am the big girl!" She wanted to make sure we all knew the truth!

Bedtime came, story time, and prayers, then everyone into their beds with kisses and cuddles. We just hoped and prayed Becky would settle and stay in her new bed and we kept opening the door to the hall just to see if she had come down. She hadn't. It had worked! We looked in on them when we went up to bed. They were fast asleep and, snuggled under the duvet in Becky's bed, were Becky—and Daniel. I guess he wanted to sleep in the new bunk beds too. The bunk beds were the answer. Becky never came downstairs again and quite often Daniel would climb into bed with her; they looked so sweet all snuggled up.

Daniel was such a busy little fellow. Greg had bought him a ride-on tractor and trailer and he would ride up and down the conservatory if it was raining or in the garden if dry. We would have to call him Farmer Dan and when he was playing this game he would make Ben and Becky be his helpers. They could sit in the trailer and have a ride but they were never allowed to actually drive the tractor. He was Farmer Dan, not them.

Our garden was small but we crammed lots into it. Greg brought some pallets home and I made a sandbox. We bought a second-hand swing and I made a slide and fixed it onto a pair of steps. I painted them all blue and orange and they looked fabulous. The kids so enjoyed playing in the garden. This was what family life was all about. Nancy, Ray and Ben were part of our family too and when the kids weren't in our garden they were in Nancy's. Nancy's parents bought Ben a climbing frame, so between our two gardens we had it all.

I had noticed with Daniel that he found thing much harder than Naomi had. She had learned her colours almost in a week but Daniel was finding it so difficult. I just put it down to the difference between boys and girls. He loved to be read to, as they all did, but found writing difficult. We would sit at the dining table and write his name but he seemed to see something different to what I had written, and would get very upset if I said, "Let's do it again."

He was so excited about starting school. Naomi was loving it and was so excited that Daniel was going to be starting at *her* school soon! We had bought his school uniform, name tapes were all sewn in, and he looked just the sweetest little man when we put it all on! He was all ready for his first day in September.

Naomi was being a really good big sister, telling him she would look after him and what he would have to do. He wasn't nearly as confident as she was, so I was a little worried about how he would settle in. He was starting with lots of his friends from playgroup, so when we arrived in the playground on that first morning, there was his mate David and several others he recognised. He relaxed a little but clung onto my hand like a vice. Becky was in the buggy, holding Daniel's PE bag. When the whistle blew and we were told to take the new children into reception, Naomi gave Daniel a big kiss and told him she would see him at playtime.

Becky, Daniel and I went into the classroom. Daniel looked anxious and was still holding tightly onto my hand. He had been so excited, now it was all a bit scary for him. The teacher told us mums to say our goodbyes so, bending down, I gave him a big kiss and a squeeze. I told him he would love it and Naomi would play with him at playtime and I would be in the playground when it was time for him to come home. His little eyes filled with tears as the teacher was saying, "Go now, mums."

I stood up ready to go and realised Becky was still holding Daniel's PE bag. I took it from her and she screamed, "MINE!"

Daniel's face changed. "No Becky, it's mine," he said, took it from me and hung it on his peg. The tears had gone and when he saw his friend Wayne sitting on the mat, he went and plonked himself down next to him. He gave me his best big boy smile and I could go! Becky was still creating a fuss, she wanted the bag, and she wanted Daniel, but by the time we got home, it was just her and me. It was very weird. The house seemed odd with just us in it but we had a lovely day, just the two of us.

When it was time for Daniel and Naomi to come home, we walked around to school. I heard Daniel before I saw him. He was laughing—a good sign I thought—and he bounded out into the playground and gave me such a hug and a squeeze! "I missed you, mummy, but I had a nice time." He was a happy boy. Naomi appeared and told me how she had looked after him and played with him, and he was such a good boy. This was another achievement—Daniel happy in school!

By the time he started school, Dan could read his name, just knew his colours and could count, but it had taken an awful lot of hard work on his part to get there. I thought it was just how boys were and that learning really wasn't on their agenda. Football, wrestling, cars, and just larking about; that's what he wanted to do.

He did settle well into school and was very popular and had lots of friends but he struggled with the learning process. It broke my heart when he would bring home flash cards with words like mummy, daddy, house, garden and so on, and we would sit after dinner and read them. He just couldn't get it and it wasn't because he didn't try. He did, so hard bless him, that his little face was screwed up in concentration. One morning when I was making his bed I found a pile of flash cards under his pillow, all torn up. I was heartbroken for him and told him it didn't matter—we would sort it out. He sobbed into my chest as I cuddled him. He was such a dear little man and he so wanted to please his teacher and all this was so hard for him.

I spoke to his teacher about maybe trying something else. She was quite rude to me and told me he was just a slow learner and he would get it eventually. I know I am not educated and am definitely not clever, but I do know my children and she didn't know my Daniel, so I said, "This is not happening because he's a slow learner, he's putting so much effort into this and getting nowhere. There must be another way for him to learn this stuff!" I just didn't want him to get to the stage of hating school and not wanting to go.

She told me to leave it for now and see how he managed for the rest of the term and, like a fool, I did. It got worse and Daniel started to pull his hair out—literally. I was so worried. At the weekend he was a bundle of fun but come Monday morning, he was a sad little man.

I went back to see his teacher but she still wouldn't do anything to help him so I went to see the headmaster. He organised for Daniel to have some tests and they showed very clearly that Daniel was dyslexic. I had no idea what this was or meant and I was sad for Daniel, but also relieved, because now we could get help for him.

I found out all about it and how best to help him learn. The headmaster was brilliant and got help in the form of Miss Lavender, who transformed my little boy lost into a school-loving little boy. I will forever be indebted to her. She thought up wonderful ways to teach Daniel. She would read stories onto tape, then he would bring home the book and the tape and we would listen and read at the same time. He never did flash cards again but learned fabulously with phonics. What a difference she made to my little Danny boy.

Unto Us a Son Is Born

JOHN AND SHARON HAD MOVED FROM THE FLAT above their kitchen shop in Ringmer and had bought a three-bed semi in Mill Mead. It was a lovely house and had a fabulous garden. Paul and Ben were settled into school and loving it. Stevie was at playgroup when Sharon rang to say she was pregnant. How exciting! Their lives were changing again.

John had been designing and fitting kitchens for a few years when he met a guy he got on with like a house on fire, Andy Hemmington. He was a Christian too and they had the same work ethic and sense of humour. They started working together doing windows and soon they had shops in Ringmer, Lewes and Seaford. They loved it, were great mates and had great times working together for a few years.

Then Andy married and went to live in Canada so John went on to set up a business in Haywards Heath. He was an amazing man, providing work for many as well as providing for his lovely family and, quite often, for the wider family too.

Sharon, bless her, was hugely pregnant and went into labour. She knew her body and said, "Come on John. We've got to go…NOW." So they set off for Cuckfield Hospital but labour came quick and fast and they just made it to Newick. John pulled in by the little chapel on the bend. Sharon was saying, "The baby is coming"—and he did! Aaron Lancaster was born in the van and delivered by his very proud and emotional Dad on 10th April 1983. Sharon said after Aaron was born that John had reached into the back of the van for something to wrap Aaron up in. "You are not wrapping my brand new baby in a mucky dust sheet!" she said, but he pulled out fresh clean towels that he had thrown in just in case! He was prepared for every eventuality. John said it was so wonderful and peaceful, just the two of them, and the moon shining, and then Aaron was born, very calm and very quiet. "Beautiful," he said. They gave thanks for this little one and then drove on to the hospital. He also said that on the wall outside the chapel was an old poster saying UNTO US A SON IS BORN. He smiled and said that if ever I needed a midwife, to give him a call. It was a doddle and he could turn his hand to owt!

We didn't see so much of Mam and Dad after moving to Uckfield. Things were changing all round. Dad was being asked to preach at various churches up and down the country. He would give his testimony and tell how God had transformed his life. He was asked so many times to write a book about it that eventually he decided he would. So, after much prayer, he set to and wrote it with help. When it was published he was out most weekends preaching and talking about his book. Mam found this very difficult. She was an incredibly jealous woman and hated Dad talking to any other woman. She would sit in the congregation seething as people listened to Dad and when a woman asked him to sign the book she would accuse him of having an affair with her. We all thought she was mad to think that; now he was a Christian he was different.

Their marriage was strained because of this and Dad seemed to have changed but not in a good way. When he was telling us about where he had been preaching the emphasis had shifted from praising God to praising himself. It was all "I did this" or "I did that." He seemed to forget that it was all God's doing. Mam said he had gone from being a preacher to being an 'I specialist'. It was a very strange time because the life we had lived since Dad was saved was really like stepping out of a dark room into bright sunlight in comparison to the life we led before. Since then he had been so committed to Christ. He wasn't perfect by any means but his heart belonged to God and this was hard to deal with. It made us all nervous and none of us had the courage to talk to him about it. We were all praying that he would come through it. But his pastor was a very discerning man and he saw a change in Dad too. He went round to see Dad and said that he should cut back on his speaking engagements for a while and come back to chapel. Errol very tactfully said that Dad had been 'giving out' for too long and he needed to 'take in' and be built up again. Dad was incensed. He said he had a 'calling' and no one would stop him. He almost threw Errol out and then spent the rest of the evening ranting and saying, "How dare he tell ME what I should or shouldn't do." He said he would resign his membership and just do his own thing. Dad didn't tell us about this, Mam did, and it was as if she gloated on the fact that he wasn't doing the right thing. She wanted him back all to herself and this way it took the shine off him.

He continued with his preaching though things had definitely changed. Whenever he used to come over to see us he would usually sit with his cuppa and talk about what he had been reading. He loved the Old Testament and would talk endlessly of the exploits of David's mighty men of valour and Elijah. He would always bring out something that we had never seen before. When he talked about the valley of dry bones he was so animated and his awe of God shone out. He would always pray with us before he went and the question he asked every time was, "How is it with thy soul?" The answer we all gave was "it is well." It sounds a daft thing but it was how he was and he always used The King James Bible and loved the language. Well that was changing. Now his talk was all about him and where he had preached and how he had them enthralled and eating out of his hand. This talk made us all nervous.

The thing about Dad was, we were all still scared of him. We all knew what he *had* been and were aware that it was God who made the difference in him. Well, if he wasn't going to church what would happen to him now? Would God still make the difference? We all got a little uneasy around him. Whenever he came, we would immediately stop whatever we were doing and drop everything. If I had visitors they had to go. I couldn't cope with trying to keep him happy and have someone else to deal with, unless it was my brothers or sister. We, of course, all knew the rules: sit with him, make him tea, get him an ashtray. No one else was allowed to smoke in my house but I never had the courage to tell Dad not to and generally made sure he was kept happy. I would be a bit nervous in case Greg would say something that would upset him. Greg wouldn't do it purposely because he too knew not to upset Dad but he didn't know how to 'keep him sweet' like we did. By that I mean we would agree with him, look extremely interested in everything he was saying, laugh at his jokes and just be his audience. When he went he would usually already have folded a £5 note into a little square and as he kissed me goodbye he would put it in my hand so on one else would see. I would smile gratefully and off he would go. He did the same with all of us children. He would 'bung' us money like that but it was always sneaky. Mam knew he did this and was always angry with whoever the recipient was. Mind you, we were always very chuffed about it. As soon as he had gone we would open our hand to see how much it was. Sometimes, when he was 'flush', it would be £10 or £20. Then, once we had thrown open all the windows to get rid of the smell of smoke, I would argue with Greg, telling him off for not being as attentive to Dad as he should have been or for saying the wrong thing. Poor Greg, he didn't know what to do, but he was learning!

Meanwhile, Phil had been doing all sorts of dodgy deals and knocking about with some dubious characters. He and Kenny were still into drugs and making quick money. Phil knew a bloke who had been to Thailand, bought heroin, smuggled it back, sold it and made a fortune, so this was now his plan. With a bloke called Mark, who had done this before, Phil flew to Thailand where Mark had contacts I think. Anyway, they were in a cheap hotel room and had bought a bit of heroin for personal use. They were raided, tested and proved positive for heroin, so were arrested and sentenced to six months in Chiang Mai Prison. The thing was, they hadn't bought the heroin they were going to smuggle, which was a miracle, because had they been caught with it they were sentencing drug smugglers to 90 years!

This was not the story Phil told Mam and Dad. He said he had been arrested and was awaiting sentence, telling them he could go down for 90 years! They were very scared for him, as we all were. He was so far away and we had seen these prisons on tell with people all squashed into one cell, not much food, beatings—scary. But none of us knew he had actually gone out there to smuggle heroin. I don't know what reason he gave for actually being in Thailand. Anyway, he told them that the prison system was so corrupt you could bribe your way out if you had enough money! Mam told me he asked for either £2,000 or £3,000. Dad was speaking in churches here and there at this time, so they told the congregation about Phil's predicament. I wish I could recall what they shared with these dear people but the truth is Mam and Dad actually believed Phil needed this money so they were worried for him. People very kindly gave money to help and then a lovely couple who had just sold their house actually gave them £2,000! Mam sent the money to a missionary who would go into the prison and give it to Phil.

In fact, the prison was very lax. Phil was able to buy heroin in there and became very addicted to it. I think the money he had taken out to actually buy heroin was used to keep him and Mark comfortable in prison. When they had done their six months they were released and Phil then used the money Mam sent to buy more heroin and smuggle it back here! When they got back to England they never spoke again. I think the reason was that Mark was telling the truth about what happened while Phil was sticking to the story of having to bribe his way out of prison. I always thought it odd that when he got home he had presents for everyone and looked incredibly tanned and toned, though he had lost weight. I'm sure that was down to the heroin, though he never injected but smoked it. Unlike Kenny he was able to get clean quite easily!

Phil and Maggy had moved from their flat to a brand-new house in Sandy Vale, Haywards Heath and we were so excited for them; they made it so cosy. When they came over to see us they told us they were expecting a baby and we were thrilled. It was so lovely that we were all having our babies around the same time and they would all grow up together. Emily Zoe Lancaster was born on 30 July 1980 and she was beautiful, we all fell in love with her. Mags was loving being a mummy and Phil was a very proud daddy but poor Emily had an underdeveloped valve and she would projectile vomit every time she was fed. My goodness, she could cover a bloomin' carpet! This was very stressful for Mags who worried Emily would starve but grew out of that as soon as she turned one and it was a huge relief to them both. Phil was brilliant with Emily and adored her.

Kenny was well into drugs at this time. I always thought it was his way to escape his life. He was such a lovely boy and had the best sense of humour, even though it was a bit black. We would all be in hysterics as Ken would tell us about jobs he had done that went wrong! We loved him but underneath I think he carried all sorts of hang-ups and hurts. He was madly in love with Susie and they were living in a flat in Haywards Heath. Kenny was doing heroin and it scared me so much. He was so skinny and every penny he had went on heroin. Susie begged him to give it up and he went onto methadone. I had no idea how strongly heroin grips you—it destroys lives—but he loved Susie and the methadone programme was a start. We were thrilled he was going to come off and be clean. He had asked Susie to marry him, so there would be a new beginning for them both.

Their wedding day was lovely. Susie looked beautiful, Kenny very handsome and they were both happy as we all were for them. After the registry office we all went up to Mam and Dad's house and a friend of Dad's who was a minister blessed their marriage. Then we all went down to the Triangle pub to celebrate! Another Mr and Mrs Ken Lancaster. We prayed they would be happy and have a fabulous future together.

Phil was home from prison and it was lovely to have him in our lives again. For Ken's wedding he decided to cut a black shirt and a white shirt in half and sew one-half black and one-half white. It looked odd but that was Phil! He and

Mags had a big row outside the pub. He couldn't cope with confrontation and Mags had stunned us all by standing up to him. Phil was very like Dad in some ways. He was the man of the house and what he said went! He was never wrong. Mags was very sweet and usually complied with his rules but not today! He was gobsmacked, as we all were. Well done Mags!

Phil was up to no good again. I was always sad about the fact that if he had been to art college his life would have been so different. He would have been able to make an honest living doing something he was passionate about and was proud of. But he didn't, he wanted money. He always thought he could make money quickly and robbery was his preferred crime. In fact he was a rubbish robber. Very occasionally he got away with it and when he did he wanted to share his bounty. He was always generous. I vividly remember him coming over to see me when he had done a robbery and had a fair bit of money. We were struggling and he gave me a bundle of notes. "Here you go, Fay, cop for that," he said, with a big grin on his face.

I looked into my hand and there was a fat wad of £20 notes. "Phil," I said, "I can't take that."

"Yes you can," he said. "You need it."

"No darlin, I can't. I know it's nicked and I can't take it. Thank you for thinking of me though." I handed the wad back to him.

"Yes, it is nicked, but you didn't nick it. Go on. Ave it!"

"I can't, Phil. I'm a Christian."

He looked really sad that he couldn't help me, bless him. Then he looked at Naomi and Dan and said, "Come on kids. I'm taking you two out." With that he put them both in the double buggy and said he would be back in a bit! He was gone ages and when he did arrive back, he was carrying a yellow ride-in pedal car on his back and a drum kit strapped to the buggy. He had taken the kids down to the toy shop and told them they could have anything they wanted.

Naomi picked the pedal car with headset—it was a yellow taxi, and Dan the drum kit! He had a kind heart and wanted to help us but he just didn't understand why I wouldn't take the money, bless him. The kids thought Christmas had come early! They thought Uncle Phil was brilliant.

Phil on the Carpet

NOT LONG AFTER THIS, PHIL DID A ROBBERY and he had a gun. Phil was arrested and the police had been to search the house, looking for the gun which they didn't find. Maggy rang me and said the gun was under the bath. Phil was under such mental stress that we definitely thought he couldn't cope with prison again. I said that I would go over the following day, pick up the gun and throw it into Piltdown Pond. Here was I, a Christian woman, as was Maggy, but we said we would just have to carry this to our graves as we could tell no one!

That night I had the most awful dream of me throwing the gun into the pond when up from behind the surrounding bushes jumped Greg and my kids, my pastor and the police, all pointing fingers at me and saying, "Fay Summers. Christian woman. Aiding and abetting and interfering with the course of justice. How could you?" I woke up all sweaty and frightened. I had made my mind up to do it, because I felt Phil couldn't handle another stint in prison. I told God that I was sorry but I had to do it!

The next day, my tummy was turning over all the time. I was going to go over to Maggy after the kids were in bed. As I came downstairs the phone rang. Maggy was saying that the police and Phil had come into the house and Phil had told them where the gun was! I nearly fell over! In all his life he had never volunteered any information to the police. I was staggered as was Maggy. We didn't have to keep the secret of the gun to our graves, thank the Lord.

But Phil was sent down for several years and as he was a violent criminal he finished up in Parkhurst on the Isle of Wight. There they tried all kinds of drug therapy to calm the side of Phil that he couldn't control; the violent aggressive side. He told us about dreadful things that had happened to him in various prisons. He was hung on the back of a door in a straitjacket for three days, beaten black and blue, and went on dirty protests when you strip naked and wipe your own faeces all over your body and the walls of your cell. The problem with Phil was he had bowel trouble and couldn't poo, so he asked the bloke in the next cell for some of his. Can you imagine? No, don't! Then the screws would come, open the cell door and with a power hose just blast all this revoltingness off them and their walls, leaving them winded and wet but clean!

The awful thing was, when Phil was finally released from Parkhurst he was very different and very damaged. All the drugs he'd been given had changed this cocky, aggressive, creative, couldn't-care-less bloke, into a mentally unstable, institutionalised, frightened, odd man, who couldn't cope with noise. He thought the central heating system was bugged and that 'they' were listening to everything. I vividly remember going to see him the day after his release. He looked different and had a haunted look about him. I was thrilled he was home. I loved him very much but he worried me when he kept telling me to shush and, pointing at the air vent, whispered, "They are listening."

The sad thing too was that Phil had no medication to help him cope. When he left Parkhurst he should have had a psychiatric referral. Medical notes from the prison should have followed him to his local doctor. In fact it was 15 years later when Phil himself said he needed help that he was finally given an appointment with a psychiatrist who did help him, but he was still very mentally ill.

Poor Emily had lived all these years with just her mum and now this nutter is here. He's her daddy, but they don't know each other. Emily was very strong-willed and wasn't going to be told what to do by him! He couldn't cope with her noise and so a very strained relationship developed. She, bless her, wasn't old enough to understand her Dad was mentally ill. Phil was so mentally incapable of being flexible and accepting the noise, the playfulness, the stroppiness of a child, that he was incapable of parenting. He had been institutionalised for so long that he now accepted that punishment was the way and he came down on Emily like a ton of bricks.

Poor Mags was in a state. She was thrilled Phil was home and she loved him very much but with Phil and Emily, she was in the middle of a war zone. Dad came to the rescue and would pick up Emily and take her with him if he was going to do an estimate. He had been the man in her life all the time Phil was away and she loved him. She certainly wasn't having any of this other bloke's nonsense!

I thought this was the saddest thing because when he went inside he had loved and adored her. It was what they had done to his mind that changed him and what he could cope with—heart-breaking. Mags always looked like she was walking on eggshells with Phil, but she loved him and was a faithful loving wife. Sometimes when I heard him talk horribly to her I would tell her to leave him but she wouldn't, bless her.

Phil needed to work. He was so different now. He wanted to be completely above board but, really and truly, he wasn't capable of looking for a job or going for an interview. John, bless him, came to the rescue. He bought an industrial carpet cleaner and a van, had a sign written on the van and had business cards printed. Swiftclean was the name. However, Phil had never passed his driving test. This had never stopped him driving before but now he wanted to be legal. John asked me if I would work with Phil; I could drive the van and talk to the clients. I agreed, so John put an ad in the local papers and we waited. We had a few calls.

Remember, we were a pair of numpties who didn't try the machine before taking it out. John told us how to work it but did we have a practice? No, we did not. John also gave us a clipboard with a price list of the different carpets we could clean: wool, shag pile, nylon, and so on. Each cost a different price per square yard. Brilliant we thought! We even had overalls with the Swiftclean logo on the back and we looked the part. I was on maternity leave as Becky was a few months old.

Our first job was in Mayfield. I put Becky in the van in her carrycot, just behind the driver's seat. All the machinery and cleaning fluids were in boxes too. I drove over and picked Phil up. He was very nervous, telling me, "You speak to the lady, Fay."

"I will, darlin. Don't worry, we can do this." At the address we put on our overalls. Phil had the clipboard and Becky was fast asleep. We went into this beautiful house where the gentleman showed us around from room to room, different carpets needing different prices. Phil, with his clipboard and pen, was feverishly writing while the man was trying to look over his shoulder, but Phil was not letting him.

I looked at Phil's face and realised there was a problem. "Phil," I said, "we need to check the cleaning fluids. Would you excuse us for a moment," and we went out to the van. "What's up, Phil?" I asked. "Don't you know how to work out this square footage and different carpet stuff?"

"Haven't a clue," he said.

I said, "I hardly went to school, thick as a brick me." So we decided we'd have one price, not all these different prices. We went back in and Phil told him we'd do the lot for £40. A proper bargain!

The next hurdle was deciding how to work the machine. For a start we filled the wrong tank and had to pour it out and Phil was getting very stressed. But eventually, we cracked it. I left Phil to do the carpets and went and sat in the van with Becky. It took ages but was finally finished. Phil came out and got me to go and speak to the man who was thrilled and gave us £45. We were chuffed! We laughed in the van on the way home about the list of prices and how we were both idiots. He showed me the clipboard on which he had written 'I haven't an effing clue how to do this'. We roared with laughter at the fact that I assumed he knew how to do it and he assumed I could do it. We were definitely related! I did love him.

We did several more jobs and Phil got a bit more confident each time. We went to clean a suite for a lady in her 80s and all of a sudden Mr 'I don't want to talk to clients' says, "Excuse me missis. If you don't mind me asking, are you a pensioner? Because if you can show us your pension book, you can get a 25% discount, it's company policy." She scuttled off, came back and showed Phil her pension book. "Fine," he said, "25% off for you."

He made all this up as he went along. It was the first time this company policy had been mentioned! It made me smile but then he was a sucker for old folk! He seemed to enjoy doing this and I certainly enjoyed being with him; we did have a laugh. If only he would lighten up with Emily.

Phil and his love of dogs seemed to take over his life. He had English bull terriers, Staffies and pit bulls, with no discussion with Mags. Dogs would just appear and he was obsessional about them and fighting them. He even wrote and self-published a book called *The Standard Procedure for Separating Fighting Dogs* and he was very proud of it! It caused a real problem between Phil and John, because at the same time as Phil wrote this book, John opened a shop in Lewes called The Lewes Glass Shop.

Phil was incensed and went over to see John. "How dare you," he said to John.

"What are you on about?" John said.

"You stole my THE!" he said, and he really meant it. He really thought that the word *the* was his. Poor John! Try as he might, there was no changing Phil's mind. He really was crazy, bless him. He was furious with John and called him worse than muck for a fair while! We all teased John and took the mickey every time he used the word THE. Sharp intake of breath, then, "John, you will be in big trouble." Poor John. He helped Phil and Kenny lots but they never appreciated what he did and always expected him to pay them far more than they were worth. But he never stopped trying to help them! He bought an industrial leather furniture repair kit and thought it would be good for Kenny to start his own business.

"Not for me," Kenny said. Bless him, John was always thinking of ways to help them.

As Emily grew, the rows got worse. She had Phil's stubborn streak and would never back down. Phil neither, but he was the one with the power. I went round once and he had all Emily's clothes in black bin liners except her school uniform and one change of clothes. He was taking all her clothes away because she was mouthy to him and he knew her clothes were important to her. I said, "You can't do that, Phil. That's too harsh. It's the sort of thing our Dad would do, and you don't want to be like him." He was furious with me and told me I couldn't tell him what he could and couldn't do. She was his kid and he would punish her however he wanted. Then he told me to piss off and mind my own business! Well, I tried.

One dog Phil had was a massive brindle English bull terrier called Solomon. He was huge. Phil used to wind him up when Greg and I went round and tell Solomon to get Greg. Greg was petrified and as he sort of reminded me of the dog we had as kids, Laddie, I was very wary of him. I would tell Greg to sit still and tell Phil to knock it off. Phil would laugh and call the dog off, to Greg's relief as it was eating Greg's foot! This dog came to a sad end. Phil was driving along with Solomon behind him in the car when he suddenly went stiff-legged, like Laddie, and started growling that deep throaty growl that you know means business! Phil was talking gently and softly to try to calm him as he had his mouth right at the back of Phil's neck. He slowly pulled over and talked this massive beast down. Very scary. He took Solomon to the vets and it turned out he had a brain tumour and had to be put down. Dangerous doggy!

Dad's Confession

IT WAS JUST BEFORE CHRISTMAS and Dad had been up to Leeds. He was preaching and giving his testimony at various venues. He was away for a few days and when he came home he brought a young couple with him. I can't remember her name but the husband, if I remember right, was called Ernie. They were in awe of Dad. They had just become Christians and she had been a prostitute and he had been her pimp. They had no idea how to celebrate a Christian Christmas so Dad invited them to spend it with him and Mam and they jumped at the chance to be with this wonderful evangelist.

Kayla was still going through her Goth period; black eyes, black clothes and sulky. She and Stuart were together at every spare moment so when Dad arrived home with this couple Kayla wasn't best pleased, though she was oddly fascinated by them. They both smoked. That was fine, Mam and Dad smoked like chimneys, but this woman had the oddest habit of instead of flicking her fag ash into the ashtray she would stick her tongue out, flick her ash onto it and eat it!

Mam and Dad almost forgot Kayla and Stuart as they tried to make this young pair welcome. Well, on the surface anyway. Mam was furious. She was her usual jealous self, accusing Dad of just bringing them home to boost his ego. They were a dear couple and wanted to serve God. What they didn't know, and why should they, was that Dad couldn't, or should I say shouldn't, drink. They had brought bottles of booze with them to celebrate with. Dad had made a covenant with God not to drink again and here he was drinking with this couple. Kayla hadn't seen Dad drunk since she was a toddler and this was all a bit scary. She was in the kitchen when she heard Ernie saying how terrible he felt that he had prostituted his wife and Dad, in an almost bragging way, said, "That's nothing Ernie mate. I sexually abused my daughter for years."

Kayla was dumbstruck! 'He hadn't, he's a liar.' She thought he was talking about her, then she realised he was talking about me. She said she felt sick. She ran out of the house, bless her, and went to Stuart's mum's house. She rang me from there and told me the whole saga and asked me if it were true. I told her it was but we were all Christians now and we had to forgive. God had forgiven him so we had to forgive those who sin against us. She was crying, bless her. This was a lot for her to take in.

I told her I loved her and to come over when she could and we could talk. She said she would. I was glad she was with Stuart. I think she told him what had happened and stayed there for several days. Mam had been standing in the kitchen with Kayla and also heard what Dad and Ernie had said.

When Christmas was finally over Mam came over to see me. It was quite bizarre because she was asking me if it were true when she already knew it was.

I had told her about it all those years ago when it had just begun. We talked about it and I told her everything. She had a knack of making everything about her and now this was about her too. She never once said she was sorry for not doing anything to stop it, for not protecting me, for hitting me and telling me not to tell anyone else, for allowing it to carry on. Oh no, this was all about her, about how Dad had brought these people without asking her. It was about him drinking and getting so drunk he told his dirty secret and embarrassed her.

I wanted to scream, "Can't you see, woman, this is not about you, it's about me and what was done to me! I was a child, think about it." But in fact I don't think she was capable of thinking of anyone but herself—and Dad of course. This is a horribly painful thing for me to dredge up, to remember and I needed her to love me, to say she was sorry, to hug me. But she didn't do any of those things. She asked if she could stay with us till she got her plan of action sorted and asked if I would ask my pastor to come and pray with her. I rang Ray, our pastor, told him the whole story and, bless him, he came over and prayed with us all.

It was such a difficult time for me. I had tried to forgive and forget all of this and, just when my life was the happiest it had ever been, it all surfaced again. It had often leapt into my mind when I wasn't even thinking about it and it would take me a few days to stuff it back into the box in my mind I kept it in. But there was no stuffing it back now; it was out in full view of everyone. The weird thing was, it was Mam who was crying, not because of what Dad had done to *me* but because of how he was treating *her*.

Mam always made stuff appear to be about her. In all this, she never once asked me how I was, how I was coping—the whole thing was about her! She had wanted him to come running over to Uckfield begging her to go back to him. He hadn't done that. He said he was ashamed of himself for drinking—no mention of what he had said to Ernie—and he would leave Mam to make up her own mind as to what she wanted to do.

Ever the drama queen, Mam stayed with us for another week to teach him a lesson and that was that. Not once did she say anything to me regarding Dad abusing me. I was deeply hurt by her lack of love and her inability to mother me. She went back to Dad and all was honky dory there while I was left with a head full of nightmares. It was months before I slept properly again, before I could stuff it all back in the box. Poor Greg didn't know how to cope with me, but he did, bless him.

Our lives were changing. Naomi was going to the local playgroup where we both made friends. I met Jill who had two boys, James and David, the same ages as my two. Jill was a gorgeous, bubbly, friendly girl. They were a lovely family and she lived just up the hill from us with her husband Peter. Jill and I would take it in turns to pick up the kids from playgroup and some days we would meet up for coffee; she was such a kind friend.

We were finding our place in the church too. It was such a change from our old church. It was great to have other young families. The pastor and his wife Hazel had four children, they were so friendly and loving. I am not saying our last church wasn't but there we were Ken and Laura's daughter and family while here we were Fay and Greg and family. It was great. We joined a house group and we would have Sundays where everyone brought food and after the service we would all eat together. It was wonderful. We would all go for walks through some of the prettiest countryside. The children would run and play together as we adults talked and laughed. One of the elders was a chap called Hedley. He and his wife Renee had five girls and, apart from being a Dad and an elder, he also had a farm not far from the chapel. In fact the chapel had been known as Cornwells Chapel for years because his father Luther and mother Ella and their family had kept the chapel going for years.

At harvest time we would take all the kids to the farm and go on hayrides. At lambing time we would all go to see the lambs. It was such a lovely time; a time of growth in us all. We learned about God's father heart towards us and we grew together as a church family. This wasn't just a Sunday faith, this was faith for life. As we watched our children grow, we were growing too. Ray's preaching was life-changing; it challenged us, we understood it and we lived by it. He

255

opened the Bible up for us all and we loved it. God was most certainly in the midst of us.

John and Sharon had three boys, Paul, Ben and Stephen. Their little family had moved up to Shildon in Durham but they were in the midst of selling their house and moving back down to Sussex. We missed them a lot and were praying they would be down soon. Phil and Maggy had Emily, Ken and Susie hadn't any babies as yet and Kayla was aunty to all of them and loved it. She was still going through her sort of Goth look; lots of black clothes and the blackest eye makeup ever, and she was in love with Stuart. He was a gangly youth with massive hair and she would bring him over to our house most weekends and stay. It was great to have her and she was great with the kids. Naomi adored her. They would come with us to chapel and always seemed to enjoy it.

I loved her lots and she seemed so happy now. She had had a completely different childhood to ours because Dad had been a Christian more or less since she was born but, even so, her growing up had been difficult. His rules for her life were very harsh and he would still thrash her—but only when she deserved it! That was his reasoning, so she had to walk on eggshells around him.

Also Mam, as I have said, was a very jealous woman and if Dad showed any affection to anyone other than her she hated it. That included Kayla, so if Kayla was in any way naughty Mam couldn't wait to tell Dad so Kayla would be in trouble and out of favour. Also, all through her childhood Mam had privately fostered children, mostly Africans whose parents were training in London. I was always shocked that these educated people training to be doctors and nurses would come into Mam and Dad's house, which reeked of fags and dogs and was in no way hygienic, and think, yes, this is the perfect environment for my precious child! They would leave these little babies with Mam and Dad for years. Anyway, mostly they would have at least two extra babies. Two in particular were with them for years and Kayla was always vying for attention. It always amazed us that Mam would choose to look after children. She was rubbish with us and now people were trusting her with their children! What amazed us all was that Mam adored one of the babies, a real character, but because Dad loved the other baby she didn't like her at all, she just had her for the money. She was a dear little girl and she left when she was about five.

Kayla wasn't allowed to do any of the things her friends were doing. She had to be at home helping Mam and, on a whim, Mam would ground her, not for a week but for months! She was totally unreasonable and was like a child in that she would gloat if Kayla was told off, beaten or grounded by Dad. A very odd woman, she really had no idea about mothering at all. Kayla also said she always felt left out because she hadn't grown up with us. She said she felt like the odd one out. Bless her heart, it's a sad thing when you wish your childhood had been worse than it was so that you would fit in.

I always tried to include Kayla when we were doing stuff so she and Stuart would come over regularly. As this little romance progressed I was aware of the temptation so when Greg and I went to bed we would leave them alone for five minutes to have a bit of a kiss and cuddle, then I would bang on the ceiling. That was their cue for Kayla to come up to her bed and Stuart to make his bed on the sofa. This worked very well although a couple of times I would bang again and she would come running upstairs, a bit stroppy, saying, "Alright, alright, we heard you the first time!," but it usually worked very well.

They were in love and spent every moment they possibly could together. Stuart wanted to be a rock star. He was a drummer and he looked the part—long curly hair, tall and scruffy seemed to be the look he was going for and he had mastered it with ease! He played in a band and Kayla would go to his gigs and be so awestruck by him and his talent! Kayla was still a bit Gothy but no matter what look she was going for, she always looked gorgeous! She would put on a pair of old jeans and one of Dad's old shirts, sometimes with a belt, sometimes not. Collar turned up, not a lot of make-up on and—stunning! Mags and I said, "We can do that look," but we looked like a pair of scruffy gypsies wearing their husbands' clothes!

Mam on the Make

MAM WAS A REAL WHEELER DEALER, always on the lookout for a good deal. She was very astute and squirrelled money away for a rainy day. When Margaret Thatcher offered everyone the opportunity to buy their council house, she jumped at it and bought 22 Glebe Road for £3,000!

A few years later she met an elderly lady who lived alone in a very big house. She told Mam she needed some jobs done: the roof was leaking, a tap wasn't turning off, bits like that. "Don't you worry," said Mam, "My husband will come and fix them for you." So Dad went and did all the odd jobs.

In the meantime, Mam would go and sit with this elderly lady, who was in her eighties, found out that she had no family whatsoever, and talked this dear lady into selling the house to her. They would do all the repairs and she could live in the house until she died. "Wonderful," the old lady said. "This has been my worry. I want to die in my own home. I have lived here all my life, it was my parents' house." I think I am right in saying that the old lady never had the house valued. Mam offered her £3,000 and the old lady was thrilled.

Mam got everything rolling with solicitors. I truly don't think Dad had anything to do with it—he just believed Mam. She bought the house, let the lady stay for a few weeks, then rang Social Services saying she was worried about this old dear living on her own, very vulnerable and not eating properly. The old lady became unwell and finished up in hospital. Mam went to visit her, only to tell her they were going to put the rent up and, poor thing, she couldn't afford it! Can you imagine how she felt?

She was rehoused in a council flat for the elderly just along the road from her old house. Mam was chuffed. She sold 22 and they moved into this beautiful Victorian detached house with two reception rooms and four bedrooms. It did need lots doing to it but, my goodness, she robbed that lady and had no qualms about doing it! I think we were all shocked and ashamed when we found out.

I remember walking in the front door to see Dad dragging Kayla down the stairs by her hair. I was shocked, he was calling her worse than muck. He said she had been flirting with some bloke he had brought home! Poor Kayla was sobbing. I didn't know what to do. I just said, "What's going on?" Dad told me to shut it and mind my own business. He was dealing with it. He dragged her into the sitting room and berated her, then slapped her a few times, then told her she was grounded for a month! It was all or nothing with Dad. Poor Kayla, she always said she had a different childhood to us but the fear was the same, the intimidation was the same, the bullying was the same, the beatings brought the same pain. The abuse was different but it was still abuse!

Kayla and Stuart were desperate to be together; they were so young and in love. I remember them coming over to us for the weekend and saying they had got engaged! Kayla was so excited showing off her ring and Stuart was grinning like the cat who had got the cream. It made me quite sad that this big milestone in their lives had not been marked. I can't imagine any of my children getting engaged without a celebration, but Mam and Dad did nothing. So I went and bought a cake and a bottle of sparkly wine. We had a lovely meal and then celebrated their engagement. Nothing flash, but we loved them and wanted to mark this occasion!

They wanted to get married but didn't have a penny to their names. Stuart was working at St Frances as a kitchen assistant and Kayla was training to be a mental nurse. But they knew they were going to get married, so why not now? Mam and Dad said they could—they were 19! So Kayla was to get married in Cuckfield Baptist Chapel and Errol would marry them. We set about planning the wedding and got my wedding dress out of the box I had packed it in. Kayla tried it on. It was too big, so I altered it and made it fit her. Naomi was to be her bridesmaid, so I made the bridesmaid's dress. The reception was to be in The Church of the Ascension, so I made a poster of Kayla and Stuart and Maggy, Greg and I decorated the hall. We did a buffet for the reception and had friends making quiches, potato salads and rice salads, and we cooked and sliced a turkey and a gammon. We had a table laden with food!

It was a lovely day and everyone was so happy, except Naomi who, after walking down the aisle and being handed Kayla's bouquet, burst into tears! The pressure of being the perfect bridesmaid had just got to her. Bless her, she was only seven. She so wanted to get it right and she did but the pressure got to her!

She made us all laugh after the reception was over and we came out of the church. My brother John said, "What is this church called?"

"The Church of the Ascension," I said.

Naomi laughed. "Don't be silly, mummy. It's The Church of the Reception!"

"Of course it is, darling," we said—and that's what it's known as in our house to this very day!

I had to buy Mam a frock because she was going to wear an old one. She was not a snappy dresser our Mam, that's for sure. I ordered it from a catalogue and I wanted her to look nice for Kayla, and she did. It was a lovely, happy day.

They lived together in the nurses' quarters, Linden House. We were not sure they were supposed to but they did until Kayla finished her training. Then she worked for about a year as a staff nurse, until she had beautiful Rachel Dyer, born on 1st November, a little dolly. They then moved into a lovely house in Colwell Gardens and she made it into a lovely cosy home.

Stuart was still working as a kitchen assistant and Kayla was at home looking after Rachel who was such a little cutie pie. Both Stuart and Kayla adored her. She was so easy to love with her beautiful little face and her mop of curly hair. Things seemed to be going along beautifully for them and they seemed happy. Stuart was still working at St Frances while Kayla was working nights in nursing homes for the mentally ill. Money was tight but they managed. Stuart was still playing in the band and working at the hospital but did not want to be a kitchen assistant for ever.

Kayla was expecting again and it was all very exciting, but all was not as it seemed. Stuart was having an affair with a lady he worked with and told Kayla he was leaving her. Kayla rang me in the most dreadful state. I went over and she was broken, bless her, and sobbed and sobbed. I arranged to meet Stuart in Victoria Park. I wanted to punch him but I knew that wasn't the answer. I prayed that God would give me the right words to say. We sat and talked for ages. I told him he was a husband, a father and a Christian and he needed to get his act together. Kayla was having his baby and he needed to be a man, get back to Kayla and talk things through. I invited them both over to our house for Sunday lunch. A very close friend of mine, Jill Young, came round and she and Stuart went for a walk and she talked to him. She is an awesome Christian woman, who I love dearly. Anyway, when they came back, he apologised to Kayla and said, "Let's try again." We prayed and they went home together.

Hannah Dyer was born on the 26 January 1990 and she was just a little poppet. Kayla has never forgiven me for looking into the little hospital cot and saying, "Oh Kayla, she looks like a little monkey." I meant that she hadn't unfurled yet; her little face was still all squished up. She was utterly beautiful when she unfurled but I had said the M word! Sorry Kayla. Hanny, I love you, you are beautiful. Kayla—am I forgiven?

It was while they were living here that Kenny and Phil decided to rob chemists. They were after the dangerous drugs cupboards as they were both well into drugs. Ken's attempts to come clean came to nothing, he just couldn't do it, so this was the plan. They would go out in the early morning, break into a chemist and do all they could to pry open the drugs cupboards or pry them off the wall. But they were rubbish robbers and failed at most attempts or got caught!

I remember them telling us years after the events that in one chemist they entered through a skylight and dropped a good 12 feet to the ground. They managed to get the drugs cupboard off the wall, but it was very dark. They knew the chemist sold watches, jewellery and perfume, so they filled up their bag with boxes that they pulled off the shelves. When they were done and wanted to get out they realised they had no rope ladder to scale the 12 feet drop! They really were that daft! They tried to open the door but it had deadlocks. They eventually decided the only way out was through the window, but it was toughened glass!

They threw themselves at the window, kicked it and punched it and eventually it cracked. Then they just kept throwing themselves at it and finally got out. All this time the alarm was going and they thought they were deffo going to get captured! They didn't and went back to Mam and Dad's. Everyone was in bed and they never locked their doors. They got the drugs cupboard open, took some drugs and then decided that the best bet was to bury the drugs and all the watches. On opening the bag the only things they found were sanitary towels! They went over to Blunts Wood—remember they are now off their faces! They buried the drugs in the cupboard, to keep them dry, and, feeling very pleased with themselves, they went home.

The following day they met up and talked over the night's drama. Then they decided to go over to Blunts Wood for a cheeky pill or two. The only trouble was neither of them could remember where they had buried them! For weeks afterwards they would go over there with a shovel and dig for the cupboard, but they never found it! Poetic justice.

Visiting Gran

NOW THAT WE WERE MOBILE, we decided to drive up to Durham to show off our new baby to my Gran and Grandad and Greg's family. I had never driven out of Uckfield and here we were planning a trek to Durham. We got map books and planned our route. We put all the seats down in the back of the car, put a single mattress in, a duvet for Naomi and Danny and the carrycot directly behind the driver's seat for Becky. We decided to drive through the night, thinking the children would sleep most of the way. We were all so excited. We set off at about 11pm carrying the children out to the car in their pyjamas and tucking them in under the duvet. They were wide-eyed with wonder. Becky fed well and was tucked into her carrycot. We prayed that God would give us journeying mercies and watch over us, not let us get lost and that the car would make it there and back!

It wasn't long before we hit London. Greg was navigating and it was at this point that I realised he was a rubbish navigator! We were lost in London. Scary! I was panicking, he was panicking, I was shouting, "Where do we go now?" and he was making funny umming noises. I prayed one of those prayers that go something like, "Lord, this pillock has got us lost. Please help us find our way to the A1," and almost as I said Amen, we both saw a sign saying A1. Thank you, Lord. I am sure that in spite of Greg's terrible navigation skills, God definitely guided us.

After much yelling and stroppy whispering as the children were trying to sleep, we made it up to Durham. We arrived at 6am just in time for Becky's feed, so we sat in the car outside my Gran's house as I fed her. Danny, bless him, looked up at the sky and saw the fading moon. "Look everyone," he said, "the moon came on holiday with us."

Naomi was awestruck. "It did mummy," she said.

"So it did," I said. "We must remember to take it back with us when we go home." It was agreed that we would and Daniel would be in charge of remembering.

At 7am sharp Gran's bedroom light came on. We hadn't told them we were coming; we wanted it to be a surprise! Well, believe me, it was! Grandad was always up first so we let him get downstairs and put the kettle on. I tapped on the backdoor so Gran wouldn't hear. Grandad opened it. "Well I'll be..." he said and flung his arms around me. I shushed him. I wanted to sneak upstairs and surprise Gran in bed. I had Becky in my arms and crept upstairs.

Gran was awaiting her morning cuppa and was sitting up in bed. The look on her face as we walked through the door was priceless. She beamed. "Good morning Gran. Look what we've brought you, your new great granddaughter," and I lay Becky in her arms.

"Eee lass, what a surprise. How did you get here? Where are the other bairns? What time is it? Eee, isn't she bonny." And with that she kissed Becky on her head and squeezed my arm. "Eee lass, it's good to see you," she said. I wanted to cry. I loved my Gran and Grandad so much and it was so lovely to be back with them again. They loved me and they loved my children.

As Gran cradled Becky, whose second name is Charlotte after her, I ran downstairs to fetch Naomi and Dan up to see her too. "Nay lass, don't bring 'em up. I'll come down." So I went up and got Becky, brought her down and handed her to Grandad—he was a sucker for babies.

"Eee, she's a bonny bairn," he said and gave her several kisses. This was how it should be, I thought. They were so proud of me and I felt it. Grandad handed Becky to Greg and then made a huge fuss of Naomi and Dan, telling them how much they had grown and how grown-up they were. I poured the tea and we all sat at the kitchen table, Grandad beaming from ear to ear, Gran mumbling about not having anything in for dinner.

"We'll have a walk up to the shops later and get some grub in Gran," said Greg.

"Aye lad, we will," she answered. She loved to cook for us. I had come to realise over the years that it was her way of showing love.

We spent a week with them and it was wonderful. We visited Greg's Mam and all his family. They all made us very welcome and it was good to see everyone and catch up with family news. The night we were travelling back we loaded up the car and kissed Gran and Grandad. I was trying not to cry; I had always hated leaving them. We sat in the car with Naomi and Dan wrapped up in the duvet and Becky fast asleep in her carrycot and we waved to Gran and Grandad as we drove up Luxmore Avenue. Suddenly, Daniel jumped up from under the duvet. "The moon, mummy. We mustn't forget the moon."

"You are so right, darling," I said. "We'll take it back with us. Come on Mr Moon, our holiday is over. It's back to Uckfield with you."

Dan settled back under the duvet, stuck his thumb in his mouth and watched the sky. Every so often a little voice from the back would say, "He's coming with us, mummy." Bless him, he made my heart fill with love—well they all did with their funny little sayings and ways. I so loved being a mummy. Our little family was everything to me but it filled me with awful memories of my own childhood and how my mother was with us. It would make me sad to think that my Mam never found any joy in us, that we were always a nuisance to her and that we never did anything as a family. I remember sitting in the park watching my children play and laughing at their antics. Mam never took us to a park or did anything fun with us. She missed so much, but her life revolved around Dad.

I found myself thinking back to my childhood quite a bit while my children were growing and wondering what went through my Mam's mind as she beat us or was particularly cruel to us. We were defenceless kids. What did she gain from her cruelty?

Greg was working at American Express and was very happy there. He would ride his little moped to and fro and be home by 6.00 every evening. It was great. He was a real 'hands on' daddy. He loved his children and would take great joy in playing with them. Dan was his little man and would want to wrestle with him at every opportunity. He and Naomi would jump all over Greg as soon as he had taken his coat off with cries of, "Come on daddy, you'll surrender first" and Greg was on the floor, two excited children wrestling him for all they were worth. After about ten minutes Greg would beg them to stop, feigning pain and injury and they would make him surrender to squeals of delight and shouts of, "We won. We beat daddy." I would be getting dinner onto the table as they finished. Then we would all sit together as Greg said grace, giving thanks for all that God had provided for us.

I loved sitting down to eat as a family. We would talk about the day and the children would tell their daddy what they had done. We would plan the next day's activities. It was important to me to include the children in every aspect of family life and for them to feel important. After dinner Greg would bath Naomi and Dan and I would feed Becky and get her ready for bed. Our little routine worked very well. Greg was a brilliant daddy, which made life so easy for me. I loved him so much.

We were travelling over to Barcombe Baptist Chapel every Sunday and for midweek prayer meetings. Our little church family was growing and it was decided that we needed to extend our chapel. It would cost lots of money. I can't remember the amount but, needless to say, we didn't have it. However, we prayed that if it was the right thing to do, if it was God's will, the money would come and, slowly but surely, it came. A list was made up of how much it cost for a brick, a bag of cement etc. and even the children got involved. I think at that time a brick cost 13 pence so children would give out of their pocket money to buy bricks. This really was a family venture! The plans were passed and the building started. It was so exciting.

We would start to panic when a bill was due to be paid and we didn't have the money but somehow at the last minute the money came in. It was awesome seeing God's hand in it all. I remember vividly going to an early morning prayer meeting and when I say early morning, I mean it—6 am! We had a particularly large bill to pay and no money. There were about twenty of us at this particular meeting, and others joined us as the morning passed. We were asking God to provide. At around 11am Hedley came into the chapel holding a cheque for the amount needed. It had arrived in the post. We really praised the Lord for that and it happened often; it was so faith-building.

When our lovely new chapel was finished it seemed enormous. It has the most beautiful arched window, high pine-clad ceilings, comfy chairs, not pews, and we had a piano, not our wheezy old organ—though, to be honest, we loved that old organ. Boy, we were posh!

It was such an exciting day when we were allowed in for our first service and we were all there bright and early. Ray had asked Dr Martin Lloyd-Jones to open it for us and he said he would, bless him. He preached his last sermon that day so we were very privileged to have been there. God was really blessing our little chapel and we were so thrilled to be part of it. Our children, too, were happy to be part of this lovely church family.

Lindsay and I, with our kids, would meet up regularly and it was great. Naomi, Dan and Emily played so well together and Charlie and Becky would take their naps together. We would drive over about 11.00 and the kids would play in the garden. Simon and Lindsay lived in Crink Cottages.

They were farm cottages and the barn was right next to the cottages so the kids loved to go play in it. One day we were heading back home, We shouted for the kids to come in and got them organised; shoes on, clobber collected together. I went out to the car and put Becky in her car seat and had her all strapped in but when I looked on the seat next to her I saw a huge dead rat! I jumped out and shrieked. Lindsay peered in the window, "Where did that come from?"

We both looked at Daniel. Emily jumped in. "Mummy, we've got lots of them and Naomi and Daniel haven't got any so I gave them one." She was so pleased with herself and she had a big grin on her dear little face. She was being kind to her friends!

"What do you mean you've got lots of them?"

"We have, mummy, look," and we all walked into the barn. They had been playing hospitals using dead rats! They had put them on bales and covered them up with straw! We rushed them all into the house, washed their hands frantically and told them not to play with dead animals anymore!

Christmas was around the corner. I just loved Christmas and I wanted it to be magical for the kids. We would put the tree up on the first Saturday in December and the kids would decorate it. The theory of less is more didn't come into it; our tree always looked like it belonged in a tart's boudoir! There was so much stuff on it, but that was all part of our Christmas.

We worked so hard all year to buy everything the kids wanted. I would buy stuff all year round and put it in the attic and I would make things too. It was so important to me that my kids had the Christmas that I would have loved, that I dreamed of. So on Christmas Eve, once the kids were in bed and I had given them a magic sleeping pill (a fresh breath mint), I would tell them it would make them fall asleep quickly so they better run upstairs quick sharp. One year Naomi fell asleep on the stairs, but then she was always the drama queen!

Greg would get everything down from the loft and we would spend the evening wrapping everything up, making sure they had equal piles of presents. It was a mountain of stuff. Far too much really, but to me it meant they were wanted, important and, most importantly, loved.

The kids would put a glass of milk and a mince pie out for Father Christmas and carrots and water for the reindeer. Once the presents were all piled up, I would get a tin of glitter and sprinkle it all over the pile, and then sprinkle some all the way upstairs and into their bedrooms and Greg would put their stockings on the bottom of their beds. This is known as sprinkle dust in our house, it's what falls off Father Christmas and it's what helps him fly—it's magic! I remember Daniel getting the dustpan, sweeping up the sprinkle dust and putting it all over himself, then trying to fly! I had to tell him that once it falls off Father Christmas it loses its magic!

Christmas morning was fabulous. As the kids woke they would come squealing into our room and jump on our bed. "He's been! He's been!," they would be yelling. They would bring their stockings into our room and open all the little pressies. Also I always put in an apple, an orange, nuts and foil-covered chocolate money. I don't really know why I did all this but I think I saw a film where a posh family did it. Not that I was trying to be posh, I just wanted to do the right thing for my kids, and for their Christmases to be normal!

Once that was done Greg and I would get up and, as we were coming down the stairs, there would be squeals of, "Look. Sprinkle dust!" As Greg opened the door and put on the light, revealing the mountain of presents, their little faces showed pure joy!

Our rule was that they could choose one present to open now and the rest after we had been to church. After all, it *was* Jesus's birthday. So we would have breakfast, then a great Christmas service at church, back home for lunch, then opening-presents time! The whole day was full of fun and excitement and I loved seeing their faces as they opened presents and found the very thing they had asked for! I just loved being a mummy. This was how family life should be. Well, that's what I thought. I had a fabulous husband who loved me, he was a great daddy and our kids were the best!

Greg was still working at American Express. He was happy in his work and he and his little moped would be back and forth to Ridgewood. When it was time for the prayer meeting his trusty little moped would get him there and back—until one fateful evening. He was driving through the country lanes when he heard a BANG! And the next thing he knew he was face down in the road! Thankfully, no one was close behind him. His back tyre had exploded! He was shaken but not broken, thankfully. John Cornwell arrived in his pick-up truck, bless him, and between them they got the moped into the truck and both continued on to the prayer meeting. Dear John then brought my battered Greg and his broken moped home. Greg got the tyre fixed, but this was to happen several more times, which was very scary. It made Greg nervous when driving it, and me worried every time he went on it! I kept saying he should take his test in a car, but he just didn't want to or, rather, he had no confidence at all. At a chapel tea once Simon asked Greg why he didn't drive a car. He said, "Well, the width of a car would worry me. On a moped all you have to worry about is between your legs!" We all fell about laughing, but I knew what he meant.

I hated it when he was asked to work in Brighton or Burgess Hill. I was so worried about the wretched moped and would pray from him leaving home to getting to work and from work to home in the evening!

Becky was growing up too. She was such an easy child, such a happy little soul, but very stubborn. She and Ben would play funny little games. She was happiest being post office lady, just moving bits of paper from one pile at this side of the table to another pile at the other side of the table. Greg had brought home an old adding machine and she would press buttons for hours. Ben would get bored. He liked playing a travel game but not Becky, she would play for hours, so Ben would invariably end up sliding down the stairs on his tummy. He and Dan would do that for hours too! You buy all kinds of toys and this is what they do! I didn't mind as they were laughing and having fun.

A Crisis for Kenny

BECKY STARTED PLAYGROUP. She went to a different one from the others. It was called Spire and was in the church hall and run by some of the mums from Naomi and Daniel's school. It was lovely. Ben and Becky started together and they both loved it. It was three hours in the morning so I decided I would try to get a job. My friend Gail had got a job working for Social Services as a home help and she said I would love it so I went for an interview and got the job! I was thrilled. I had no confidence in myself or my ability, and the fact that I had no qualifications made me feel stupid and thick, but I knew I could clean and I had an affinity with older people, so this was the perfect job for me, and God knew that.

I was to go to different homes and, depending on the client's needs, I would do shopping, cleaning, cooking, or whatever the client wanted. Sometimes they would want to be taken to the shops and do their own shopping with my help. Gail was right—I did love it. I met some absolutely lovely people. I also met some rotters but, on the whole, I loved it.

I worked part-time and once Becky started school I upped my hours. It worked really well. I could drop the kids off at school, go to my first client and make sure I finished my last client by 3.00 so I was able to be outside school in time to pick up the children. I did this for many years and it fitted into my day very well. It was hard work sometimes but, as I said, I met some lovely people. We were not supposed to get emotionally attached to our clients but my nature is to do just that! I would have little old ladies ringing me at all hours, asking me to pop round. So I and the kids would visit. They loved the kids and the kids loved them.

I would sometimes collect three old ladies and take them down to Eastbourne for fish and chips, followed by a lovely ice cream on the front! We had such fun! Lots of them had no families and hadn't been out for years. It made me realise how important family was. These old ladies became part of our extended family.

It was 4am and Greg and I were in bed. The phone rang and it was my sister-in-law Susie. She and Kenny had moved up to live in Willington, near Gran and Grandad. Her voice was full of panic. Kenny had been in a car crash, no one else involved, but he was in a critical state. He had crashed through a five bar gate and fence and one of the bars had smashed through the windscreen and through his forehead, smashed his skull and gone three inches into his brain. The force was such that it had brushed him from the driver's seat into the back seat. The irony was that if he had been wearing his seat belt he would have been killed instantly. As it was, he was conscious and impaled on the fence post. Unable to move but alive!

This happened at 2am on a country road and, fortunately for Kenny, a lady in a cottage a few hundred yards away, had been unable to sleep. She thought she heard a noise, looked out of her window and could see Ken's headlights in the field so, bless her heart, she phone for an ambulance, assuming someone was hurt. How right she was!

Ken was taken to Newcastle General Hospital. The fire brigade had to cut him out of the car and saw the fence post down to a manageable size, leaving it still embedded in his brain, to get him into the ambulance.

Susie was in a desperate panic when she phoned. She had two small children, two-year-old Adam and baby Dawn. She couldn't go to the hospital with them. I calmed her down a bit and told her I would ring the rest of the family. We would organise something but, right now, we would be praying for them and I would ring in a little while to find out what was happening. It didn't dawn on me that she had no car and couldn't get to Newcastle. Bless her, she must have been so frightened.

I was now in a mad panic! I leapt out of bed, told Greg to start praying for Kenny while I phoned Mam, Dad, John, Phil and Kayla. I couldn't rouse Mam and Dad and I was crying with frustration and panic. I phoned John and Sharon and John answered. Through sobs I explained what had happened. "We must pray. He can't die, he's not saved." John was in shock too. The thought of my little brother spending eternity in hell terrified me.

Greg had gone downstairs and I joined him. He was praying for Ken and Susie while I was sobbing and still trying to get Mam and Dad on the phone. I had managed to get everyone else. They were all shocked and those who prayed were praying. Every time Greg tried to talk to me I would say, "Don't talk, pray." I was worried that if he stopped praying Kenny would die. Irrational I know but

I was just frightened for Kenny. I was praying too when the doorbell rang and I ran to the door. It was 5am and there stood my lovely brother John. He took one look at me and said, "I'll put the kettle on. You put a frock on." I was stark naked! It just hadn't come into my thinking, I was in such a state of panic.

John was such a darling boy. He was a rock and though he was one of my younger brothers, he had such a wise head on his very broad shoulders. I loved, valued and respected him highly. Well, frock and kettle both on, we sat with our tea and talked over the possibilities and we prayed for hours. We decided that when God made Kenny, He had put some spare bits in his brain, because he knew what was going to happen to him.

We finally got through to Mam and Dad, who decided to go up to Willington which we thought would be a great help to Susie. In fact it turned out to be anything but! They went up by train because Dad didn't like driving out of his little area, his comfort zone, so they couldn't drive Susie to the hospital. They wouldn't stay with Susie, because Ken and Susie had bought a house that needed lots of work doing and they were in the middle of renovating it—a work in progress. So they stayed with Gran and Grandad and were neither use nor ornament to poor Susie.

Mam and Dad went once to see Ken and were so upset they didn't go again! They were a weird pair and seemed to make Kenny's accident all about them and how they couldn't bear to see Kenny in such a dreadful state. This was their youngest son in intensive care! Not a thought for Susie and the children or supporting Kenny and his little family. When they said they were coming home it was a relief to Susie but she felt quite alone and frightened up there. We were all furious with Mam and Dad. What on earth was the point of going up!

Greg and I prayed about me going up but we really couldn't afford it. We only just met all our commitments and sometimes there was more months left at the end of the money! We had asked our church to pray for Kenny and it was a great comfort to know that so many faithful Christian brothers and sisters were praying for him.

We were sat at the dinner table when the doorbell rang. It was Keith, one of the church leaders. He said, "I'm not stopping. Just called by to give you this and to say that we really feel you should go up to Durham to be with your brother." He handed me an envelope, prayed with us and left. There was £50 in the envelope, which today isn't a huge amount of money but 30 years ago it was a lot. We were so touched and astounded. We hadn't told anyone that we felt I should go or that we were short of money but God knew our need and met it yet again. What a wonderful God we serve.

I rang work and told them I didn't know how long I would be away. They were brilliant and said not to worry and my job would be there when I got back. Nancy and Ray said they would help out with the kids and the church family rallied round. We had great neighbours who also helped Greg.

We prayed together as a family after explaining to the kids where I was going and why and I told them that as soon as Uncle Kenny was better I would come home. I would ring them lots and I needed them to be really helpful to daddy. They all said they would. There were big hugs and kisses all round and off I went. I drove through the night and arrived early. Susie didn't know I was coming and so she was so pleased to see me and I her.

That afternoon her friends Ron and Rita looked after the children and I took Susie and drove to Newcastle to see Kenny. What a shock it was to see him. He had tubes and pipes in all sorts of places and machines with lights flashing. He looked so poorly, weak and feeble. He was unconscious. The surgeon had taken the wood out of his head and they told us that was a dangerous time and he could so easily have died. He didn't but he looked very close to death. We sat at his bedside and prayed.

What I haven't said was that Kenny was still a heroin addict. He was actually coming home from a friend's house the night of the accident. He had been drinking and using drugs and was off his face when the crash happened. Now here he is in intensive care. The surgeon told us he had removed a lot of damaged brain when they took out the wood which had gone three inches into his brain. A huge chunk of his skull was missing, smashed to pieces, and his face looked terrible. He had two black eyes swollen shut and his face was distorted and yellow and purple, and covered with cuts. His head was a mass of bandages, his chest was black and blue and his fingers were swollen like sausages. These were just the injuries we could see. The whole extent of his injuries was not really apparent to us as yet.

Susie found this so hard, not knowing how Ken's injuries were going to affect him and their life together. It was all very frightening. I would go to the hospital most days and sit with him and would pray for him to be healed. Susie would come with me on the days she could get someone to watch the kids.

Ken regained consciousness and was very chatty. We were thrilled and very thankful. He never asked why he was in hospital or what happened but he did ask where we were. "Newcastle," I said.

"Oh. I've never been here before," he replied.

I had taken photos of Adam and Dawn to show him but, it was shocking to me, he didn't know who they were! He didn't remember he was married. It was heart-breaking. He thought he lived in Haywards Heath which he had left three years before! I got a scrapbook, put photos in it and would write in what we talked about every day. I would also write what Susie and I had been doing at the house—a bloomin' lot! We decorated the bedrooms and, in the evening, when the kids were in bed, we finished off jobs Kenny had started. I am a dab hand at wallpapering, thanks to all those years working with Dad, so we flew through the rooms. We laughed as much as we worked and it was lovely to be there and be useful.

I missed Greg and my kids. I would ring two or three times a week and chat to each of them. They were desperate to tell me how they were helping daddy and what they had done at school. It would make me so homesick. Greg would be all upbeat and telling me he was missing me but after hearing all about Kenny and what Susie and I were doing he was convinced I was in the right place and God was using me. I would come out of the phone box all teary-eyed but determined to do all that I possibly could to help both Kenny and Susie.

We spent a day and a night delivering a litter of puppies which was a wonderful blessing as they were pedigree Staffordshire Bull Terriers and were to be sold. That would pay the mortgage as Ken was self-employed so, no work, no money. As each one those puppies popped out we prayed there would be yet another. In fact there were six but one was very weak. I stayed up all night rubbing this little scrap of life to keep it breathing and putting it to Bodie's teat. Eventually he made it! I felt a real sense of achievement.

Ken was getting stronger each day but the doctor would come and say, "Don't hope for too much. A lot of his brain was damaged. We removed a substantial amount and we're not sure what his limitations will be." It was quite depressing but I decided that right back at the beginning when John, Greg and I prayed, we thought God had made spares for Ken. So I prayed that every time the doctor said he wouldn't be able to do something he would do it!

His memory was terrible so, as I said, I wrote everything in his scrapbook. He would read it over and over and eventually his memory improved. They said he might have difficulty walking so I prayed for his legs to work. He walked! It was such a time of miracles!

I would say to him, "You are a bloomin' miracle, Kenny," and, bless him, he would tell anyone who would listen to him, "I'm a bloomin miracle, I am. I should be dead, but I'm not." The biggest miracle was that he didn't remember that he was a heroin addict and because the hospital had been giving him huge amounts of painkillers and slowly over the weeks cutting them down, by the time he came home from hospital, he was clean. How wonderful!

I had been up in Durham for six weeks. I had missed my Greg and my lovely babies and couldn't wait to see them all, though I had enjoyed getting to know Dawn and Adam, such adorable little munchkins. Adam was full of fun and chatter and we had so much fun together. Little Dawnie was such a cuddler and would climb into bed with me first thing in the morning and snuggle up—too cute! I would miss them when I went home.

I had rung home regularly and Greg would tell me all was well and to stay until I felt it was time to come home. They were all praying for me, Kenny, Susie and the kids. The church was being wonderful but my babies were missing having mummy around. They would all say, "Mummy, when are you coming home?" and I would feel so sad.

When the doctor told Susie and me that Ken could come home we were thrilled. His head wound had healed beautifully. The hole had been a good three inches across by three inches high but they had cobbled the skin together. Almost his whole forehead was like a baby's fontanelle and you could see his brain pulsating. It was very weird! They were going to put a plate in but it couldn't be done for a year so he had to be very careful not to bang his head or have a two-year-old poke it—which was far more likely to happen!

The day before Kenny came home from hospital, Susie and I went to Social Services and asked for help for Ken. He had to keep his wound sterile so we asked if we could have vouchers to buy new bedding, sheets, duvet, pillows—the lot. They were brilliant and gave us vouchers for it all. The house looked lovely, Susie looked lovely, the kids looked lovely, though we were a little nervous as to how Ken would cope. He had some very funny ways with him now. He seemed to have no filters and would say exactly what he thought, such as, "She's fat" or "That's a horrible dress." We would discover that he had lost his sense of smell too and would say quite inappropriate things.

I went to hospital to pick up Ken and all the paraphernalia that he needed to bring home. It was a long journey and I drove very slowly and carefully and we chatted easily. He was scared of coming home because he didn't know what he was expected to do. I told him he didn't have to do anything, just get well and enjoy being a daddy and a hubby. I told him how Adam had been my best mate and I had taught him a few big and very clever words for a little fella. There were three large pylons on the way to Bishop Auckland, so he learned pylon, also viaduct, and another one was antenna. It was so sweet hearing this little fella say, "Aunty Fay I can see the viaduct." If anyone heard him they had a look of amazement on their face; he was a delightful little man. Dawn was just toddling and would walk on her tippy toes, arms outstretched towards me and say, "UP!" As I picked her up she would put her little arms around my neck and give me a big squeeze. I loved it. She was such a little poppet and I had so enjoyed getting to know them.

We arrived home. Adam and Dawn were so excited to see their daddy and Susie was so thrilled to have Kenny home, though a little apprehensive as to how this would all pan out. I felt I should leave this little family to find its feet and get back-to-back to *my* family. So, after having a lovely meal together and lots of cuddles and kisses from Adam and Dawn, we all prayed together, I gathered all my bits and began the long drive south. I was sad to be leaving them but I couldn't wait to cuddle my little ones.

I drove through the night and arrived at home around 4.30am. I crept into the house and went upstairs. I looked into Naomi and Becky's room and they were both fast asleep. It was so lovely to see them and I sneaked a kiss on their cheeks. They looked adorable, all snuggled down. I went into Daniel's room where he was snuggled down like a little hamster. I kissed his head and he turned and looked at me. "Mummy," he said. I kissed him again and said, "Yes it's me darlin'. Now go back to sleep." He closed his eyes and I slipped out of his room. I got undressed in the dark and slipped into bed. Greg was fast asleep and I snuggled up to him. I was home. Thank you, Lord.

The next thing I knew it was 7.30 and Daniel came running in. "I dreamed you came home and you did," he said as he leapt onto me, hugging me tightly and laughing. Naomi and Becky soon joined us. "You are home mummy," they shouted and bounced onto the bed. They were adorable! I had missed them so much and there were lots of kisses and cuddles. It was lovely. I was back where I belonged.

Greg had gone downstairs to get breakfast ready and he came up with a cuppa for all of us. A real treat! The kids were full of questions and then all talking at the same time, telling me stuff that had happened while I had been gone. It was chatter, chatter, chatter and I loved it.

Greg came up and said, "Right, you lot. Come on and show mum how we get ready." They were reluctant but ran to their rooms and got on with their morning routine. I got up, went downstairs. My home looked different but, boy, it felt good to be home. The kids were down in no time and breakfast was on the table. We all sat round.

Naomi said grace and added, "Thank you God that mummy is home safe." We all said Amen.

Greg said how glad he was to have me back—he had missed me. I soon got back into my routine; poor Greg had found being mum *and* Dad a real struggle. The washing machine had baffled him. He didn't realise washing had to be sorted into light and dark so when I looked into the washing basket, everything was blue! He said it made it all easier, it all matched! Also the kids, especially Naomi, had talked daddy into letting them do things they knew I wouldn't let them do. Apparently, Naomi said that after school they were allowed to eat snacks while watching telly, instead of doing their spelling or reading. Also, they told Greg they were allowed to wear jelly shoes to school and he fell for it all. You can't blame them for trying, can you?

I would phone Susie regularly to see how Kenny was doing. It seemed he was struggling with life and was getting quite angry with her and the kids. She wasn't coping with him either. This was not good and certainly not what I had expected.

We had decided to change a few things in the house, so we asked Kenny, who was a builder, and his mate Dutch, who was a brickie, to come down and give us an estimate to do the work. They both jumped at the chance to earn a few quid and it got Kenny away from Susie and the kids to give them a break. They would live with us while they did the work. We had a huge conservatory on the back of the house which was falling apart. We had to do something, so a friend came round and drew up plans to move the kitchen and put a shower room and loo where the conservatory was. The plans were fabulous. It would make a huge difference to our living space, freeing up the old kitchen to make a large dining room too. We were very excited and extended our mortgage. Ken and Dutch arrived and work started. It was manic, with them working and living with us.

We were all squeezed in together, Daniel sleeping on the floor in the girls' room with Dutch and Ken in Daniel's room. It was a very long two months!

But in that time Ken and I had some long, meaningful conversations. He was still clean and was asking about God. He came to church with us and really seemed to want to find God and find peace. I told him he needed to ask God to forgive him for all the wrong things he had done—and he had done some really bad stuff. He seemed to take it all in.

Ken went to stay with Mam and Dad for the weekend. He talked with Dad well into the night about Christianity and when he went to bed that night, he told us, he sat in bed, put his bins (glasses) on the bedside table, turned off the light, put his hands together and prayed, pouring his heart out to God and asking God to forgive him. He said he opened his eyes and the room was filled with light! In the corner of the room at ceiling height was a ball of light and, as he looked, it came towards him and seemed to burst on his head. He felt joy like never before. He had a sense of God's love and forgiveness and he also had a feeling that the hole in his head had been healed. He put his hand up to his head. It hadn't but he realised that the hole in his heart and soul had been filled! He knew he was forgiven, he knew he was loved, and he knew he was a Christian. It was a life-changing moment and what a difference it was to make to his life and his marriage.

When our building was finished and Dutch and Kenny went home, Kenny was a completely different man. Susie and the kids had to get used to living with him all over again and their lives were to change out of all recognition. Kenny joined the church with Susie, they made friends and were very involved with church life. We were all thrilled when Kenny decided to be baptised and we all drove up on Saturday and went to the baptism on the Sunday. It was joyous! Ken gave his testimony and it was a wonderful privilege to be there. We all went back to Kenny and Susie's and had a wonderful time!

Phil had been making phone calls all the time. He disappeared and came back with a white English bull terrier pup! We were all shocked and said that Maggy would go mad. "Nah, she'll be OK," said Phil but we weren't so sure. John said Sharon would kill him if he came home with a bull terrier!

After saying our goodbyes to Kenny, Susie and the kids, we set off. The journey back home was interesting as this pup was passed around like a parcel and the little fella had a real wind problem! Not good in a confined space. Phil thought this was hilarious, at least until the pup weed on him, then we all thought *that* was hilarious! Fun times.

A Pain in the Neck

KENNY AND SUSIE WERE SETTLED IN THEIR LITTLE HOUSE IN HELMINGTON ROW, but life was tough for them as Ken couldn't seem to get back into the swing of work. Susie was coping with the kids, the dog, the house *and* Ken. She loved living in Durham and the church, but Ken wanted to move back south although the houses in Durham were so much cheaper than Sussex. John had bought a nightclub in Lewes and was ripping the guts out of it, turning it into two houses. He told Kenny he could have one of them cheaper so he could move back. They were both thrilled. The houses were not quite finished but Kenny said he would finish bits off anyway. So they sold their home in Helmington Row, packed their furniture into a van and travelled down to Lewes.

We were all thrilled they were back down south. It was lovely to have them back in the family and joining in parties and gatherings. Adam and Dawn were growing up. Adam started school and he was such a little geezer. Dawn was running around like a little tornado. Kenny worked for John for a while. John was brilliant at giving his brothers work, always there for us all, bless him, but eventually Kenny started working for himself.

They were attending The Kings Church in Lewes and settled in brilliantly. Life was looking good for them all. They lived in this house for a few years, then decided to move to Ringmer into a lovely house on the Broyle. It was a three-bed semi with a beautiful big garden. The kids would love it as the Lewes house only had a yard. This was fabulous!

Ken was growing as a Christian, Susie too. They still had their old dog Bodie and Susie's joy was walking her over the fields. She was working in nursing homes and then the hospital. Ken was still working for himself but finding life difficult. He did his back in and the doctor gave him some heavy painkillers. This was a big mistake. Having been a heroin addict, as soon as he started on the painkillers he craved them and this would cause him and Susie so much heartache. He then started buying codeine. The kids were growing, both of them at Ringmer schools, and were watching their Dad becoming very ill. It must have been very scary for them.

I was going to work one morning after dropping the kids off at school, when I had a strange sensation in my fingers. I was holding the steering wheel but I couldn't actually feel it—very odd. This sensation was to happen a lot. Then one day I was driving and couldn't feel my feet—it was very scary. I had been getting lots of headaches, so finally I went to the doctor's who seemed to think I had a trapped nerve. I can't quite remember the sequence of events, but I had physiotherapy. I had my head put in a traction contraption and was pulled this way and that, all to no avail. This went on for months. The doctor had given me a soft collar to wear which didn't really do anything except make people give me a wide berth and stop people bumping into me! I wore it to remind the kids not to jump on me too.

My dear friend Jill suggested I go to a healing meeting and get prayed for and I did. Actually it was quite funny. Here I was wearing my neck collar, I went up to be prayed for and the chap praying said, "Now what's your problem?"

I was so tempted to say I had a bad foot! I know, I am a sad old woman! I explained about my neck and he proceeded to pray for me. I didn't feel any different but the next day I didn't have the numb feelings in my hands, so I thought, "I've been healed!" I met up with various friends and told them I had been healed. I felt great. Naomi was learning to skip, so there I was skipping to show her how to do it. I was lifting the kids up, just behaving like I had prior to my neck giving me problems.

Two weeks later an appointment arrived to see the specialist about my neck in Haywards Heath. I was going to cancel it as I had been healed but Jill said it would astound the doctor to see that God had healed me. So I kept the appointment. I was told I was to have dye injected into my spine and they would be able to see what the problem was. I was to be sedated and it would be all over before I knew it.

Well, I remember waking up unable to move my head! I had a buzzer in my hand, so I pressed it.

A lovely nurse came and explained that the doctor would come and tell me what they found as soon as possible. He told me that a disc in my neck had broken and was pressing on my spinal cord! He explained that the spinal cord is like a thin straw inside a fat straw, and the broken disc had cut through the fat straw and was pressing on the thin straw—my spinal cord. Scary. He told me I was in a very precarious state and he would operate on me that day. He said I could have been paralysed from the neck down if the cord had been severed! Here I was thinking I had been healed and I was a sneeze away from being paralysed!

I lay there thinking about what I had been doing over the last few weeks. Skipping, chasing the kids, driving, carrying huge shopping bags—how stupid I had been. I had a picture of God with his finger on the broken disc, protecting me from myself. He must think I am such a plonker! He had looked after me, when I hadn't looked after myself.

I had the operation that day and woke up in intensive care feeling gruesome but very thankful to God. The op was a success but my blood pressure dropped dramatically, hence I was in intensive care with the worst headache I have ever had in my life! I felt dreadful. My Mam was helping Greg by looking after the kids for the afternoon but, unbeknown to Greg, she had decided it would be a good idea to bring my children into intensive care to see me! Dozy woman! Here was I, my neck all stained with iodine and bandaged up. I was connected to machines, looking like death and she brings them in—but not before telling them, "This might be the last time you see your mummy, so be good!"

They were six, eight and ten. I remember waking up and seeing my babies' faces looking so terrified. I told them I was fine and I would be home soon. The look on their little faces will stay with me forever. I told Mam to take them out and NOT to bring them in here again! She never saw that it was such a traumatic thing to do to my kids! They have never forgotten the fear of thinking I was dying. Mam said she thought they would love to see me. That woman hadn't one ounce of sense!

I was in hospital for a couple of weeks. When I came home the ambulance drivers were on strike so Kayla, bless her, came and picked me up and drove me home. She was so nervous in case she broke me! She had made a sign and stuck it in her back window. It said CARRYING A POST-OP PATIENT. PLEASE PASS and she had packed me into the seat with cushions. She packed me in like a delicate china doll, bless her heart, and we drove from Haywards Heath to Uckfield at about 15 miles per hour, with her hazards flashing. She was so scared she would damage me!

She didn't damage me of course and in fact she came over and would help me bathe and generally look after me. She was a nurse and a brilliant one to boot! She would scuttle around tidying up and make my bed. My house drove her crackers—she is such a minimalist. I on the other hand am a maximumist! I just love stuff. It all stems from our Mam who was, as you have probably gathered by now, a mucky mare who never threw anything away. She collected stuff as though her very life depended on it. That was OK but she was not a woman of discernment and her house was always stuffed to the rafters with stuff that could mostly be described as crap! Cupboards were full, drawers were stuffed so full that the bottoms broke, and you couldn't open them. Under chairs, behind sofas, behind almost everything was stuff.

Because of this, Kayla had made a conscious decision never to have stuff! I, on the other hand, had made an unconscious decision to have stuff and lots of it! But nice stuff—at least I think it's nice!

So poor Kayla was driven mad by my stuff and she was always telling me that I didn't need this or that and she would sneakily sling stuff in the bin. I knew, Kayla but, as you rightly said, I had more than enough stuff for both of us!

I was very scared about my neck. The surgeon had taken out the broken disc and fused the two vertebrae together with super glue. My brother John said he could have sorted my neck out; he was a dab hand with super glue. Working with glass he was always cutting himself and he just super-glued himself together. But I think my surgeon used a special surgical super glue—not B&Q special!

John, bless him, would pop in to see how I was doing when he had a job in Uckfield and would bring cream cakes or chocolate. The best visitor ever! He would make us a cuppa and we would sit and chat about all sorts of things, from his plans for his business, what the boys were up to, to what the sermon was about on Sunday and how he disagreed with this or that point. I loved his randomness and his visits. Well actually, I just loved him.

Greg and the kids were all very gentle with me. Greg was doing all the housework and helping me with the cooking. I was not allowed to lift for a few weeks. Naomi decided the hoover was too heavy for me so, bless her, she decided hoovering was *her* job. Danny, not to be outdone, would do the sweeping in the kitchen, dining room and bathrooms, and Becky would do the dusting. My little troupe of cleaners were keen as mustard and would try to outdo each other in their enthusiasm. I remember sitting in the living room and Naomi walking in (she was 10 at the time) saying, "My goodness mum. This floor is disgusting and I only did it yesterday" and she tutted at me! I had a job not to laugh but this was no laughing matter. She dragged the hoover out and began running it around the room. Becky was straight in the kitchen for her duster and polish and was squirting everything liberally with Pledge. Danny was sweeping the kitchen floor vigorously. They were like little mice scurrying round, all trying to help. Even after I was up and about and back to being mummy, they all wanted to keep their jobs. They were not quite as enthusiastic but they still did them.

Over the years I went on to have several more spine operations. Discs removed and metal put in. My neck has been a proper pain in the neck! But I think it's all part of life in a fallen world and it's how we deal with it. I have tried not to be a whinger—in life other people cope with far worse—and just because I am a Christian I don't think God should give me the perfect life. In truth I have learned so much through pain and to accept help graciously to know a little of Christ's suffering. All this sounds terribly holy but it's true. It has taught me that I need Jesus to help me through. He is my strength and I am sure that without Him I wouldn't be here at all. He has lifted me up when life seemed all too much.

Birthdays and Bonfires

As FAMILIES, WE WERE ALL GROWING, and our kids were growing up, but whenever we had a birthday or a celebration of any kind we would get together and have fun. John and Sharon were brilliant and would have the whole family over for Christmas when John would think up painful games for us all to play. 'Where are you, brother?' was a typical Lancaster party game. Two competitors lay on the floor holding each other's right hand and with a rolled-up newspaper in their left hand. Blindfolded, each player takes it in turn to say, "Where are you, brother?"

"Here I am," says the other, and then the one asking has to try to hit the other with the rolled-up newspaper. Hilarious, but made even more so by removing the blindfold of one of them, so they always hit their opponent!

John was brilliant at organising us all. 'Pass the parcel' had forfeits. Stevie's was to 'put lipstick on the person to your left', who happened to be Uncle Phil! To raucous laughter, Steve went to put it on him and, to everyone's amazement, Phil let him! They were always such fun. All the kids loved it and the adults enjoyed it immensely.

Bonfire Night was always a great event. John and Sharon, bless them, did that too. Many a life was almost lost at these evenings. John using an old toilet to set the fireworks off in, but the toilet exploded and porcelain shards flew through the air, missing children and adults by fractions. We all laughed! Sharon was very cross with John but he laughed and did his 'What?' face. We sat and ate burgers, chatting and laughing together, not realising how precious these times together were. I loved them all so much. Birthday parties were equally fun. The birthday boy or girl would be the centre of attention and loving every moment.

We loved being together and Mam and Dad would be included at every do. They seemed to enjoy it too. Their 40th wedding anniversary was a big celebration and we all clubbed together to buy them a clock and a massive bouquet of red roses for Mam. We made a video with all of us saying our thanks to them for various things, including leading us to Jesus, teaching us various skills and for being our parents. We had a party at our house and everyone brought something towards the grub. We left the camera rolling as we sat and ate. We were all there with our kids apart from John and Sharon and the boys. They had done a house swap and gone to New Zealand for three months. We missed them but they were having the best time, apart from Paul who had appendicitis. He had it removed in Rotorua, bless him. But what a fabulous thing for them to do as a family. We couldn't wait for them to get back and hear all about it.

I digress! At the party we chatted, laughed, and presented Mam and Dad with our gifts. It was only on watching the video that we saw that Dad, who when Greg was saying grace was faffing about with the clock, seemed totally uninterested in what Greg was praying. It scared me to see that!

Life in the Dyer home was full on. They moved to a little house down Hanbury Lane and were there for a couple of years when the house next door but one to Phil and Mags became vacant. They applied for it and got it! Wonderful! They moved in and it was just a very cosy little home. They would come over to us for Sunday lunch. The girls were adorable and my three treated them like living dollies. They loved our toys and cats and when we had a litter of kittens I remember the girls begging Kayla if they could have one. Not a chance! Our toys were different to theirs and we had masses! We had the most wonderful Christmas together when they stayed with us and we loved them so much.

I remember going over to Kayla and Stuart's and she had found a lump in her breast. As I had had four lumps removed, all benign, I said, "Don't worry, darling. You are probably lumpy like me." It was a small lump; you could actually see it. I thought it would be a cyst, so I really wasn't worried about it. "It'll be nowt," I said, "but do get it checked out."

Bless her, she went to the doctor who sent her to Haywards Heath Hospital. I think she had a biopsy and had to go back to get the results. Bless her heart, she went on her own. Stuart was working and didn't take a day off to go with her. They told her it was cancer! How terrible to get that news on your own and she was only 33! She rang and told me and I was in shock. Rachel and Hanny were ten and eight and they needed their mummy. I needed my sister! It was a scary time but, bless her, she was so brave. She went into hospital, they did a

285

lumpectomy and she had to have radiotherapy every day for six weeks in Brighton Hospital. I drove her down and my heart ached for her.

It was very unpleasant but, as always, she was very brave. She would go in and I would mostly wait in the car and pray for her. In my memory I thought Stuart had left but in fact he was still with Kayla at this time. Maybe he was a bit detached. We all thanked God that the cancer had gone and she recovered well. She's not one to sit and mope, she just got on with it for her girls. Don't get me wrong, we both cried a fair bit on the way home from hospital from time to time and she felt ill and rotten, bless her. She would put the seat right back and lie down, feeling energy-less and poorly. As she did that, I would pray silently that God would help her and lift the sick, listless feeling.

It made me so sad to see her like this. I tried to stay strong for her and Mam, Dad and Maggy were there to try to help and support her. John and Shaz too, but no one could take away that feeling of no energy and still having two little girls to put on the 'I'm fine' face for. She is only little on the outside but she is massive in spirit! I do love her so much.

Stuart had started teacher training and Kayla was working and supporting him through this. We were thrilled, because Stuart had a good brain and being a kitchen assistant wasn't using his brain and challenging him. They were going along happily for a few more years, or so we thought, with Stuart teaching and loving it. But he was also having another affair. Kayla was shattered and after talking to each other, pastor and friends, Stuart finally moved out. They had been married for 21 years—so sad! But God didn't leave Kayla and she and the girls carried on life in Vale Road and attending the Baptist church in Haywards Heath. The girls still saw their Dad. He was a fabulous Dad and he loved his girls but he was just a rubbish husband to Kayla.

It was at the Baptist church that Kayla met Richard Harlow. He was the chaplain at the hospital and they started seeing each other. We could see she was falling in love with him and he with her. They came over to ours for dinner and we deduced he was a lovely man. They were married on 4th August 2007 and I can honestly say I had never seen her happier. They have grown together. Both of them were hurting people but God brought them together and over the years they have grown closer. Richard's love has healed Kayla. She is secure in his love, trusts him implicitly and they are serving God together in Tadley. They're as happy as pigs in muck, love 'em!

Nancy Leaves and John Thrives

NANCY WAS GOD'S GIFT TO ME. We saw each other most days and we discussed everything from kids to family to church. She knew everything about me and she loved me as a friend and I her. She would look after my kids and I hers, we were like family. We laughed together, cried together and ate together. Ben went to Chicago to Moody Bible College to study and the inevitable happened—he met a beautiful American girl, Pam Day, and fell in love. They married and Becky and I went to his wedding in Seattle; a beautiful wedding.

Nancy and Ray decided they were moving back to America. She said she had been on the wrong side of the Atlantic to her family for 25 years and she didn't want to be on the wrong side of the Atlantic to Ben, Pam and any grandchildren that may come along. I totally understood that but, boy, I would miss her. They went in the January just as Dad's trial was about to happen. She was the one I shared everything with and prayed with and I cried buckets on the day they went. I have been over several times to see her and she has been back here but I still miss her although we Skype regularly—such a dear dear friend.

John had built up his business and was making an awesome success. He always said he worked so hard for Sharon and his boys; he loved them all dearly and they loved him. There were times when he could have cheerfully strangled each one of them for stuff they had done and I am sure each of them had moments when they wanted to strangle him, but thankfully neither happened. He and Sharon raised four wonderful boys whom I love dearly—we have had some fun times together. I remember vividly John and Sharon going away for the weekend. Paul was 16 so they left him in charge of his brothers but rang me and asked if I would keep an eye on them.

The first evening they were gone Paul rang me in a state. "Aunty Fay, they won't listen to me, and they are doing all sorts." I was in agony with my back and couldn't drive as I had taken heavy pain-killers. "I can't come over Paul but I will come as soon as I can drive."

At 10am the next morning I drove over to Ringmer, my back still hurting, so I was not a smiley Aunty Fay. I also picked up Danny's baseball bat as I left our house. I turned into Springet Avenue to see Ben and Stevie walking up, video in hand. I pulled up and they were all smiles. "Hello Aunty Fay, we're just going up to the shop."

"No you're not. Get in!" They both climbed into the back of the car and I could see the video being pushed from one to the other. If they could have, they would have shoved it up their bum! On getting to the house, I got out, picked up the baseball bat and opened the back door. They sheepishly climbed out and I grabbed the video—a mucky one! I tutted and we all walked into the house. There were kids in the lounge, the kitchen and more upstairs. Fag ends, beer cans, dirty plates—the house was a mess. I walked through, slapping the baseball bat into my hand. To the kids who were sat on the sofa eating cereal I said, "Do you live here?"

"No," they said.

"Well, go home then. Anyone who doesn't live here GET OUT!" They scuttled off.

Paul, Ben, Steve and Ron stood in a line and I told them how disgusted I was. The house was filthy, people stayed over, there was beer and fags and, worst of all, a mucky video. They all looked at the floor. "I am ashamed of you all!" I shouted and scowled as I yelled. I hoped they, too, would feel ashamed.

Then cheeky Stevie says, "It's only a mucky video, Aunty Fay. We haven't raped anybody!" and he stuck his square chin out and looked me dead in the eye.

"No Stevie, you're right, you haven't raped anybody. But you have raped your mother's house!" They all looked ashamed. I seem to remember Ben crying at this point, although he says he didn't. But they all looked at the floor. I said that I was going home and would come back later and the house better be spotless! "And you all need to think about your behaviour. You were trusted by your mum and Dad and it turns out you are not trustworthy!" On that I flounced out; it was about 6 o'clock.

When I went back the house was spotless, not a whiff of fags or beer, and everything shining like a new pin. After I had looked around, they all stood before me heads down. "We're sorry, Aunty Fay. Please don't tell mum and Dad."

"Well, I'll have to think about that," I said. John and Sharon were due home the following day. I left the boys not knowing what I would do. I didn't tell them and for years after I would say to John and Sharon when the boys were around, "Did I ever tell you about…" and their faces were a picture! It was pure power and I loved it! I love them all vast amounts. They were lovely boys and they have grown into awesome men whom I am so very proud of.

John, bless him, worked like a machine. He was always working and he was doing it for Sharon and the boys. He wanted them to have a business to take over from him and to provide for Sharon. He also helped us all over the years, bless him. Money to him was just a tool to be used or given to someone who needed it. He was as generous as the day is long.

He was running the glass business in all three shops with great blokes working for him. He took the boys with him to work and they all said they hated it! He had Stuart, Greg, Daniel, Kenny, Phil and Adam all working for him over the years. He was always reaching out to help those who needed it; he had a heart as big as a bucket. But Phil and Kenny both had inflated ideas about their worth. John would pay them £60 a day but they called him a bread head and said they were easily worth £80 to £100 a day. Truth was they weren't worth £60, he just wanted to help them.

He was such an entrepreneur, always inventing things and looking into new businesses. I recall him talking about a substance you sprayed on glass and it never needed cleaning again. I keep thinking he had a franchise and did a cruise ship in Southampton with this stuff, always willing to give a new idea a go. He was passionate about three things: his family, his Lord and paragliding, a bug he got many years ago. He bought a second-hand one and we all went over to Whiteman's Green in Cuckfield to try it out. He could have killed us! He didn't and we all loved it and loved him. I have a photo of Daniel when he was about 10 up in the paraglider with John holding the rope which was all that tethered him to earth! He was effectively using Dan as a kite!

Everyone had a go and any one of us could have been killed because he had no real clue how to do this! But we all trusted and loved him. It was great fun—actually half the fun was us all being together. We always laughed a lot when we were together.

This was the beginning of a love affair with flying that never left him. He actually took lessons, became a very accomplished paraglider, and went all over the world leaping off mountains. Sharon would go with him sometimes, as long as there was a beach and a nice hotel. She would sit by the sea or pool, read her book and relax while John would be up and off to find a mountain. Then they would have a lovely meal together in the evening. It was the only way Sharon could get him to go on holiday! He bought into a paragliding company, Airworks, where he was an instructor and he loved it. He made great friends in the flying world. They were all as crazy as he was with the same passion for flying. He said being up in the sky was the best place to worship God, with buzzards flying alongside you. Wonderful!

Whenever he called in to see any of us, he was half listening to what was going on, but his attention was on the sky and the wind! He was always looking at his weather app. When he could take it no more he would say, "Gotta go. Great flying weather." And off he would go! He would drive Sharon crazy!

Sharon had started a mother and toddler group at Eastgate Baptist Church, not long after they started going there. Kingfishers it was called. Bless her, she ran it for 20 or more years which was a good job as she had somewhere to pour all her energy and time, as well as her boys and then her grandchildren, because John was either working or flying. She has only recently stepped down from running it. Such a successful group with waiting lists for people wanting to join.

I have said on many an occasion how John had helped us all financially. He gave each of us a wad of money one Christmas, turning up about a week before and shoving an envelope into my hand and giving me a kiss and a squeeze. "Have a good Christmas, darling," he said and then, "Gotta go!," and he was off! There was £500 in the envelope and he had been to each one of the brothers and sisters and Mam and Dad and done the same thing! He was so generous and he didn't want money just for having money.

Money was just a tool to him that enabled him to bless his family, his church, his wider family and many more in between, and to do things he fancied doing. He bought houses and made them into flats, run-down buildings and made them into homes—such a gifted man. He was never still, always looking for the next project. He was so thrilled when, after years of the boys working Saturdays and holidays for him in the factory or the shop, Paul joined the RAF. "A bit radical, just so you don't have to work with yer Dad, Paul!"

In all truth John and Sharon couldn't have been prouder. Stevie had gone to the States to do Camp America. He loved it and fell in love with a gorgeous Kentuckian, Kim Widmann. He had won her heart and she his, so they were married and Stevie moved out to Kentucky. Also radical so as not to work with yer Dad! Truth is, John and Sharon fell in love with Kim too and were so thrilled to welcome her into the family and to give Stevie to *her* family!

Ben was a wanderer. With a guitar and much hair, he went to Europe busking. "Rather sleep on the streets than work for yer Dad!" Harsh man! He had a great time making enough money to feed himself and see the world. What a time he had. He met lovely friends and met a girl, but then tragedy struck— and that is Ben's story to tell not mine. But Ben came home and after a time went to work with his Dad and continued to for 15 years. They were great mates as well as father and son. John and Ben love a discussion, whether deep and meaningful, or light and ridiculous. The mickey was taken on a regular basis but John and Ben loved every minute, so this was perfect.

Then there was Ron. He too had worked Saturdays and holidays. With Ben working in Lewes, Seaford needed Ron and, bless him, he realised resistance was futile so he runs the Seaford shop. These boys do the most wonderful job; with all the teams of fitters they run a wonderful business. John was as proud as punch of all that they did, even telling us, "Oh yes, the boys really know what they're doing!"

So even if he didn't tell you, boys, he knew the business was safe in your hands and now, after 22 years in the RAF, Paul has retired and joined Ben running the Lewes shop. You can run, Paul, but you can't hide! The glass business will get you!

Emily's Secret

OUR THREE GREW INTO TEENAGERS and we enjoyed life as a family and had fun holidays. We even took Paul, Ben, Stevie and Ron with us to Centre Parc and had such a great time. We just loved these boys and they all got on so well together. We took Emily too. She was a character and we love her too. The girls all got on fabulously, though at one point I could have strangled her. We were in a restaurant, Greg was paying with his card and Emily was standing next to him, reading his card. Just as the bloke was giving Greg the machine, Emily says, "That's not your name, Uncle Greg!" Fancy trying to explain that his real name is John in front of a bloke who is thinking we are using someone else's card!

We were a close extended family and, as I said, we enjoyed each other's kids and birthdays were still a great gathering. But as they got older, they didn't want to include us oldies!

When Emily had her 18th birthday, Naomi, Daniel and Becky went. I was waiting up for a phone call to say, "Muuuummm. Can you come and pick us up!" But the call didn't come and at 1am they all came home. The girls went straight up to bed but Daniel came into the sitting room. I knew something was wrong; his face crumpled and he burst into tears. "What's wrong, darlin'?" I said.

"Mum, I have just learned the worst thing ever but it's a secret and I don't know what to do!" He was absolutely inconsolable.

"Well darlin', you can share the secret with me, and whatever needs doing we will do. If it is to be kept a secret, I promise I will keep it with you. If something needs doing we'll do it." Over the next half an hour, Dan shared with me, through his sobs, that Emily had told him that Grandad had been sexually abusing her since she was six! I felt sick in my stomach.

Daniel adored his Grandad. He was a Christian tough guy, though he had seen a side to my Dad when he was around 10. His dyslexia was making him think he was useless and Grandad suggested that Dan spent time with him and learned practical stuff. Dan was very keen to do this, so for a few Friday evenings

292

I would drive him over to Grandad's house. He would sleep over and help Grandad do bits of jobs, learn which tools were which. Emily also slept over, so they got to spend time together, but not very long after doing this, Dan said he didn't want to go, but he was scared to tell Grandad. "Don't worry, darling. I will tell him." So when I rang and told Dad Dan wouldn't be coming any more, I was quite shocked that he didn't ask me why, just "OK."

When I asked Dan why he didn't want to go, it transpired that Dad had taken great delight in shouting at Dan and humiliating him in front of Emily! I was so upset for Dan and I apologised for all that Dad had said and done, but I never confronted Dad because, just like Dan, I was scared of him too!

But this was something that needed confronting. I told Dan he did the right thing sharing this and we would do the right thing. I gave Dan a hug, told him to go to bed and we would talk tomorrow.

I sat for ages just mulling this all over in my head. I prayed about it, then went up to bed. The following day I talked it over with Greg and I decided I needed to talk to Emily, so I rang her. I explained that Dan hadn't wanted to betray her by sharing her secret but couldn't cope with it and had shared it with me. I was shocked and so very sorry. She jumped in and said, "No one will believe me, will they?"

"Yes darling. I believe you." We both cried.

"What do we do, Aunty Fay?" she said.

"I think we need to get the whole family to meet up." So we did and we decided that we had to tell them all what Grandad had done to her. Kayla had two little girls, Rachel and Hannah, and Susie had Dawn. We couldn't just leave it in case he was also abusing them too!

We both knew that I would have to tell Phil separately, so we rang everyone, set an evening and everyone came, older kids too. Emily was nervous of what everyone would think or say, but we prayed before everyone arrived. It was a sombre evening. I said I had some dreadful news to share and we needed them to just listen. So I told them what had happened to Emily. Faces dropped, sadness and shock filled the room. John said, "Girls, I am so sorry" and he hugged Emily. "So what do we do now?"

We said, "He can't get away with this again." Everyone agreed. Kayla and Susie had to ask their girls if Grandad had ever touched them inappropriately. What a thing to have to ask! Thankfully, the answer was No.

We decided we should go to the police. He had got away with abusing me as a child, but he wasn't a Christian then. Today was a whole different thing. He had used his Christianity to hide behind and do dreadful things to an innocent child—despicable!

We went and spoke to Mam and told her. She was quite odd in that she said how sad and shocked that he had abused me. I told her, "But you knew that, Mam. I told you at the time."

"Oh, oh yes, and now Emily. This is despicable." We said we were going to the police and she said she would come and give a statement too. We were thrilled she was standing with us. "He deserves hanging," she said! She called him worse than muck. I felt that she was being a proper Mam, defending me and Emily, wanting what was right, and I liked it.

Mam, Emily and I went to the police and Emily gave her statement. They asked if he had done it before because the more evidence we had the more likely it would be to go to court. I said he had abused me and gave my statement. Thankfully, I had been writing stuff down over the years to help me deal with what he had done, so they wanted my written stuff too. Mam went in and gave her statement. She actually told them she had recollections of him abusing me but that it was a difficult and different time.

The hardest part was going to see Phil and telling him. I was very worried about what he would do. He exploded! Though he and Emily had a very strained and difficult relationship, because Phil was a schizophrenic and was very irrational a lot of the time, here he was going crazy because of what his father had done to his child! He said he would kill him. Maggy and I begged him not to, saying he would be sent down for years and we wanted Dad sent down not him, so let the law deal with him. He agreed after much swearing and shouting, which I totally understood. Kenny told me months later that Phil had a shotgun that he had buried in the garden. He had separated the stock from the barrel and wrapped them in plastic. Apparently, he dug up the stock but, try as he might, he couldn't find the barrel! I am so thankful that he didn't find it.

The awful thing was we had to carry on as normal with Mam and Dad as if everything was tickety boo, until the police had got everything in place to arrest him. It was dreadful. Poor Uncle Lou had died and his funeral was being arranged. We all had to be round at Mam and Dad's knowing what we knew and pretend all was well. It was really hard but we did it. Uncle Louie was buried and we went back to Mam and Dad's.

Uncle Louie left his money to Mam, bless him. He didn't have lots, about £10,000, and she didn't want Dad to get his hands on this money, didn't even want him to know about it, so she asked Phil if he would put it in his account till Dad had been arrested and sent down. "No problem," said Phil. He adored Mam and actually they had a very odd relationship, a bit Oedipus-like. He would go up to see her every day, he trusted her implicitly and she manipulated him and used him. Now we were waiting for the police to arrest Dad, Phil was with her a lot. When the police arrested Dad, he was working on a job not too far from where they lived, up a ladder painting. Dad must have been shocked rigid. He thought he had got away with it all! He was charged and sent to a bail hostel in Southampton until the trial.

Phil and Mam made up posters saying PAEDOPHILE with a picture of Dad and Emily. They had written stuff about him too. I didn't see them but Emily did and said it made her feel dirty. They put them all over Haywards Heath, even opposite their house near the school. There were complaints so the police told then to take them down. I think it was illegal and they wouldn't help our case, so they did take them down. Mam wasn't good for Phil because she would feed into that nasty side of him and this was probably one of her ideas.

As the weeks went on Emily and I had to go to court in Haywards Heath when Dad was to make his plea. We went in and up the stairs and sat right in front of us in the waiting room was Dad! We nearly had heart attacks! What terrible organisation. Surely this should not happen! We shot downstairs and waited until he was called, then we went up and into the courtroom. Dad looked a very angry man. The judge asked him how he pleaded. "Not guilty, your honour!" And that was it.

He left and we waited and then walked out. This meant he would go to trial. We went and had lunch and talked things over. Emily was very stressed, bless her, and we didn't know what would happen next. The case took months to come to trial and all the while Dad was in the bail hostel in Southampton. Mam seemed to be coping OK and would go up every other weekend and stay with Uncle Bill in Bedfordshire. We all popped in to see her during the week, just to make sure she was alright.

Finally, we got a letter to say the trial date was to be 10th January 2000. Emily rang me. She had had her letter to say the trial was to be at Lewes Crown Court. She didn't want anyone to be in the courtroom hearing all the details and neither did I, so we didn't tell anyone when it was. I would pick her up and we would go together, just the two of us. It was weeks away but we were both nervous. He was still pleading not guilty which would mean we would be cross-examined and neither of us were looking forward to that!

John came over to see me. "Darlin', how are you doing?" he said. I told him the cross-examination was worrying us both, but it was necessary to get justice. Bless him, he prayed with me that God would give me everything I needed to get through it all.

The morning of the 10th came and I picked Emily up. We had told no one, not even Greg, and as we were the only ones involved, no one else knew. But as we walked into the court, there was Mam and Kenny. We were shocked! "What are you doing here?" we said. Mam said she just wanted to know what he got. "You can't come into court," we said. We couldn't cope with them hearing the details.

"OK," they said, "we'll stay out here." We wondered how they knew.

We went into the courtroom and sat, just the two of us. I was praying we would both be brave and be able to do this. After sitting through the trial before Dad's, they brought him in. We were sitting just to the side of him and if I had leant across I could have touched him. My tummy was doing cartwheels and by the look of Emily, hers too. We held hands. *We have nothing to be ashamed of. Heads up! He should hang his head in shame*, I thought.

The judge came in and we all rose, then sat. The clerk of the court read out the charges and his name. Then Dad's brief stood and said, "My client would like to change his plea to guilty, your honour!" We were dumbstruck! Thank you, Lord! What a relief! It was then just a matter of the judge reading his charges and sentencing him. The judge asked if he had any support.

Then his brief said, "Mrs Lancaster has withdrawn her statement and has been visiting Mr Lancaster in the bail hostel on a regular basis. She intends to support him whilst in prison and on his release." We were gobsmacked! She hadn't been going to Uncle Bill's but down to see Dad and withdrawn her statement. How could she do this to us—again?

Dad did play the pathetic old man, saying he couldn't stand and he couldn't hear. The judge said, "Taking into consideration that you are not a young man, and not a well man, I sentence you to 18 months and to be placed on the sex offenders register for a long period." I can't remember the exact amount of time, but it was significant.

He was taken down to the cells by a policeman. Emily and I were shocked; glad it was over, glad he didn't get away with it, but dumbstruck by the revelations about Mam! She had been running him down to Phil and everyone. We came out of court and Mam and Kenny were stood outside having a fag. As soon as she saw us, she said, "What did he get?"

"18 months," I said.

"Oh, not too long," she said.

Emily could hold it in no longer. "You lying two-faced bitch!" she yelled.

"What are you talking about?" said Mam.

"You know full well what I'm on about. You're standing by him. You've been visiting him! Withdrawn your statement!." At that point Emily lunged at Mam.

I grabbed her. "Don't Emily, she's not worth it," I said. "As far as I'm concerned I don't have a father, and it seems I don't have a mother either."

She looked me in the face and said, "Well that makes you a f*****g orphan then, doesn't it?" Kenny looked very uncomfortable and shrugged his shoulders. He had driven Mam and had to drive her home. The thing about Kenny was, he was back on drugs, and Mam would use him. She had obviously paid him to drive her to and fro. He was always on the lug for money.

"Come on, Emily," I said. I took her arm and we walked back to the car. Emily was shaking with rage. She so wanted to hurt Mam. Her granny had just betrayed her and she was hurt, angry, broken by what they both had done. In the car we just held each other and cried. Then we prayed that we could both move forward.

I took Emily home, then called into Phil and Mags to tell them what sentence he had been given and what had occurred with Mam. Phil was livid—with me! He had so wanted to go to court to see Dad sentenced and shout obscenities at him and throw rotten fruit at him. I know—mad! And because we hadn't wanted anyone there, I said to Phil that this wasn't about you, it was about Emily and me. With that he said, "Get out of my house. Go on, f... off, I'm done with you." I begged him not to do this but it was done and once said, he can't go back on his words. I left knowing that he would cut me dead now and that broke my heart. I cried all the way home. I loved him.

I got home deeply sad in my heart about Phil, told Greg and the kids about the sentence, rang John and Sharon and told them what had happened and about Dad changing his plea. Then Sharon told me that John had been down to

Southampton to talk to Dad, telling him to change his plea. He told him he had put us through the abuse once, so not to put us through it again, having to be cross-examined, and he did! What a lovely brother.

Then the proverbial really hit the fan, because now Phil knew Mam had been lying to him for months and he was not happy. The saddest thing for Phil was that he loved Mam and they were always up to something. He would do anything for her, like hiding the money from Dad. Well, she shot herself in the foot there, because she had given Phil a letter saying the money was a gift to him. Phil got a solicitor's letter asking for the money back—jog on! Then another one asking for just half—not a hope. Then he had a letter from her saying it was a gift! He frittered the lot away on rubbish, but what I found sad was she was more upset that she lost £10,000 than she was about losing her children and grandchildren!

Mam was in a mess with not having Phil to lean on and to manipulate. We all felt utterly betrayed by her. I felt I had no relationship with her and I didn't want one. She had hurt me so much and this was the straw that broke the camel's back. Life was difficult. We were all coming to terms with life without them in it. We had been such a tight family and this just shattered us. She was now scared of Phil. She knew she had betrayed him and knew what he was capable of, so as soon as she could she sold the bungalow, moved up to Blackpool, bought several houses and let them out. Apparently, when Dad finished his sentence, he went up to Blackpool too. They went back to the life they lived before becoming Christians; boozing, fighting, dogs, and eventually drugs, selling the houses one by one to fund their lifestyle.

We got back to life but it was different not having them in our lives and, in truth, we all missed them. They were the only parents we had and we all loved them in our own way. It was not a normal family by any means, but it was ours, and all we had ever known. But this was now life. We all felt the loss and the children all reacted in different ways. My children all rejected Christianity, saying it was fake like Grandad. John and Sharon's boys, too, didn't want much to do with church after this. Kayla's girls were young and didn't grasp the severity of what had happened, and Ken's too. It was a very difficult time as we all came to terms with life without them in it.

Kenny Leaves and Mam Dies

KENNY HAD BEEN STRUGGLING WITH DRUGS for a long time and he was taking codeine. He had a bad back at one time and the doctor gave him codeine or coproxamol, and in a very short time he was craving them. It was the saddest thing because they had a lovely family life up to that point! They were very involved with the church where he had a couple of good mates, he and Susie were working and Adam and Dawn were doing well in school. They had moved to Ringmer and all was well, until he started going round all the chemists from Haywards Heath to Brighton to buy pills. If you went too many times to the same chemist they wouldn't sell them to you. He would call in to see me but the real reason was to see if I had any pills. As soon as he pulled up I would rush upstairs and hide my pills. He would always say he needed the loo and dash upstairs, bless him. I felt so sorry for him but I couldn't be an enabler!

His life was falling apart and he couldn't work, so poor Susie was working all hours to pay the mortgage and all the bills. This was a very hard time for them all. Dawn and Adam were old enough to know what was going on but too young to do anything about it, bless them. They must have been very worried and frightened. It came to a head after a couple of years of things getting worse when Susie woke to find Kenny had left. He had got up at 4am and driven to Blackpool. He stayed with Mam and Dad for a while before he got himself on benefits and got a flat of his own. His slow decline back into heroin was one of the saddest things in my life. He would ring me in such a bad way, crying and regretting everything, and saying how much he loved Susie. I would tell him to get clean and, you never know, maybe Susie will have you back. He was always going to do it. I would send him a Tesco delivery once a month, because after I went up to see him he had no food in the flat. I took him to a cafe and we had lunch. I wouldn't give him money because I knew fine well what he would do with it, so a food delivery was the best option. Although I always had to make sure he had butter not marge, bless him. He hated marge!

He wanted a divorce, not because he didn't love Susie, because he certainly did, but he wanted the house sold and his half of the money! Poor Susie was left with the task of selling the house and buying a little flat, all so that Kenny could feed his addiction. He said he was going to buy a place but he just blew the lot on heroin, pills and drink. Those things are such liars, promising fabulous times but they rob you of everything you ever loved. They suck the life out of relationships, empty your bank balance and take everything you ever held dear, even your body. You can't eat, can't be bothered to wash or clean your teeth, change your clothes or clean your surroundings. You are consumed with your next hit or drink and yet every time I saw him or rang him, he would tell me he wanted to get clean and wanted Susie back. I would say, "Get clean Kenny. Just as you love Susie, she still loves you and would have you back if you got clean."

"I will, Frow," he would say, but then he would cry because he couldn't do it and he knew he didn't have the inner strength needed to do it. He wanted God to do it for him. He was no good with pain and couldn't handle anything. I guess heroin is the ultimate painkiller and he had felt nothing for years so suddenly to feel pain—he couldn't do it. It was just too sad.

He rang to tell me that Mam was very ill. She had stomach cancer, had had a stroke and was in a nursing home. Greg and I were driving up to Durham that weekend; it was *his* mum's birthday. So after we had visited all Greg's rellies I decided to drive over the Pennines. I rang Kenny to get the address and told him we would call in to see him too and go and visit Mam before she died. It was a long old drive. We arrived at the nursing home, only to find that Kenny must have told Dad we were going to see Mam, because when we got there Dad had taken Mam out and told the staff I was not allowed to see her! We went to Kenny's flat and *he* wasn't there either! I rang him but he didn't answer so we just drove home, exhausted!

Mam didn't die and a few months later Kenny rang and said Dad said if we wanted to see Mam before she died, we should go up soon. I rang Kayla and John. John couldn't cope with seeing her but Kayla said she wanted to go. I couldn't face driving all that way so we decided to go on the night coach and come back the following night. What a mistake that was! We couldn't sleep and couldn't get comfy. We had a backpack with bits for Kenny, some towels and sheets and stuff like that. Well, we were trying hard to sleep and put the backpack between us on the seat for us both to lean on.

Then we realised the backpack had more room on the seat than we had and we got the giggles. Everyone was cross with us and started tutting at us, which made us giggle all the more. We were like a pair of sleep-deprived school kids! Finally, we arrived but no sign of Kenny. He finally arrived and had big hugs and kisses. It was lovely to see him. We all went for breakfast then got a taxi to go to see Mam. We walked into the nursing home and the nurse said Mam was in the lounge.

Kayla said, "That's Mam," pointing to a skinny little lady walking in front of us.

"No," I said. Then she turned and it *was* Mam, but she looked so old and tiny, like great granny. She had had a stroke so one arm just hung; dementia too. We all walked her out into the garden and we were crying. She wanted a cigarette and Ken gave her one. Kayla and I were in shock at the size and state of her—this was all too sad. If she had stood by us and stayed in Sussex, we would all have looked after her. She looked so very ill and didn't seem to know who we were.

Apparently, Dad couldn't cope with looking after her. She had loved him all her life, put him before anything and anybody, had always looked after his needs and given up everything and everyone for him. Yet here she was in a smelly nursing home. We prayed with her, kissed her and left her, all anger towards her dissipated. She looked so pathetic and we cried buckets. She was a rubbish Mam, but she was the only one we had and it was hard to see the stroppy, bolshy, mouthy, large Mam brought to this end. She died a couple of weeks later and we don't even know where she is buried.

Dad apparently was devastated on her death. Mam had been the money-maker, always on the make, but their lifestyle had dwindled. Mam had sold all the houses she had once owned to fund the drinking and drugs that Dad was into. He seemed to have let go of all his Christian principles and I think he thought he was an apostate—someone who has committed the unforgivable sin—so if he was going to hell he may as well go for living the most sinful life possible.

Now he was alone except for Kenny, who would go to see him when he needed something. They both used each other. Kenny knew the dealers and would get the drugs. Dad would pay and they would share the drugs! Vodka was drunk by the litre too. They were both in a dreadful state. And prostitutes…you name it, Dad was into it.

The Dream

EMILY WAS STRUGGLING TO DEAL WITH LIFE, but that's Em's story to tell, not mine. Knowing she was struggling, I wanted to help her and felt she was blaming herself for what Dad had done. She felt she had broken the family and no amount of telling her that her Grandad broke the family, not her, seemed to help. Not knowing how to help, I prayed for clarity from God, that he would show me what to do.

I woke after such a vivid dream. I had walked into Mam and Dad's house. I went into the kitchen, which was filthy with a round table in the middle with a dirty white plastic doily type table cloth. It was tea-stained, with dirty cups, used tea bags and tea spoons stuck with sugar to the tablecloth. At the other side of the table was Dad who shouted at me. I stood tall and looked him square in his face and said, "You damaged Emily. She needs you to own what you did to her," and I took paper and pen out of my bag, put it on the table in front of him, and said, "Write to her," and he wrote the letter! I woke up in a sweat.

Greg woke. "What's up, love?" he asked. I told him my dream. "Wow," he said, "that was vivid!"

It certainly was! "Do you think it was God showing me what to do?"

"Nah," he said.

I got up and made a cuppa, sat and prayed. I had never had anything like that before but I still wondered if this was God showing me how to help Emily. "Was that you Lord? If it was, show me please," I prayed. I went up to church to the coffee shop and as I walked through church, Andrew Cornes, our lovely vicar, was walking towards me.

"Fay," he said. "Do you ever see your father?"

"No," I said. "Not since the court case. Why do you ask, Andrew?" He said he was thinking about me and the whole situation. He had never asked me about Dad before, so I told him about my dream and said that I wondered if it was God telling me to go, but I told him Greg didn't think it was. He prayed with me and

302

said, "Trust God. Let's pray that if it is from God that Greg will change his mind."

I didn't talk about it with Greg again. We were going on holiday with our dear friends Tony and Christine Holcombe to their lovely timeshare in Tenerife. We had the most wonderful time. We laughed, ate, drank, walked, saw beautiful places, swam in fabulous pools and I continued to pray about my dream. When we got home after this fab week Greg said, "You know your dream. I was wrong to say it wasn't from God. I've been thinking about it and praying, and I really think it was from God and you should go!"

Wow! I told him what Andrew and I were praying. This was definitely a God thing so I booked train tickets to Blackpool for the following week, Greg's day off. I told Andrew we were going and he said he would pray for us. We dressed very smart. It may seem silly, but I felt we were about God's business and we needed to dress the part. I put paper and pens in my bag, along with the newspaper with Dad's trial on the front, just in case. I had some leverage—to threaten to show the neighbours if he wouldn't write the letter. Talk about lack of faith! I was ready for all eventualities! We sat and prayed, asking for courage and strength to face the day and to face Dad.

It was a long day. We arrived in Blackpool and took a taxi to Dad's house. I had never been to the house so had no idea where it was. My tummy was doing backflips but as soon as we pulled up outside the house my tummy stopped. I felt calm and strong, and I knew God was with us.

I knocked on the door and Kenny answered. He was as shocked to see us as we were to see him. "Hello Frow, Dad's in there," he whispered.

"Good," I said. "I've come to see him," and we walked into the lounge. Dad was standing at the far end of the room and he turned. "Hello Dad," I said.

"I don't know you. F… off!" he said and rushed towards me.

"Yes you do," I said. I thought he was going to punch me but I stood my ground and braced myself. He pushed past me; he was running away from us! I tried to stop him leaving by pushing the door but he barged me out of the way and f'd me off again He ran out of the house. We were stunned. He was afraid of me! This was such a strange experience. All my life I had been afraid of him, and now he was afraid of me! I think it wasn't me he was scared of but who I represented.

Kenny looked at me and said, "Well Frow, he's f'd off and he ain't coming back!"

"Yes he will, cos we will pray him back. God told me to come, so he will come back."

"What do you want?" Kenny asked. I told him. "Well, if you could squeeze it out of him, you might stand a chance, but no way, Fay."

Greg and I sat and prayed that God would bring him back—and in he came. Kenny's face was a picture. But he ran straight upstairs and I could hear him pacing back and forth. I stood at the bottom of the stairs and shouted, "Dad, I need you to come down and write a letter to Emily, owning what you did. Because of you, she is very damaged and ill. If you write owning what happened, she may be able to move on. Come down Dad and do this. She loved and trusted you, and you betrayed her in the worst possible way—own it! Please Dad, you are her Grandad. You were trusted with her!"

Kenny said, "I think you've got your answer, Fay."

He paced some more, then came down the stairs muttering stuff that I could barely hear. He was eye level with me and said, "You are a lying cow and a stirring bitch."

"No I am not," I said. He pushed past me and went into the kitchen and I followed him in. It was exactly like the kitchen in my dream—exactly—down to the doily tea-stained plastic tablecloth, sugar spoons and dirty cups. I felt a real surge of strength and confidence that he would write it because God was with me!

Dad was looking out of the window with his back to me. "It's all cobblers what you're saying about me. You are lying!"

He turned and I stood tall and looked him full in the face. "There's only you and me in here, Dad, and we both know I am not lying!" He looked away. I took the paper out of my bag and the pen, laid it on the table and said, "Dad, write it."

He turned and picked up the pen and wrote it! "Is this a trick?" he said.

"Before God, it is not," I said.

"Don't you go calling on higher powers," he said as I watched him write 'Dear Em, for what it's worth, I am sorry' and he signed it Ken Lancaster. I had hoped for more but was grateful for this.

I said, "Thank you" and then, "You have never asked for my forgiveness, Dad. I have always wanted you to, because I would give it, if you asked." We stood there for a few moments. I looked at him, he looked at the table. Nothing! OK then. I went into the lounge where Greg and Kenny were, kissed and hugged Kenny and said goodbye and Greg and I walked out! It was an amazing feeling to have the letter. We got back to the station and sat and just gave thanks to God for his leading, for being with us, for the dream. I so hoped the letter was going to help Em.

When we got back home, we were exhausted, but elated too. I couldn't wait to give Emily the letter. I phoned Andrew Cornes to tell him and he was elated too. He had been praying for us throughout the day. I think God used this time to show me that in God I am strong, and that Dad was scared, not because of Fay Summers, he was scared of God who was with me and in me and Dad could see that.

A few years went by and we were all still coping badly with the fallout of what Dad had done. John missed him very much and was hurting. Kayla was lost and hurting. Phil was angry and Emily still struggling. I was seeing a psychiatrist and having counselling. I knew Dad wouldn't do anything off his own back to make the situation better for anyone so I wrote everyone an envelope with their name and address on, put a stamp on each and a plain sheet in each and went back to Blackpool to Dad's.

We were quite shocked with the way Dad looked. He was thin and old and dirty, but he let us into the house and there was no shouting or swearing. He asked why we had come, so I told him how he had not only damaged Emily and me, but everyone was damaged by what he did. They had all trusted him, loved him, believed him, looked up to him. All his grandchildren were shattered by what he had done and no one could understand how he could just abuse Emily and throw God out of his life, when God had saved him, given him a new start and a life worth living.

How could he abandon his family and run away, back to his old life? The Bible says it's like a dog returning to its vomit. How could he not try to help those hurting ones, those he once purported to love and care for? I said, "On your release, you just left, with no attempt to apologise, to try to make this terrible situation better, to mend those broken people. We all need to hear you say sorry Dad, and you never have."

He sat with his head in his hands and said he would put it right. I gave him the envelopes and said, "This would be a great way to start. Write to each one of these and say how sorry you are." He took them, looked through them, nodded and said he would. I believed him. We went to the shop, bought some groceries and took them back to his house. He looked a very pathetic figure as we left. I felt a deep sadness and, as I looked back, I was very aware of how far he had fallen. It reminded me of the prodigal son who finished up with the pigs, except the prodigal son realised where he was and returned to his father repentant. Here was Dad, sat in such a filthy place, living a vile life and was happy to stay there. To give him his due, he wrote to me and Emily with an apology for what he had done, but no one else. I was saddened by that but thankful Emily had an apology. But it made me think it was an empty apology or he would have wanted to help everyone he hurt to move on.

Emily is the most amazingly strong woman, whom I love very much and stand in awe of. She has pulled herself up with the help of God, her mum and Mike, and she has two amazing children, Ellis and Ela. She is married to Mike whom we love immensely and they have made a fabulous life together.

Ellis was such a little fella. Maggy and Phil looked after him while Emily worked. We all wondered how Phil would cope with this but we needn't have worried. Ellis crawled into his arms and melted his heart. I think as a family, we saw the love of this little boy change the hard man into a complete softy. Phil's greatest joy was being a Papa and when Ela came along, he just fell head over heels in love with her as soon as he clapped eyes on her, as we all did. These two little people never saw an angry Phil; they had him wrapped around their little fingers and he knew it, loved it and loved them with everything in him.

Kenny Inside

I REMEMBER MAGGY CALLING and telling me Phil had been to the hospital; he had bladder cancer. It had been 10 years since Dad's trial and it broke my heart that he would have nothing to do with me. I would see him quite often if I was going in to Kayla's house and he would be working on his car. I would always say, "Hiya Phil. You OK?" He would look up, scowl at me and carry on with whatever he was doing, never saying a word. I would carry on to Kayla's, sad that he just couldn't let this go. He wasn't speaking to Kayla either. Her Stuart had done something that upset Phil, so he cut him off, then Kayla stuck up for him and he cut her off. He didn't speak to Kayla for 12 years though he still spoke to Hannah and Rachel. So it was all on poor Mags. Thankfully he didn't stop Mags seeing us or talking to us.

Phil had to have his bladder removed in Brighton County Hospital and I was so worried about him. He actually said to Maggy, "If you tell our Fay she can come to see me, I would like that." Maggy called and told me and I was thrilled. The following day Greg and I went to see him. He was sat in ICU looking very bright and breezy. Maggy was sat with him.

I walked over and gave him a kiss. "Hello Phil. Good to see you."

"Hello Fay," he said and that was that, no apology, nothing. But I was fine with that, I was just glad to have my brother back. We talked for ages and he told us all about his operation. He had had an ileostomy as his bladder had been removed. He was in ICU for a while. Kayla asked if she could visit too. "Yes of course," he said, and John and Sharon too. So we were all allowed back into his life. Good job we were a forgiving bunch!

The thing with Phil was that he didn't know how to back down or apologise. He sort of locked himself into these situations and the longer it goes on the harder it gets. This dreadful cancer gave him a way out without having to back down or apologise, and we were all glad to have him back in our lives.

He came home from hospital and had to come to terms with his bag and all the paraphernalia that came with it. Maggy was amazing in the way she changed his bag and kept him infection-free. They seemed to be happier than they had ever been. Phil seemed to really appreciate all that Maggy did for him and he had taken her for granted for so many years, that this was lovely to see.

Phil invited Greg and I to afternoon tea and we were in for a shock. When we got to their house, we found he had made beef paste sandwiches, scones with jam and cream, and cream cakes too. It was so lovely and we ate, chatted and laughed lots. Then Phil suggested we go on holiday together. We were thrilled. Yeah let's! He wanted to go back on the Norfolk Broads and told us all about it. We would talk about what we would do, who would steer and who would jump off the boat to tie it up. We talked about lock opening and closing, pub meals, and the great breakfasts we would have. Mags and Phil booked it (I just learned this today). John had given Phil money for his birthday and he used it as the deposit. He wouldn't let us go halves, so we said we would do all the food and meals out. We would argue about this but we were all so excited about going. Every time we were together we talked of nothing else and were so looking forward to it, no one more so than Phil.

Kenny had been living in Blackpool for years. Adam his son had been playing up at home and his mum Susie was at the end of her tether with him. He had pulled some awful strokes and his mum couldn't cope with him so he finally moved up to be with his Dad. This was not a good move as Adam had dabbled in drugs and, being with Kenny, he plunged headfirst into Blackpool's seedy side. Before very long he was as bad as Kenny. I vividly remember going up to see them and being shocked at the state of them both; dirty, skinny, pallid junkies. I cried buckets over them and took them out for lunch. We finished up in McDonalds where there were little families of healthy-looking children and adults. Here I was with these two boys, whom I loved dearly, but they stuck out like sore thumbs—junkies. I was so sad for them. Blackpool is not a good place for anyone with an addiction. It's all too readily available and they were in a dreadful state. I drove up to see them on several occasion.

Adam and Kenny fought a lot and eventually Adam moved down to London and we didn't see him for a long time. I am thrilled to say that at the time of writing Adam has become a Christian, is in rehab and is finally clean after many years lost to drugs. He met a girl called Isabelle, fell in love and they had a beautiful baby girl who is just gorgeous. Hopefully he and Isabelle will be able to be back in a relationship soon.

Kenny just deteriorated. His tummy was so distended and his liver was inflamed—sclerosis I think. He would periodically come down to Sussex to visit us all but he was lonely and sad. It was always lovely to see him and we would all beg him to move back down south. Finally he said yes. He bought an old van, piled all his stuff in it and drove it down as far as Bedford where it broke down! He had to get it towed to Haywards Heath. Phil rang me and said, "Have you got £300 cash? Can you get it over to mine? Ken's skint and this bloke needs paying." Credit card to the hole in the wall produced £200 and I borrowed £100 from a friend and took it over and paid the man. Kenny looked awful. He had swapped heroin for vodka and pills, and was drinking vodka by the litre. His capacity for drink was unbelievable!

He had parked his van in the car-park next to Phil and Kayla's houses and was going to live in the van until he got a place. Phil, bless him, was very ill at this time as his cancer had travelled into his bones and walking was so painful for him. But he was on the case. He loved Ken and wanted to get him settled. Ken living in the van annoyed the allotment association who rang the police and they turned up. Ken was down and very maudlin. He told the police that he wanted to kill himself, his life was shite. They thought he was a danger to himself. Richard and Kayla persuaded him to go with them to a mental health unit in Crawley so, bless him, he went. He rang Phil that evening to go get him. He hated it and as he hadn't been sectioned they couldn't keep him there against his will. But now he was known, they sort of had a duty of care as he was vulnerable. Phil was on his case and he rang everyone. The council, telling them he couldn't live in his van as it was disgusting. He rang the housing association, private landlords, and eventually the council found him this flat in Burgess Hill.

It wasn't perfect but it was definitely better than the van and was just what he needed. There were some bits of furniture and we all gave him stuff. Maggy, Kayla and I went over and made the bed up. We went shopping and bought everything we thought he would need. We put curtains up, his TV and stereo were sorted and he was all set. We sat and had a cuppa with him. We were all thrilled he was back down here where we could keep an eye on him.

It was fine for a while but his drinking was getting worse. Then he would go out into the town, forget his keys and break a window to get back in. We would phone John and, bless his heart, he would send Ben or Ron over to measure up and fix him a new window. He must have done this half a dozen times over the time Ken lived there. He was very thankful and had Zippo lighters engraved with their names on to say thank you.

He had a fall while he was drunk. It didn't hurt him at the time but, on sobering up, he was in a lot of pain; his jaw was agony. He had bashed it on the table. He took himself to the doctor and wanted morphine, but the doctor would only give him paracetamol. He gave the doctor a mouthful of abuse and left! He would walk into Haywards. Heath and go to see Phil and Mags. The thing was, he couldn't make friends. All his junkie mates were dead, so he only had family; he was very lonely.

Phil was getting more and more ill, bless him, and Kenny arrived, having bought vodka on the way to take the pain away. By the time he got to Phil's it was pouring with rain and he was soaked to the skin and grumpy. He was always cross with God for not helping him; he always wanted everything to happen now! God had to take his pain away, get him money, heal his addiction, get him and Susie back together, all with no effort from him. Phil and Mags were out. How very dare they be out when he had come to see them! He waited at the side of the house until they arrived back. "WHERE HAVE YOU BEEN," he growled. "I am coming in." Phil realised he was drunk and he was not a nice drunk. "No, you're not coming in," Phil said. Ken was evil mad and gave Phil a load of mouth. Phil ignored him and went in and shut the door. Ken wandered off shouting abuse. Phil and Mags had a cuppa and Phil said, "I better go find him," so off he went driving around looking for Ken. He found him lying in someone's drive in the pouring rain. Phil, having such difficulty walking himself, helped him up, got him in the car and drove him back to the flat!

Ken, still in lots of pain with no relief, rang me. I took him some of my coproxamol—only one strip and I think there were 12 on the strip. I gave them to him thinking they would last him a few days. "Cheers Frow," he said and popped every one of them out of the pack and took the whole lot at once! I was so angry with him and frightened he would die. Needless to say he didn't; his body was so used to large amounts of drugs.

The following day he was in such a state that he went to the chemist armed with a hacksaw and a screwdriver and threatened the poor chemist. The police station was just across the road so the terrified chemist pressed his silent panic button, which went straight to the police station. Ken was shouting at the chemist to give him the drugs as the policemen burst into the shop!

They yelled at him to drop his weapons but he didn't, so they bashed him with truncheons and he was arrested. I feel sad that the poor chemist was put through such a terrifying ordeal but Ken was desperate. He had been having seizures and collapsing and I got a call saying he was found unconscious in the town. Poor Ken. I think when the policeman said "Drop your weapons", he was half dazed, because he would have known what would follow if he didn't—and he hated pain.

He was charged with aggravated robbery, I think, and allowed home on bail. He called me and he was in a sorry state. I took him home, made him a drink and he showed me all the bruises on his body and told me to photograph them. I told him that we could see his damage. The poor chemist would carry what Ken did to him for a very long time. He was sorry. He wouldn't have hurt him, he said, he was just desperate!

When it came to court, it was in Hove. I picked him up early and he was in a dreadful state. His tummy was swollen and he was in a lot of pain. We stopped at a chemist on the way to get some codeine and he took loads. At court he went to see his brief. I kissed him and said we would see him after the trial. We went upstairs to the courtroom, where he was sentenced to four years! We were shocked but not as shocked as Ken; he went to Albany Prison on the Isle of Wight. I rang Phil who was on the way to Brighton Hospital for treatment. He was shocked too! We worried about how he would cope in prison.

Mags, Kayla and I went over to Ken's flat to empty it. Phil took stuff to the tip and we sorted through clothes. It was all filthy, the flat was disgusting, but we all set to and scrubbed it sparkly! We handed the keys back and took all Ken's bits and Phil took his tools. Kayla had sorted his DVDs and we packed them in a box—I think they went to a charity shop. Nothing much was worth saving and that, too, was sad. Kenny didn't cope well at all. There was a lot of bullying in the prison and it really messed with his head. He was very scared of two blokes in particular.

Phil and I went to see him. I wanted to drive but Phil wouldn't let me. "You can navigate." I took the satnav but no, he wanted me to read instructions from the AA route finder! We were lost even before we left Haywards Heath. Mags was really good at this but I was rubbish. And he told me so many times! But we did laugh a lot! We made it to Portsmouth and got the hovercraft over. Then we were to catch the bus to the prison which was due in 15 minutes. Then Phil said, "Look, that bus goes to Albany. Come on."

"No, let's wait for the proper bus."

"Nah, this one's going now." So like a fool I followed him and this bus went the entire way around the island! I kept saying, "We're gonna miss visiting," but he just tutted at me and rolled his eyes.

Finally, we were at the prison with half of visiting gone. Poor Phil was worried about his wee bag and had to empty it on the grass verge or it would have burst. He was walking really badly. He had a crutch and it looked so painful and such hard work as we climbed the hill to the gate. Finally we were in, were searched and let into the visiting room. Kenny was brought in and he was very pleased to see us. Big hugs and kisses, then I got us all a cuppa and Ken was telling us what a hard time he was having being bullied. He needed some gear brought in and asked Phil if he would smuggle some.

"You could put it under your ileostomy bag. They won't look there!"

I went mental at him. "Don't you dare ask Phil to do that! Don't you do it, Phil!" I couldn't believe he would ask that but, when I think back now, he was so scared of the two blokes who were making his life miserable that giving them drugs would alleviate the situation—but even so!

The drive home was easy. Phil had not printed out the return journey so my satnav was a godsend. We both noted how much better Kenny looked physically but his mental state was sad. He had been in the hospital wing for a while and his tummy was a lot better. His seizures seemed to have stopped. They had had him on some epilepsy medication which had really done dreadful things to his body.

Before his release we had been trying to get him into rehab or someplace where he would be cared for, as he was very vulnerable. I was ringing councils and social services. Dawn was on the drug abuse trail, ringing various places, bless her. She finally got him into an ex-offenders and drug users halfway house but it was in Blackpool and we had no other choice. He was booked in on the day of his release. Greg and I went down to Portsmouth and said we would meet him at the railway station. I had bought him some clothes and bits so took a suitcase and, when he arrived at the station, I was so upset. He was so frightened; he said he could still hear the blokes that had been bullying him. They could talk to him telepathically and they were threatening him now! "Ken, they can't," I said. "It's not possible. You talk to me telepathically—you can't!" I realised he was really struggling. We went to the café and sat and chatted for a while. It was good to see him. I did love him, but this was heart-breaking.

He showed me his papers and the address he was going to and I wrote down the address and phone number and told him I would ring that night to make sure he got there. We prayed with him and I hugged him tight, his train came and he was gone. He looked like a little boy lost. I cried so much and was very glad Greg was with me. It turned out Ken was now schizophrenic and those wretched voices would torment him for the rest of his life.

Goodbye, Phil

PHIL WAS HAVING TREATMENT FOR HIS CANCER which had spread to his bones. Walking was so painful and he would hobble around and the pain showed on his face. We were all still hoping to be able to go on holiday, but the cancer specialist said, "No Phil, you can't." We were all so disappointed, none more so than Phil who was so looking forward to cooking breakfast for us all. He had become quite the dab hand at cooking now!

Sharon had gone off somewhere and Phil asked John to come and have steak with him. He bought the finest fillet steak and the brothers ate this delicious meal together, Phil, I am sure, trying to make up for all those years not speaking! John had invited Phil and Mags over for a cream tea. John made sandwiches and did scones and jam and they had a wonderful time. That's where Phil got the idea to invite Greg and I for the very same meal—precious times.

Phil bought a wheelchair as walking was almost impossible. He was also having trouble breathing, bless him. It was hard to see him in such pain. It got so bad that they rang 111 and an ambulance took him to Brighton, where the cancer unit was. They got his pain under control a bit and he came home. Then for some reason he was taken to Haywards Heath Hospital and I went over to see him; in fact we all went, Kayla, Mags, John and I. The drugs Phil was on did something to his chin and this enabled him to grow a beard. All his life he had wanted to grow one and just couldn't. He had looked like the bloke from Scooby Doo with a few scrappy tufts, but now he had a full-on beard! He let me trim it and called it his magnificence which made us all laugh! We had some lovely times and talked about love. Kayla, bless her, told Phil she loved him and to everyone's amazement he said he loved her too. This was a special moment as Phil was not one for expressing his emotions.

I forget the sequence but Phil went to the hospice. He had been before and it was a beautiful tranquil place which he liked. He had his own room with French doors that overlooked the field, and there were donkeys. I can't see a donkey

314

without thinking of Phil; he was a bit of a stubborn donkey too! We all visited him there and they had definitely got him pain free. He looked very rested and I was very worried about him—we all were. It was just him and me one afternoon and I asked him if I could pray with him. He looked at me and said, "No thanks Fay," as if I had offered him a biscuit. I prayed for him silently anyway.

Naomi was working for an elderly lady in the evenings, helping her to get into bed. She was a Christian. I had told Naomi how worried I was that Phil would die without Jesus. And I couldn't bear it. Well, this lady was having a prayer meeting the following day and Naomi asked her if they would pray that I would get a chance to pray with Phil. That was so sweet of her but she knew how important it was to me.

The following day was May 1st. I drove over, picked up Mags and we went to St Peters and St James. It was a beautiful day and we sat in Phil's room. He was chatty and desperate for a fag. One of the nurses had been so kind and stuck a nicotine patch on him when he first went it there. As his pain was easier, they would get him into the wheelchair and push him through the French doors and he would sit out and have a fag. He was too poorly to do that today and as we sat and chatted he was struggling to get enough breath in and wanted his asthma pump, but it did nothing to help. We felt useless and he flopped back into his pillow and dozed a bit. Mags and I went and got a cuppa. I stayed till about 7.00 and Mags said she would stay a bit longer. I gave Phil a kiss and told him I would see him tomorrow. As I drove out, John was driving in, bless him. I waved, blew him a kiss and he caught it and smiled.

It was 9.00 when Kayla phoned and asked me if I was on my own. "NO," I said. "NO, not yet, not now!" Apparently, Mags and John had stayed a good hour after I left. John dropped Mags home and she got a call about half an hour after they left. Phil had just slipped from life into death. Greg and I drove back to the hospice. Kayla and Richard, John, Mags and Emily came and we were all in shock. We knew Phil was ill, knew he was terminal, but he said he would live five years after the specialist give him his diagnosis and we believed him. It hadn't been a year!

He looked so peaceful and we were all in tears. We kissed his little face and hugged each other. This was too soon, too sad. We were all back in relationship, all loving having Phil back in our lives, and he was so enjoying life with Mags and the grandkids. It seemed like a sad end. We stood around his bed, I held his hand and Mags held his other hand and we all joined hands. Richard, bless his

315

lovely heart, prayed and committed Phil to God. We all prayed, then we kissed Phil, kissed and hugged each other and went to our various homes with really sad and heavy hearts.

I rang Naomi the following day to tell her Uncle Phil had died. She was shocked and very sad. She loved him very much and they had got on since she was small. "Did you get to pray with him mum?" she asked. "No darling, I asked him but he said no but I prayed for him silently." She asked what happened and I told her about going back and us all holding hands and praying for him. She said she had asked if we prayed for him because the elderly lady she worked for had given her a piece of paper. One of the other ladies at her meeting had prayed for me and Phil to pray together and, as she prayed, a picture had come into her mind of Phil lying on his bed and everyone around him holding hands and praying and the words of the grace were written above Phil. The lady had drawn the very scene of us in Phil's room, all holding hands. That gave me such confidence that God had heard the cries of our hearts and taken Phil to himself.

It was a terribly sad time. Mags was trying to organise the funeral and we were all trying to help. Phil hated, I mean really hated, to be looked at. He once told me that he even hated the birds looking at him. When his schizophrenia was bad he said he could hear the birds saying, "Look at him. Let's shit on him" so, bless him, he would have hated a last ride in a hearse with windows on all sides and people able to see his coffin. We asked if it were possible that John, Greg, Ben and Dan could collect Phil from the undertakers and drive him to the crematorium in Ben's van. They could, so that's what they did. Greg took a crem service booklet from church and just the four of them read and prayed together, before Phil was cremated. It was perfect for Phil.

Then everyone gathered at the Baptist Church in Haywards Heath, where Kayla and Richard had organised tea and cake. Kayla made the cakes, we had boards with photos and some of Phil's artwork. Ben, bless him, played his guitar as people wandered in and sat. The church was full of family and friends. Richard led the service and he asked if anyone had anything they wanted to share—a memory of Phil. Naomi stood up and told of the time she had boasted to Stuart about her amazing Uncle Phil's sculptures.

He had done heads of different mental illnesses. Paranoia was a head looking terrified with eyes all over the head looking everywhere. Anorexia was actually Naomi's head with tiny arms coming out of her neck and her hands were a knife and a fork. In front of her was a plate with a slice of her own face and her eye on it—she was effectively eating herself. There were lots of other heads, each depicting an illness and there were also animal heads. He had a full-size iguana on the lounge floor at one time and the details was amazing! So she took this boy to see Uncle Phil's sculptures. They were all in the kitchen covered with cloths. Phil said, "Yeah Nao, show him," and as she pulled the cloths off each of the sculptures, she saw that Phil had added a very large-veined erect penis to every head.

She was mortified but had to admit that they were beautifully done. Phil went on to tell Stuart about his time in Parkhurst, which was really a big thing for Phil as he didn't share much with anyone outside of family. He must have had a real connection with Stu! We all laughed. Paul also said how he loved his Uncle Phil and always enjoyed being with him. He would miss him. One or two friends shared how much the appreciated Phil and his kindness to them. It really was a lovely service. It just seemed unreal that my brother, my big brother, was dead. I miss him.

A Shrinking Family

KENNY WOULD PERIODICALLY RING ME at silly o'clock in the morning. He would be either drunk or depressed or both and, bless him, he was always regretting his life choices, always wanting life to be different. He said he didn't have the strength to change and I would tell him we would all help him if he went to rehab. But he said he couldn't do rehab, that was the reason he had left Susie. She had got him a place in rehab and it scared him, so he left his wife, his children and his home because he said he knew he couldn't do it! This was the decision that he regretted for the rest of his life. It had set him on a path to destruction.

He loved Susie and was always asking me if she would have him back. "Get clean Ken. She loves you but she hates the drugs and the drink. I'm sure you could work things out if you got clean." He would cry and it would break my heart. I would pray with him over the phone but he would always say he was no good. "But Jesus came for us no-goods Ken. He loves us. He loves you. Ask him to help."

"Nah Frow. I know I can't do it."

I would talk to Greg and we would go up to see him. He had been moved from the unit he went into when he came out of prison and was in a little flatlet. The block had a warden who just kept a weather eye on the residents. It was in Fleetwood and it was lovely. The last time we went up, we bought groceries, cream cakes especially, and went to his flat. We rang but no answer, so buzzed the warden. She let us in and took us up to Ken's flat. She knocked but no answer, so she opened with her master key. Ken was lying on his bed and jumped up and grabbed his specs. He had an angry face but then he saw me and melted. He wrapped his arms around me and gave me such a hug. It was lovely to see him.

"Oh Frow, what are you doing here? Don't waste your money coming to see me—I'm not worth it. Greg mate, I'm sorry she's dragged you up here."

Greg said, "She didn't drag me, Ken. We both wanted to come to see you."

318

When I got a good look at him, he was stick thin with such a distended belly. His hair was scruffy, his beard was scruffy, but he was smiling and he was pleased to see us. I did love him. I made a cuppa and we sat and chatted. He always asked about everyone; Susie, Dawn and Adam first, then everyone else and their kids. Bless him, he remembered everyone's kids' names and even who they were married to. He always said to give them all his love.

I put away the groceries and he rolled his eyes and smiled at me. I thought, *He's not going to eat any of this.* I found some scissors in his drawer, so I said, "Come on Ken. Let's tidy you up a bit." He looked like a proper tramp. He was not happy with me but he let me do it and he looked so much better when I finished. The warden told us he had been having seizures and had collapsed a couple of times in the high street, which worried me.

When we left, Ken was tired but he gave us both big hugs. He always told me he loved me and I him. I was so sad to see him in such a state. We had talked about his tummy. He said it was his liver and he was taking medication but it wasn't really doing much. There were empty vodka bottles in the kitchen. He was a very sick man. He told us not to come again, then we prayed with him and left. That was November 2014 and was to be the last time I would see Ken alive.

The following February I got a call from Blackpool Hospital to say Ken had been found collapsed and was taken in. He was a very sick man they said. I was going into hospital myself to have yet another procedure on my neck. I desperately wanted to go up but in reality I knew I couldn't. I rang Susie and Dawn and, bless 'em, they were as shocked as I was. The nurse had said there was no way Ken was going to recover and if we wanted to see him we had to come now. Dawn drove Susie up and they got to Ken just in time. He was in a coma and they were with him for three hours. Dawn was shocked that Ken was unconscious but Susie told her that he could still hear, so she sat and talked to her Dad, Susie too. Then Dawn realised Ken was actually dying and said, "Say a prayer for him mum." Susie prayed and Kenny slipped from life into death, very peacefully, and with the two women whom he loved the most in all the world. He was just 57. Too young, too sad.

Dawn and Susie arranged for Ken to be cremated up in Blackpool and his ashes to be sent down to Dawn's in Lewes. Kayla's husband Richard said he would lead the service which Greg organised for us to have at All Saints Crowborough. It was a lovely service, with all the family together to say a last farewell to Kenny. It was a sad day because he died too young; his life robbed

319

from him by addiction. I so remember the beautiful, clear bright-eyed boy, who had the quickest, funniest, sharpest mind and wit. I loved him so much but he was so damaged by what our parents had done to him. He never sought help for all his emotional damage. He self-medicated and finally killed himself—heartbreaking. His ashes were put into the garden of remembrance to the side of the church and Greg and I have booked the plots next to Kenny.

It was in the same year in June that Maggy called me to say that Aunty Kath had rung her to say that Dad had been taken into hospital. I was indifferent to him and had no feelings about visiting or not but Greg said, "What do you want to do?"

"Nowt," I said. Before we went to bed, we prayed together as we always do and I thought, 'I should pray about Dad and what I should do'. When I woke the next morning, I just knew we should go to Blackpool to see him because I knew he was dying.

So we booked a coach to Blackpool—it's so much cheaper than the train. We arrived at 11pm and we had booked at the Premier Inn. We woke early, had breakfast, then prayed. I didn't know why we had to come, I just knew we had to. We asked God to be with us and went to the hospital. It was enormous, like a bloomin' city! We found the ward, went in and there lying in a bed was my Dad. This great man, strong as an ox, was reduced to skin and bone. I was shocked because he looked so small in the bed, hardly a bump in the blanket! But there was no mistaking that face, that jaw. He opened his eyes and looked up at me. "Fay," he said, and he puckered his lips. I didn't kiss him. "What are you doing here?"

"God told me to come."

His face dropped. "How is everyone?" he said.

"Phil is dead, Kenny is dead, John and Kayla are broken. Maggy, Sharon, Susie, Emily, all the grandchildren, are damaged by what you did. Why didn't you write to everyone? Why did you just leave everyone hurting? You should have tried to put things right." I was shouting at this point.

"I will do it when I get out of hospital," he said.

"You are not getting out. You are dying."

Greg poked me in the back and said, "That's a bit strong, love!"

Dad looked shocked. "Who told you?" he said.

I think he thought I would say the doctor but I said, "God."

He went completely white and looked shocked, then he started to pray out loud, pleading with God for forgiveness. I was incensed! I wanted to stop him, I wanted to put a pillow over his face. "Oh no you don't!" I was filled with anger. "You can't do this. You can't get forgiven for what you have done! You deserve to go to hell!" But then the most surreal thing happened. I felt as though God placed a blanket of peace over me and I heard a voice say, "I will lose none that the father has given me." So I watched my Dad pleading with God. Half the time I couldn't hear what he was saying but that didn't matter, he wasn't talking to me. I saw grace in action and God's love poured out.

He prayed for ages and when he had finished, I said, "We have to go. I won't see you again, unless I see you in glory." He puckered his lips and I bent and kissed him.

We got home from Blackpool at midnight and the next morning there was a call from the hospital to say Dad had died in the night. How gracious was God to send us to tell Dad he was dying and to give him the opportunity to repent and ask for forgiveness. In truth, if I had known God's plan I probably wouldn't have gone, because I thought he deserved hell. But in truth I deserve hell too, and God has forgiven me. What a loving father he is.

Now Dad was dead, we had to decide what to do with him. John, Kayla and I drove up to Blackpool in Ben's car as all of us have rubbish motors that would never have got us there! We had to sort the house out. They had taken all the equity out of the house and it now belonged to some building society. It was actually lovely being together. We had to register Dad's death so John, bless him, paid for everything: the cremation, the certificates and everything. We said we'd do it between us but, "Nah, don't be daft. I've got this," said John. We had to go to the hospital to see the registrar and get several death certificates, collect Dad's belongings and organise the undertaker to sort out the cremation and have Dad's ashes couriered to Kayla.

Then we went to the house. They were both shocked at the filthiness and the sadness of how our parents had ended in this mucky home. We all stood and hugged each other and just wept. This was not how it was supposed to be! We pulled ourselves together and sorted through the few bits that were left and then we drove home, John, bless him, serenading us from Blackpool to Reading! He found such joy in singing. We had enjoyed it too until about Birmingham. From there on we took the mickey but it didn't stop him. He sang his heart out! We loved it really and we loved him.

Crowborough

AFTER 22 YEARS, GREG WAS MADE REDUNDANT FROM AMERICAN EXPRESS. One of the other chaps had also left just a few months before and was running a warehouse in Maidstone. He rang and offered Greg a job. Greg was thankful for the job but, having only just passed his driving test, he found the travelling very stressful. He worked there for a few months, then was offered a job in Tunbridge Wells. He jumped at it, only because of the travelling. After he had worked there for just a few months, Nancy came over and said, "Greg, there's the perfect job for you at our church." Having just built a £2,400,000 extension, the church needed a verger\building manager.

Greg said, "Nancy, I have only just got this job."

"But Greg, this is perfect for you," she said. Greg went into work the following day to be met by all the bosses. They had sold the business to a Chinese firm and everyone was handed their P45 and redundancy money. He arrived home in shock! We sat and talked about what had happened and we prayed that God would lead us and Greg would find the right job. This was all very unsettling for him.

Nancy came over for a cuppa and said, "Greg, the job at church. You should have gone for it. I think the deadline for applications has passed but let me drive you up there and have a look around. You would need to see the administrator, Jim Wheeler, but he's not there today. Come on," and with that she was off with Greg following. I sat and prayed that if this was the job for Greg, he would know it.

Apparently, the first person they met when they walked into church was Jim Wheeler. Nancy introduced Greg and told Jim that Greg would be the perfect man for the job. Greg and Jim talked, then he said, "We're interviewing on Monday." He gave Greg an application form, showed him around and Nancy brought him home. Application form filled in, Nancy took it into church and gave it to Jim on Sunday. We were still attending Kings Church at that time.

On Monday morning Greg went up to Crowborough and there were four applicants for the job, one being a builder. The interview went well and the vicar, Andrew Cornes, asked if he was a committed Christian and was he a member of a church. They had his application form so they could see his skills and, talking to him, realised he was a very personable bloke.

One of the questions was about Greg's DIY skills and, very honestly, he told them he was rubbish. He came home not knowing if he had got the job. They would let him know as soon as they had interviewed everyone and the interviewing panel had talked it over. We had prayed that if this was the right job for him, he would get it, so we just left it with God.

The phone call came the following morning saying they would love to offer him the job! Thank you, Lord. Well, this was all change for us, as we decided that if Greg was to work for All Saints Crowborough, we should worship there. It was weird after years of attending a Baptist church and the evangelical churches and believing that the Church of England was dead and filled with nominal Christians. I was worried about joining but I had been very wrongly informed! This church was very much alive and filled with Bible-believing Christians! Forgive me Lord. How arrogant we were, thinking the churches we had attended were the only ones filled with real Christians! We loved it and settled into church life with relish! Greg loved the job. Nancy was right, bless her heart. After around three years Greg was wanting to be closer to the church, as he had to go back and forth in the evening. Although Uckfield is not far, it swallowed up time and petrol, so we decided to sell our house and move to Crowborough.

The children were all living independently so we thought we would sell our four-bed semi, buy a little bungalow and have some money left over. For the first time in our lives we would have spare money! We looked in all the estate agents in Crowborough and there were no bungalows. We kept looking and then a friend from church rang to tell us that one was coming on the market. We went to look at it, just from the outside. It was small but we decided that as long as it had two bedrooms we could manage. When we found out the price we were stunned! This little bungalow cost more than our house was worth! We went into the church coffee shop feeling rather fed up where we met a friend, Marion. "Don't give up," she said, "keep praying." I said, "If God wants us in Crowborough He will have to find us something a lot cheaper than that!" She laughed and said she would pray too.

That evening Marion's adopted daughter, Mya, went to a prayer meeting, Central Focus, at her church in London. The chap who ran it had rung Phil Haughton, who used to attend, and asked him if he was OK. Phil told him his mother had died. She had owned a bungalow and he wanted someone to live in it, rent free, and look after the bungalow and the garden. He thought he was asking the impossible, but God was in this because my friend Marion's daughter was at this meeting. She asked where the bungalow was. "Crowborough," he said.

"I used to live there. I'll ring my mum. She may know someone." She rang Marion who rang us and we rang him. We could hardly believe it!

We arranged to meet him at the bungalow which is just down the hill from the church. It had three bedrooms and a huge garden. We talked with Phil the owner. He was very trusting and we were trustworthy, so we moved in just before Christmas 2004. We decided to rent our house out as we didn't know how long we would live there. We worked hard decorating the bungalow and sorting the garden out—we wanted Phil to be glad he let us live in his mum's bungalow. After three years he asked us to pay rent which we do and are so happy living in this beautiful bungalow. We have looked after all our grandchildren over the years and this garden has been such a blessing to us all. We are very thankful to Phil, and to God for bringing us together. Phil says we were the answer to his prayer and he definitely was the answer to ours!

Greg worked at All Saints for 19 years and he was happier than he had ever been in his job. He is so brilliant with people, whether they are Christian or not. In fact he welcomed all who came into the church and made everyone feel comfortable, loved and cared about. He prayed with anyone who needed prayer. Many of the clubs met in the church and they all just loved him—he really was the face of All Saints. Nothing was too much trouble for him. He would be up at church at 11.30 at night to lock up after parties and he never moaned. I did! "It's all part of the job darling," he would say. He was Father Christmas at the nursery and many of the schools around town. His easy way is such a gift, and God used it. He knows everyone and everyone knows him. "I am Mrs Greg," I used to say and I love the fact that he was just where God wanted him.

In October 2018, he was 67 and was finding some things quite difficult. We had discussed when he would retire and Bertie Pearce, one of the church wardens, came to see us to talk about retirement. We decided that the end of March 2019 would be a good time. Once the decision was made it felt right, but odd to think he wouldn't be working at church after that. The months passed quickly and Bertie organised a Do for us both on the last Saturday in March. We arrived at church and all our children and grandchildren came. John and Sharon, Kayla and Richard drove up from Hampshire and the church was packed—we were both so emotional.

Greg was\is so loved by the church family. It was the most amazing evening. John and Greg sang, the staff all did a fabulous sketch, taking the mickey and all loving him. So many people did skits and Rob Dillingham made me cry with what he said about us both. Zan Alexander made the most amazing cake with a picture of us both on it and the church family gave us a gift of £7,000 pounds! We were blown away. It was such an emotional evening and the church was full of love for us both, our family and church family together. So special.

The Continuing Story

WHERE TO NOW with the Lancaster/Summers/Harlow/Baulu/Gunn/Kinsella/
Patchin/Husband family story? Well, wonderfully, we are the chain breakers. You know the old saying that those who have been abused go on to abuse? Well, not in this family, thank you very much. Because of those of us who became Christians, we had a new beginning and that particular chain was broken! My children, Naomi, Daniel and Becky, had a fairly OK childhood I think. We did our very best. We didn't have much money but we had loads of love. We put good Christian values into them, laughed a lot, cried a bit, struggled sometimes, but in spite of us they all turned out to be fabulous people! We are very thankful to God for them all and their partners.

When **Naomi** decided she wanted to be a teacher at five, she worked towards that from then onwards, always sitting her dollies and teddies in a classroom setting and teaching them everything they knew! So all through school this was her career choice and we were the proudest parents when she went off to Chichester Uni. She was the first in my family to go to university and she studied hard. But when she went on placement to a school with a mature student, the teachers at the school would relay everything to the older woman, who was supposed to pass all the info on to Naomi. She didn't, so Naomi would go into school quite unprepared because of the mature student, who would look fabulous.

Poor Naomi was so unhappy and would ring me crying. I was so upset for her because she had lost her desire and love of being a teacher because of this selfish woman. She came home and we talked and prayed about what she wanted to do. I certainly didn't want her to be in a career that she no longer wanted and she didn't want to finish the teaching part of her degree. She was so unhappy and we were heartbroken for her, because this had been her dream forever! We agreed with her and she talked to the uni and dropped the QTS part and finished her Religious Studies degree. She then went to Lewes Tertiary College and did a one-year private secretarial diploma on finishing that.

She got her first job in London for a firm called Redbus but the company folded after she had worked there for two years and she was made redundant. She then got a job in Donaldsons where she met Susie and worked there for five years. Then she went to work for a local building firm called C.J Gowing where she has been for 13 years and absolutely loves it. She works with such a lovely bunch and they get on like a house on fire.

Stuart Gunn started his career at 14 with an old lawn mower. He would go around cutting people's lawns for a couple of quid to earn a bit of pocket money and he built up quite a few clients. When it came to choosing a career at school, he told the careers officer he didn't know what he wanted to do but knew he wanted to work with his hands. The officer suggested being a mechanic, so he said OK, got a job in a garage and went to Lewes Tertiary College for two years. Then the garage went bust so that was when he went to work for Greg at American Express.

After two years, he joined Systematic, installing telephone wiring. After two years he decided he hated office work and hated working for other people. He had kept up his grass cutting at weekends and people had got to know him and asked him to do gardening too, so he decided to work for himself. He was very nervous to start with in case he couldn't earn enough but he needn't have worried. His reputation as an excellent worker soon spread and he had more work than he could handle. He had a couple of lads working with him on several jobs, he bought machinery and vans, and having done the mechanics course he is able to maintain and service them all himself.

He's built up a fabulous little business and started his company, Great Gunns, 23 years ago. He has two blokes, Keith and Dale, who are regular helpers and work alongside him. He's a perfectionist, so his clients know that when they ask him to do a job it will be tip top. He loves the outdoor life and I wonder if **Harry** will work with his Dad. He has just started cutting lawns for extra money so, like father like son? Watch this space.

Naomi started to go out with Stuart when he worked for Greg at Amex. I had heard all sorts of stories about him and wasn't sure he was right for my daughter—she was 17 and he was 20. They were very keen on each other and it worried me a bit. After two years they got engaged and then saved like mad for three years to buy a house. Stu came to live with us for a while and I got to know him better. Because we were Christians we wouldn't have them living together in our house. I am sure he thought we were weirdos but he was OK with it and we started to get on better. They were married in July 2001. Naomi looked so beautiful and Stu looked very handsome. It was such a lovely day and yet….

They had bought their house in Jefferies Way and they made it very beautiful and were very happy. Then, on 5 March 2003, **Lucy Abby Gunn** burst into the world. She was our first grandchild and we fell headlong in love with her; she was just beautiful! Her birth made us grandparents, Nana and Pops, a whole new role and relationship and we loved it. We loved Lucy and I had the privilege of looking after her when Naomi went back to work. I loved it and we became great mates, Lucy and I. We did all sorts of things together and I loved every moment.

It's funny; when you are a young mum, you worry about all sorts of things, about the house being tidy and putting everything away before daddy gets home, getting the dinner ready on time, but as a nana you just enjoy being with this lovely little person. There were toys everywhere and we never put them away; no point, she'll be here in the morning.

One time Naomi and Stu had taken Lucy to Marwell Zoo, so when she came over to us, we got the Lego out and built Marwell Zoo in the lounge. We added to it for weeks and it was a talking point when anyone came. I didn't care how long it was there; she so enjoyed it and so did we! We had paddling pools in the garden, bought a trampoline and swing set. We loved having her and she loved coming, which filled our hearts with love and joy. I would take her up to the church coffee bar and she got to know all the regulars and would high five everyone. They all loved her and one very elderly gent who was a retired vicar would come in and whenever he saw Lucy would exclaim, "Hello Lucy girl!"

One day she just shouted, "Well hello Johnny boy!" His face was a picture and he threw his head back and laughed. That was how they always greeted each other after that. She was three and he was 86! They were great mates. He was such a gent and Lucy the only one ever to call him Johnny boy!

Three years later on 16 May 2006, **Harry Stuart Gunn** also burst into the world. How could we possibly love another grandchild like we loved Lucy? But on meeting Harry for the first time, we fell headlong in love with him too! I also had the pleasure of looking after Harry. What a character he was; such a gorgeous little fella. He loved the trampoline and would be on it for hours. He liked anything that was messy—painting, mud—and he would always try to make us laugh; such a comedian!

In the summer, one of the best games was Pops squirting them with the hosepipe as they squealed and ran around the garden! Or pouring water down the slide to shoot down as fast as possible and adding plastic sheets to the end of the slide so they would go further! Harry worked out you went further if you took your trunks off, so they were all starkers in the garden! They had water bomb fights, water pistol fights with so much laughter and giggles. Harry was always the one doing the daftest stuff to make everyone laugh. He asked me if he could have a whole watermelon and I gave it to him. He took it outside with everyone following, smashed it on his head and yelled, "WATER MELLOWN!" Everyone was in hysterics; he is a born entertainer! I so love him and love being a nana.

It was watching Stuart with his children and with Naomi that I realised how they were right for each other and he was a fabulous daddy. I realised how wrong I was and I have loved him like a son ever since. Forgive me, Stu—I really do love you!

As I write this, Lucy is 17 and Harry 14. They are amazing kids and have had a wonderful childhood. They are very loved, secure and have confidence gushing out of their ears! Stu and Naomi have done a wonderful job as parents and I am so very proud of them all.

Daniel had gone to Eastbourne College after finishing school. He went on the car bodywork course because he went to the wrong class! He was going to do mechanics but stayed on the bodywork course only because he was too embarrassed to say, "I'm not supposed to be here"! But he did amazingly well and it seemed he most certainly had a gift for it. He worked at Paragon Porsche as a Saturday boy from 15, and when he finished his course worked full-time. He loved it and had great banter with all those he worked with, particularly Sam Corke. After many years working together, they decided to leave and work together. Impact was the name of the company and they have worked together since that day to this. He is so good at what he does and still enjoys it, which has to be a blessing.

Susie worked in London and trained as a surveyor. She values commercial property all over the country and thinks nothing of driving up to Leeds or Manchester or down to Devon and back in a day. She is amazing and loves her work. She has worked for Allsop for 13 years and is an associate partner.

While Naomi was working in a London office she made several friends, one of whom was Susie Mitson. Susie came down to stay with Naomi for carnival weekend in September. I'm not sure if it was at this time that she met Dan but I

329

remember the Christmas when everyone came to our house. Susie came too and I watched as she and Dan were all snuggly and seemed to really like each other. I thought she was lovely and would be good for Dan. That relationship blossomed. It's very odd watching your children fall in love, but it's lovely too, because all you want for them is to find the right one and to be happy, and here she was. And Dan seemed to be the right one for her too. It was all very exciting and they were so happy. Susie had a house in Lingfield, Dan moved in and life was wonderful for them.

Maisy Kate Summers burst into our world on 1 October 2008 and we fell headlong in love with her too. This grandparenting is amazing; you just have more love for everyone who comes along. It was my privilege to look after Maisy too while mummy and daddy worked. We too became great mates, doing all manner of things together. Maisy loves crafts and we enjoyed making all manner of wonderful things for mummy and daddy. She was such a cuddler and just a little cutie.

When Dan and Susie decided to get married, we were thrilled. It was on 17 June 2010. Susie looked beautiful and Dan looked so handsome. It was a fabulous day, enjoyed by one and all—well except Maisy, who was a diddy bridesmaid. She found it all too much. There's a fabulous photo of Dan and Susie looking beautiful, with heads thrown back laughing, and Maisy sat between them, face screwed up and crying! Hilarious!

Maisy was a little shy around people she didn't know and one Christmas we took all six grandkids to the local panto. Maisy had on her Cinderella dress and, as the panto was Cinderella, the lady on the door welcomed us all, bent down and said to Maisy, "You should be on the stage."

Her little face was a picture. We all sat and watched the show. The intermission came and a man came out on stage and said, "There are some special people in the audience today." Maisy was sat on Lucy's knee and she jumped down, pushed past us all, walked over to the stage, up the steps and there she was, holding her Cinderella dress out on both sides so that everyone saw her in all her glory. She walked up to the bloke on stage, who was quite flustered by her arrival. "What's your name?" he asked.

"Maisy Kate Summers but today I am Cinderella," she said and smiled. We were all in hysterics! This was so unlike Maisy. The bloke was looking down his list for a Maisy but there wasn't one, so he gave her a selection box anyway and made everyone applaud her. Off she walked like a queen bee! What a little character! I'm sure she did it because the lady on the door had said she should be on the stage!

The following year on March 3rd, **Charlie Edward Summers** burst into our world and we all fell headlong in love with him too. When Susie went back to work, I had the privilege of looking after Charlie too. Now, this little fella loved nature. Any animals and he wanted to know all about them. He was the dinosaur king; I had a million books on dinosaurs and he learned all their names and whether they were carnivore or herbivore. We learned all this together. He always had an animal book in his hand and devoured knowledge about them all. We were once coming over the forest when we came over the brow of a hill and a beautiful stag was standing in the middle of the road. We stopped and it stood staring at us.

"It's magnificent," I said.

"Yes," said Charlie. The stag moved on and we chatted about it for the rest of the journey home. As we got in, he said, "Nana. What's magnificent?" I explained it was the most beautiful, the best ever, just fabulous. Everything we had or saw for the rest of the week was a magnificent chicken nugget, a magnificent tee shirt, a magnificent drink. Charlie was a little character and what fun we had. Dan and Susie are wonderful parents and have a fabulous life together. Maisy and Charlie are awesome children and I love them all and am so proud of the Summers family part two!

Becky was living in her flat above the HSBC bank in Uckfield. She was working at Buxted Park Hotel and life was stressful. Dan met up with **Neil Kinsella** whom Becky had gone out with before he went to Uni. "How's Becky?" he asked.

"Why don't you give her a call," said Dan, and he gave Neil her number. He rang, took her out and love blossomed again. We met Neil for the first time at Christmas and very soon realised he was perfect for Becky. He made her very happy and we loved him for that. We have loved him ever since. He moved into the flat with her and on 28 January 2007 they married—what a fabulous day. Becky looked beautiful and Neil very handsome. It was such a lovely day.

Alfie Connor Kinsella burst into our world on 18 July 2007, bright-eyed and very aware. We were there immediately after his birth along with Bill and Judy, Neil's parents. We felt very privileged to be allowed in the room—it was magical. All of us grandparents fell headlong in love with Alfie and there is an amazing photo of Bill holding Alfie with both of them staring intently at each other—beautiful. I would love it in school holidays when I would get to look after Alfie and Harry together. They were the most adorable, beautiful boys and they loved each other. Harry would do daft stuff to make Alfie laugh. I have many photos of these two darling boys together: in the paddling pool, in the bath, running naked around the garden in the summer. They would sleep over one night a week and what fun we would have: dinner together giggles, bath together giggles, film night giggles, story time, prayers and bed.

They were and still are the best of mates and I love those boys. Alfie was the one who talked me into putting a tent onto the double bed and letting them all sleep in it together. They all piled in and snuggled down. It was an adventure! Alfie was such a kind little fella. Well he still is, but as a little one he was always keen to make sure everyone was OK and he always looked after Ellie in such a sweet way. He melted my heart with his gentleness and thoughtfulness.

Then, on 27 March 2010, **Ellie Summer Kinsella** burst into our world and was a pickle from the moment she arrived. Almost born in the car-park but for a nurse's ability to push Becky in a wheelchair very quickly into the foyer of the hospital where she arrived! We rushed over to meet her and, bosh—headlong in love again! She was beautiful. Neil and Becky had decided they would try to look after the children by themselves, so I only got to have Alfie and Ellie in school holidays but we certainly had fun together.

We would have all our grandchildren together. They all love each other and had such fun together with sleepovers at nana and pops, eggy bread for breakfast and chocolate pancakes, picnics, roller blading, sledging, trampolining, painting and crafting. Ellie was always the crafting queen; she really is brilliant at art and loves making stuff. We had stories, film nights and every summer we would make a video and they would dress up. We would make up stories or sing to popular songs and Ellie would throw herself into the part—such a little actress! We would make props for the video. This was a great project and we all loved it! Ellie and Maisy were the best of friends and would spend hours with the Barbie dolls, or baby dolls and pushchairs.

When they were old enough we would walk up to church, all pushing prams or riding bikes or scooter. They progressed to roller boots and rollerblades. The two girls would love to serve in the coffee bar and took turns to do the money. They were all allowed to get a sweetie pot from Nana's cupboard at home to take up to church. Ellie had special sweeties and would be so sweet saying, "I can only put a few in my pot nana, cos I'll be sick." Bless her, so sensible. We would get all the toys and equipment from the charity shop in Jarvis Brook and they all loved to go and have a rummage. I would give them all a quid each and come home with a car full of stuff that they would play with all summer, then back it goes to the charity shop and another quid's worth next holiday—wonderful stuff! It has been such a joy to be involved in our grandchildren's lives and we thank all of our children, their hubbies and wife, for allowing us to be such a lovely part of their, and your lives. We thank you all, we love you and we thank God for each and every one of you.

Becky continues to work at Buxted Park Hotel. She has been there for 22 years and has worked in many departments. She enjoys working there and is brilliant at what she does, from wedding planning to receptionist to housekeeping to office work. Neil has worked for Freedom Leisure in many of their leisure centres, including Uckfield, East Grinstead, K2 Crawley, where he was the operations manager, and Bewbush. He has worked his way up in the company and is now Contract Manager at The King Alfred Leisure Centre in Brighton as well as General Manager of Portslade Sport Centre. He loves his job and seems to enjoy every aspect of it.

Where do I start with **Emily**? She is one awesome woman! She has had to battle through so much—but I will start with **Giles**. Ems met Giles at a party. He asked for her number and rang her. That was the start of their relationship and they were very happy for a while. On 13 August 2006, **Ellis David Welsh** arrived in the world. He was soooo tiny but perfect! Emily was a mummy and she was wonderful! But after a while Giles and Emily realised that they didn't love each other but they both loved Ellis so they made arrangements for them both to share custody of Ellis. Life was tough for Ems. She was trying to get better jobs and decided to do bookkeeping and accountancy and she worked very hard to do this training.

When Ems was 14, she had met **Mike Baulu** and they dated for a while until Phil got wind of it and put the kybosh on the relationship. Here we are all those years later and Mike friended her on Facebook! It was lovely to be back in touch and they met up and began a relationship. She fell head over heels in love with him and he with her. It was so lovely to see her so happy. Then on 26th February 2010 **Elalane Rae Baulu** arrived into the world and what a little darling she was. We all fell in love with her, she was beautiful. Mike and Emily decided to buy a home together in Burgess Hill and then in August 2015 they got married. What a wonderful day that was. Emily looked like a princess and Mike her handsome prince.

We were all so thrilled for them both but my heart was bursting with joy for Emily. What a journey she has been on and what sadness and heartache she has been through. But she is a chain breaker and a strong, spirited woman who, despite all that she has been through, found love and her soul mate in lovely Mike. They are such a loved up happy pair. Their little family is growing up and their house is fabulous. Mike has been working so hard on doing an extension and it has made such a difference to them having the extra space. Mike is a perfectionist, so you know when he does something it will be wonderful. They not only have Ellis and Ela, but cats Reggie and Ronny. Granny Annie and Nana Maggy all help to make this little family work well.

Paul joined the RAF, loved it and made some fabulous mates. One in particular, Sam, invited him up to his place on New Year's Eve 1998\99 and that was where and when he met Sam's sister Holli. It was meant to be and they fell in love. Paul proposed to Holli while he was in the Falkland Islands in 2000— very romantic—and they were married in March 2002 at the most amazing place; the wedding venue was an actual castle! Fairytale stuff! Such a fabulous day. Holli looked amazing and Paul looked handsome and we all had a great time. John did his usual, which was the kung fu fighting dance. He had loved Bruce Lee since we were teenagers and we went to Brighton to see *Enter the Dragon*. John came out and stated leaping about, kicking everything at head height, and that was where it all began.

So whenever he heard the song *Everybody*, he thought he was Bruce Lee and we all loved watching him. He had never seen himself doing this dance until someone videoed him at Paul and Holli's reception. I did say, "Don't show John," but they did, and his illusion was broken. He saw a 45-year-old bald fella, not a 20-year-old Chinese bloke and he was shocked, bless him. I don't think he danced that dance again. Sad.

Anyway, after the beautiful wedding they moved into married quarters in Burghfield, near Reading, and were very happy. They were made even happier when on 2 July 2008, **Isaac James Lancaster** arrived in the world; a beautiful boy loved by all who clapped eyes on him. They lived happily in Burghfield for 15 years and Isaac went to school there. Then Paul was stationed in Beaufort, South Carolina, for three years, after which he retired from the RAF having served for 22 years.

Ben was the last of John and Sharon's boys to marry, but the girl he married was definitely worth the wait. Ben met **Deborah Henderson** in December 2014 and I remember meeting her in June the following year at John's birthday bash over at Airworks in Glynde. It was plain to see that Ben was all loved up and it seemed mutual. Deb had baked lovely cakes and I liked her already! They got engaged in August 2015 and married on the Isle of Wight on 27 May 2017. It was a beautiful day and Deborah looked stunning in her black lace dress with Ben so handsome in his very flash tweed suit. They have been as happy as it's possible to be and lived on the Isle of Wight until they sold that house and moved into a cottage on the green in Ringmer, with Midget the dog. They love village life and each other, and the dog.

Stephen Lancaster went to Camp Pinewood in North Carolina in the summer of 1999. He had the most wonderful time and met the most wonderful girl, **Kim Widmann**. This gorgeous girl won his heart and they got engaged in the summer of 2000 and were married in June 2001. It was a fabulous day and Greg and I went over to the States to stay with Nancy and Ray in Indianapolis. We were driving down from there to Florida and we timed it so that we could go to Steve and Kim's wedding in Bowling Green.

Greg, being the plonker that he is at times, went fishing with Ray in the lake by their house with no shoes on, no sun cream either, all day in full sun by the water. By the evening his feet had swelled to look like they had been blown up like a rubber glove! I was worried but we set off for the wedding and everywhere we stopped for lunch or coffee break, people would say, on seeing Greg's feet, "Put Aloe Vera on"; "Put vinegar on"; "Put flour on"; "Put butter on"—all kinds of crazy remedies. We did try the Aloe Vera, only to find he was allergic and it made the feet worse! By the time we got to Bowling Green, his feet were enormous and he couldn't get his shoes on! We put flip flops on his feet with black socks over them—he could hardly walk—but I think he got away with it!

It was a fabulous service. Kim looked beautiful and Steve looked handsome. It really was a wonderful day. After a few years with just the two of them, the beginning of the American Lancaster clan began with the birth of **Samuel John** on 11 August 2009. What a beautiful boy! Then on 19 September 2011, along came **Mia Rose**, a little beauty with killer dimples, loved by all who meet her.

Ron, the youngest of John and Sharon's boys, moved out to share a flat in Seaford with his cousin Adam, who was also working for John at that time, but things went awry for Adam and he moved out. Ron was on his own in the flat for a while, then found a new flatmate. He had a girlfriend **Coreena**. They had gone to school together and got together in the 5th year. She is a fantastic girl and perfect for Ron and they seemed to be together for ever.

After a while Ron moved into his brother Paul's flat until he was able to buy his own. He was 18, definitely his father's son! He continued working for John until John sold Seaford Glass and Coreena went up to Nottingham to uni. Ron went up to Nottingham too—this was true love! He worked in a bar for a year and a half until Coreena graduated, then they both moved into Ron's flat in Seaford.

Seaford Glass had gone bust and was empty, which was so sad as it had been a thriving little business. So John reopened it as Johnson's Glass with Ben and Ron. It has been a wonderful business since, run by Ron.

Ron and Coreena got engaged in 2006 and married in 2007 and that was another wonderful day. Coreena looked beautiful, Ron so handsome, the service was perfect and the reception was epic. Aunty Susie and Stu were the talk of the dance floor—they could really bust some moves! I love family weddings and this one was fabulous!

They enjoyed a few years getting their home just perfect, then in May 2011 **Grace Lancaster** was born. I so remember John telling me he was a Gramps and he finally had his girl, he was ecstatic! Gracie had him wrapped around her little finger and he loved it and so did Grandma! Grace was a little beauty. Then in September 2011 along came **Douglas Lancaster**, a little belter! And what a fabulous little family they are.

Adam Lancaster moved out of home and into a flat with Ron, to work for John but after a while things went wrong. (I have Adam's permission to say this). He was struggling with addiction and couldn't cope with life very well. He moved back to live with his mum and, bless her, she did all that she could. Eventually Adam went up to Blackpool to live with his Dad. This was a bad move as he and Kenny were not good for each other and they both went downhill. I so remember visiting them and seeing two skeletons walking! I cried buckets. Adam went to prison a couple of times and in and out of psychiatric wards for treatment.

Granny asked him to clean for her, which he did. He found a jar with money in so he took it. The following day he was in the shower when granny and Grandad burst into the bathroom and both of them battered him black and blue!

What deep family love all round—him nicking the money and them beating their grandson!

The last time Adam went to prison in Blackpool, he realised he couldn't stay with his Dad anymore so on his release he went to say goodbye to his Dad and Grandad, granny having died. They both wished him well and each gave him £100. He went to his mum's flat but he could only stay a little while before heading for Bournemouth where he went to a treatment centre. I think this is where he met **Fleur** and a relationship started. Fleur got pregnant and **Isabelle Grace Sullivan** was born on 1 January 2010. This relationship was not to last but beautiful Isabelle was here. Adam went to London and into a treatment centre for two months, moved out, lived on the streets, then into a psychiatric hospital and ended up in St Thomas's Hospital, almost losing his legs and his life!

He was extremely ill, with seizures, blood clots on his lungs and a fade on the brain. On his release he went home to his mum, very paranoid. Poor Susie couldn't cope so John and Sharon said he could stay with them and work with John. He told them he was clean but he wasn't. John was doing all he could to help, but Adam was an addict and just lied. He moved out and a chap in Susie's church arranged for him to go to a Christian festival. He had a bag of drugs with him and as he was walking along a man said, "Can I pray with you?" He did and Adam slept for 15 hours straight and woke up with all symptoms gone!

He then went to the rehab centre, has been clean for two years, has become a Christian and is on step 11 of the 12-step programme. As I write he is trying to reconnect with his family. He is repentant and knows people have heard all this before but this time it's genuine. He is healthy and fit and wants to put right the things he has done wrong. Bless you Adam, you can now have a life worth living.

Dawn Lancaster is another awesome woman. She has coped with so much on her own and achieved so much on her own! I remember little Dawney in such a terrible state when Kenny was off his head, trying to put his head through the greenhouse and Dawn only about 10 years-old, hanging on to her Dad and desperate to stop him. Susie called an ambulance and they were desperately trying to stop him hurting himself. Not the sort of thing you want your 10 year-old to cope with. Then when Kenny left, it was devastating for Dawn; she and Kenny had a great relationship and he just left her.

She was a young teenager, such a difficult time for girls anyway, and this must have been heart-breaking for her. But Dawn kept things very close to her chest. Adam went off the rails but Dawn studied hard and did amazingly well at school—such a bright girl. She then went on to university at Brighton to study criminology and applied psychology, bless her. Of course, she had a bit of inside knowledge on criminology! She really got stuck in and graduated with a First! What an achievement when you think of all she had coped with.

She met **Lee Payne** in 2001 in Ringmer. Love blossomed and they bought a flat in Seaford and it was there that **Archie Lee Payne** was born on 11 March 2010. What a little bruiser—gorgeous boy. They were happy with their little family. Then, on 11 November 2012, **George David Payne** arrived to complete their family. They had moved from Seaford and bought a fabulous house in Lewes, so Susie was just around the corner to help with child care, which she loves! Lee is a fabulous daddy and partner and they make such a lovely family.

Rachel was the eldest of Kayla and Stuart's girls and she is beautiful and smart. The girls were young when Dad's fall from grace happened and they continued in their faith, bless 'em. Then their own family fell apart when Stuart left, but Kayla and the girls closed ranks and became a tight little unit, the three of them against the world. The girls would say mum was too strict, but she was keeping her girls close and safe, and did an amazing job. Rachel decided she wanted to study design and advertising at Northampton University. She moved up there and loved it.

She joined a fabulous church and it was there that she met **Jon Patching**. He was the bass player in the band and they both attended the same house group. They got to know each other properly when they got together to run a youth group in 2007 but didn't start dating until 2008. Love blossomed, Jon asked Rachel to marry him and they got engaged in March 2009—actually the same day that her sister got engaged too! They married in June 2010 and she looked so beautiful. It was a fabulous day and we were all there to celebrate with them. No one was happier that Jon and his speech at the reception was just full of declarations of love for his beautiful bride. All the men in the room were rolling their eyes and Uncle John was doing a winding handle motion. But Jon, bless him, was so thankful to God and to Rachel. We women thought it was just beautiful!

They stayed in Northampton because Jon has a good job and their very dear friend Mr Marsh needed someone to rent his house; perfect for them. They have since bought the house and have lived happily in their home for 10 years. This year, after many, many heartaches, their family was completed when **Scarlett Emma Patching**, born 2 November 2017, and **Mia Harlow Patching**, born 18

December 2018, were finally adopted by these two lovely people on 9 April 2020. What a wonderful day that was! Life for the Patching family is exciting, messy, fun and stressful—just like every other young family!

Hannah was 15 when Stuart left. She didn't cope well with his leaving and did what all teenagers do—rebelled doing all manner of daft stuff. Kayla was at the end of her tether and arranged for Hannah to see a counsellor, Annie Hance, who was amazing and guided her through all manner of stuff over the next year. She came back to her faith and realised you can't be a part-time Christian; you are full-time or nowt! So she committed her life to Christ and wanted to live a godly life. She thought mission might be good for her, so Annie helped her look for mission training colleges, and Redcliff Bible College popped up. This was the college for her. She also went on a mission to Thailand with OMF and on her return she was baptised in February 2008. John did a Bible reading and Kayla prayed a blessing.

Hannah moved to Gloucester which was where she met **Liam Husband** and was smitten immediately. Beautiful blue eyes were the clincher apparently! They began a relationship, though Liam was warned off as Hannah was young. He took no notice and they continued. Then Liam went on placement to Guyana and on his return he proposed in March 2009 by a fountain in Gloucester with a ring he had made for her. They were madly in love and she left the college to go home and earn some money. They decided to bring the wedding plans forward. Kayla and Richard were wonderful and so supportive, and they married in August 2009. It was a beautiful day and Hannah looked beautiful and Liam very handsome.

This was the beginning of an adventure and a wonderful little family for both of them. Liam finished his degree and on 17 March 2010, **Samuel Isaiah Husband** was born in Gloucester; a beautiful boy! Liam started a training course in Kidderminster, where he did split hours with Willowdene Farm, a rehab centre in Shropshire, where Liam had been a resident before Bible College. They had housing for them there too. Liam worked like crazy and it was here that **Zachariah John Husband** arrived on 7 July 2011. Three years of hard work later, God provided a car for them so they could now join a toddler group and church, make friends and meet people.

They met the pastor and his wife of Riverside Church, who needed an associate minister. After much discussion he asked Liam to join him and he could finish his MIT (minister in training) course. Everything fell into place at

Riverside with a house with a garden and then on 20 November 2014, along came **Elizabeth Rose Husband**, a beautiful girlie. They had happy years there but in 2016 they felt God telling them to move on.

Liam had finished his training and was ordained. They prayed, put their names on a list for a church, and waited. They had an offer of a church near Bournemouth, had an interview, were offered the job and moved in August 2016. On 8 March 2018, **Beatrice Grace Husband** burst into the world, another beautiful girlie. They have been at Hope Church for four years and love it. Their little family is growing and blossoming as is Liam's ministry and the church family. What a blessing!

John and Kayla

JOHN EDWARD LANCASTER was the biggest of my brothers in many ways. Not in age, but he was big in stature, big in heart, big in love, big in kindness, big in generosity, big in ideas, big in work, big in family, big in song, big in paragliding, and big in Christ. He was an all-round big man and was loved and admired and looked up to by many people. I most certainly have loved and admired him all my life. He was my little brother only for about 11 years, when I looked after him. Then he shot up and became the big brother who looked after *me*—and everyone else too.

He was a workaholic and threw himself into everything he did wholeheartedly, from the moment he started work at 15. He loved it. He had worked with Dad, so he learned wallpapering, and painting skills. He worked at Hiltons in Haywards Heath where he learned bricklaying and plastering. He just loved to learn new skills. He worked for Graham Slegg and learned so much from him about being a Christian businessman and having a good work ethic.

After he and Sharon married he was the happiest man on earth. He loved and adored Sharon and when his boys arrived one by one, he loved being a family man. It was Sharon who raised the boys as John was out all day working and earning money for the family and he was a brilliant provider. He was such an entrepreneur, always thinking up ways to earn. He bought old houses and converted them into flats, doing lots of the work himself, as well as running the glass shop, double glazing too. They moved up to Durham where he learned more skills; kitchen fitting, designing kitchens and bathrooms—there was nothing he wouldn't have a go at. Back to Ringmer in Sussex as a kitchen fitter and, after a few years, meeting Andy Hemmington, a lovely Christian man with whom he worked doing windows in Ringmer, Seaford and Lewes. They had a fantastic friendship that John likened to David and Johnathan's relationship in scripture. Andy married and went to live in Canada and John really missed him and the banter they had.

341

He was always reaching out to help one or another of us: Phil and Ken, his son Adam, Kayla's first husband Stuart, and odd mates of the boys. My Dan worked for him for a bit too. He employed them all, always willing to give a helping hand and also give someone the benefit of the doubt. He was a great teacher and wanted the boys to acquire skills; he taught them all so much. When Phil died, he reached out to Maggy and created a job for her, which she loves. Family was very important to John. He wanted his Dad to be proud of him, but Dad would always pull him to bits, criticise him and pull him up on things, then laugh when John suggested something! It was horrible, and John's countenance would fall! In truth I always thought Dad was jealous of John's success and his abilities, but poor John was desperate to hear Dad say, "Well done son" and he never did! When he would pop into our house on his way to a job or just for a cuppa, he would tell me about his latest venture. I would be spellbound as he told me what he was up to and would tell him how clever and gifted he was and how proud I was of him. He would grin like a Cheshire cat—but it wasn't me he needed to hear that from.

He so wanted to be a good provider, for his boys to be able to earn a living, for Sharon to have everything she wanted, and for there always to be food on the table and plenty in the cupboards. He never wanted them to be hungry like we were as kids. If you had ever shared a meal with John, you would have been amazed at the speed he could clear his plate—a legacy from childhood and always being hungry. He would eat all our breakfast porridge because Phil, Ken and I hated it made with salt. What's that all about? But John was always hungry and even though he didn't like it made with salt, he would eat it to feel full and he could finish all our bowls off in no time at all! He never wanted that for his boys.

He threw himself wholeheartedly into everything he did, like his paragliding. He went all over the world, jumping off mountains. He loved it so much. He said there was a freedom and a closeness to God when he was flying. He came to singing late in life but he just loved it. He got such joy from singing and he had a beautiful voice. He sang at home, at work, in the car, in church, at church events; he sang at Greg's retirement do at our church and it was beautiful. He even sang at Glyndebourne Opera House on the stage in an opera called *Imago*. We were all so very proud of him and he loved every moment of it. We all miss that voice and I can't hear *Nessun Dorma* without crying. Luciano Pavarotti had nothing on our John.

I can't believe he has died. It all seems unreal. It was 4 November 2019. We were in bed and the phone rang; it was Sharon. I knew her Dad had been very unwell and so when she said she had some sad news, I thought she was going to tell me her dear Dad John had died.

But she didn't. She said, "Darling, I have some really sad news. John died tonight!" NO HE DIDNT! That's not right. He can't have, not John! "I'm sorry darling, he did," she said.

I leapt out of bed, sobbing. No, not John. Not John. Greg was saying, "What's happened? What's happened?"

"Sharon said John died." I was getting dressed. Greg was in shock too. We both dressed and got into the car. How I drove to Ringmer I don't know, crying the whole way. We ran into the house, Sharon was in shock but very calm. I hugged her. Ben and Ron were both there and I fell into Ben's arms and we both sobbed. Then Ron's Deb was there too and we hugged and cried. Sharon, bless her, was holding it all together and her pastor was there too. "John is upstairs if you want to see him." I went up and the ambulance man was sat on the bed. John was on the floor looking like John! I sat on the floor, held John's hand, kissed him and just wailed. Greg stood behind me looking ashen. I couldn't believe our John, this great big little brother, was dead! It was like being in a nightmare and I felt sick.

I asked the ambulance man if there was anything else they could do but he shook his head. "I'm so sorry," he said. I kissed and stroked John's lovely face and sat and hugged his huge shoulders. We stayed for a while, then went back downstairs, still sobbing. We all sat waiting for the police, hugging and crying. This was the saddest night of my life, the biggest shock. John always said he would live to be 90 and when he wasn't able to do the things he wanted to do, he would paraglide into the side of a mountain. We all believed him! Flying straight into heaven! We all laughed and thought that would be fitting. Not this; not so young, not so fit!

When Phil died, he was so ill we knew he was dying and we cried buckets. It was hard and very sad, but we were expecting it. The same with Kenny, but John was just taken from us and it was shocking! Even knowing he was a Christian and had gone to be with his Lord didn't help. I didn't want him to go yet, none of us did; he was the patriarch of our family. We were all broken-hearted. Grief is tangible, painful and horrid and it's said the greater the love the greater the grief. Never a truer word was spoken and we miss him terribly.

Sharon and the boys organised his funeral and it was such a sad day. We first went to the crem in Brighton, then to a thanksgiving at Eastgate Baptist Church, John and Sharon's church. It was full to bursting! All the boys—Paul, Ben, Steve and Ron—did beautiful tributes to their Dad. Andy and Donna Hemmington had come from Canada and Andy did a beautiful tribute to his dearly-loved friend. His paragliding buddy, Steve Purdie, gave a lovely tribute too and I did the family eulogy. It was such a difficult thing to do but it was my privilege to let people know where my brother John came from and how he became the amazing man, Christian, husband, father, brother, uncle, friend and workmate that he was.

John was a very insecure person, needing lots of reassurance and love. Well, we're all a bit like that, thinking we are unlovable, because we weren't loved by the ones who were supposed to love us. It leaves you quite needy, even after becoming a Christian. There is still a big hole in us that needs to be filled. It is hard to live with, but now I know that John is fully loved, completely fulfilled and at peace with himself and with his Lord. I dream that my three brothers are all united in heaven—how wonderful.

When Dad died, I found a letter in his belongings that John had written. In it he thanked them for being his parents, even for the thrashings. He said he had learned many things through them. He thanked Dad for the strength he had inherited from him, which enabled him to work hard and provide for his family. He thanked Mam for the business acumen that he inherited from her, which enabled him to build his businesses together. How gracious he was.

The difference was that John didn't use his strength to bully, beat and intimidate his family. He used it to build up, to teach, to provide for his family. As for the business acumen, he didn't rob, steal, or manipulate the vulnerable to build up his bank balance. He used it to bless and help his wife, his sons, brothers, sisters, nephews, nieces, and various people and charities and his church. If he saw a need he would meet it, he was generous to the end. He leaves an enormous hole in our family. How we miss him. Even though he never got his, "Well done son, we are so proud of who you are and what you have achieved," from Mam and Dad, I know that when John arrived in heaven his heavenly father said, "Well done you good and faithful servant. Welcome home!" Though I still wish he were here.

As I am writing this, my lovely little sister is going through a dreadful time. She found a lump in her breast, after all this time. I couldn't believe it when she told me. I was scared for her. She said it was in the same breast as the cancer had been all those years ago. I told her to get to the doctor and she was going to but we were in the middle of a pandemic and everything was so difficult because everything was shut down. We were all praying and because of her history of cancer she got seen really quickly. The doctor referred her to an oncologist, and she had a scan and blood tests. It was cancer! I was so frightened. "Me, not her! Please Lord, don't take my sister!"

Richard was as strong as iron for her. Death to the cancer, life to Kayla was his and our prayer. He is her rock and was the most supportive husband. He took her to Basingstoke Hospital for the scan and the oncologist decided she needed a mastectomy. Because the hospital had the Covid virus, she was to have her op in Winchester in a Covid-free private hospital. Wonderful! They both had to isolate for two weeks, then she went into the hospital. She was very scared she would die, bless her heart. Her main fear was leaving Richard alone and not being around for her girls and her grandchildren.

She was to be there at 7.30 and Richard took her. She facetimed me in her surgical stockings and nighty all ready, her little face swollen from crying. We talked for a bit and I said God was deffo in this because people were having their operations cancelled because of the virus and here she was, seen, scanned and operated on in less than a month—a minor miracle! She finally went down to the theatre at 1.30 which was a long time to sit in your nighty and anxiously wait! But everything went well and Richard brought her home that same evening, drains in and all. She is now five weeks post-operative and healing well. The consultant told her they got every bit of cancer! Yay! Thank you, Lord.

She was having pain in her hip and worried that it was secondaries. The consultant rang her as she was going on holiday. She told her which medication she was putting her on and Kayla told her about the hip pain. "I am looking at your scan and I can see your hips. There is NO cancer in them!"

Hallelujah! So we all breathe out and say an enormous, "Thank you, dear Lord!" Kayla is recovering well, is looking wonderful and feeling so much better. She will be around, God willing, for many more happy years with those lovely girls and grandchildren and, of course, the lovely Richard.

Chain Breakers

I STARTED WRITING THIS BOOK as a help in coping with all that had happened to me as a child, on seeing a psychiatrist who said it could be cathartic. I wrote a bit, left it for years and then, when ugly things popped into my mind over the years, I wrote some more. Really I thought it might help my kids to understand why I was such a mad mother! And as I wrote more, I could see God's hand on our lives. I have tried to write about all of us but I haven't written everything. Just enough to give you all an idea of Lancaster life before and after Dad's conversion.

When I see how God definitely changed my Dad all those years ago in prison and how our lives changed. Then how John became a Christian and shared his love of God with me. Then how I became a Christian, and then Maggy, then Greg, then Susie and Kenny, then Kayla—lives transformed by a loving God. And how, because of that, we all had new principles to live by; out with the old ways and in with the new. No more shoplifting, fighting, deceiving, burglary, out and out thievery, car stealing, bike robbing, bullying, beating—all gone. Replaced by love, honesty, truth, kindness, gentleness, faithfulness, and much more. We are far from perfect, that's for sure, but if you look at what our lives were before God changed Dad, that would have been our template for living and our role model. So your lives would have been very different.

They do say that if you have been abused then in most cases you go on to abuse. Well, we didn't. We are all chain breakers—with God's help we broke the chains that bound us, and because we did that, you all live in the good of that, and all your lives are blessed because you are free from those chains. How wonderful to see you all, every one of you, wonderful partners and parents. You have all been prayed for every day of your lives by all of us who love God. We give Him all the credit and all the thanks for all of you: nephews, nieces, great nephews and nieces, children and grandchildren. You are all the result of much prayer and your lives are fabulous because of His love. Please don't dismiss the work of God in our lives. He is what has held us together all these years and healed deep hurts. My prayer is that one day you all will know and love Him as we do.

LOVE AND FORGIVENESS

Very much love to you all from Mum, Nana, Aunty Fay or Great Aunty Fay.

I hope this helps you all to understand who we are and where we have all come from.

Maybe it will help you to forgive us for sometimes getting it wrong and sometimes being a little crazy!

xxxxxxx

from PSALM 71

For you are my hope, O Lord my God;
You are my trust from my youth.
By You I have been upheld from birth;
You are the one who took me from my mother's womb.
My praise shall be continually of You
And to this day I declare Your wondrous works.
Now also when I am old and grey-haired,
O God, do not forsake me,
Until I declare your strength to this generation,
Your power to everyone who is to come.

Phil and me—love his safety pin!

Kenny, John and me at 22
Glebe Road.

John and me at Dollcliffe Road, where
I looked after him.

Dollcliffe Road. Mam in such amazing surroundings!

When Phil and Ken came back to live with us.

Phil and me at Dollcliffe Road.

Mam and Dad at the prefab.

Phil and me in his pedal car.

Uncle Mossy and Dad—
drinking partners.

Dad aged 17.

Dad in the garden of 22.

John, Kenny and Kayla.

The five of us and Taurus.

Me and my darling Kayla.

Dad ready for a fight.

Left: Phil, John, Ken and
Mam
Right: John, me and Kenny.
School photo: I'm 3rd from
left, 2nd row up—with no tie!

Mam and Kenny on one of the bikes before it was buried!

Maggy and John.

Dad painting 22.

John and Sharon's wedding.

Grandad coming home from the pit.

Me and Greg on our wedding day.

John, Susie and Kenny on their
wedding day

Me with Nanna wiping her nose
on my veil

Mam and Dad on Kenny and
Susie's wedding day.

John and Sharon

All five of us with Phil saying Persil
washes whitest and it shows!

Maggy, Mam and Susie.

Kayla and Richard's wedding day.

Phil, Maggy and Emily before things went wrong.

Me and Phil.

Kenny aged 19.

Ray and Nancy.

Errol Hulse.

The five of us.

Me and my formidable sisters-in-law.

Granny, Grandad and all of us.

Mam, just before she died, with me and
Kenny.

My little winner, Punk Rocker
Naomi.

Mam, Dad, Kenny and Adam.

Top: My little darlings,
Dan, Becky and Naomi

Naomi's newspaper cutting.

Right: one of the funny notes Kenny
would leave me at the flat

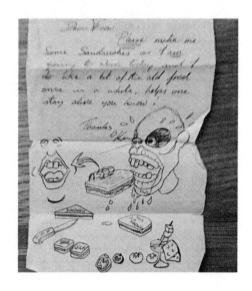

 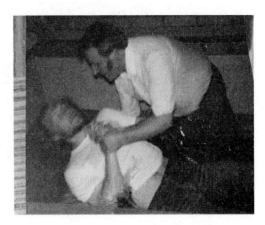

A family gathering with Granny, Mam and Aunty Jessy

Kenny's Baptism

John in his favourite place – paragliding.

Dad and Kenny. You can see the hole in his forehead.

The whole family—except Dan's family.

My darling grandchildren.

Lancaster/Summers party.

The whole family.

Greg's retirement cake.

Naomi, Dan and Becky.

John and Cathy singing at Greg's
retirement celebration.

Me and Kayla.

The All Saints staff at Greg's retirement.

A family meal.

Greg's 'do'.